# EXPERT RESUMES™ FOR COMPUTER AND WEB JOBS

**SECOND EDITION**

DISCARD

## Wendy S. Enelow and Louise M. Kursmark

JIST Works
America's Career Publisher

# *Expert Resumes for Computer and Web Jobs,* Second Edition

© 2005 by Wendy S. Enelow and Louise M. Kursmark

Published by JIST Works, an imprint of JIST Publishing, Inc.
8902 Otis Avenue
Indianapolis, IN 46216-1033
Phone: 1-800-648-JIST     Fax: 1-800-JIST-FAX     E-mail: info@jist.com

Visit our Web site at **www.jist.com** for information on JIST, free job search tips, book chapters, and how to order our many products! For free information on 14,000 job titles, visit **www.careeroink.com**.

Quantity discounts are available for JIST books. Please call our Sales Department at 1-800-648-5478 for a free catalog and more information.

Acquisitions and Development Editor: Lori Cates Hand
Cover Designer: designLab, Seattle
Interior Designer and Page Layout: Trudy Coler
Proofreaders: Linda Seifert and Jeanne Clark
Indexer: Kelly D. Henthorne

Printed in the United States of America
09 08 07 06 05          9 8 7 6 5 4 3 2 1

Library of Congress Cataloging-in-Publication data

Enelow, Wendy S.
  Expert resumes for computer and Web jobs / Wendy S. Enelow and Louise M. Kursmark.-- 2nd ed.
     p. cm.
  Includes index.
  ISBN 1-59357-127-5 (alk. paper)
  1. Résumés (Employment) 2. Electronic data processing personnel--Employment.
  I. Kursmark, Louise. II. Title.
  HF5383.E47876 2005
  650.14'2'024005--dc22                    2005007784

ISBN 1-59357-127-5

# TABLE OF CONTENTS

# ABOUT THIS BOOK

The Technology Revolution of the past two decades has impacted the employment market on a scale even more dramatic than the Industrial Revolution. Everything about work is different today and will be forever! As a result of these dramatic technological advances, three remarkable things have happened:

1. **Virtually everyone in every place is, or can be, part of the Technology Revolution,** from the graduate student who has just earned his Master of Science in Information Technology to the 55-year-old grandmother whose expertise in C++ programming keeps her in demand for a wide variety of temporary/contract positions.

2. **There are now thousands of new careers in technology.** Twenty years ago, who had heard of Web site designers, Java scripters, C++ programmers, database administrators, CIOs, CTOs, or CKOs? Now, there is a wealth of new career opportunities, and every economic projection indicates tremendous and continuous growth in the demand for technology professionals.

3. **Hundreds of new professions have emerged,** from Internet Web site hosting to the design and manufacture of advanced telecommunications and networking technologies. Most of these professions did not exist 10–15 years ago. In turn, they are further adding to the number and diversity of careers that are now available within the technology industries.

It is critical to note that these new occupations and professions are not restricted to the technology industry. In fact, they exist in virtually every industry, from old-line manufacturing to emerging health-care ventures; from hundred-year-old utility companies to your local grocery chain; from major retail conglomerates to small real-estate brokerages; and every other industry imaginable. Perhaps, most important, there are dramatically more employment opportunities than there are qualified professionals, and that's great news for you!

To take advantage of all of these opportunities, you must first develop a powerful, performance-based resume. To be a savvy and successful job seeker, you must know how to communicate your qualifications in a strong and effective written presentation. Sure, it's important to let employers know essential technical details, such as the programming languages or operating systems with which you are experienced. But a powerful resume is much more than just a list of technical competencies; it is a concise yet comprehensive document that gives you a competitive edge in the job market. Creating such a powerful document is what this book is all about.

We'll explore the changes in resume presentation that have arisen as a result of the tremendous surge in technology. In years past, resumes were almost always printed on paper and mailed. Today, e-mail has become the chosen method for resume distribution in many industries. In turn, many of the traditional methods for "typing" and presenting resumes have changed dramatically. This book will instruct you in the methods for preparing resumes for e-mail, scanning, and Web site posting, as well as the traditional printed resume.

By using *Expert Resumes for Computer and Web Jobs* as your professional guide, you will succeed in developing a powerful and effective resume that opens doors, gets interviews, and helps you land your next great opportunity!

# INTRODUCTION

According to the U.S. Department of Labor, technology is the fastest-growing industry and fastest-growing segment of the employment market. It is anticipated that this trend will continue for years to come—through 2008 at least. We are in the midst of a Technology Revolution that has clearly surpassed the Industrial Revolution in terms of the volume of change, the speed of change, and the long-term results of those changes.

In turn, this revolution has created a wealth of new career opportunities for the following types of workers:

- **Technology professionals** (hardware and software engineers, programmers, systems analysts, database administrators, network administrators, Web site designers, field service technicians, and so on)

- **Technology support professionals** (sales and marketing professionals, e-commerce business development experts, training specialists, field support personnel, technical writers, and so on)

- **Technology management professionals** (CIOs, CKOs, and CTOs; vice presidents, directors, and managers of technology, systems, and MIS; and so on)

To take advantage of these opportunities, you must be an educated job seeker. That means you must know what you want in your career, where the hiring action is, what technical skills you need to attain your desired career goals, and how best to market your qualifications. It is no longer enough to be a talented technologist! Now, you must be a strategic marketer, able to package and promote your experience to take advantage of this wave of employment opportunity.

There's no doubt that the employment market has changed dramatically over the past decade. According to the U.S. Department of Labor (2000), you should expect to hold between 10 and 20 different jobs during your career. No longer is stability the status quo. Today, the norm is movement, onward and upward, in a fast-paced and intense technology market. And to stay on top of all the changes and opportunities, you must proactively control and manage your career.

## Technology Job Search Questions and Answers

Whether you're currently employed in the technology industry or looking to enter the industry for the first time, the following sections offer some practical advice.

## How Do You Enter the Technology Profession?

As with any other industry, education, credentials, and experience are the keys to entry and long-term success. It is difficult to obtain a position in the technology industry without some related work experience, relevant education, or technical credentials. Here are a few pointers:

- **If you're just starting to plan and build your career,** consider a four-year degree in a technology-related discipline (such as Information Systems, Information Technology, Computer Science, or Engineering) or completion of a technology certification program. Be advised, however, that you must stay current on new technical certification programs and how they are accepted in the market. What's hot one day is passé the next!

- **If you're a technology professional who wants to make the move to a true technology company,** sell your technology knowledge and experience in order to "connect" yourself to the industry. Perhaps you're a network administrator, database administrator, programmer, or MIS manager in a traditional, nontechnology industry. The technical skills and experiences you've acquired are real and valuable to others. Make the case that you're not an outsider, but rather an insider who understands technology and its applications.

- **If you're a successful sales and marketing professional, customer service specialist, or trainer** but have no technology experience, focus your resume on your revenue performance and the people skills you bring to an organization. "Sell" the fact that you built and managed customer relationships, improved revenues, designed innovative training programs, and the like. Place the emphasis on you and your performance, not unrelated products or services.

- **If you're an experienced business manager or executive** but have never worked in the technology industry, highlight the value you bring to an organization: your leadership skills, achievements, financial contributions, and more. Many companies seeking talented and effective leadership are more than willing to provide technical training to the "right" candidate.

## What Is the Best Resume Strategy if You're Already in the Technology Industry?

If you're already employed in the technology field but are interested in moving onward and upward, remember one critical fact:

> **Your resume is a marketing tool written to sell YOU!**

If you're a C++ programmer, *sell* the fact that you've helped to manage development projects, restored nonperforming systems, and created new, user-friendly applications. If you're a technical consultant, *sell* major projects, key clients, and innovative technologies. If you're a CIO, *sell* your achievements—financial, operational, and technological.

When writing your resume, your challenge is to create a picture of knowledge, action, and results. In essence, you're stating "This is what I know, this is how I've used it, and this is how well I've performed." Success sells, so be sure to highlight yours. If you don't, no one else will.

## WHERE ARE THE JOBS?

The jobs are everywhere—from the technology giants such as IBM, Cisco, and Hewlett Packard seeking well-qualified hardware, software, and network engineers to the small manufacturing company recruiting a Webmaster and an MIS director.

- The jobs are in **development** of new products, technologies, systems, and applications.
- The jobs are in the **manufacture** of these products and technologies.
- The jobs are in the **sale, marketing,** and **support** of these products and technologies.
- The jobs are in the **installation, operation, maintenance,** and **management** of these technologies in nontechnology companies—virtually every other company in the world.
- The jobs are in the **delivery** of technology services, as either an employee or a contractor/consultant.

The jobs are in every market sector, every industry, and every profession. Technology is everywhere.

## HOW DO YOU GET THE JOBS?

To answer this question, we need to review the basic principle underlying job search:

**Job search is marketing!**

You have a product to sell—yourself—and the best way to sell it is to use all appropriate *marketing channels* just as you would for any other product.

Suppose you wanted to sell televisions. What would you do? You'd market your products using newspaper, magazine, and radio advertisements. You might develop a company Web site to build your e-business, and perhaps you'd hire a field sales representative to market to major retail chains. Each of these is a different marketing channel through which you're attempting to reach your audience.

The same is true for job search. You must use every marketing channel that's right for you. Unfortunately, there is no single formula. What's right for you depends on your specific career objectives—type of position, type of industry, geographic restrictions, salary requirements, and more.

Following are the most valuable marketing channels for a successful job search within the technology industry. These are ordered from most effective to least effective.

1. **Referrals.** There is nothing better than a personal referral to a company, either in general or for a specific position. Referrals can open doors that, in most instances, would never be accessible any other way. If you know anyone who could possibly refer you to a specific company, contact that person immediately and ask for his or her assistance.

2. **Networking.** Networking is the backbone of every successful job search. Although you may consider it a chore, it is essential that you network effectively with your professional colleagues and associates, past employers, past co-workers, suppliers, neighbors, friends, and others who may know of opportunities that are right for you. Another good strategy is to attend meetings of professional associations in your area to make new contacts and expand your professional network. And , most important, in today's nomadic job market— where you're likely to change jobs every few years—the best strategy is to keep your network "alive" even when you're *not* searching for a new position.

3. **Responses to online job postings.** One of the greatest advantages of the Technology Revolution is an employer's ability to post job announcements and a job seeker's ability to respond immediately via e-mail. In most (but not all) instances, these are bona fide opportunities, and it's well worth your while to spend time searching for and responding to appropriate postings. However, don't make the mistake of devoting *too* much time to searching the Internet. It can consume a huge amount of your time that you should spend on other job search marketing efforts. Even if you're a technologist, job search is *not* just about technology!

   To expedite your search, here are a few of the largest and most widely used online job posting sites—presented alphabetically, not necessarily in order of effectiveness or value:

   www.careerbuilder.com

   www.chiefmonster.com

   www.computerjobs.com

   www.dice.com

   www.hotjobs.com

   www.monster.com

   www.nationjob.com

   www.sixfigurejobs.com

   www.tech-engine.com

   See the Appendix for a more complete list of relevant job search Web sites.

4. **Responses to newspaper and magazine advertisements.** Although the opportunity to post jobs online has reduced the overall number of print advertisements, they still abound. Do not forget about this "tried-and-true" marketing strategy. If they've got the job and you have the qualifications, it's a perfect fit.

5. **Targeted e-mail campaigns (resumes and cover letters) to recruiters.** Recruiters have jobs, and you want one. It's pretty straightforward. The only

catch is to find the "right" recruiters that have the "right" jobs. Therefore, you must devote the time and effort to preparing the "right" list of recruiters. There are many resources on the Internet where you can access information about recruiters (for a fee), sort that information by industry (information technology, software, communications, and so on), and then cross-reference with position specialization (programming, Web design, sales, executive management, and so on). This allows you to identify just the "right" recruiters who would be interested in a candidate with your qualifications. Because these campaigns are transmitted electronically, they are easy and inexpensive to produce.

When working with recruiters, it's important to realize that they *do not* work for you! Their clients are the hiring companies that pay their fees. They are not in business to "find a job" for you, but rather to fill a specific position with a qualified candidate, either you or someone else. To maximize your chances of finding a position through a recruiter or agency, don't rely on just one or two, but distribute your resume to many that meet your specific criteria.

6. **Online resume postings.** The Net is swarming with reasonably priced (if not free) Web sites where you can post your resume. It's quick, easy, and the only *passive* thing you can do in your search. All of the other marketing channels require action on your part. With online resume postings, once you've posted, you're done. You then just wait (and hope!) for some response.

7. **Targeted e-mail and print campaigns to companies.** Just as with campaigns to recruiters (see item 5 above), you must be extremely careful to select just the right companies that would be interested in a candidate with your qualifications. The closer you stick to "where you belong" in relation to your specific experience, the better your response rate will be. You can also conduct these campaigns via e-mail, but only when you are targeting technology companies. If you are looking at companies outside the technology industries, we believe that print campaigns (paper and envelopes mailed the old-fashioned way) are a more suitable and effective presentation—particularly if you are a management or executive candidate.

8. **In-person "cold calls" to companies and recruiters.** We consider this the least effective and most time-consuming marketing strategy for technology jobs. It is extremely difficult to just walk in the door and get in front of the right person, or any person who can take hiring action. You'll be much better off focusing your time and energy on other, more productive channels.

## WHAT ABOUT OPPORTUNITIES IN TECHNOLOGY CONSULTING AND CONTRACTING?

Long gone are the days of the "9 to 5 job," and nowhere is that more true than in the technology industries. Although, of course, the vast majority of people still have (and want) full-time jobs, there are now a wealth of opportunities for work as a technology consultant or contractor. Consulting generally refers to an individual who moves from company to company, and from project to project, where his or her particular expertise is most needed and most highly rewarded (and compensated).

In fact, more and more people—in technology and in most other industries—are flocking toward these types of working arrangements because of the tremendous flexibility they offer. And, what a great phenomenon for companies! They can now hire the people they need, when they need them, and *only* when they need them.

Give careful thought and consideration to the prospect of "contract" work. It's a rapidly emerging career track all its own and is becoming extremely prevalent within the technology industries. How great to be able to work on the projects that interest you and then move onto to something else. There are definite benefits to consider as well as the perceived negatives of "not having a permanent job." However, in today's transitory work culture, not having a permanent job is not such a negative! Working as a contractor or consultant allows you to control your own destiny.

## How Can I Overcome the "Offshoring" Trend?

Offshoring—the practice of sending U.S. work to foreign countries—has had an impact on many professions, most notably computer jobs. Perhaps you lost your last position when your company decided to move its call center to Panama or its programming operation to India. You might be feeling that you don't have a chance of landing another great job because "all the jobs are going to other countries." In fact, there is still a huge demand for technology workers in the U.S., and as we've noted, this demand is predicted to grow.

Rather than worry about the state of the industry, focus your job search on existing opportunities—perhaps in emerging technology fields. Focus your resume on what you have contributed to past employers. And be sure you are prepared to communicate these value messages during your interviews. We predict that you will successfully land a new, challenging, and exciting opportunity in a technology field.

## Conclusion

Career opportunities abound within the technology industries and professions today. What's more, it has never been easier to learn about and apply for jobs. Arm yourself with a powerful resume and cover letter, identify your most appropriate marketing channels, and start your search today. You're destined to reach the next rung on your career ladder.

# PART I

# Resume Writing, Strategy, and Formats

# CHAPTER 1

# Resume Writing Strategies for Technology Professionals

If you're reading this book, chances are you've decided to make a career move. It may be because:

- You're graduating from college or technical school and are ready to launch your professional career.

- You've just earned your graduate degree and are ready to make a step upward in your career.

- You're ready to leave your current position and move up the ladder to a higher-paying and more responsible position.

- You've decided on a career change and will be looking at opportunities in new media and other emerging technology industries.

- You're unhappy with your current company or management team and have decided to pursue opportunities elsewhere.

- You've been laid off, downsized, or otherwise left your position and you must find a new one.

- You've completed a contract assignment and are looking for a new "free-agent" job or perhaps a permanent position.

- You're relocating to a new area and need to find a new job.

- You're returning to the workforce after several years of unemployment or retirement.

- You're simply ready for a change.

There may even be other reasons for your job search besides these. However, no matter the reason, a powerful resume is an essential component of your search campaign. In fact, it is virtually impossible to conduct a search without a resume. It is your calling card that briefly, yet powerfully, communicates the skills, qualifications, experience, and value you bring to a prospective employer. It is the document that will open doors and generate interviews. It is the first thing people will learn about you when you forward it in response to an advertisement, and it is the last thing they'll remember when they're reviewing your qualifications after an interview.

Your resume is a sales document, and you are the product! You must identify the *features (what you know* and *what you can do)* and *benefits (how you can help an employer)* of that product, then communicate them in a concise and hard-hitting written presentation. Remind yourself over and over as you work your way through the resume process that you are writing marketing literature designed to sell a new product—*you*—into a new position.

Your resume can have tremendous power and a phenomenal impact on your job search. So don't take it lightly. Rather, devote the time, energy, and resources that are essential to developing a resume that is well-written, visually attractive, and effective in communicating *who* you are and *how* you want to be perceived.

## Resume Strategies

Following are the nine core strategies for writing effective and successful resumes.

### RESUME STRATEGY #1: WHO ARE YOU AND HOW DO YOU WANT TO BE PERCEIVED?

Now that you've decided to look for a new position, the very first step is to identify your career interests, goals, and objectives. *This task is critical,* because it is the underlying foundation for *what* you include in your resume, *how* you include it, and *where* you include it. You cannot write an effective resume without knowing, at least to some degree, what type or types of positions you will be seeking.

There are two concepts to consider here:

- **Who you are:** This relates to what you have done professionally and/or academically. Are you a programmer, network administrator, systems analyst, or telecommunications engineer? Are you a technology sales professional, field support specialist, or technical training manager? Are you a recent graduate from the DeVry Institute of Technology with a certificate in computer programming? Who are you?

- **How you want to be perceived:** This relates to your current career objectives. If you're a computer analyst looking for a position in project management, don't focus just on your technical qualifications. Put an equal emphasis on projects, personnel, schedules, team leadership, and more. If you're a technical sales engineer interested in a product-management position, highlight your involvement in product development, product support, multidisciplinary teaming, and other skills related to the design, creation, commercialization, and launch of new products.

The strategy, then, is to connect these two concepts by using the *Who you are* information that ties directly to the *How you want to be perceived* message to determine what information to include in your resume. By following this strategy, you're painting a picture that allows a prospective employer to see you as you wish to be seen—as an individual with the qualifications for the type of position you are pursuing.

> **WARNING:** If you prepare a resume without first clearly identifying what your objectives are and how you want to be perceived, your resume will have no focus and no direction. Without the underlying knowledge of "This is what I want to be," you do not know what to highlight in your resume. In turn, the document becomes an historical overview of your career and not the sales document it is designed to be.

## RESUME STRATEGY #2: SELL IT TO ME... DON'T TELL IT TO ME

We've already established the fact that resume writing is sales. You are the product, and you must create a document that powerfully communicates the value of that product. One particularly effective strategy for accomplishing this is the "Sell It to Me... Don't Tell It to Me" strategy that impacts virtually every single word you write on your resume.

If you "tell it," you are simply stating facts. If you "sell it," you promote it, advertise it, and draw attention to it. Look at the difference in impact between these examples:

**Tell It Strategy:** Assisted in development of company Web site and e-commerce capability.

**Sell It Strategy:** Member of 8-person technology team credited with the design and implementation of company Web site and launch of e-commerce capability (now generating $2.1 million in annual product sales).

**Tell It Strategy:** Increased sales revenues within the Northeastern U.S. region.

**Sell It Strategy:** Delivered a 45% revenue increase and 22% gain in customer base while managing technology sales throughout the $8.4 million Chicago sales territory.

**Tell It Strategy:** Improved systems performance, reliability, and functionality.

**Sell It Strategy:** Reengineered all system hardware and software, implemented quality assurance standards, upgraded supporting business processes, and significantly improved overall IT performance, reliability, and functionality.

What's the difference between "telling it" and "selling it"? In a nutshell...

| Telling It | Selling It |
| --- | --- |
| Describes features. | Describes benefits. |
| Tells what and how. | Sells why the "what" and "how" are important. |
| Details activities. | Includes results. |
| Focuses on what you did. | Details how what you did benefited the company, department, team members, customers, and so on. |

## RESUME STRATEGY #3: USE KEYWORDS

No matter what you read or who you talk to about job search, the concept of key-words is sure to come up. Keywords (or, as they were previously known, buzz words) are words and phrases specific to a particular industry or profession. For example, keywords for technology include *architecture, artificial intelligence, CASE tools, C++, functionality, hardware, Internet, software, systems analysis, technical training, user support,* and many, many more.

When you use these words and phrases—in your resume, in your cover letter, or during an interview—you are communicating a very specific message. For example, when you include the words "software development" in your resume, your reader will most likely assume that you have experience in user needs analysis, software engineering, testing, prototype development, troubleshooting, hardware interface, and more. As you can see, people will make inferences about your skills based on the use of just one or two individual words.

Here are a few other examples:

- When you use the words **multimedia technology,** people will assume you have experience with videoconferencing, teleconferencing, CD-ROM, graphic interfaces, Internet broadcasting, and more.

- When you mention **e-commerce,** readers and listeners will infer that you have experience with the Internet, online technology, online advertising and promotion, secure shopping carts, and more.

- By referencing **systems architecture** in your resume, you convey that you have experience with hardware, software, systems configuration, systems migration, applications, functionality, systems performance, and more.

- When you use the word **network,** most people will assume you are familiar with LAN and WAN technology, network protocols, network interfaces, network administration, and the like.

Keywords are also an integral component of the resume scanning process, whereby companies and recruiters electronically search resumes for specific terms to find candidates with the skills, qualifications, and technical expertise for their particular hiring needs. In many instances, electronic scanning has replaced the more traditional method of an actual person reading your resume (at least initially). Therefore, to some degree, the *only* thing that matters in this instance is that you have included the "right" keywords to match the company's or the recruiter's needs. Without them, you will most certainly be passed over.

Of course, in virtually every instance your resume will be read at some point by human eyes, so it's not enough just to throw together a list of keywords and leave it at that. In fact, it's not even necessary to include a separate "keyword summary" on your resume. A better strategy is to incorporate keywords naturally into the text within the appropriate sections of your resume.

Keep in mind, too, that keywords are arbitrary; there is no defined set of keywords for a Web site developer, Novell network administrator, or any other profession. Employers searching to fill these positions develop a list of terms that reflect the specifics they desire in a qualified candidate. These might be a combination of technical skills, education, length of experience, and other easily defined qualifications, along with "soft skills," such as leadership, problem-solving, and communication.

> **NOTE:** Because of the complex and arbitrary nature of keyword selection, we cannot overemphasize how vital it is, especially in the technology industry, where resume scanning and other electronic tools are so frequently used, to be certain that *all* of the keywords that represent your experience and knowledge are included in your resume!

How can you be sure that you are including all the keywords and the right keywords? Just by describing your work experience, projects, technical qualifications, and the like, you will naturally include most of the terms that are important in your field. To cross-check what you've written, review online job postings for positions that are of interest to you. Look at the precise terms used in the ads and be sure you have included them in your resume (as appropriate to your skills and qualifications).

Another great benefit of today's technology revolution is our ability to find instant information, even information as specific as technology industry keywords! Refer to the appendix for a listing of Web sites that have thousands and thousands of technology keywords, complete with descriptions. These are outstanding resources.

## RESUME STRATEGY #4: USE THE "BIG" AND SAVE THE "LITTLE"

When deciding what you want to include in your resume, try to focus on the "big" things—new products, new technologies, system enhancements, productivity and quality gains, major projects, major customers, improvements to functionality, new applications, sales increases, profit improvements, and more. Give a good broad-based picture of what you were responsible for and how well you did it. Here's an example:

> Managed a $12 million robotics development project in cooperation with the company's largest retail customer. Orchestrated the entire project, from initial planning and design through prototype development and final customer delivery. Matrix-managed a 42-person development team.

Then, save the "little" stuff—the details—for the interview. With this strategy, you will accomplish two things: You'll keep your resume readable and of a reasonable length (while still selling your achievements), and you'll have new and interesting information to share during the interview, rather than merely repeating what is already on your resume. Using the above example, when discussing this experience during an interview you could elaborate on the design process, your involvement with marketing, the specific technologies that were involved, and the long-term benefits of the system.

## RESUME STRATEGY #5: MAKE YOUR RESUME "INTERVIEWABLE"

One of your greatest challenges is to make your resume a useful interview tool. Once you've passed the keyword scanning test and are contacted for a telephone or in-person interview with a real person, the resume becomes all-important in leading and prompting your interviewer during your conversation.

Your job, then, is to make sure the resume leads the reader where you want to go and presents just the right organization, content, and appearance to stimulate a productive discussion. To improve the "interviewability" of your resume, consider these tactics:

- Make good use of Resume Strategy #4 (Use the "Big" and Save the "Little") to invite further discussion about your experiences.

- Be sure your greatest "selling points" are featured prominently, not buried within the resume.

- Conversely, don't devote lots of space and attention to areas of your background that are irrelevant or about which you feel less than positive; you'll only invite questions about things you really don't want to discuss.

- Make sure your resume is highly readable—this means plenty of white space, an adequate font size, and a logical flow from start to finish.

## RESUME STRATEGY #6: ELIMINATE CONFUSION WITH STRUCTURE AND CONTEXT

Keep in mind that your resume will be read *very quickly* by hiring authorities! You may agonize over every word and spend hours working on content and design, but the average reader will skim quickly through your masterpiece and expect to pick up important facts in just a few seconds. Try to make it as easy as possible for readers to grasp the essential facts:

- Be consistent: For example, put job titles, company names, and dates in the same place for each position.

- Make information easy to find by clearly defining different sections of your resume with large, highly visible headings.

- Define the context in which you worked (for example, the company, your department, the specific challenges you faced) before you start describing your activities and accomplishments.

## RESUME STRATEGY #7: USE FUNCTION TO DEMONSTRATE ACHIEVEMENT

When you write a resume that focuses only on your job functions, it can be dry and uninteresting and will say very little about your unique activities and contributions. Consider the following example:

> Responsible for the development and administration of all database functions for the company.

Now, consider using that same function to demonstrate achievement and see what happens to the tone and energy of the sentence. It becomes alive and clearly communicates that you deliver results.

> Reengineered the corporation's database systems, introduced new applications, and improved user satisfaction by 18%.

Try to translate your functions into achievements and you'll create a more powerful resume presentation.

## RESUME STRATEGY #8: REMAIN IN THE REALM OF REALITY

We've already established that resume writing is sales. And, as any good salesperson does, one feels somewhat inclined to stretch the truth just a bit. However, be forewarned that you must stay within the realm of reality. Do not push your skills and qualifications outside the bounds of what is truthful. You never want to be in a position where you have to defend something that you've written on your resume. If that's the case, you'll lose the opportunity before you ever get started.

## RESUME STRATEGY #9: BE CONFIDENT

You are unique. There is only one individual with the specific combination of employment experience, technical qualifications, achievements, and educational credentials that you have. In turn, this positions you as a unique commodity within the competitive job search market. To succeed, you must prepare a resume that is written to sell *you*, and highlight *your* qualifications and *your* success. If you can accomplish this, you will have won the job search game by generating interest, interviews, and offers.

# There Are No Resume Writing Rules

One of the greatest challenges in resume writing is that there are no rules to the game. There are certain expectations about information that you will include: principally, your employment history and your educational qualifications. Beyond that, what you include is entirely dependent upon you and what you have done in your career. What's more, you have tremendous flexibility in determining how to include the information you have selected. In chapter 2, you'll find a complete listing of each possible category you might include in your resume, the type of information in each category, preferred formats for presentation, and sample text you can edit and use.

Although there are no rules, there are a few standards to live by as you write your resume. The following sections discuss these standards in detail.

## CONTENT STANDARDS

Content is, of course, the text that goes into your resume. Content standards regard the writing style you should use, items you should be sure to include, items you should avoid including, and the order and format in which you list your qualifications.

### Writing Style

*Always* write in the first person, dropping the word "I" from the front of each sentence. This style gives your resume a more aggressive and more professional tone than the passive third-person voice. Here are some examples:

**First Person**

> Lead 12-person team in the design and market commercialization of next-generation SAP technology.

**Third Person**

> Mr. Jones manages a team of 12 in the design and market commercialization of next-generation SAP technology.

By using the first-person voice, you are assuming "ownership" of that statement. You did such-and-such. When you use the third-person, "someone else" did it. Can you see the difference?

### Stay Away From...

Try *not* to use phrases such as "responsible for" or "duties included." These words create a passive tone and style. Instead, use active verbs to describe what you did.

Compare these two ways of conveying the same information:

*Duties included* the development, implementation, and marketing of an innovative intranet system offering a secure portal with centralized access to records, test results, and medical information. *Responsible for* training and customer-service staff, vendor-employed network engineers, and Web developers. *Also responsible for* $1.3 million operating budget.

*Managed* development, implementation, and marketing of an innovative Intranet system offering a secure portal with centralized access to records, test results, and medical information. *Supervised* training and customer-service staff. *Directed* the activities of vendor-employed network engineers and Web developers. *Developed and administered* $1.3 million operating budget.

## Resume Style

The traditional **chronological** resume lists work experience in reverse-chronological order (starting with your current or most recent position). The **functional** style de-emphasizes the "where" and "when" of your career and instead groups similar experience, talents, and qualifications regardless of when they occurred.

Today, however, most resumes follow neither a strictly chronological nor strictly functional format; rather, they are an effective mixture of the two styles, usually known as a "combination" or "hybrid" format.

Like the chronological format, the hybrid format includes specifics about where you worked, when you worked there, and what your job titles were. Like a functional resume, a hybrid emphasizes your most relevant qualifications—perhaps within chronological job descriptions, in an expanded summary section, in several "career highlights" bullet points at the top of your resume, or in project summaries. Most of the examples in this book are hybrids and show a wide diversity of organizational formats that you can use as inspiration for your own resume.

## Resume Format

Resumes, principally career summaries and job descriptions, are most often written in a paragraph format, a bulleted format, or a combination of both. Following are three job descriptions, all very similar in content, yet presented in each of the three different formats. The advantages and disadvantages of each format are also addressed.

### Paragraph Format

**Team Leader—Client/Server Implementation Project**   2002 to 2005

**BELL ATLANTIC CORPORATION,** Baltimore, Maryland

Co-led $950 million investment to develop client/server order-entry system to service operations in 50 locations throughout 6 Northeastern states and

*(continued)*

*(continued)*

> support 1,600 users processing 140,000 orders per year ($32 billion in revenue). Directed a staff of 73. Wrote and presented the business case for $7.9 million in board-approved funding.
>
> Planned and orchestrated a successful technology development and implementation project, achieving all performance goals and objectives and delivering the project on time and within budget. Most notably, increased billing accuracy from 80% to 91% and coordinated integration of $1.2 million of capital equipment into existing data center. Delivered major cost reductions including 66% savings in development of technical specifications (through competitive RFP and subsequent negotiation of offshore development contract) and 15-person reduction in client staffing expense.

## Advantages:

Requires the least amount of space on the page. Brief, succinct, and to the point.

## Disadvantages:

Achievements get lost in the text of the second paragraph. They are not visually distinctive, nor do they stand alone to draw attention to them.

### Bulleted Format

> **Team Leader—Client/Server Implementation Project**   2002 to 2005
>
> **BELL ATLANTIC CORPORATION,** Baltimore, Maryland
> - Co-led $950 million investment to develop client/server order-entry system to service operations in 50 locations throughout 6 Northeastern states and support 1,600 users processing 140,000 orders per year ($32 billion in revenue). Directed a staff of 73.
>
> - Wrote and presented a business case for $7.9 million in board-approved funding.
>
> - Planned and orchestrated a successful technology development and implementation project, achieving all performance goals and objectives and delivering the project on time and within budget. Most notably, increased billing accuracy from 80% to 91%.
>
> - Coordinated integration of $1.2 million of capital equipment into existing data center.
>
> - Delivered major cost reductions including 66% savings in development of technical specifications (through competitive RFP and subsequent negotiation of offshore development contract) and 15-person reduction in client staffing expense.

**Advantages:**

Quick and easy to peruse.

**Disadvantages:**

Responsibilities and achievements are lumped together with everything of equal value. In turn, the achievements get lost further down the list and are not immediately recognizable.

## Combination Format

> **Team Leader—Client/Server Implementation Project**   2002 to 2005
>
> **BELL ATLANTIC CORPORATION,** Baltimore, Maryland
>
> Co-led $950 million investment to develop client/server order-entry system to service operations in 50 locations throughout 6 Northeastern states and support 1,600 users processing 140,000 orders per year ($32 billion in revenue). Directed a staff of 73.
>
> - Wrote and presented a business case for $7.9 million in board-approved funding.
>
> - Planned and orchestrated a successful technology development and implementation project, achieving all performance goals and objectives and delivering project on-time and within budget. Most notably, increased billing accuracy from 80% to 91%.
>
> - Coordinated integration of $1.2 million of capital equipment into existing data center.
>
> - Delivered major cost reductions including 66% savings in development of technical specifications (through competitive RFP and subsequent negotiation of offshore development contract) and 15-person reduction in client staffing expense.

**Advantages:**

Our recommended format. Clearly presents overall responsibilities in the introductory paragraph and then accentuates each achievement as a separate bullet.

**Disadvantages:**

If you don't have clearly identifiable accomplishments, this format is not effective. It also may shine a glaring light on the positions where your accomplishments were less notable.

## E-Mail Address and URL

Be sure to include your e-mail address prominently at the top of your resume. As we all know, e-mail has become one of the most preferred methods of communication in job search, particularly within the technology industry.

We advise against using your employer's e-mail address on your resume. Not only does this present a negative impression to future employers, it will become useless once you make your next career move. And since your resume may exist in cyberspace long after you've completed your current job search, you don't want to direct interested parties to an obsolete e-mail address. Instead, obtain a private e-mail address that will be yours permanently. A free e-mail address from a provider such as Yahoo!, Hotmail, or NetZero is perfectly acceptable to use on your resume.

In addition to your e-mail address, if you have a URL where you have posted your Web resume, be sure to also display that prominently at the top of your resume. For more information on Web resumes, refer to chapter 3.

To draw even more attention to your e-mail address, consider this format for the top of your resume:

---

**JOHN L. GREEN**

**johngreen23938@aol.com**

999 Old Mill Lane                                   Phone: (888) 556-1238
Smithville, VA 22890                                   Fax: (888) 556-1239

---

## PRESENTATION STANDARDS

Presentation regards the way your resume looks. It regards the fonts you use, the paper you print it on, any graphics you might include, and how many pages your resume should be.

### Font

Use a font (typestyle) that is clean, conservative, and easy to read. Stay away from anything that is too fancy, glitzy, curly, and the like. We've listed a few recommended fonts at the top of the next page. Other fonts that work well for resumes include Franklin Gothic, Myriad Roman, Helvetica, Univers, Palomino, Souvenir, and Fritz.

Although it is extremely popular, Times New Roman is our least preferred font simply because it is overused. More than 90 percent of the resumes we see are typed in Times New Roman. Your goal is to create a competitive-distinctive document, and, to achieve that, we recommend an alternative font.

Your choice of font should be dictated by the content, format, and length of your resume. Some fonts look better than others at smaller or larger sizes; some have "bolder" boldface type; some require more white space to make them readable.

| | |
|---|---|
| Tahoma | Times New Roman |
| Arial | Bookman |
| Krone | Book Antiqua |
| **Soutane** | Garamond |
| CG Omega | Century Schoolbook |
| Century Gothic | Lucida Sans |
| Gill Sans | Verdana |

Once you've written your resume, experiment with a few different fonts to see which one best enhances your document.

## Type Size

Readability is everything! If the type size is too small, your resume will be difficult to read and difficult to skim for essential information. Interestingly, a too-large type size, particularly for senior-level professionals, can also give a negative impression by conveying a juvenile or unprofessional image.

As a general rule, select type from 10 to 12 points in size. However, there's no hard-and-fast rule, and a lot depends on the font you choose. Take a look at the following examples:

### Very readable in 9-point Verdana:

Designed an easy-to-navigate Web page for a retail company, using a version of Netscape Composer with limited capabilities; included a home page, product page, and order form, with strong graphics and hyperlinks.

### Difficult to read in too-small 9-point Gill Sans:

Designed an easy-to-navigate Web page for a retail company, using a version of Netscape Composer with limited capabilities; included a home page, product page, and order form, with strong graphics and hyperlinks.

### Concise and readable in 12-point Times New Roman:

**Primary focus:** European rollout of SAP system, implementing new functionality into a live, productive system. Project manager and chief architect of Euro currency conversion project: Security, Systems Testing, and Training. Manage virtual, cross-functional team of 20.

**A bit overwhelming in too-large 12-point Bookman Old Style:**

---

**Primary focus:** European rollout of SAP system, implementing new functionality into a live, productive system. Project manager and chief architect of Euro currency conversion project: Security, Systems Testing, and Training. Manage virtual, cross-functional team of 20.

---

## Type Enhancements

**Bold,** *italics,* <u>underlining</u>, and CAPITALIZATION are ideal to highlight certain words, phrases, achievements, projects, numbers, and other information you want to draw special attention to. However, do not overuse these enhancements. If your resume becomes too cluttered, nothing stands out.

> **NOTE:** Resumes intended for electronic transmission and computer scanning have specific restrictions on font, type size, and type enhancements. We discuss these details in chapter 3.

## Page Length

A one- or two-page resume is preferred. Use three or more pages only in a particularly unusual circumstance. For instance, if you're an experienced CIO with a 25-year career and a host of major accomplishments in every position, don't short-change yourself by insisting on a two-page resume. If you're a free agent with many diverse projects under your belt, a longer resume that includes just about all of your projects could give you a competitive edge over other less experienced freelancers.

If you must create a resume that's longer than two pages, consider making it more reader-friendly by segmenting the information into separate components. For instance, you might summarize your project-management experience on page 1 of the resume, then create an addendum that provides more detail about each project. Or you could write an all-encompassing technical summary, then detail a long list of specific technologies on a separate page.

## Paper Color

Be conservative. White, ivory, and light gray are ideal. Other "flashier" colors are inappropriate for individuals in the technology industry.

## Graphics

An attractive, relevant graphic can really enhance your technical resume. When you look through the sample resumes in chapters 4 through 10, you'll see some excellent examples of the effective use of graphics to enhance the visual presentation of a resume. Just be sure not to get carried away... be tasteful and relatively conservative.

### White Space

We'll say it again—readability is everything! If people have to struggle to read your resume, they simply won't make the effort. Therefore, be sure to leave plenty of white space. It really does make a difference.

## ACCURACY AND PERFECTION

The very final step, and one of the most critical in resume writing, is the proofreading stage. It is essential that your resume be well written, visually pleasing, and free of any errors, typographical mistakes, misspellings, and the like. We recommend that you carefully proofread your resume a minimum of three times, and then have two or three other people also proofread it. Consider your resume an example of the quality of work you will produce on a company's behalf. Is your work product going to have errors and inconsistencies? If your resume does, it communicates to a prospective employer that you are careless, and this is the "kiss of death" in a job search.

Take the time to make sure that your resume is perfect in all the little details that do, in fact, make a big difference to those who read it.

# CHAPTER 2

# Writing Your Resume

For many technology professionals, resume writing is *not* at the top of the list of fun and exciting activities! How can it compare to solving a programming bug, developing a new technology, advancing an e-commerce application, cracking a longstanding systems malfunction, or launching a global systems upgrade? In your perception, we're sure that it cannot.

However, resume writing can be an enjoyable and rewarding task. Once your resume is complete, you can look at it proudly, reminding yourself of all that you have achieved. It is a snapshot of your career and your success. When it's complete, we guarantee you'll look back with tremendous self-satisfaction as you launch and successfully manage your job search.

The very first step in finding a new position or advancing your career, resume writing can be the most daunting of all tasks in your job search. For most of you in technology, writing may not be your primary skill. In fact, writing is a right-brain skill, the exact opposite of what you do when you use your left brain to develop theory, analyze, synthesize, extrapolate, plan a process, or handle a variety of other functions related to the technology industry.

Therefore, to make the writing process easier, more finite, and more "analytical," we've consolidated it into five discrete sections.

- **Career Summary.** Think of your Career Summary as the *architecture* of your resume. It is the accumulation of everything that allows the system (you) to work. It is the backbone, the foundation of your resume.

- **Technical Qualifications.** Your technical qualifications are equivalent to the functionality, the underlying foundation of the system and of your career. This section is a consolidated yet comprehensive summary of your specific technical qualifications and expertise.

- **Professional Experience.** Professional Experience is much like the software and applications of your system. It shows how you put all of your capabilities to work… in ways that benefit "users" (employers).

- **Education, Credentials, and Certifications.** Think of this section as the *system specifications*, the specific qualifications of the system and of your career.

- **The "Extras"** (Professional Affiliations, Civic Affiliations, Publications, Public Speaking, Honors and Awards, Personal Information, and so on). These are the *bits and bytes* of your resume, the "extra stuff" that helps distinguish you from others with similar technical qualifications.

## Step-by-Step: Writing the Perfect Resume

In the preceding section, we outlined the five core resume sections. Now, we'll detail the particulars of each section—what to include, where to include it, and how to include it.

### CONTACT INFORMATION

Before we start, let's briefly address the very top section of your resume: your name and contact information.

### *Name*

You'd think this would be the easiest part of writing your resume… writing your name! But there are several factors you may want to consider:

- Although most people choose to use their full, formal name at the top of a resume, it has become increasingly more acceptable to use the name by which you prefer to be called.

- Bear in mind that it's to your advantage to have readers feel comfortable calling you for an interview. Their comfort level may decrease if your name is gender-neutral, difficult to pronounce, or very unusual; they don't know who they're calling (a man or a woman) or how to ask for you. Here are a few ways you can make it easier for them:

> Lynn T. Cowles (Mr.)
>
> (Ms.) Michael Murray
>
> Tzirina (Irene) Kahn
>
> Ndege "Nick" Vernon

### *Address*

You should always include your home address on your resume; not your employer's address. If you use a post office box for mail, include both your mailing address and your physical residence address.

### Telephone Number(s)

Your home telephone number should be included. If you're at work during the day, when you can expect to receive most calls, consider including a work phone number (if it's a direct line and you can receive calls discreetly). Or you can include a mobile phone number (refer to it as "mobile" rather than "cellular," to keep up with current terminology) or a pager number (however, this is less desirable because you must call back to speak to the person who called you). You can include a private home fax number (if it can be accessed automatically), but do not include your work fax number.

### E-Mail Address

In chapter 1, we addressed positioning your e-mail address and URL at the top of your resume. Without question, individuals in technology professions should list a private e-mail address. Do not use your employer's e-mail address, even if you access e-mail through your work computer. Instead, if you don't already have an e-mail address, you can obtain a free, accessible-anywhere address from a provider such as Yahoo! or Hotmail.

As you look through the samples in this book, you'll see how resume writers have arranged the many bits of contact information at the top of a resume. You can use these as models for presenting your own information. The point is to make it as easy as possible for employers to contact you!

Now, let's get into the nitty-gritty of the five core content sections of your resume.

## CAREER SUMMARY

The Career Summary is the section at the top of your resume that summarizes and highlights your knowledge and expertise.

You may be thinking, "But shouldn't my resume start with an Objective?" Although many job seekers still use Objective statements, we believe that a Career Summary is a much more powerful introduction. The problem with Objectives is that they are either too specific (limiting you to a "C# Programmer position" or too vague (doesn't everyone want a challenging opportunity with a progressive organization offering the opportunity for growth and advancement?). In addition, they can be read as self-serving, since they describe what *you* want rather than suggesting what you have to offer an employer.

In contrast, an effective Career Summary allows you to position yourself as you wish to be perceived and immediately "paint a picture" of yourself that supports your current career goals. It is critical that this section focus on the specific skills, qualifications, and achievements of your career that are related to your current objectives. Your summary is *not* a historical overview of your career. Rather, it is a concise, well-written, and sharp presentation of information designed to *sell* you into your next position.

This section can have various titles, such as the following:

| | |
|---|---|
| Career Achievements | Management Profile |
| Career Highlights | Professional Qualifications |
| Career Summary | Professional Summary |
| Career Synopsis | Profile |
| Executive Profile | Summary |
| Expertise | Summary of Achievement |
| Highlights of Experience | Summary of Qualifications |

Or, as you will see in the first example format (Headline Format), your summary does not have to have any title at all.

Here are five sample Career Summaries. Consider using one of these as the template for developing your Career Summary, or use them as the foundation to create your own presentation. You will also find some type of Career Summary in just about every resume included in this book.

### Headline Format

**SENIOR INFORMATION TECHNOLOGY EXECUTIVE**

Information Systems / Telecommunications / Web / Voice & Data

Harvard University MBA—Specialization in Information Systems and Technologies

### Paragraph Format

**PROFILE**      Highly skilled and experienced **Database Developer / Technical Project Lead** with a track record of managing on-time, on-budget projects that deliver substantial business benefits. Solid business background and innate understanding of how technology systems impact business processes. Known for ability to rapidly assess business needs and quick-start technology solutions.

## *Core Competencies Summary Format*

### PROFESSIONAL SUMMARY

**PRODUCT DEVELOPMENT, SALES & MARKETING PROFESSIONAL**

**Advanced Technology Industries**

| | |
|---|---|
| Technology Development & Commercialization | Marketing & Business Development |
| Technology Design, Engineering & Manufacturing | Market Planning & Competitive Positioning |
| Technology Transfer & Commercialization | New Product & New Technology Launch |
| Integrated Systems & Technology Solutions | Negotiations, Presentations & Consultations |
| Advanced Telecommunications & Satellite Systems | Partnerships, Alliances & Joint Ventures |
| Operating Management | Sales & Customer Management |
| Plant Operations & Profit/Loss Management | Sales Team Building & Team Leadership |
| Performance, Productivity & Quality Improvement | Key Account Development & Management |
| World Class Production & Manufacturing Practices | Multimedia Customer Communications |
| Reengineering & Process Improvement | Territory Development & Management |

Guest Speaker, 2003 Technology Roundtable Conference

Winner, 2002 Technology Sales Council Award for Excellence

### Bullet List Format

## PROFESSIONAL QUALIFICATIONS

- Network Administrator/Database Administrator with 10 years of professional experience.

- Proficient in the use of TCP/IP, WAN and LAN networks, and network protocols.

- Expert in the design, integration, and management of multi-tiered databases.

- Outstanding project-management and team-building/team leadership skills.

- Project budget responsibility for up to $2.5 million annually.

- Keen problem-solving, troubleshooting, and communication skills.

### Category Format

## CAREER HIGHLIGHTS

| | |
|---|---|
| **Experience:** | 12 years in IT Systems Design, Analysis, Programming & Operations |
| **Education:** | MS—Information Technology—University of California |
| | BS—Computer Operations—California Institute of Technology |
| **Publications:** | "Enhancing Systems Functionality," *DPMA Annual Journal,* 2004 |
| | "Power In Performance," *Computing Weekly,* 2002 |
| **Awards:** | Technologist of the Year, Dell Corporation, 2004 |
| | Product Design Award, Dell Corporation, 2002 |
| | Recognition of Outstanding Project Leadership, Dell Corporation, 1999 |

## TECHNICAL QUALIFICATIONS

The Technical Qualifications section is a vital component of just about every technology professional's resume. It is here that you will summarize all of your technical skills and qualifications to clearly demonstrate the value and knowledge you bring to an organization.

There are instances, however, for which a Technical Qualifications section may *not* be appropriate. These may include the following:

- Senior technology executives (CIO, CTO, CKO, MIS Director, VP of Information Technology)

- Technology sales and marketing professionals

- Technology support professionals

For these individuals, technical qualifications are not the *focus* of the resume, although their technical experience is vital. For senior executives, the resume should focus on organizational development and leadership, financial and operational achievements, and other general management functions and achievements. For sales and marketing professionals, the resume should highlight performance, numbers, and revenue/market growth. For support professionals, the emphasis is on customer relationship management, troubleshooting, and problem-solving.

For all of the rest of you who will include this section in your resume, here are five samples of Technical Qualifications that you can use as a model. More inspiration can be found in the sample resumes in chapters 4 through 10.

### *Technical Skills Summary Format*

## COMPUTER / NETWORKING SKILLS

| | |
|---|---|
| **Operating Systems:** | Windows XP, 2000 Workstation; Novell NetWare 6.5; |
| **Protocols/ Networks:** | TCP/IP, NetBeui, IPX/SPX, Ethernet 10/100Base-T |
| **Hardware:** | Hard drives, printers, scanners, fax/modems, CD-ROMs, Zip drives, Cat5 cables, hubs, NIC cards |
| **Software:** | *Commercial:* Microsoft Office Modules, FileMaker Pro, PC Anywhere, MS Exchange, ARCServe, Artisoft ModemShare, Norton/McAfee Anti-Virus, Ghost |
| | *Industry-specific:* e-Credit, ICC Credit, Energizer, Midanet, Flood Link, Greatland Escrow, Allregs, Echo Connection Plus, Contour (Handler, Closer, Tracker, and LP Module) |

### Double-Column Bullet Format

## TECHNOLOGY PROFILE:

Programmer / Systems Analyst / Project Manager with expert qualifications in

- Systems specification, design & analysis
- Voice & data communications
- Data systems engineering & integration
- Application architecture & deployment

- Multimedia & videoconferencing systems
- Internet & intranet solutions
- C++ programming & HTML coding
- Project planning & team leadership

### Multiple-Column List Format

## TECHNICAL SKILLS

| | | | |
|---|---|---|---|
| • Oracle | • Delphi | • Enterprise Technologies | • TELNET |
| • PMRS | • Windows XP | • MIS IIS | • ARC Serve |
| • HP900 Database | • Novell NetWare | • UNIX | • TM1 Database |
| • SunSparc | • Banyan | • FTP | • ADP |
| • JAM | • TCP/IP | | |

### Combination Technical Qualifications/Education Format

## COMMUNICATIONS EDUCATION/KNOWLEDGE

**Bachelor of Science in** Telecommunications, University of Missouri, Columbia, Missouri

- Graduate, ABC Technologies Career Path Program, 2004

- **Certifications:** Panduit, Mohawk, Bertek, Belden, and ABC Technologies fiberoptics; ABC Technologies Systimax certification in Installation, Sales, and Design/Engineering

- **Training:** New Bridge on basic LAN environments, Bay Networks, and AT&T Pardyne DSU/CSU

- **Installation/Repair:** System 75/G3, Merlin and Partner; Dimension PBX 100, 400 & 600 Installation and Repair of Tier 1/Tier 2 Levels

- **Call Center Applications:** UCD & DGC Groups

- **Other:** All Comkey products; all other AT&T vintage PBX switches; UNIX language; basic/advanced electronics

## Combination Career Summary/Technical Skills Summary Format

### — TECHNOLOGY PROFILE —

Highly motivated and enthusiastic **IT professional** with proven experience in both team- and project-management capacities. Outstanding analysis, programming, and debugging capabilities. Ability to work autonomously and as a team player, with demonstrated strengths in leadership and mentoring situations. Easily adaptable to change, with an eagerness to learn and expand capabilities. Industry expertise includes

2D / 3D Graphing          Geometry Management

Speech Recognition       Taxation Software

**Languages:** C#, C++, C, Visual C++, MFC, ATL, ASP, Java, COM, Windows

## PROFESSIONAL EXPERIENCE

Your Professional Experience is the meat of your resume—the "software and applications," as we discussed before. It's what gives your resume substance, meaning, and depth. It is also the section that will take you the longest to write. If you've had the same position for 10 years, how can you consolidate all that you have done into one short section? If, on the opposite end of the spectrum, you have had your current position for only 11 months, how can you make it seem substantial and noteworthy? And, for all of you whose experience is in between, what do you include, how, where, and why?

These are not easy questions to answer. In fact, the most truthful response to each question is, "it depends." It depends on you, your experience, your achievements and successes, and your current career objectives.

Here are five samples of Professional Experience sections. Review how each individual's unique background is organized and emphasized, and consider your own background when using one of these as the template or foundation for developing your Professional Experience section.

## Achievement Format

Emphasizes each position, overall scope of responsibility, and resulting achievements.

---

### PROFESSIONAL EXPERIENCE

**ABC TECHNOLOGY INTERNATIONAL, INC.,** Tokyo, Japan

**Board Member / Senior Consultant** (2003 to Present)

**President & Chief Executive Officer** (2001 to 2003)

Recruited by corporate joint-venture partners to launch the start-up of a new technology company to market remote radar systems technology and imagery worldwide. Given full leadership, negotiating, and decision-making responsibility for creating a strategic business plan, negotiating complex government approvals and funding, developing market vision and tactical business development plans, staffing, establishing a global distributor network, and building an operating infrastructure.

- Created and commercialized Japan's first radar satellite company (replacing less reliable optical/solar technology), requiring a massive initiative to educate the marketplace in the functionality of this pioneering technology. Far exceeded the financial, technological, and operational objectives of investors, the Japanese government, and the industry.

- Devoted five years to obtaining government funding ($600 million), negotiating sales and distribution rights, establishing business operations, and developing advanced technologies.

- Launched operations in 2001 and achieved profitability by end of first year. Built sales to $25 million with a staff of 150. Major clients included Georgia Pacific, BP, Lockheed Martin, Canadian Coast Guard, and Swedish and Norwegian governments. Won business in Indonesia, Singapore, and Colombia.

- Structured and negotiated a second round of government financing ($250 million) to fund the development of a second satellite system. Spurred further growth and expansion throughout new markets.

**EXCEL TECHNOLOGIES,** Washington, DC

**Vice President—Marketing** (1997 to 2001)

Recruited to provide executive marketing and business-development leadership for an innovative RCA / Sony joint venture to commercialize satellite remote sensing technology from government to the private sector. Created the entire marketing organization, established a "for-profit" business culture, and recruited talented sales professionals.

- Established a worldwide sales and marketing division and built revenues to $22 million. Delivered phenomenal growth in international markets (60% of total company sales). Negotiated profitable sales in China, Germany, UK, Spain, Israel, Japan, and Brazil.

- Personally structured and negotiated marketing agreements, partnerships, and alliances with foreign governments, international sales agents, and product/technology development firms worldwide.

- Built in-house software and applications development group to eliminate reliance on third-party vendors.

- Reduced workforce from 300 to 150, recruited 70+ professional staff, introduced field sales automation, and restructured field sales teams. Rationalized and balanced technology offerings.

## Challenge, Action, and Results (CAR) Format

Emphasizes the challenge of each position, the action you took, and the results you delivered.

### PROFESSIONAL EXPERIENCE

**Director of Networking & Telecommunications** (2000 to Present)

**Telecommunications Project Manager** (1999 to 2000)

**Telecommunications Engineer** (1996 to 1999)

**PACBELL TECHNOLOGY SERVICES CORPORATION,** Los Angeles, California

**Challenge:** To transition an antiquated organization into a state-of-the-art telecommunications organization to support PTSC's rapid market growth and services expansion. Working to position the company as one of the top 5 players in the global technology market.

**Action:** Built an entirely new telecommunications organization with new architecture, hardware, software, and network protocols. Restaffed with experienced telecommunications operators, engineers, and project managers. Full P&L responsibility.

*(continued)*

*(continued)*

**Results:**

- Orchestrated the selection and implementation of a T1 backbone to support the implementation of a global telecommunications network. Invested more than $2.8 million to build one of the nation's most sophisticated networks.

- Achieved/surpassed all corporate objectives for system performance, functionality, reliability, and quality. Earned top rankings from internal and external audit teams evaluating the corporation's technological competencies.

- Dramatically increased user/customer responsiveness and satisfaction. Closed 2004 with less than .2% customer complaints and a better than 98.7% customer retention rate.

- Partnered with HP, IBM, and Dell to integrate their systems architecture with proprietary networks and network protocols.

- Contributed to a more than 125% increase in annual gross sales and a 150%+ increase in bottom-line profitability.

## Functional Format

Emphasizes the functional areas of responsibility within the job and associated achievements.

### EMPLOYMENT EXPERIENCE

**Chief Information Officer (CIO)** RADIO TECHNOLOGIES, INC.
1999 to Present

(High-growth, $300+ million company with 35 locations in the US & UK)

CIO, Vice President of Business Technology, and member of a 6-person Corporate Executive Board credited with transitioning this $35 million company into one of the nation's premier special-events companies. Given full strategic planning, leadership, and decision-making authority for building the corporation's entire IT organization, infrastructure, and operations. Led technology organization through $100 million public bond offering (Jamestown) and $65 million venture capital funding (XYZ Ventures).

Built the entire IT organization from concept into a state-of-the-art centralized IT/IS model with distributed services worldwide. Recruited, trained, and developed a staff of 37 technologists, including remote IT managers, a centralized network and operational team, and a matrix-managed finance/business team. Control over $100 million in annual operating and capital expense budgets.

**Infrastructure Development:**

- Partnered with MIT, Cisco, and an independent software company to develop high-speed **WAN technology**, one of the most critical drivers in the company's sustained and profitable growth. Developed a 20-node T1/T3 WAN within 2 years and achieved/maintained 99.9% uptime.

- Directed technology integration for **16 acquisitions** (30 sites) over 30 months. Built IT systems where none existed, replaced obsolete technology with legacy systems, and achieved Y2K compliance for all operations. Introduced and achieved corporation-wide technology standardization.

- Built **data center** from start-up into a 24x7 operation supporting high-end SUN UNIX systems and an NT platform primarily hosting Oracle databases (ERP applications).

- Designed **LAN** models and standardized voice communications using a mix of open-standard PBXs, voice mail, and voice over IP. Built MCI back-up **ISDN** network and multiple secure Internet protocols.

**Solutions & Applications:**

- Revitalized fledgling **Oracle implementation** and took ABC "live" in less than 10 months. Modules included AP, AR, GL, Purchasing, Inventory, Project Management, and HR.

- Designed "new" **Internet computing architecture,** migrating Oracle applications onto a 3-tier Web-based environment. Delivered 100% migration of 92 customizations within 60 days.

- Integrated 13 **e-mail systems** (Lotus Notes, Eudora) into one system (Microsoft Exchange) to facilitate collaborative participation among all ABC companies and operating sites.

- Led the selection and implementation of AT&T's VPN solution for direct access to ABC's **private network**.

**Internet/Intranet Development:**

- Led the design, development, and execution of five major Internet/Intranet sites. Developed business and market strategies, financial plans, Web site interfaces, and e-commerce transactional processes that supported successful launches, solid functionality, and consistently strong performance.

  intranet.abc.com (ABC Intranet deployed to 1,000 users)

  www.nightstar.com (independent LLC company)

  www.industry.com (e-commerce site)

  www.lite.poly.edu/html/milso_case.htm (sponsored research with Merrill Lynch)

  www.abc-link.com (password-protected outsourced server—"Certnet" for ABC project management)

## Consulting and Project Format

Emphasizes clients and project highlights.

### PROJECT HIGHLIGHTS

**DEVELOPER:** Maxx Data Applications

**CLIENT:** Value Enhancement Services, Inc., June 2002–Present

**PROJECT:**

- Prepare system and design requirements for the Maxx system.
- Write specifications and database definitions.
- Work with development team and end users to complete system development.
- Continue to modify and enhance the system.

**PLATFORMS:**

- Microsoft Access XP, VBA, ADO, SQL Server
- Microsoft Excel XP, UML Use Case Studies, UML Use Case Diagrams

**BENEFITS:**

- System helps clients recover "lost" money by identifying oversights, overpayments, and missed opportunities following an expense audit conducted by Value Enhancement.
- On the first project following implementation, slashed audit time in half—from 3 months to 6 weeks—and doubled recovered funds, thereby doubling revenue to the firm.

**DEVELOPER:** Microsoft Access database

**CLIENT: City of Plano,** Texas, May 2000–June 2002

**PROJECT:**

- Stepped in on short notice to identify enhancement requirements and then define, specify, and complete enhancements to the Construx project-management system.

**PLATFORMS:** MS Access XP, VBA, MS Excel XP

**BENEFITS:**

- Responded to client urgency to complete system modification within a rapid timeframe… completed using only 23 of the 40 hours allocated.

**Y2K PROJECT COORDINATOR**

**CLIENT: CompUSA** (through Rent-a-Tech consulting firm), May 1999–May 2000

**PROJECT:**

- Work with employees and contractors in all CompUSA business areas to define requirements for system functions and required results.

- Develop MS Access systems to analyze and compute project metrics.

**PLATFORMS:**

- MS Access XP, MS Excel XP, ABT

**BENEFITS:**

- Completed project on time, with no errors or incidents, and $3 million under budget...ranked by *Dallas Morning News* as one of the best-conducted Y2K projects in the Dallas/Fort Worth area.

## Technology Skills Format

Emphasizes technological expertise and notable projects/achievements.

## —PROFESSIONAL EXPERIENCE—

**HONEYWELL IAC**      July 2002–August 2004

**Applications Engineer, Specialty Chemicals Division,** Cincinnati, OH

*Procter & Gamble Shampoo and Conditioner Plant Expansion,* Mariscala, Mexico—January–August 2004

- Assisted in definition of HPM and PLC logic for core control box.

- Developed software (CL, control language) to simulate batch production of shampoo and conditioner.

*B.F. Goodrich Carbopol Plant Upgrade Project,* Paducah, KY—January–June 2003

- Implemented and adapted old TDC 2000 MFC database, interlocks, and complex control loops into current TPS (Total Plant System) control system.

*(continued)*

*(continued)*

- Implemented and adapted old GE FANUC PLC ladder logic to a series of logic points in the Honeywell system that wrote and read to the PLC through a serial interface.

- Developed installation qualification and operational qualification documentation for testing procedures.

- Assisted in startup and commissioning of new control system—loop checking, troubleshooting wiring problems, and testing complex control schemes.

**Control System Engineer, North American Projects Division,** Phoenix, AZ

*TCO Project,* Tengiz, Kazakhstan—April–December 2003

- Translated and then implemented Control Bailey control schematics into current TPS control system.

- Assisted in creating serial interface points on Honeywell system to connect to Wonderware system.

- Developed software to simulate a nitrogen-generation unit for expansion area added to Tengiz plant.

- Assisted in establishing termination drawings that entailed segregation of IS and non-IS field wires.

- Created intelligent P&IDs of the refinery using Rebis and AutoCAD software.

- Came on board mid-stream while project was in danger of being lost due to client dissatisfaction. Met critical deadlines through intensive team efforts; contract extended for contingency phase.

**Control System Engineer, CSCC,** Ashland, KY

*Ashland Petroleum Steam Project,* Catlettsburg, KY—July 2002–March 2003

- Established real-time steam model for Catlettsburg refinery using G2-based Visual-MESA (a steam optimization program).

- Developed real-time control schematics for G2-based ASM (Abnormal Situation Management).

- Created a search program for ASM using G2 code.

- Calculated boiler efficiency curves for all boilers in the refinery.

- Worked with interface technology between G2 and Microsoft products.

- Rapidly learned G2 programming on the job. Became primary project engineer mid-stream. Contract extended.

## EDUCATION, CREDENTIALS, AND CERTIFICATIONS

Your Education section should include college, certifications, credentials, licenses, registrations, and continuing education. Be succinct, and be sure to bring any notable academic credentials or certifications to the forefront—either in your Education section or in your Career Summary, as demonstrated in the first Career Summary example shown previously. If you have attended numerous continuing education programs, list only the most recent, most relevant, and most distinguishing.

Here are five sample Education sections that illustrate a variety of ways to organize and format this information.

### *Academic Credentials Format*

**EDUCATION**

**MBA—Information Systems & Technology**—Xavier University—2002

**BSEE—Electronics Engineering & Systems Design**—The Ohio State University—1998

**Highlights of Continuing Professional Education:**

- Robotics & Systems Automation, Rensselaer Polytechnic University, 2004
- Advanced Computer Science Applications, The Ohio State University, 2004
- Executive Leadership Skills, Dale Carnegie, 2003
- Web Systems Design & Integration, University of Cincinnati, 2002

Microsoft Systems Certified Engineer (MSCE), 1996

FCC Registered Mobile Radio Operator, 1996

### *Executive Education Format*

**EDUCATION**

| | |
|---|---|
| **Executive Development Program** | STANFORD UNIVERSITY |
| **Executive Development Program** | UNIVERSITY OF CALIFORNIA AT IRVINE |
| **Bachelor of Science Degree** | UNIVERSITY OF CALIFORNIA AT LOS ANGELES |

## Certifications Format

### TECHNICAL CERTIFICATIONS & EDUCATION

**Microsoft Certified Systems Engineer (MCSE)**, 2003

**Microsoft Certified Professional (MCP)**, 2001

**Cisco Certified Network Associate (CCNA)**, 2001

**Computer Systems Management Major**, University of Michigan, 1998

**A.A.S. Degree in Computer Technology**, Michigan Community College, 1996

## Professional Training Format

### PROFESSIONAL TRAINING & DEVELOPMENT

**Computer Statistics & Methodologies**, Baruch College, 2002

**Computer Operations Management**, Baruch College, 2002

**C++ Programming for Technology Professionals**, University of Maryland, 2001

**Voice & Data Systems Design**, New York University, 2000

**Network Administrator**, New York University, 2002

**Anne Arundel Community College**, Arnold, Maryland, 1998-2000

## Non-Degree Format

### TECHNICAL TRAINING & EDUCATION

**UNIVERSITY OF ILLINOIS**, Urbana, Illinois

**BBA Candidate—Management Information Systems** (senior class status)

**UNIVERSITY OF MICHIGAN**, Ann Arbor, Michigan

**Dual Major in Computer Systems & Programming** (2 years)

**Graduate**, 200+ hours of continuing professional and technical education through DPMA, Chicago Technology Institute, IBM, HP, and DePaul University.

## THE "EXTRAS"

The primary focus of your resume is on information that is directly related to your career goals. However, you also should include things that will distinguish you from other candidates and clearly demonstrate your value to a prospective employer. And, not too surprisingly, it is often the "extras" that get the interviews.

Following is a list of the other categories you might or might not include in your resume, depending on your particular experience and your current career objectives. Review the information. If it's pertinent to you, use the samples for formatting your own data. Remember, however, that if something is truly impressive, you may want to include it in your Career Summary at the beginning of your resume in order to draw even more attention to it. If this is the case, it's not necessary to repeat the information at the end of your resume.

### Affiliations—Professional

If you are a member of any professional, leadership, or technology associations, be sure to include that information on your resume. It communicates a message of professionalism, a desire to stay current with the industry, and a strong professional network. Here's an example:

> **PROFESSIONAL AFFILIATIONS**
>
> - Member, Data Processing Management Association (Training Program Chairperson—2004)
>
> - Member, Institute for Technology Enterprise (Convention Chairperson—2002)
>
> - President, Project Management Institute (New York Chapter—2000–2001)

### Affiliations—Civic

Civic affiliations are fine to include if they fall into one or more of the following categories:

- Are with a notable organization
- Demonstrate leadership experience
- May be of interest to a prospective employer

However, things such as treasurer of your local condo association and volunteer at your child's day care center are not generally of value in marketing your qualifications. Here's an example of what to include:

- Volunteer Chairperson, United Way of America—Detroit Chapter, 2002 to Present

- President, Lambert Valley Conservation District, 1999 to Present

- Treasurer, Habitat for Humanity—Detroit Chapter, 1996 to 1997

## Public Speaking

Experts are the ones who are invited to give public presentations at conferences, technical training programs, symposia, and other events. So if you have public speaking experience, others must consider you an expert. Be sure to include this very complimentary information in your resume. Here's one way to present it:

- Keynote Speaker, 2004 Conference of Internet Executives—Las Vegas

- Presenter, 2003 International DPMA Conference—Dallas

- Presenter, 2001 IBM Technology Training Symposium—New York

## Publications

If you're published, you must be an expert (or at least most people will think so). Just as with your public speaking engagements, be sure to include your publications. They validate your knowledge, qualifications, and credibility. Publications can include books, articles, Web site content, manuals, and other written documents. Here's an example:

- Author, "Winning Web Marketing Strategies," *TechBusiness Magazine,* January 2004

- Author, "Web Marketing 101: Compete To Win," *TechBusiness Online,* February 2002

- Co-Author, "Op-Cit Technology Training Manual," Op-Cit Corporation, December 2001

## Honors and Awards

If you have won honors and awards, you can either include them in a separate section on your resume or integrate them into the Education or Professional Experience section, whichever is most appropriate. If you choose to include them in a separate section, consider this format:

- Winner, 2003 **"President's Club"** award for outstanding contributions to new product development.

- Winner, 2000 **"Innovator's Club"** award for outstanding contributions to technology innovation.

- Named **"Graduate Student of the Year,"** Hofstra University, 1996

- **Summa Cum Laude Graduate**, Washington & Lee University, 1984

## Teaching and Training Experience

Many professionals in the technology industry also teach or train at institutions and organizations other than their full-time employer. If this is applicable to you, you will want to include that experience on your resume. If someone hires you (paid or unpaid) to speak to an audience, it communicates a strong message about your qualifications and credibility. Here's a format you might use to present this information:

- Adjunct Faculty—Information Technology, Contra Costa Community College, Spring 2003

- Instructor—Programming Principles, Contra Costa Community College, Fall 2001

- Instructor—Systems Architecture, Valley Mead University, Fall 1999–Spring 2000

**NOTE:** If teaching or training is your primary occupation, you will not include this section in your resume. Rather, your teaching and training will be in your Professional Experience section.

## Personal Information

We do not recommend that you include such personal information as birth date, marital status, number of children, and related data. However, there may be instances when personal information is appropriate. If this information will give you a competitive advantage or answer unspoken questions about your background, then by all means include it. Here's an example:

- Born in Argentina. U.S. Permanent Residency Status since 1987.

- Fluent in English, Spanish, and Portuguese.

- Competitive Triathlete. Top-5 finish, 1987 Midwest Triathlon and 1992 Des Moines Triathlon.

### *Consolidating the Extras*

Sometimes you have so many extra categories at the end of your resume that spacing becomes a problem. You certainly don't want to have to make your resume a page longer to accommodate five lines, nor do you want the "extras" to overwhelm the primary sections of your resume. Yet you believe the "extra" information is important and should be included. Or perhaps you have a few small bits of information that you think are important but don't merit an entire section for each "bit." In these situations, consider consolidating the information using one of the following formats. You'll save space, avoid overemphasizing individual items, and present a professional, distinguished appearance.

#### PROFESSIONAL PROFILE

| | |
|---|---|
| **Affiliations** | American Management Association |
| | Data Processing Management Association |
| | Information Technology Executives Leadership Council |
| **Public Speaking** | Keynote Speaker, AMA Leadership Conference, Dallas, 2004 |
| | Presenter, DPMA National Conference, San Diego, 2002 |
| | Panelist, DPMA National Conference, Chicago, 2000 |
| **Foreign Languages** | Fluent in English, Spanish, and German |

#### ADDITIONAL INFORMATION

- Founder and Program Chair, Detroit Technical Professionals Association.
- Bilingual—Spanish/English.
- Available for relocation.

## Writing Tips, Techniques, and Important Lessons

At this point, you've done a lot of reading, probably taken some notes, highlighted samples that appeal to you, and are ready to plunge into writing your resume. To make this task as easy as possible, we've compiled some "insider" techniques that we've used in our professional resume writing practices. These techniques were learned the hard way through years of experience! We know they work; they will make the writing process easier, faster, and more enjoyable for you.

### GET IT DOWN—THEN POLISH AND PERFECT IT

Don't be too concerned with making your resume "perfect" the first time around. It's far better to move fairly swiftly through the process, getting the basic information organized and on paper (or on-screen), rather than agonizing about the perfect phrase or ideal formatting. Once you've completed a draft, we think you'll be surprised at how close to "final" it is, and you'll be able to edit, tighten, and improve formatting fairly quickly.

## WRITE YOUR RESUME FROM THE BOTTOM UP

Here's the system:

- **Start with the easy things**—Education, Professional Affiliations, Public Speaking, and any other extras you want to include. These items require little thought, other than formatting considerations, and can be completed in just a few minutes.

- **Write short job descriptions for your older positions, the ones you held years ago.** Be very brief and focus on highlights such as rapid promotion, project highlights, notable achievements, technology innovations, industry recognition, or employment with well-respected, well-known companies.

  Once you've completed this, look at how much you've written in a short period of time!

- **Write the job descriptions for your most recent positions.** This will take a bit longer than the other sections you have written. Remember to focus on the overall scope of your responsibility, major projects, and significant achievements. Tell your reader what you did and how well you did it. You can use any of the formats recommended earlier in this chapter, or you can create something that is unique to you and your career.

  Now, see how far along you are? Your resume is 90 percent complete with only one small section left to do.

- **Write your career summary.** Before you start writing, remember your objective for this section. The summary should not simply rehash your previous experience. Rather, it is designed to highlight the skills and qualifications you have that are most closely related to your current career objective(s). The summary is intended to capture the reader's attention and "sell" your expertise.

That's it. You're done. We guarantee that the process of writing your resume will be much, much easier if you follow the "bottom-up" strategy. Now, on to the next tip.

## INCLUDE NOTABLE OR PROMINENT "EXTRA" STUFF IN YOUR CAREER SUMMARY

Remember the "bits and bytes" sections that are normally at the bottom of your resume? If this information is particularly notable or prominent—for example, you won a notable award, spoke at an international technology conference, invented a new product, or taught at a prestigious university—you may want to include it at the top in your Career Summary. Remember, the summary section is written to distinguish you from the crowd of other qualified candidates. As such, if you've accomplished anything that clearly demonstrates your knowledge, expertise, and credibility, consider moving it to your Career Summary for added attention.

Refer to the sample Career Summaries (especially the third and fifth ones) earlier in the chapter for examples.

## USE RESUME SAMPLES TO GET IDEAS FOR CONTENT, FORMAT, AND ORGANIZATION

This book is just one of many resources where you can review the resumes of other technology professionals to help you in formulating your strategy, writing the text, and formatting your resume. These books are published precisely for that reason. You don't have to struggle alone. Rather, use all the available resources at your disposal.

Be forewarned, however, that it's unlikely you will find a resume that fits your life and career to a "t." It's more likely that you will use "some of this sample" and "some of that sample" to create a resume that is uniquely "you."

## STICK TO THE HIGHLIGHTS

If you have more information than will fit comfortably into a single category on your resume, include just the highlights. This is particularly relevant to the "extra" categories such as Professional Affiliations, Civic Affiliations, Foreign Languages, Honors and Awards, Publications, Public Speaking, and the like. Suppose you have won 10 different awards throughout your career, but you're limited in the amount of space available at the bottom of your resume. Instead of listing all 10 and forcing your resume onto an additional page, simply title the category "Highlights of Honors & Awards" or "Notable Honors & Awards" and include just a sampling. By using the words "highlights" and "notable," you are communicating to your reader that you are providing just a partial listing.

## INCLUDE DATES OR NOT?

Unless you are over age 50, we recommend that you date your work experience and your education. Without dates, your resume becomes vague and difficult for the typical hiring manager or recruiter to interpret. What's more, it often communicates the message that you are trying to hide something. Maybe you haven't worked in two years, maybe you were fired from each of your last three positions, or maybe you never graduated from college. Being vague and creating a resume that is difficult to read will, inevitably, lead to uncertainty and a quick toss into the "not interested" pile of candidates. By including the dates of your education and your experience, you create a clean and concise picture that one can easily follow to track your career progression.

If you are over age 50, dating your early positions must be an individual decision. On the one hand, you do not want to "date" yourself out of consideration by including dates from the 1960s and 1970s. On the other hand, it may be that those positions are worth including for any one of a number of reasons. Further, if you omit those early dates, you may feel as though you are misrepresenting yourself (or lying) to a prospective employer.

Here is a strategy to overcome those concerns while still including your early experience: Create a separate category titled "Previous Professional Experience" in which you summarize your earliest employment. You can tailor this statement to emphasize just what is most important about that experience.

If you want to focus on the reputation of your past employers, include a statement such as this:

> • Previous experience includes several programming, applications-development, and project-management positions with **IBM, Tandem, and Hewlett Packard.**

If you want to focus on the rapid progression of your career, consider this example:

> • **Promoted rapidly through a series of increasingly responsible project management positions** with Digital Equipment Corporation, earning six promotions in eight years.

If you want to focus on your early career achievements, include a statement such as

> • Led the design, development, and market launch of X-TEL's second-generation software, now a **$2.1 million profit center** for the corporation.

By including any one of the above paragraphs, under the heading "Previous Professional Experience," you are clearly communicating to your reader that your employment history dates further back than the dates you have indicated on your resume. In turn, you are being 100 percent above-board and not misrepresenting yourself or your career. You're focusing on the success, achievement, and prominence of your earliest assignments without specifying exact dates.

If you are over age 50, we generally do not recommend that you date your education or college degrees. Simply include the degree and the university with no date. Why exclude yourself from consideration by immediately presenting the fact that you earned your college degree in 1958, 1962, or 1966—about the time the hiring manager was probably being born? Remember, the goal of your resume is to share the highlights of your career and open doors for interviews. It is *not* to give your entire life story. As such, it is not mandatory to date your college degree.

However, if you use this strategy, be aware that the reader is likely to assume there is *some* gap between when your education ended and your work experience started. Therefore, if you choose to begin your chronological work history with your first job out of college, omitting your graduation date could actually backfire, because the reader may assume you have experience that predates your first job. In this case, it's best either to *include your graduation date* or *omit dates of earliest experience,* using the summary strategy discussed above.

## ALWAYS SEND A COVER LETTER WHEN YOU FORWARD YOUR RESUME

It is expected, and it's appropriate job search etiquette, to include a cover letter with your resume. When you prepare a resume, you are writing a document that you can use for each and every position you apply for, assuming that the requirements for all of those positions will be similar. The cover letter, then, is the tool that allows you to customize your presentation to each company or recruiter, addressing their specific hiring requirements. It is also the appropriate place to include any specific information that has been requested, such as salary history or salary requirements (but see the following section for a caution on this). See chapter 11 for more about creating cover letters with impact.

## NEVER INCLUDE SALARY HISTORY OR SALARY REQUIREMENTS ON YOUR RESUME

Your resume is *not* the proper forum for a salary discussion. First of all, you will never provide salary information unless a company has requested that information and you choose to comply. (Studies show that employers will look at your resume anyway, so you may choose not to respond to this request, thereby avoiding pricing yourself out of the job or locking yourself into a lower salary than the job is worth.)

When contacting recruiters, however, we recommend that you do provide salary information, but again, only in your cover letter. With recruiters you want to "put all of your cards on the table" and help them make an appropriate placement by providing information about your current salary and salary objectives. For example, "Be advised that my current compensation is $75,000 annually and that I am interested in a position starting at a minimum of $85,000 per year." Or, if you would prefer to be a little less specific, you might write, "My annual compensation over the past three years has averaged $50,000+."

## ALWAYS REMEMBER THAT YOU ARE SELLING

As we have discussed over and over throughout this book, resume writing is sales. Understand and appreciate the value you bring to a prospective employer, and then communicate that value by focusing on your achievements. Companies don't want to hire just anyone; they want to hire "the" someone who will make a difference. Show them that you are that candidate.

## CHAPTER 3

# Printed, Scannable, Electronic, and Web Resumes

After you've worked so tirelessly to write a winning resume, your next challenge is the resume's design, layout, and presentation. It's not enough for it to read well; your resume must also have just the right look for the right audience.

## The Four Types of Resumes

In today's employment market, job seekers use four types of resume presentations:

- Printed
- Scannable
- Electronic (e-mail attachments and ASCII text files)
- Web

The following sections give details on when you would need each type, as well as how to prepare these types of resumes.

### THE PRINTED RESUME

We know the printed resume as the "traditional resume," the one that you mail to a recruiter, take to an interview, and forward by mail or fax in response to an advertisement. When preparing a printed resume, you want to create a sharp, professional, and visually attractive presentation. Remember, that piece of paper conveys the very first impression of you to a potential employer, and that first impression goes a long, long way. Never be fooled into thinking that just because you have the best qualifications in your industry, the visual presentation of your resume does not matter. It does, a great deal.

### THE SCANNABLE RESUME

The scannable resume can be referred to as the "plain-Jane" or "plain-vanilla" resume. All of the things that you would normally do to make your printed resume look attractive—bold print, italics, multiple columns, sharp-looking typestyle, and more—are stripped away in a scannable resume. You want to present a document that can be easily read and interpreted by scanning technology.

Although the technology continues to improve, and many scanning systems in fact can read a wide variety of type enhancements, it's sensible to appeal to the "lowest common denominator" when creating your scannable resume. Follow these formatting guidelines:

- Choose a commonly used, easily read font such as Arial or Times New Roman.

- Don't use bold, italic, or underlined type.

- Use a minimum of 11-point type size.

- Position your name, and nothing else, on the top line of the resume.

- Keep text left-justified, with a "ragged" right margin.

- It's okay to use common abbreviations (for instance, scanning software will recognize "B.S." as a Bachelor of Science degree). But, when in doubt, spell it out.

- Eliminate graphics, borders, and horizontal lines.

- Use plain, round bullets or asterisks.

- Avoid columns and tables, although a simple two-column listing can be read without difficulty.

- Spell out symbols such as % and &.

- If you divide words with slashes, add a space before and after the slash to be certain the scanner doesn't misread the letters.

- Print using a laser printer on smooth white paper.

- If your resume is longer than one page, be sure to print on only one side of the paper; put your name, telephone number, and e-mail address on the top of page two; and don't staple the pages together.

- For best possible results, mail your resume (don't fax it), and send it flat in a 9 × 12 envelope so that you won't have to fold it.

Scannable resumes are becoming less common and less in demand as the majority of career documents are transmitted by e-mail or pasted into online applications. It is only when your resume pages need to physically pass through a scanner that you will need a scannable resume. We recommend that you not worry about this format until and unless you are required to produce one for a specific company. For electronic resume guidelines, see the next section.

## THE ELECTRONIC RESUME

Your electronic resume can take two forms: e-mail attachments and ASCII text files.

### E-Mail Attachments

When including your resume with an e-mail, simply attach the word-processing file of your printed resume. Because a vast majority of businesses use Microsoft Word, it is the most acceptable format and will present the fewest difficulties. However, given the tremendous variety in versions of software and operating systems, not to mention printer drivers, it's quite possible that your beautifully formatted resume will look quite different when viewed and printed at the other end. To minimize these glitches, use generous margins (at least 0.75 inch all around). Don't use unusual typefaces, and minimize fancy formatting effects.

Test your resume by e-mailing it to several friends or colleagues, and then having them view and print it on their systems. If you use WordPerfect, Microsoft Works, or another word-processing program, consider saving your resume in a more universally accepted format such as RTF or PDF. Again, try it out on friends before sending it to a potential employer.

Although employers can easily open, view, and print a PDF (Portable Document Format) file, we do not recommend this as your primary electronic format. A PDF file is viewed as a graphic rather than an editable file, and therefore the data from your resume cannot be read into a company's resume-storage system unless it is printed and physically scanned. PDF is an excellent option if your resume has an unusual design, and especially if design skills are an important part of your qualifications. But for the most part, the PDF format will be less useful than a word-processing file format (such as .doc) for the companies receiving your resume.

## *ASCII Text Files*

You'll find many uses for an ASCII text version of your resume:

- To avoid formatting problems, you can paste the text into the body of an e-mail message rather than send an attachment. Many employers actually prefer this method. Pasting text into an e-mail message lets you send your resume without the possibility of also sending a virus.

- You can readily copy and paste the text version into online job application and resume bank forms, with no worries that formatting glitches will cause confusion.

- Although it's unattractive, the text version is 100 percent scannable.

To create a text version of your resume, follow these simple steps:

1. Create a new version of your resume using the Save As feature of your word-processing program. Select "text only" or "ASCII" in the Save As option box.

2. Close the new file.

3. Reopen the file, and you'll find that your word processor has automatically reformatted your resume into Courier font, removed all formatting, and left-justified the text.

4. To promote maximum readability when sending your resume electronically, reset the margins to 2 inches left and right, so that you have a narrow column of text rather than a full-page width. (This margin setting will not be retained when you close the file, but in the meantime you can adjust the text formatting for best screen appearance. For instance, if you choose to include a horizontal line to separate sections of the resume, by working with the narrow

margins you won't make the mistake of creating a line that extends past the normal screen width. Plus, you won't add hard line breaks that create odd-length lines when seen at normal screen width.)

5. Review the resume and fix any "glitches" such as odd characters that may have been inserted to take the place of "curly" quotes, dashes, accents, or other nonstandard symbols.

6. Remove any tabs and adjust spacing as necessary. You might add a few extra blank lines or move text down to the next line.

7. If necessary, add extra blank lines to improve readability.

8. Consider adding horizontal dividers to break the resume into sections for improved skimmability. You can use any standard typewriter symbols such as *, -, (, ), =, +, ^, or #.

To illustrate what you can expect when creating these versions of your resume, on the following pages are some examples of the same resume in traditional printed format, scannable version, and electronic (text) format.

## THE WEB RESUME

This newest evolution in resumes combines the visually pleasing quality of the printed resume with the technological ease of the electronic resume. You host your Web resume on your own Web site (with your own URL), to which you refer prospective employers and recruiters. Now, instead of seeing just a "plain-Jane" version of your e-mailed resume, with just one click an employer can view, download, and print your Web resume—an attractive, nicely formatted presentation of your qualifications.

What's more, because the Web resume is such an efficient and easy-to-manage tool, you can choose to include more information than you would in a printed, scannable, or electronic resume. Consider separate pages for achievements, technology qualifications, equipment skills, honors and awards, management skills, and more, if you believe they would improve your market position.

For those of you in technologically related professions, you can take it one step further and create a virtual multimedia presentation that not only tells someone how talented you are, but also visually and technologically demonstrates it. Web resumes are an outstanding tool for people seeking jobs in technologically or visually related professions.

Your Web resume can also include all of the items (and more) that you would normally include in your professional portfolio. If you are an elementary teacher, you might include lesson plans, thematic units, customized curriculum, photographs, and other artwork. If corporate training is your expertise, your portfolio could showcase some of your handout materials, group exercises, and summary reports of your post-training evaluations. Testimonials and letters of reference can be another powerful part of your professional portfolio.

Depending on your technology skills, you might decide to create and manage your own Web resume/portfolio. Another option is to outsource this project to a firm that specializes in career portfolios. A few we like are Blue Sky Portfolios (www.blueskyportfolios.com), Brandego (www.brandego.com), and Portfolio Vault (www.portfoliovault.com).

A simplified version of the Web resume is an online version of your Microsoft Word resume. Instead of attaching a file to an e-mail to an employer, you can include a link to the online version. This format is not as graphically dynamic as a full-fledged Web resume, but it can be a very useful tool for your job search. For instance, you can offer the simplicity of text in your e-mail, plus the instant availability of a printable, formatted word-processing document for the interested recruiter or hiring manager. For a demonstration of this format, go to www.e-resume-central.com and click on "SEE A SAMPLE."

---

**T. RICHARD POLAWSKI**

5252 Memory Lane — Shuffletown, NC 28217 — 704-365-1818 — trpolawski@carolina.rr.com

**CAREER GOAL**

Position as Instructor in an environment focused on education, enlightenment, and encouragement.

**KEY BENEFITS**

- Exceptional ability to communicate technical information to end users. Have provided end-user training and ongoing support in network, Internet/Web, and various Microsoft applications (Windows, Outlook, Exchange).
- Offer a unique, valuable perspective gained from longevity in the field (11 years with Microsoft Corporation), complemented by a passion for technology, an enjoyment of training delivery, and an inner drive to remain on the cutting edge.
- Expertise in systematically troubleshooting network messaging problems, upgrading hardware/ software, and performing service work; received superlative grades in courses in Pascal, Advanced Pascal, FORTRAN, COBOL, and C languages.

**INFORMATION TECHNOLOGY COMPETENCIES**

- *Microsoft Certified Systems Engineer (MCSE),* 1997; *Microsoft Certified Professional (MCP),* 1994: Design, install, maintain, troubleshoot, test, and repair computer systems. Experienced in building and rebuilding computers and related peripherals.
- Strong background in developing and evaluating new products and implementing "best practices." Extensive experience in writing technical (including user-training) procedures.

**RECENT EMPLOYMENT HISTORY**

**MICROSOFT CORPORATION** — Charlotte, NC                          1993–Present
*Product Support Engineer*

Currently provide product support for MS Exchange: Troubleshoot message-flow problems across various networks and the Internet, to include interfacing with Lotus Domino and Novell GroupWise servers. Previously provided support for MS Word for Windows and Macintosh. **Wrote technical procedures for user functions,** including repair, optimization, and other customer requirements.

---

*The print version of the resume section.*

T. Richard Polawski
5252 Memory Lane, Shuffletown, NC 28217
704-365-1818 — trpolawski@carolina.rr.com

CAREER GOAL
Position as Instructor in an environment focused on education, enlightenment, and encouragement.

KEY BENEFITS
- Exceptional ability to communicate technical information to end users. Have provided end-user training and ongoing support in network, Internet/Web, and various Microsoft applications (Windows, Outlook, Exchange).
- Offer a unique, valuable perspective gained from longevity in the field (11 years with Microsoft Corporation), complemented by a passion for technology, an enjoyment of training delivery, and an inner drive to remain on the cutting edge.
- Expertise in systematically troubleshooting network messaging problems, upgrading hardware/software, and performing service work; received superlative grades in courses in Pascal, Advanced Pascal, FORTRAN, COBOL, and C languages.

INFORMATION TECHNOLOGY COMPETENCIES
- Microsoft Certified Systems Engineer (MCSE), 1997; Microsoft Certified Professional (MCP), 1994: Design, install, maintain, troubleshoot, test, and repair computer systems. Experienced in building and rebuilding computers and related peripherals.
- Strong background in developing and evaluating new products and implementing "best practices." Extensive experience in writing technical (including user-training) procedures.

RECENT EMPLOYMENT HISTORY
MICROSOFT CORPORATION, Charlotte, NC, 1993–Present
Product Support Engineer
Currently provide product support for MS Exchange: Troubleshoot message-flow problems across various networks and the Internet, to include interfacing with Lotus Domino and Novell GroupWise servers. Previously provided support for MS Word for Windows and Macintosh. Wrote technical procedures for user functions, including repair, optimization, and other customer requirements.

*The scannable version of the resume section.*

```
T. Richard Polawski
5252 Memory Lane, Shuffletown, NC 28217
704-365-1818 — trpolawski@carolina.rr.com

=========================================
CAREER GOAL

Position as Instructor in an environment focused on education, enlightenment, and
encouragement.

=========================================
KEY BENEFITS

* Exceptional ability to communicate technical information to end users. Have
provided end-user training and ongoing support in network, Internet/Web, and various
Microsoft applications (Windows, Outlook, Exchange).
* Offer a unique, valuable perspective gained from longevity in the field (11 years
with Microsoft Corporation), complemented by a passion for technology, an enjoyment
of training delivery, and an inner drive to remain on the cutting edge.
* Expertise in systematically troubleshooting network messaging problems, upgrading
hardware/software, and performing service work; received superlative grades in
courses in Pascal, Advanced Pascal, FORTRAN, COBOL, and C languages.

=========================================
INFORMATION TECHNOLOGY COMPETENCIES

* Microsoft Certified Systems Engineer (MCSE), 1997; Microsoft Certified
Professional (MCP), 1994: Design, install, maintain, troubleshoot, test, and repair
computer systems. Experienced in building and rebuilding computers and related
peripherals.
* Strong background in developing and evaluating new products and implementing
``best practices.'' Extensive experience in writing technical (including user-
training) procedures.

=========================================
RECENT EMPLOYMENT HISTORY

MICROSOFT CORPORATION, Charlotte, NC, 1993-Present
----------------------------
Product Support Engineer
----------------------------
Currently provide product support for MS Exchange: Troubleshoot message-flow
problems across various networks and the Internet, to include interfacing with Lotus
Domino and Novell GroupWise servers. Previously provided support for MS Word for
Windows and Macintosh. Wrote technical procedures for user functions, including
repair, optimization, and other customer requirements.
```

*The electronic/text version of the resume section.*

# The Four Resume Types Compared

This chart quickly compares the similarities and differences between the four types of resumes we've discussed in this chapter.

| | PRINTED RESUMES | SCANNABLE RESUMES |
|---|---|---|
| **TYPESTYLE/ FONT** | Sharp, conservative, and distinctive (see our recommendations in chapter 1). | Clean, concise, and machine-readable: Times New Roman, Arial, Helvetica. |
| **TYPESTYLE ENHANCEMENTS** | **Bold,** *italics,* and underlining for emphasis. | CAPITALIZATION is the only type enhancement you can be certain will transmit. |
| **TYPE SIZE** | 10-, 11-, or 12-point preferred... larger type sizes (14, 18, 20, 22, and even larger, depending on typestyle) will effectively enhance your name and section headers. | 11- or 12-point, or larger. |
| **TEXT FORMAT** | Use centering and indentations to optimize the visual presentation. | Type all information flush left. |
| **PREFERRED LENGTH** | 1 to 2 pages; 3 if essential. | 1 to 2 pages preferred, although length is not as much of a concern as with printed resumes. |
| **PREFERRED PAPER COLOR** | White, Ivory, Light Gray, Light Blue, or other conservative background. | White or very light with no prints, flecks, or other shading that might affect scannability. |
| **WHITE SPACE** | Use appropriately for best readability. | Use generously to maximize scannability. |

| ELECTRONIC RESUMES | WEB RESUMES |
|---|---|
| Courier. | Sharp, conservative, and distinctive... attractive onscreen and when printed from an online document. |
| CAPITALIZATION is the only enhancement available to you. | **Bold,** *italics,* and underlining, and color for emphasis. |
| 12-point. | 10-, 11-, or 12-point preferred... larger type sizes (14, 18, 20, 22, and even larger, depending on typestyle) will effectively enhance your name and section headers. |
| Type all information flush left. | Use centering and indentations to optimize the visual presentation. |
| Length is immaterial; almost definitely, converting your resume to text will make it longer. | Length is immaterial; just be sure your site is well organized so viewers can quickly find the material of greatest interest to them. |
| N/A. | Paper is not used, but do select your background carefully to maximize readability. |
| Use white space to break up dense text sections. | Use appropriately for best readability both onscreen and when printed. |

# Are You Ready to Write Your Resume?

To be sure that you're ready to write your resume, go through the following checklist. Each item is a critical step that you must take in the process of writing and designing your own winning resume.

❏ Clearly define "who you are" and how you want to be perceived.

❏ Document your key skills, qualifications, and knowledge.

❏ Document your notable career achievements and successes.

❏ Identify one or more specific job targets or positions.

❏ Identify one or more industries that you are targeting.

❏ Research and compile key words for your profession, industry, and specific job targets.

❏ Determine which resume format suits you and your career best.

❏ Select an attractive font.

❏ Determine whether you need a print resume, a scannable resume, an electronic resume, a Web resume, or all four.

❏ Secure a private e-mail address.

❏ Review resume samples for up-to-date ideas on resume styles, formats, organization, and language.

# PART II

# Sample Resumes for Computer and Web Jobs

CHAPTER 4

# Resumes for Computer Operators and Technicians

- Computer Operators
- Computer Analysts
- Computer Systems and PC Technicians
- Hardware Technicians
- Electronics Technicians
- Systems Installation and Configuration Technicians
- Field Service Technicians
- Field Engineers
- Systems Technicians

# John B. Lankford

2020 West Main Street, Apt. 231 — Hendersonville, Tennessee 37075

Home: (615) 555-5466 — E-mail: jblankford@home.com

## COMPUTER OPERATIONS AND SYSTEMS PROFESSIONAL

IBM PCs – Compatibles – Microsoft Office

Linux – Windows 9x/NT/2000/XP

DSU/CSU – Routers – Hubs

## QUALIFICATIONS SUMMARY

- Solid computer operations background involving installation, maintenance, and troubleshooting of PC hardware, operating systems, LAN and WAN equipment, and numerous software applications.
- Experienced as a technical trainer/instructor with strong knowledge in hardware repair and technical training.
- Ability to translate technical information and make it more easily understood by nontechnical audiences.
- Learn new systems and software readily. Strong desire to expand computer knowledge and apply it to improving business performance.

## PROFESSIONAL EXPERIENCE

**Field Engineer / Inside Sales Support** ...................................................................................1999–Present
**DIGITAL COMMUNICATIONS, INC.** — Hendersonville, Tennessee

- Configuration, installation, and troubleshooting related to connecting 120 LANs to WAN equipment in Birmingham for AmSouth Bank.
- Work with inside sales staff to determine customer needs and provide sales support.

**Senior Field Engineer** ........................................................................................................1997–1999
**TECH SYSTEMS** — Marietta, Georgia

- Tested and repaired Packard Bell hardware for both personal users and small- to medium-sized businesses.
- Installed, operated, and troubleshot hardware and software, providing on-site support.

**Personal Systems Help Center / Technical Support Group** ...........................................1994–1997
**IBM** — Marietta, Georgia / Research Triangle Park, North Carolina

- Provided information and technical support via telephone for users with software problems.
- Accurately and successfully identified customer problems and offered solutions.
- Served as an effective Team Leader and liaison between Technical Support Group and management.

## EDUCATION

**Bachelor of Science, Economics** — 1994 ................................... Florida State University, Tallahassee

*This individual's 10-plus years of directly related experience are summarized in brief "responsibility" statements, whereas his qualifications are presented "front and center" as his greatest selling points.*

# Joseph E. Boyce

7115 South Rosendale Drive • Franklin, Wisconsin 54315
Phone: (414) 487-2678 • Email: jeboyce@hotmail.com

## PROFILE

**Computer Operations & Systems Professional** with 25+ years of experience. An extremely loyal and dedicated employee who has served as lead person for 10 years. Strong mainframe expertise; currently training for support of desktop systems. Commended for producing high-quality work with solid attention to detail. A team player with effective decision-making skills and the ability to operate independently.

## TECHNICAL SUMMARY

- **Software:** MVS, JES2, DOS, VM, CICS, TSO, DB2, Omegamon, Netview, Zeke, Autosys, UCC7, Windows, Word, Outlook, Exchange, Remedy

- **Hardware:** IBM 3090, AS/400, IBM System 360 & 370, IBM Tape Robot, IBM 3480 & 3420 tape drives, Xerox printers, IBM printers

- **Languages:** JCL, COBOL

## PROFESSIONAL EXPERIENCE

MIDWEST BREWING COMPANY, MILWAUKEE, WI                    1977 to Present
*(A subsidiary of a Fortune 500 firm, with annual beverage sales in excess of $1 billion.)*

**Senior Computer Operator** (1993 to Present)

Lead first-shift computer operator within the Information Systems Department (ISD). Supervise and assist 2 other operators on IBM 3090 mainframe system utilizing MVS and JES2 operating systems. Generate reports in a timely manner and forward to ISD personnel. Ensure an effective overall operation by carefully monitoring hardware and software and responding as a first level of support. Maintain and control supplies inventory. Perform initial program loads and back up systems using established schedules.

- Promoted after serving as Junior Operator (1977–1983) and Operator (1983–1993).

- Recognized for maintaining a nearly perfect attendance record throughout tenure.

## EDUCATION

**Associate of Applied Science Degree**—Computer Programming—1979
Waukesha County Technical College

*The clean formatting and large type of this one-page resume make it highly readable. The two bullet points under the Professional Experience section describe notable achievements.*

**RESUME 3: BY SUSAN GUARNERI, NCC, NCCC, CPRW, CCMC, CEIP, MCC**

## Jeremiah Best
32 Andrews Street, Livingston, NJ 07039
(973) 740-5555 ▪ jerbest@net.com

| | |
|---|---|
| **Objective** | A technical support position in Computer Technology and Electronics |
| **Education** | April 2005    The Computer Institute, Mahwah, NJ<br>**Certificate, Electronics and Computer Technology**<br>▪ 60-week, 96-semester-credit-hour program<br>▪ GPA 3.93 / Executive List every semester<br>▪ Work part-time to fund education while taking classes |
| **Courses** | ✓ Basic Electricity I & II<br>✓ Microcomputer Fundamentals<br>✓ Semiconductor Devices and Circuits<br>✓ Personal Computer Repair<br>✓ Integrated Circuits and Digital Logic<br>✓ Data Communications and Fiber Optics<br>✓ Systems and Networking |

**Technical Skills and Equipment**

| | |
|---|---|
| AC/DC Power Supply | PC Repair / Troubleshooting |
| Digital Logic Probe | Networking Media Installation |
| Bread Boarding Circuits | Networking Server Installation |
| Digital Voltmeter AC/DC | Workstation Software Installation |
| Oscilloscope | Data Communications |
| Function Generator | Microprocessing |
| Novell NetWare 6.5 | Windows XP / 2000 / NT |

**Work History**
2003–present

Grand Central Theatre, Livingston, NJ
Kitchen Help / Concession Help

- Prepare fast food for theatre clientele, often cooking for 200–300 orders per shift per night, as part of a team of six kitchen and concession workers.

- Serve as cashier for concession sales, filling in for absent workers; proof out $3K–$4K in sales per night.

- Selected by Manager as "Employee of the Month" in October 2004 for cooperative attitude, perfect attendance and willingness to work double shifts on short notice.

**Testimonials**

"Jeremiah is an exceptional person, and I know that anything he is a part of will be a success."
– Ellery Williams, Managing Director, Grand Central Theatre

"Jeremiah is punctual and eager to work…"
– William McCarthy, Manager, Grand Central Theatre

*This individual is a new graduate whose education and technical capabilities take up most of the resume. His work experience is less important; it is not technology based, but it does show strong capabilities and achievements. Note the effective testimonials at the bottom.*

# Lisel Roemmele

11034 Highway 1247
Waynesburg, Kentucky 40489
Voice (606) 595-1029
liselr@aol.com

*"Lisel is at the top of her class, showing a great deal of insight and enthusiasm for networking, trouble-shooting, and administration.*

*"I feel she can be of considerable help in a school environment, as she has good people skills, is willing to work wherever needed, and is tenacious in solving problems that come up day-to-day."*

*—Roger Angevine, Chair, Physical Sciences and Mathematics*

*"If there is a network problem that is not easily discovered, Lisel is willing to go the extra mile to find and resolve it.*

*"She is quite knowledgeable and has the ability to troubleshoot many PC platforms. Her extensive knowledge of operating and network systems will be an asset to any company."*

*—Troy Schlake, Network Administrator, Bondtech Corp.*

## PROFILE

Innovative, achievement-oriented computer professional with exceptional abilities in the areas of technical and systems support. Immediate goal is to provide comprehensive, high-quality support to meet the needs of a growing organization. Personal and professional strengths include the following:

- Microsoft Certification in Windows XP and XP Pro; Windows Server 2003 and Network Essentials pending.
- Conscientious and dependable in completing systems projects accurately and independently in zero-error-tolerance environment.
- Experienced in system management disciplines, including disaster recovery.
- Proven ability to meet and maintain time requirements.
- Experience developing applications/solutions for ad hoc assignments.
- Quick learner; able to grasp and master new concepts easily.
- Equally effective working independently or as part of a team.
- Extremely hardworking; dedicated to enhancing personal computer skills.

## PROFICIENCIES

Operating Systems:
Linux, Solaris 10 (UNIX), Windows 98, Windows 2000, Windows XP, NT Server, Workstation (Including User Manager), DHCP, WINS, and MS Office.

Languages:
HTML and JCL; familiarity with CVB and C

## INTERNSHIP EXPERIENCE

**2003–2004       Somerset Community College       Somerset, KY**
On-call Consultant. Installation of TCP/IP, IPX networks, and workstation for lab units and associates as required. Strengths in troubleshooting and technical support.

## EDUCATION

Network Information Systems Technology
Somerset Community College, Somerset, Kentucky
Degree anticipated—December 2005

## CERTIFICATIONS HELD

Microsoft Certified Professional, MCPID 1465546
NT Server Certified—2003
Windows 98 Certified—2004
NT Workstation 4 and Network Essentials Certifications pending

*Excellent personal and professional references will be made available on request.*

*Appropriate graphics and an interesting layout make this resume attractive and fun to read. The testimonials in the left column are highly visible, yet they don't detract from the standard format of the rest of the resume.*

## VANESSA BLYTHE

276 Wyndham Lane, Unit 10
Tallahassee, FL 32303
(850) 453-1211
E-mail: vblythe28@prodigy.com

### COMPUTER TECHNICIAN
**System Set-Up / Repair & Troubleshooting / Networking**

### PROFILE

- Results-oriented professional with 10 years of experience with computers and software; possess Microsoft Certified Systems Engineer credentials.
- Strong technical troubleshooting and analysis skills balanced with strengths in communication, teamwork, and leadership.
- Key areas of knowledge, training, and experience encompass the following:

| | | |
|---|---|---|
| Networking | TCP / IP | Local Area Networks (LANs) |
| Windows Server 2003 | Novell NetWare 6.5 | DOS |
| Windows 98 / 2000 / XP | Internet | MS Office XP |
| Mac OS X | MS Outlook | MS Outlook Express |
| Software Conversion | System Upgrades | Component-Level Repair |
| Hardware Installation | Software Installation | System Integration |
| Computer Assembly | Database Management | End-User Training |

### EDUCATION

- **Microsoft Certified Systems Engineer Credentials,** Georgia Institute of Technology, Atlanta, GA
- **A.S. in Computer Engineering,** Manatee Community College, Jonesboro, GA

### RELEVANT EXPERIENCE

**Field Technician,** ARCO Software Systems, Atlanta, GA—2001 to 2004
**Computer Consultant,** Contractor, Atlanta, GA—1999 to 2001
**Computer Technician,** ENVISION Microsystems, Atlanta, GA—1996 to 1999

- **System Design & Set-Up:** Built computer systems to customer specification for private clients, as field technician and as computer consultant at Atlantic Cellular.
  - Set up computer, forms, and database for Network Video and other private clients.
  - Assessed customer needs, ordered components, assembled computer systems, and installed and configured software and peripherals for ENVISION customers.
  - Installed and configured Mac-based desktop computers in a classroom environment.

- **System Repair & Troubleshooting:** Troubleshot and repaired computers to component and software level, establishing alternative repair procedures to meet customer needs.
  - Performed telephone and on-site troubleshooting for clients as field technician.
  - Performed Y2K system upgrades, and hardware and software upgrades as field technician.

- **Networking:** Set up local area networks for classroom projects.
  - Configured a multi-computer local area network using Windows for class project.
  - Learned to manage file systems, storage devices, network servers, and workstations.

- **End-User Training:** Provided training to end users on systems use and operating systems as a field technician and consultant.

*Note the skills-based format of the Relevant Experience section, in which all positions are combined.*

# THOMAS LEMKE

5555 Dove Drive
Citrus Heights, California 95621
(916) 788-9993

tlemke@att.net

## Computer Analyst

**PROFILE**

More than six years of combined experience in advanced computer diagnostics, continuing education, and ability to provide on-site system analysis and service. Effectively troubleshoot and install hardware/software, operating systems, networking strategy, and direction. Proven capabilities in

| Quality Standards | Team Building | Purchasing |
|---|---|---|
| Commitment and Reliability | Problem Solving | Staff Training |
| Interpersonal Relations | Customer Service | Business Solutions |

**TECHNICAL EXPERTISE**

| Windows 98, 2000, XP | PC Hardware/Software & Networking |
|---|---|
| Technical Support/Service | Basic Integrated Circuit Repair |
| On-line Technology | Computer Peripherals/Equipment |

**RELATED EXPERIENCE**

ASPER COMPUTER COMPANY, Sacramento, CA        1998 to Present

*Field Technician/Lead Technician*

Co-manage computer sales, service, and business processes. Assist as resource and problem solver for customers and local businesses to maximize benefit from equipment and applications development *(Holly Cleaners; Sacramento School District; Modular Buildings, Inc.)*. Focus on providing a high level of customer service. Troubleshoot a full range of technical issues related to installations by telephone and in person.

*Selected Accomplishments*

Supervised and developed highly involved, self-directed technicians.
Worked closely with online technical support to ensure quality installation of hardware, operating systems, and software programs.
Built strong reputation as Morris High School's resource for diagnosing and analyzing technical problems on the SASI program.
Consistently planned and completed projects on schedule.

ALDA COMPUTER, Sacramento, CA        1997 to 1998
*Manufacturing Associate*
Highly motivated participant/team player of 20-member team. Focused on working together in problem solving and decision making. Maintained safety standards and quality control for each job on production line.

**EDUCATION**

A+ Service Technician (2002)

Heald Institute of Technology, Sacramento, CA (2002)
Courses: Integrated Circuit Repair and Computer Science

*This resume uses a very traditional format and clean typestyle to present quite a bit of information on one page without sacrificing readability. Note the attention-getting headline.*

**RESUME 7: BY KRISTIE COOK**

# PENELOPE S. RICHARDS

4601 Arlington Drive, Baltimore, MD 21111
Home: (410) 521-4690
E-mail: oraclepro@hotmail.com

---

## SUMMARY OF QUALIFICATIONS

- Computer Specialist with more than 8 years of experience in IT/IS.
- Praised by superiors for Oracle expertise, ability to work as a team member, and customer responsiveness.
- Proven oral and written communication skills; comfortable delivering presentations to large groups and training both technical and non-technical people in group settings as well as one-on-one.

---

## TECHNICAL SKILLS

| | | | |
|---|---|---|---|
| ■ Oracle | ■ Delphi | ■ Enterprise Technologies 4.0 | ■ Telnet |
| ■ PMRS | ■ Windows 98/NT/XP | ■ MS IIS | ■ ARCserve |
| ■ HP900 | ■ Novell NetWare | ■ UNIX | ■ TM1 Database |
| ■ SunSPARC | ■ Banyan | ■ FTP | ■ ADP |
| ■ JAM | ■ TCP/IP | | |

---

## EXPERIENCE

**COMPUTER SPECIALIST**                                                                    2002–Present
**Web Hosts Unlimited—Baltimore, MD**
Perform system accounts maintenance; change TCP/IP protocols for security purposes and manage IP address changes under Internet Information Server (IIS); maintain active server pages (ASP); provide user support; back up TM1 database using ARCserve software; and monitor and install Microsoft security patches.
- Served as trouble desk coordinator, traveling on a moment's notice when necessary to provide onsite assistance.
- Wrote a database manual for onsite users to easily enhance the system and troubleshoot/solve problems.
- Recognized for outstanding performance.

**COMPUTER SPECIALIST**                                                                    1998–2002
**Market Researchers, Inc.—Washington, DC**
Served as Lead Senior Computer Specialist for design, development, and implementation of two customized, complex database systems; worked as Lead Database Administrator (DBA) on and off site and trained Assistant DBAs; provided onsite user support in all areas of client/server software installation and upgrades.
- Designed, developed, tested, and maintained four Oracle Version 8 databases on a SunSPARC 2.0 server.
- Created, implemented, and maintained forms, reports, and program modules using JYACC JAM 6.3.
- Received Outstanding Performance award two years straight.
- Commended by the director for going the extra mile to troubleshoot and debug customized software for offsite operations systems.

**COMPUTER SPECIALIST**                                                                    1995–1998
**Onsite Marketing, Inc.—Washington, DC**
Provided application software and database support; supervised 16 personnel; installed patches; verified nightly database changes were run and synchronized with Honolulu location; and assisted switching stations with transmission validity.
- Conducted application software training classes for new personnel.
- Participated on the qualification board for personnel as the senior software engineer.
- Recognized with outstanding performance award.

---

## EDUCATION

**Northern Virginia Community College—Alexandria, Virginia**
Computer Technology, Effective Presentation

---

*The heading style in this resume is an attractive way of clearly distinguishing different sections of information. The right margin is justified to complete the clean look.*

## ANTHONY E. CALAVETTI

1501 Crosswicks Landing • Port Monmouth, NJ 07758 • 732-706-1341
E-mail: acala@aol.com

**OBJECTIVE:  Position in Technical Support**

### SUMMARY

- Experience installing and configuring a variety of operating systems, including Windows XP Pro and 2003 Server and Novell NetWare.
- Familiar with network management tasks, including user and security administration, file/directory access, and remote access service; experience with TCP/IP and NetBEUI protocols.
- Self-directed, confident professional with effective troubleshooting, customer relations, interpersonal, and leadership skills.
- Strong academic performance (93% grade average) at a highly regarded technical school.
- Entrusted with highly confidential information; security clearance.

**O/S:**  Windows XP and Server 2003, Novell NetWare 6.5, Windows 2000
**Applications Software:**  MS Office XP (Word, Access, Outlook, Excel, PowerPoint), MS Publisher, Lotus SmartSuite, Rhino, FrontPage XP, CAD programs
**Hardware:**  IBM-compatible PCs, hard drives, CD-ROMs, video boards, NICs, multimedia devices, printers, and SCSI devices

### EDUCATION / HONORS

Computer Technical Support Program, 2000 • Computer Institute, Jersey City, NJ • 96% Grade Average
A.S. Business Administration, 1989 • Randall Community College, Randall, NJ

**Technical / Leadership Achievements**

- Performed network management and administration functions using Windows NT. Set up and managed user accounts, and handled security issues (file/directory access); configured print queues, network printers, and remote access service. Maintained registry profiles for local and roaming users and provided disk administration support.
- Designed an easy-to-navigate Web page for a retail company, using a version of Macromedia Dreamweaver with limited capabilities; included a home page, product page, and order form, with strong graphics and hyperlinks.
- Installed and configured operating systems and applications.
- Assisted in network cable layout and installation.
- Recognized frequently as a team leader; selected to summarize project work and answer questions.
- Encouraged other students to focus on project objectives and provided technical guidance.

### EXPERIENCE

**Technical Support Representative,** A.N.B., Inc., Irvington, NJ                    2003–Present
Provide hardware and software support for clients of a computer service and retail organization.

- Installed and configured computers and peripherals for clients throughout the Northeast.
- Performed a wide range of troubleshooting and repair work, including hard drive replacement, restoration of files, and video card replacement.
- Set up a peer-to-peer network with 5 workstations.
- Provided explanations for clients and demonstrated appropriate facets of system/software.

**Secure Documents Handling Clerk,** U.S. Army, VA                    2001–2003
Entered, maintained, and tracked confidential information on 400+ military personnel, including personal records, achievements, salaries, benefits, and education. Supervised a data-entry clerk.

- Reviewed records for accuracy and thoroughness, entered data into computer system, and submitted electronically to superiors for review.
- Instructed 12 trainees in various clerical functions.
- Received 2 awards for outstanding performance.

**Administrative Clerk,** U.S. Army, SC                    1999–2001
Performed diverse clerical functions, including data entry, correspondence preparation, and record keeping.

- Assisted with installation of Novell operating system and applications software after a hard drive crash.

*This individual has both recent education credentials and relevant work experience, so both are described in detail. Note how the Summary combines both overall qualifications and specific technical skills.*

# Mathew S. Michaels

417 Bettwork Street ➤ Port Orchard, WA 98366 ➤ 360-874-6519 ➤ pcpro@aol.com

## PROFESSIONAL PROFILE

Technical expert with comprehensive knowledge of Computer Information Systems operation and administration. Documented skills in technical systems configuration, installation, maintenance, and repair. Extensive experience in software development. Recognized agency-wide as "go-to-guy" for immediate resolution of critical system problems.

## TECHNICAL EXPERIENCE

➤ Trained in troubleshooting, diagnosis, installation, and modification of networked computer hardware and software components and programs.
  — Hardware: PCs and peripheral equipment
  — Operating Systems: MS-DOS, Windows 95/98/NT, UNIX, Novell, and LAN
  — Software: MS Word, Excel, PowerPoint, and Access
➤ Format and test system hardware; install operating systems and application software; replace boards; diagnose and correct hardware problems; install peripheral equipment; install PCs on network; install and upgrade hardware, software, and linkages for PC workstations.
➤ Set up, configure, use, and support Transmission Control Protocol/Internet Protocol. Use Windows utilities for diagnosing problems. Modify host files. Write batch files.
➤ Use computer-aided diagnostics and digital logic devices to locate malfunctions. Use testing equipment to troubleshoot equipment malfunction to system and board level.
➤ Provide user support for hardware, software, and operating systems.

## SELECTED ACCOMPLISHMENTS

➤ As LAN Administrator, coordinated LAN consolidation with WAN to provide Internet/intranet access and e-mail capability. Consolidation significantly improved detachment efficiency and effectiveness and reduced system downtime and denial-of-service problems.
➤ Selected by Commander, Atlantic Submarine Forces, to implement, troubleshoot, and debug new automated inventory program. Successful implementation resulted in incorporation of program on ships fleet-wide.
➤ Consistently earned awards and accolades throughout career for technical and leadership abilities, including one of four Navy Achievement Medals for directing major Magnetic Disk File repair to missile fire control computer. Repairs allowed nuclear submarine to remain at sea and complete patrol.

## COMMUNICATIONS

➤ Proven record of success working one-on-one with clients to identify and clarify product capabilities and recommend equipment and systems.
➤ Articulate in oral communications; clear and concise in written communications and technical documentation. Recognized ability to quickly generate trust and develop rapport.
➤ Professional and personable in demeanor and presentation.
➤ Successful instructor/trainer with ability to effectively convey technical information in an understandable format.

*"…superior technical knowledge and supervisory skills…*

*…exceptional drive and 'can-do' attitude…*

*…brings maturity, experience, and technical knowledge to every endeavor…*

*…demonstrates the initiative, leadership, and drive to achieve exceptional results…*

*…meticulous administrator…*

*…possesses a great deal of energy, is highly industrious, and doesn't believe in idle time…*

*…level-headed and constantly uses sound judgment…*

*…strongly encourages development of teamwork…*

*…self-starter whose initiative and leadership skills stand out from his contemporaries…"*

- excerpts from
Performance Evaluations

*This is an intriguing format in which all employment experience is relegated to page 2, while the first page "sells" the candidate with extensive technical expertise, strong accomplishments, important "soft" skills, and effective testimonials.*

**Mathew S. Michaels**                                                                                           **Page 2**
360-874-6519 ➤ pcpro@aol.com

# CAREER HISTORY

**Computer Systems Consultant**
**The PC Pro, Silverdale, WA**                                                                      **2002–Present**
➤ Concurrent to military service, provide consulting services to individuals and businesses on all aspects of computer operations, including
— System and component troubleshooting, testing and repair
— Hardware and software upgrades
— Setup of Internet ISP connections
— Networking solutions
— System assessments and recommendations
➤ Design, write, test, and install software to meet customer requirements.
➤ Maintain and enhance existing system configurations to boost productivity.
➤ Manage all aspects of business: administer budget, monitor finances, process accounts payable/accounts receivable; research and order parts and equipment; develop marketing materials; promote business in local community.

**System Administrator**
**Computer Program Configuration Coordinator**
**Nuclear Weapons Technical Inspector**
**Electronics Technician, U.S. Navy, Various Duty Stations**                              **1979–Present**
➤ As System Administrator, conduct and oversee configuration, testing, troubleshooting, and maintenance of routers, hubs, switches, cabling, and other LAN equipment for 230-hub intranet system. Perform site surveys and prepare technical solutions for LAN installation and upgrades.
➤ Set up intranet system consisting of two servers and eleven units.
➤ Established, compiled, and managed a computer-based accounting system to automate more than 1,400 classified documents, decreasing processing time by 40%.
➤ Troubleshot CPUs and Computer Maintenance Subsystem, preventing loss of training and correcting numerous equipment failures.
➤ Led training and qualification programs for seven diverse training groups. Success documented by numerous Outstanding ratings for major inspections. Student critiques cited instruction as creative, direct, and outstanding.
➤ Managed installation of shipboard security camera system consisting of more than 3,500 feet of cable, 11 closed-circuit cameras, and 7 monitors. Authored 85-page system maintenance manual.
➤ Supervised performance of and presented formal training to electronic specialists performing operation, maintenance, and repair of missiles, fire control systems, launcher subsystems, and associated support and test equipment. Planned and conducted corrective maintenance, operation of test equipment, and testing and repair of all subsystems and equipment.
➤ Assisted CEO in establishment of Command Management and Equal Opportunity Program.

# EDUCATION and CERTIFICATION

2003 – Microsoft Certified System Engineer
2003 – Microsoft Certified Professional + Internet
2002 – Marine Computer Systems Degree (two-year program)
Trident Training Facility, Bangor, WA

## TECHNICAL & SUPERVISORY TRAINING

| | |
|---|---|
| Administering Windows NT 4.0 | Digital Computer Basics |
| Internetworking TCP/IP on NT 4.0 | Basic & Advanced Electronics |
| Windows NT 4.0 Core Technologies | Computer Program Configuration |
| Supporting Windows NT 4.0 | Total Quality Leadership |
| Creating & Managing Web Server, IIS 4.0 | Master Training Specialist |
| Networking Essentials | Leadership & Supervision |

# JASON DE MARCO

1030 Saddlehorn Drive
Hendersonville, TN 37075

Home: (615) 555-1097
E-mail: jdemarco@aol.com

## A+ CERTIFIED SERVICE TECHNICIAN

Highly skilled technical professional demonstrating knowledge and skill with various PC-based operating systems, networks, and software applications. Trained to support end users in a Windows environment via telephone and hands-on support. Diagnose and troubleshoot PC and basic network problems. Install and configure software onto individual and networked systems. Set up PCs, printers, modems, monitors, and other ancillary equipment and attach them to networks. An effective communicator with solid professional abilities, a strong work ethic, and a commitment to excellence.

## TECHNICAL SKILLS

**Operating Systems & Networks**
Windows XP, 2000, 98 – Windows Server 2003

**Applications**
Expertise with Microsoft Office (Word, Excel, and PowerPoint)
Basic knowledge of Microsoft Access – Lotus 1-2-3 – WordPerfect

## ABILITIES

- Help Desk Support / Customer Service
- On-Site Technical Support

- Installation / Configuration
- Troubleshooting / Repair

## CERTIFICATIONS

**A+ Service Technician Certification** – August 1999
Career Blazers Learning Center – Delray Beach, Florida

**PC Applications** – May 1999
Edward Ross Career & Employment Institute – Deerfield Beach, Florida

## EDUCATION

**Degree Program: Associate of Applied Science** (45 credit hours) – 1993 to 1996
Broward Community College – Fort Lauderdale, Florida

## WORK EXPERIENCE

**Computer Technician** – 1999 to Present
Wireless Innovations – Nashville, Tennessee

- Perform troubleshooting, repairs, and upgrades for company's LAN system.
- Provide on-site software training and technical support to end users using Windows, MS Word, and MS Excel.

**Route Salesman** – 1990 to 1999
Blanding Brothers – Fort Lauderdale, Florida

- Serviced commercial accounts, primarily supermarkets, delis, and convenience stores.
- Prepared daily log to track inventory, sales, collections, and payment receipts.

*This individual successfully transitioned from a nontechnology sales job to a computer technician position and is ready for advancement. His resume highlights his solid and current technical skills.*

1159 Danlette Drive
North Bridge, NY 11703

# EVAN FLANDERS

(631) 008-4000
eflanders229@aol.com

**A+ Certified Technician seeking to expand career within the information technology arena**

B.A. degree in Economics, continuing education in Information Technology, and a combination of technical and diversified administrative experience gained over ten years in positions of increased responsibility

**Select strengths encompass . . .**

Project Management / Help Desk Support / End-user Training / PC/LAN Service and Support
Systems Integration / Sales and Marketing / Procedural Documentation / Business and Technical Problem
Resolution / Inventory Control / Procurement / Vendor Relations / Client Needs Assessment / Cost Management

## PROFESSIONAL EXPERIENCE

**PC/LAN Technician**                                                                                  2003–2005
FINANCIALLY SOUND, INC. (FSI), Merlin, NY

**Technical Support**

- Successfully rolled out Windows XP Pro and newly developed FSI software to 80 nationally based branch locations.

- Installed and configured 50 XP Pro workstations at Dallas branch office, providing comprehensive post-installation support including client training and provision of procedural documentation.

- Attached corporate personnel to Novell and Windows Server 2003 network; performed scheduled network tape backups.

- Provided remote and on-site end-user support on a broad scope of hardware/software problems and printing/network connectivity issues; delivered effective training and practical solutions.

- Developed MIS procedural documentation to streamline and optimize departmental/company-wide workflow.

- Built and maintained workstations and laptops; replaced and upgraded various peripherals and components.

- Restored files utilizing Backup Exec and ARCserve for NetWare and Windows Server.

- Proficiently utilized diagnostic tools to assess and troubleshoot hardware and software performance to sustain the effective use of existing and newly implemented systems technology.

- Retrieved borrower-related data for underwriters and processors through access of WAN and PC Anywhere.

**Office Management**

- Sourced and negotiated with resale vendors, achieving total cost savings of $25,000 in license renewal fees for first and second quarters of 2000.

- Handled all aspects of MIS cost center and inventory control at the corporate and company-wide level with direct responsibility for distribution of accurate and timely documentation to all impacted departments.

- Created batch files to automate pulling of monthly pipeline reports for senior management review.

- Maintained and updated equipment tracking data for accounting and reporting functions.

- Supervised and maintained company-wide user activity to ensure the integrity of multiple licensing software.

— continued —

*The "Select strengths" section combines with the technical skills summary on page 2 to create a strong "keyword summary" for this individual.*

**RESUME 11, CONTINUED**

## EVAN FLANDERS
Page 2 of 2

### ADDITIONAL WORK HISTORY

HH GROUP, Woodland, NY                                                    1998–2003
**New Accounts / Parts Administrator**

RECOVERY HOME SYSTEMS, Centralville, NY                                   1995–1998
**Administrative Assistant**

### COMPUTER / NETWORKING SKILLS

**Operating Systems:** Windows XP Pro/2000/98; Novell NetWare 4/5; MS-DOS 6.22

**Protocols/Networks:** TCP/IP, NetBEUI, IPX/SPX, Ethernet 10/100Base-T

**Hardware:** Hard drives, printers, scanners, fax/modems, CD-ROMs, Zip drives, Cat5 cables, hubs, NIC cards

**Software:**

*Commercial:*

Microsoft Office Modules, FileMaker Pro,
PC Anywhere, Norton/McAfee Anti-Virus, Ghost,
MS Exchange, ARCserve, Artisoft ModemShare

*Industry-specific:*

e-Credit, ICC Credit, Energizer, Midanet, Flood Link,
Greatland Escrow, Allregs, Echo Connection Plus,
Contour (Handler, Closer, Tracker, and LP Module)

### EDUCATION

CAREER CENTER, Garden Grove, NY
**Fall 2005 enrollment: MCSE Windows Server 2003 Track**

**Completed Coursework, 2004–2005**
Windows XP Pro
Networking Technologies / Microcomputers I & II /
PC rebuilding, upgrading, and repairing

THE UNIVERSITY AT OLD WESTERN TOWN, Old Western Town, NY
**Bachelor of Arts, Economics, 2002**
Graduated with honors—GPA 3.77

CENTER COMMUNITY COLLEGE, Bendwood, NY
**Associate of Arts, Liberal Arts and Science, 1996**
Graduated with honors—GPA 3.5

### LICENSES / CERTIFICATIONS

Comp TIA A+ Certified Technician

New York State Notary Public

# DALWIN E. TOOLMAN

1000 Court Place - Tyler, Texas 75700
(903) 979-8488 - dtoolman@etin.net

## COMPUTER SYSTEMS TECHNICIAN / SPECIALIST

*Utilizing cutting-edge technology and state-of-the-art components to build superior systems to meet needs.*

► Highly efficient **COMPUTER SYSTEMS SPECIALIST** with comprehensive knowledge and technical expertise in **PC fabrication, configuration, system networking, diagnostic testing, malfunction identification, and repair.** Excellent **customer relations / service.**

► Proficiency in **surfing Internet** to **locate vendors** and **negotiate highest quality for lowest cost.**

► Customer satisfaction– and challenge-driven. Exemplary **integrity** and **work ethic.**

| Hardware Installation | Operating Systems / Software Applications |
|---|---|
| PCs through Pentium IV / Athlon XP | Windows NT / 2000 / XP |
| Palm Pilots – Speaker Phones | MS Office (Word, Access, Excel, PowerPoint) |
| Network Cards – Sound Cards | Works – Outlook Express – Money – Encarta |
| RAM and Video Memory | Publisher – Freelance Graphics – Adobe Photoshop |
| Multiple Hard Drives – Floppy Drives | iPhoto Plus 4 – Lview Pro – Cheyenne Bitware |
| Tape Drives – CD-ROM – CD-R | Lotus 1-2-3 – Quicken – Turbo-Tax – Tax-Cut |
| Printer / Parallel / USB / Mouse Ports | Parsons Personal Tax Edge – MS Internet Explorer |
| Serial / Cable Connections – Modems | Netscape Communicator – Navigator – Eudora |
| Power Supplies – Cooling Fans | ICQ – Cute FTP – HTML (Web Page Design) |
| BIOS Upgrades – Batteries – Scanners | Norton – Check-It – WinCheckIt Pro – Dr. Hardware |
| | Ontrack E-Z Drive Diagnostics – Wintune – WinBench |

## PROFESSIONAL EXPERIENCE

A-OK COMPUTER — Tyler, Texas (2001–Present)
**Owner / Computer Technician**

► Founded and progressed viable computer business from ground level, managing all aspects of business.

► Establish trusting relationships with customers; provide high-quality, low-cost service; and "go beyond the call of duty" to ensure total customer satisfaction. Make service calls throughout East Texas.

► Build computer systems from shell up. Install, identify malfunctions through extensive diagnostics of, and repair all types of components for multilevel systems through Pentium IV/Athlon.

► Search the Internet to locate vendors and successfully negotiate lowest cost for highest quality.

► Frequently receive client kudos, such as **"excellent service," "persistence to make it right," "honest/ fair."**

SPORTSMAN'S DEN TAXIDERMY / FISH CLONES — Tyler, Texas (1991–2002)
**Owner / Manager**

► Founded and built successful taxidermy business from ground level; hired, trained, and supervised up to five employees.

► Instructed seminars and judged competitions throughout the U.S.; served as board member / vice president of Texas Taxidermy Association.

► **Won more than 140 state, regional, and national awards for excellence in taxidermy art.**

► One of eight in nation **certified by National Taxidermy Association in <u>all</u> categories** in 1995.

► One of **first in state of Texas** to achieve **"State Award of Excellence."**

*This resume is visually appealing due to its clean layout and triangle-shaped bullets. Note the "kudos" quoted in the final bullet point of the most recent position.*

# CHARLES SALONGO

2741 East Broadway
Phoenix, AZ 85048

480-549-2309
csalongo@home.com

## SUMMARY OF QUALIFICATIONS

- Experienced Field Engineer with strong business, marketing, and customer service background, coupled with experience in troubleshooting, installing, and repairing electrical and electronic systems. Proficient in

  ▸ **System Installation**          ▸ **System Development**
  ▸ **IS Service / Support Management**  ▸ **System Troubleshooting**
  ▸ **Client Relations / Support**       ▸ **End User Training**

- Extensive technical hardware and software background, with ability to independently master new software and hardware, initiate troubleshooting process, and solve variety of technical support issues.
- Expertise in network design, configuration, and integration. Ability to assist in all facets of hardware and software conversion, including customization, support, cabling, training, and installation.
- Reliable member of team organization, assessing problems and system requirements, and developing effective solutions to meet end-user needs. Network with other computer experts via Internet regarding hardware and software problems.
- Education in Computer Science, with 3000 hours lab and theory training.

## TECHNICAL EXPERIENCE

| **Systems:** | Windows XP | Novell | IBM Platforms – AS400, RS6000 |
| | DOS | UNIX | PC with Pentium Processor |
| | ZENIX / AIX | AS1 Series | Tiger |
| | | | |
| **Software:** | Corel Suite 2000 | PC Anywhere | Penbase / PenDirect |
| | Microsoft Office XP/2003 | Lotus Notes | Internet Browser / Plug-Ins |

**Certification:**   Novell Certification, System Solutions, Tempe, Arizona — 1996

## PROFESSIONAL EXPERIENCE

**Service Engineer** — MYRIAD COMPUTER, Phoenix, Arizona — 1999 to Present
- Analyze and assess problems; recommend hardware, software, and office integration; determine use to make relevant recommendations on upgrading and networking, using LAN/WAN networks and out-of-office connectivity as appropriate.
- Train clients in all aspects of system, from basic instruction in operating hardware to more complex software applications.
- Purchase computer components, maintain and control inventory levels, and implement cost controls to ensure profitability.

**Field Engineer** — FIBERMESH SYSTEMS (Division of Visys, Inc.), Phoenix, Arizona — 1996 to 1999
- Served as primary contact for technical support to client base of 90 medical and 60 commercial clients. Supplied full integration between MS-DOS, Windows, and UNIX.
- Supported / operated 10Base-T, Ethernet, and personal computers for up to 700 end users and devices.

**Field Engineer** — HVM CORPORATION, Phoenix, Arizona — 1994 to 1996
- Developed and integrated electronic alarm control system designs and programs for gas distribution networks per client requirements.
- Installed diffusion equipment in U.S. and Mexico. Experience included diffusion furnaces, temperature / pressure indicators and controllers, relay / solenoid control, and programmable logic controllers integrated into Novell network for controlled shutdowns.

## EDUCATION

**Associate Degree — Electronics Technology — 1994**
LONG TECHNICAL COLLEGE, Phoenix, Arizona

*The extensive Summary of Qualifications sells this candidate with a list of keywords along with both an experience summary and "soft skills."*

## RESUME 14: BY KELLEY SMITH, CPRW

# DON G. SHELLEY

65 Lake Green Circle ~ Stafford, TX 77477
Home: (281) 992-0663 ~ Office: (713) 565-4999 ~ dgs1159@mccn.net

## NETWORK / PC TECHNICIAN

More than 10 years of broad-based experience encompassing installation, upgrades, troubleshooting, configuration, support and maintenance of third-party software applications, hardware, servers, and workstations. Skilled at determining company and end-user requirements and designing architecture to meet or exceed those requirements. Effective leadership and training skills combined with extensive technical expertise. Highly organized, with the ability to efficiently manage projects and resources.

### *Competencies:*

TROUBLESHOOTING, ANALYSIS & RESOLUTION ~ IMPLEMENTATION PLANNING & MANAGEMENT
END-USER TRAINING ~ SYSTEM UPGRADES ~ DATABASE ADMINISTRATION ~ IT PURCHASING
STAFF SUPERVISION & TRAINING ~ EXPENSE TRACKING & CONTROL ~ VENDOR RELATIONS

## TECHNICAL SKILLS

*Hardware:* All relevant hardware, including LAN cards and Bay Networks switches, as well as fiber-optic connections and network printers

*Networks:* Microsoft Windows XP, Novell NetWare 6.5

*Operating Systems:* Windows XP, DOS 6.22

*Software:* Primavera Project Manager, Metaframe Citrix Software, Microsoft Office Suite, Aspen Plus Simulation Software, Bridge by Kemma, EPOCH, Engineer's Aid, Microsoft Exchange 5.5, Visio, Enterprise Administrator, Weather View 32, Performance 2000, WordPerfect 2000, Imagecast, Sybase SQL Anywhere

## PROFESSIONAL EXPERIENCE

MODERN INFORMATION SYSTEMS – Houston, TX                               1998 to Present
*(Contracted to Sitico Chemical Corporation)*

### PC / Application Technician

Sole on-site technician with full accountability for hardware, software, and network support for a manufacturing plant with 300 end users. Provide NetWare 6.5 system administration to include installations, maintenance, upgrades, troubleshooting, and support for servers, fiber optics, printers, software applications, and all workstations running Windows for Workgroups.

Manage installation and upgrade project schedules and work closely with management to control project risks involving schedule, technical issues, and personnel. Communicate with vendors and suppliers to purchase parts and coordinate warranty service. Provide training to system users and new technicians. Set up and maintain individual user and group accounts. Work closely with Help Desk to ensure all issues are quickly resolved and to maintain optimal system performance.

- Managed the successful migration and data transfer from LAN Manager to NetWare 6.5 with no loss in productivity.
- Planned and managed migration project from NetWare to Windows Server 2003.

*(continued)*

*This is a traditional, comprehensive resume for an experienced professional. Two full pages are devoted to his 15-year career. The Competencies listing and the Technical Skills section are effective keyword listings.*

DON G. SHELLEY ~ PAGE 2

## PROFESSIONAL EXPERIENCE
*(continued)*

COMPUTER INNOVATIONS – Houston, TX                                    1997 to 1998
*(A local computer manufacturer)*

### Service and Production Manager

Tested and troubleshot hardware and software problems of completed systems and corrected deficiencies in assembly or manufacturing. Supervised, scheduled, and trained 20 technicians. Scheduled production, work flow, and customer repairs to ensure a high level of customer satisfaction. Maintained and updated two Novell networks.

- Created database for tracking parts and service, which allowed for more efficient repairs and improved customer service.

JLM COMPUTERS INC. – Houston, TX                                    1993 to 1997
*(A national computer manufacturer)*

### PC Evaluation and Test Engineer

Evaluated all new computer systems and internal peripherals before shipment to mass merchants such as Sam's Club and Wal-Mart. Supervised 14 production personnel. Provided installation, maintenance, and support for systems at administrative offices. Installed and configured Microsoft's HCT (Hardware Compatibility Testing) on all systems to ensure complete compatibility with JLM systems. Installed EDI (Electronic Data Interface) to allow for more efficient and accurate communication with trading partners. Maintained current knowledge of major hardware and software manufacturers and technology changes.

TETRAMAX, INC. – San Jose, CA                                    1990 to 1992
*(A plastics manufacturer specializing in fluorocarbons)*

### Process Engineer

Created and administered databases for all materials, log numbers, and material properties for the Isostatic Molding Research and Development department. Interfaced all CNC machines to a common terminal. Created bar and chart graphs to exhibit control limits for major companies such as Lockheed, Boeing, and Hughes. Oversaw R&D development of the Isostatic molding process in order to improve material properties.

- Designed and built first machine on the West Coast to skive six-foot-wide Tetrafluroethylene.

## TRAINING

NETWARE 6 ADMINISTRATION – certificate

XP WORKSTATION – certificate

MICROSOFT EXCHANGE SERVER – certificate

*Please keep this inquiry confidential at this time.*

DAM TYLER, Austel Licensed No. 55555

220 Citizen Street, PCVILL 2615 ACT    0404 555 555    (02) 5555 5555    adam@adam.com.au

*"I can honestly say that Adam would be in the top 5 percent of people I have offered positions to, and by far the best installer/technician."* Manager's Reference

Telecommunications/IT installation specialist with 9+ years of experience troubleshooting faults, installing systems and components, laying cables, restoring services, and refining technical expertise throughout. Poised for leading technician or supervisory role, where client interaction is integral to ongoing client retention and satisfaction.

Cited by management for demonstrating high-level, enthusiastic customer service and willingness to achieve time-critical deadlines—resulting in increased productivity and business revenues.

Exceptional track record for quality, safety, and team leadership.

## KEY STRENGTHS

**High-level technical competencies.**
**Install, repair, diagnose, and troubleshoot**
- Personal Computers & Networks
- Telecommunications Cables
- Security Systems
- Printers & Scanners
- Software
- Plotters
- Modems

**Articulate in communicating problems and solutions to people at all levels. Noted for**
- Customer Relations Attitude
- Intuitive Hardware/Software Support
- Team Leadership/Team Building
- Rapid Conflict Resolution
- Safety & Quality Compliance
- Productivity in Deadline-Dependent Environments

## QUALIFICATIONS & ADVANCED TRAINING

AUSTEL CABLING LICENSE (General Premises), *Australian Telecommunications Authority*

QUALIFIED ELECTRONIC SECURITY INSTALLER, *Australian Institute of Technology*

## PROFESSIONAL EXPERIENCE

HEAD INSTALLER/NO. 1 TECHNICIAN, *ICU Home Security*                                      02–05

Install, test, maintain, and service security systems in domestic dwellings across Canberra. Despite no previous experience in this industry, attained security installer's certificate and was elevated to leadership role in recognition of technical expertise, thoroughness, and customer-focused communication style.

Frequently requested to contribute fault-finding expertise on troublesome or complex project assignments; quickly gained reputation for ability to identify persistent and elusive faults.

Instruct new customers on the use, operation, features, and benefits of security systems; share information on emergency procedures, company policy, servicing schedules, and routine equipment care.

Contribute to business revenues by recommending extended warranties and maintenance plans.

*"Adam's honesty, integrity, work ethic, organization and people skills are to be envied by most…his workmanship has always matched his own personal high standards…this office constantly receives mail from Adam's clients heralding his praises."* Reference Excerpt from Manager, ICU Home Security

FIELD ENGINEER, *Tekkoworld*                                      97–02

Hands-on technical role installing, configuring, and troubleshooting personal computers and peripherals (printers, scanners, plotters, modems). Established outstanding customer relationships, acquiring business-wide reputation for strengths in resolving the most complex of technical challenges.

*"We found Adam to be responsive, efficient, and meticulous in all his work activities. Indeed, one of his skills lies in the rapport he had with our customers."* Reference Excerpt from Managing Director, Tekkoworld

**REFERENCES — AVAILABLE UPON REQUEST**

*"Because his hands-on work was repetitive (he installed only telecommunication cables and security systems), it was important that we get across his broader skills. He'd been cited frequently for his customer service focus, which would be a real selling point as a team leader where he'd have quite a bit of customer contact to 'put out the fires'—therefore, that's what I focused on."*

RESUME 16: BY ALICE BRAXTON, CPRW, CEIP

# KAMARRA E. MAHON

202 Main Street • Graham, NC 27253 • (336) 227-9095 • 1mahon@trex.net

## IT SUPPORT – ACADEMIC ENVIRONMENT

### PROFILE

*Technical Skills*

- Hardware/software configuration, support, and service
- System installation and networking (LAN)
- Multiuser Interface
- Operating Systems – Mac OS X; Windows 98, 2000, XP
- Applications – AppleWorks; MS Office 2003 for Mac; Adobe Photoshop CS, PageMaker 6.5+, InDesign; MS Word, Excel, Access, PowerPoint, Publisher, and Outlook; ACT!; Corel WordPerfect, Draw 9; CAD
- Working on Network+ certification

*Sales and Public Relations*

- Key account management
- Client and vendor relationship development
- Detail and outside sales
- Problem solving and complaint resolution
- Trade shows, presentations, and special events

*Human Resources*

- Hired, trained, and supervised sales and technical staff
- Understand compensation, incentives, and benefits issues

*Personal Strengths*

- Self-motivated and dedicated
- Multitask oriented, versatile, and adaptable
- Quick and avid learner
- Organized and flexible
- Professional and diplomatic

### EDUCATION

**Alamance Community College,** Graham, North Carolina
Currently enrolled in college transfer program

**Newport University,** Newport, Virginia
Completed 1 year in Computer Engineering curriculum
GPA 3.9

**Oakville Community College,** Chicago, Illinois
Associate of Arts degree, Space Planning
GPA 3.8

### RELEVANT EXPERIENCE

**COLLEGE AND UNIVERSITY COMPUTERS, INC.**
Tanner College, Mason, North Carolina          01/03–08/04
**Computer Store Manager** (06/03–08/04)
Primary liaison with Tanner College IT Department. Acquired major accounts through outside sales efforts in addition to in-store sales and operations. Performed market research and sales forecasting, budget development, and administration; and oversaw compliance. Achieved sales, margin, and inventory targets and minimized loss. Created and designed advertising communications, promotions, incentives, and special events. Served as service manager/technician responsible for hardware/software installations and repairs.

- Concurrent responsibility for new site development, build-out, budgeting, and product line rationalization.
- Co-authored store operations manual and new store set-up manual.

**Marketing Assistant** (1/03–6/03)
Collaborated with a Marketing and Sales Team on projects including brochures, flyers, advertising, promotions, web development, and trade shows.

- Developed a wide variety of multimedia promotional materials

**Other Experience**

**THE GUILD HALL OF WILLIAMSBURG**
Williamsburg, Virginia          07/00–05/02
**Executive Assistant**
Designed an inventory control system to track purchasing, receiving, on-hand inventory, and P&L. Supervised receiving department. Project planning, development, implementation, and management. Hands-on administrative support activities.

- Restructured operations and wrote manual for receiving and front-end procedures.
- Wrote job descriptions; retrained employees on new policies and procedures.

**HOMEBASE**
Lacey and Vancouver, Washington          01/98–07/00
**Interior Design Specialist**

**PREFERRED CARE NETWORK, INC.**
Lincolnwood, Illinois          01/90–12/97
**Client Relations Assistant**

*"Using this resume, my client got an interview with a school system that has a new Information Technology department that services the entire school system's network. She is an 'uneducated genius' who recently returned to school to get her degree in IT."*

## RESUME 17: BY DIANE BURNS, CPRW, CCMC, CCM, CEIP, JCTC

### James M. Pantell
3409 Blue Tree Drive, Baltimore, MD 21047
Tel: (410) 575-5095    Email: JMP@yahoo.com

**Information Technology & Information Systems Technician**
*Clearance: TS/SCI*

**Certified through Microsoft: MCSE & MCP**
**Certified through Novell: CNA and CNE (NetWare 5 & 6)**
**CISCO Certified Network Associate**

Skilled Communications Technician incorporating 14 years of in-depth knowledge of complex Communications, Computer, Network, Digital Imagery Processing, and local and worldwide Intelligence systems. Highly skilled with scores of network operating systems, hardware, software, networks, servers, workstations, LANs, WANs, fiber optics, and a wide variety of attached peripherals from military, commercial, and proprietary manufacturers.

Full scope of responsibilities include installation, integration, configuring, diagnostic testing, repair, and maintenance of systems, servers, fiber-optic termination, worldwide data communications, Cisco routers, workstations, mainframes, digital, satellite, multiplexers, and cryptographic equipment.

### Skills

| | | |
|---|---|---|
| Systems Administrator | Satellite Communications Systems | Encryption Equipment |
| Systems Analyst | Technical Hardware Support | Technical Authority |
| Secure Systems | | Troubleshooting |

### Professional Experience

Bell Atlantic, Baltimore, MD                                                    1999 to Present
*Systems Field Representative (Europe)*

- Currently participating in the implementation and administration of a Top Secret Windows Server 2003 network integrated with the in-place UNIX environment.
- Manage baselining and daily desktop maintenance of Secret and Unclassified Windows Server 2003 networks.
- Install and maintain Sun Enterprise Servers and Sun StorEdge storage devices, Sun workstations, and many personal computers. Plan and install fiber optics, Thinnet, and Cat 5 cabling.
- Efficiently provide residential, on-call, and deployed maintenance support throughout Europe. Maintain an extensive knowledge of complex U.S. military Command, Control, Communications, Computer, and Intelligence Systems. Conduct troubleshooting and maintenance on a wide variety of systems and provide technical hardware support.

Science of Computers International, Germany                                     1994 to 1999
*Systems Administrator*

- Provided technical support to four distinct networks (Novell NetWare 4.x and 5.x, and Microsoft Windows) utilizing three different Network Operating Systems (NOS) supporting classified and unclassified Local Area Networks (LANs).
- Conducted systems analysis on the networks, servers, and workstations. As a member of the critical integration team, installed and configured new hardware and software into existing networks. Conducted a full range of testing and analysis of the compatibility of new and old components, configurations, functionality, and expandability, ensuring full support for the new system.

*(continued)*

*In this resume, extensive lists of technical training and proficiencies are relegated to page 2 to allow the individual's high-level experience to shine on page 1. Note the brief "a short list" notation under Technical Training; this is an effective way to convey only the highlights.*

RESUME **17,** CONTINUED

James M. Pantell, Page 2

Bell Atlantic, Baltimore, MD                                                    1989 to 1994
*Field Service Representative (Europe)*

- Installed, integrated, and conducted diagnostic testing and repair at the European Node of the Joint Worldwide Communication System (JWCS). The system included secure high-speed data communications and simultaneous video-teleconferencing.
- Installed, tested, and repaired communication circuits and maintenance of three separate video-teleconferencing studios.
- Precisely calculated and ensured that the sparing level for the system was properly maintained.
- Installed and terminated fiber-optic cables, Sun workstations and servers, and Cisco routers.
- Installed and administered several NET IDNX 20/70/90 Digital Exchanges for worldwide data communications.
- Instrumental in the critical installation and integration of an Ethernet LAN and ATM connecting more than 150 Sun workstations.
- Ensured the security of highly classified materials by installing, testing, and repairing encryption devices.
- Managed a team responsible for installation, integration, testing, and repair of a prototype Sun-based classified message-handling system. Ensured continuous, uninterrupted networks.

### Education

A.A. in Computer Studies, Central Texas College, 2002

### Technical Training

*A short list*

- *Certified through Comp TIA: Network+ Certification, 2004*
- *Certified through CISCO: CISCO Certified Network Associate, 2004*
- *Certified through Microsoft: MCSE and MCP, 2003*
- *Certified through Novell: CNA 5 and CNE 5, 1998; CNA 6 and CNE 6, 2003*
- Windows 2000 Network Training, 2002
- Novell NetWare 5 Administration & Advance Administration, 2000
- Novell Service and Support & 5 Design and Implementation, 2000
- Novell NetWare 5 Installation and Configuration Workshop, 2000
- Fiber-Optic Installation and Termination, 1999
- Cryptologic Equipment Limited Maintenance, 1999
- Rembrandt II/VP Maintenance and Operations, 1999
- IDNX 20/70/90 Installation, Operation, and Maintenance, 1999
- LAN Cabling Systems, 1999

### Computer Proficiencies

**Software:** Microsoft Office Suite, Novell GroupWise, Microsoft Exchange, Microsoft Exchange Server, Visio 5

**Operating Systems:** Microsoft Windows 98, 2000, XP; Novell NetWare 5, 6

**Hardware Families:** Sun Microsystems; SPARCstation 20; Ultra 1, 2, 5, 10, 30, 60; SPARCserver 1000; Sun Enterprise Servers 450; Cisco Systems (2500, 4000, 7000, 7500 series routers); Catalyst 5500 Series Switch; Compaq; Proliant 6000 Servers; Network Equipment Technologies; IDNX 20/70/90

CHAPTER 5

# Resumes for Computer Systems Professionals

- Computer Programmers
- Applications Programmers
- Programmer Analysts
- Systems Analysts
- Database Designers
- Database Administrators
- Software Engineers
- Systems Engineers

**RESUME 18: BY ANN STEWART, CPRW**

## BRENT D. BOATMAN

1836 Tameria Drive, Dallas, TX 75234 ♦ (214) 251-3415 ♦ bboatman@texas.net

---

### *Game Programmer*

| | | |
|---|---|---|
| C/C++ | Open GL | Nintendo 64 |
| Win32 API | 3D Graphics | Nintendo Game Cube |
| MFC | AI | Sony PlayStation 2 |
| DirectX SDK | Console Development | Microsoft Xbox |
| Assembly | | |

---

**PROFESSIONAL EXPERIENCE**

2002–2005 **Koala Game Studio, Dallas, Texas**
Developer and publisher of entertainment software
Console Game Programmer

♦ Participated as a graphics programmer on a cross-functional development team that published a highly successful leading-edge sports game for Nintendo 64 and Sega Dreamcast. Recognized for strong individual contribution and emerging technical leadership.

♦ Represented company on team partnered with Microsoft that successfully resolved software incompatibility issues inhibiting game's development.

♦ Currently creating leading-edge graphics technology for next-generation platforms (Sony PlayStation 2, Microsoft Xbox, Nintendo Game Cube).

*Manager's Comments: "very hard worker" ... "goes above and beyond to meet schedule" ... "instrumental in Nintendo 64/Sega Dreamcast versions of game" ... "very high-quality work."*

2001–2002 **University of North Texas, Denton, Texas**
Computer Science Department
Student Intern

♦ Helped design and code an educational game under a research grant; incorporated graphics, sound, and network play into game.

♦ Assisted professor in innovative computer game development lab.

**EDUCATION** **University of North Texas, Denton, Texas**
Bachelor of Science, 2002
Major: Computer Science
Minor: Mathematics

Attended PlayStation 2 Developers' Conference, 2004

---

*This resume is distinguished by the box design that sets off the technical skills and by the manager's comments included under the most recent experience.*

# John Percello

303 Treepark Lane
Palatine, Illinois 60067

(847) 345-7811
johnpcl@aol.com

## DATABASE DESIGNER

- Designed database for customer history
- Designed database for machine shop
- Modified spreadsheets and tied into database
- Programmed procedures to update records

- Provide technical support to employees
- Designed database to store heat numbers
- Designed database for inspection services
- Designed spreadsheet database

## EMPLOYMENT

R.W.O. METAL, Arlington Heights, IL                    1995–Present
**Shipping/Receiving Manager**

- Promoted to shipping manager to help meet ISO9002 requirements.
- Resumed using software for truck Bills of Lading, and introduced UPS shipping software for UPS shipments.
- Created MS Access database to track outbound shipments/incoming freight.
- Retained production scheduler duties.

**Inventory Control Coordinator**
**Production Scheduler**

- Created and maintained multiple MS Access databases
  - To track production and history, produce shipping manifests, and print out production reports and charts
  - For customer quality certification
  - For machine shop inspection histories
- Assisted in the creation of an Excel spreadsheet used to schedule orders.

**Note:** Throughout my career with this company, I have assisted co-workers with all computer-related problems whether software, hardware, or network. I created a backup routine when the tape drive on the server failed. When asked, I built numerous spreadsheets and small databases for others or taught them how to do it themselves.

**EDUCATION**       WILLIAM RAINER-HARPER COLLEGE, Palatine, IL
- Certificate in CIS—Microcomputers in Business
- Completed courses in Visual Basic, C, MS Access, MS Excel, MS Word, MS PowerPoint, Paradox, MS FrontPage
- Completed Micro Computer Printers
- Currently enrolled in Web Design
- Studying for MCSD certification

*A strong element of this resume is the personal "Note" below the employment summary that calls out technology-related activities in a nontechnology job.*

# Tanya Kirkpatrick

578 14th Street, #3
Tampa, FL 33609

(813) 967-1408
tanya.kirk@browsenet.com

## PROGRAMMER / SOFTWARE ENGINEER

### PROFILE OF QUALIFICATIONS

Cited as *"a keen technical intellect who consistently makes the grade through innovation and the perfect eye for finding coding flaws."* — Jerry Drake, Director

- Results-oriented software engineer who adapts easily to requirements in mainframe and PC application development.
- Consistently commended for ability to work as a team member or independently while achieving critical deadlines. Strong project leader.
- Recognized for performance and project contributions. Consistently achieve highest rating in annual evaluations for top 2% of total company personnel.

### TECHNICAL APPLICATIONS

- Programming Languages: C, C++, COBOL, SQL, CICS, Lotus Notes application development, FORTRAN, C-Shell, Java, HSPICE and Matlab.
- Platforms: Windows NT, UNIX, OS/2, Windows 95 and Windows 98.
- Software: MS Word, Excel, PowerPoint and Access; various other programs.
- Experienced in developing Graphical User Interfaces (GUIs).

### EDUCATION & TRAINING

**B.S. in Computer Information Systems,** University of South Florida, Tampa, FL
- Courses: **Coding for Tomorrow, Java, SQL and Images, Copyrights and the Web**

### PROFESSIONAL EXPERIENCE

**Senior Programmer,** Carco Corporation, Orlando, FL — 1998 to Present
Perform multifaceted programming and analysis from code development through acceptance testing on a number of projects.

- Developed special applications in C++ to customize office business systems.
- Enhanced existing software subsystems to accommodate new requirements.
- Developed a graphical user interface (GUI) for an analog design automation tool in a UNIX environment.
- Interface communicated with a range of C programs to transfer input parameters provided by user and to display programs' output on the screen.

**Software Analyst and Programmer I,** Carco Corporation, Orlando, FL — 1996 to 1998

- Analyzed all company-designed software programs for Y2K compliance.
- Led a consulting team in the analysis of customer operating systems and software applications. Made suggestions for software changes and customization to existing programs.

*The attractive boxed headline and excellent testimonial are strong lead-ins to this resume.*

**RESUME 21: BY ROSS MACPHERSON, MA, CPRW, JCTC, CEIP**

# JEFFREY J. VANBEEK

555 – 200 Masters Road West
Augusta, Ontario  A2B 2B2

Phone: (905) 555-6666
Email: vanbeek@imail.com

## Profile

Highly motivated and enthusiastic **IT professional** with proven experience in both team and project management capacities. Outstanding analysis, programming, and debugging capabilities. Ability to work autonomously and as a team player, with demonstrated strengths in leadership and mentoring situations. Easily adaptable to change, with an eagerness toward learning and expanding capabilities. Industry expertise includes

- **2D / 3D Graphing**
- **Speech Recognition**
- **Geometry Management**
- **Taxation Software**

## Languages

C++, C, Visual C++, MFC, ATL, ASP, Java, COM, Windows SDK, Visual Basic, Delphi

## Experience

**2002–Present**

**C++ / ActiveX Template Library / Microsoft Foundation Classes / COM / ASP**

TECHNICAL PROJECT MANAGER — XYZ Group Inc., Augusta, Ontario

- Managed programmers, technical writers, and release engineers from design and implementation through testing and delivery during several major release cycles.
- Produced charting and geometry management components for Windows developers.
- Researched and prototyped geometry management tool based on design by Chief Technology Officer.
- Led development of an ASP version of the charting components.
- Provided estimates and technical expertise to sales force to develop and close source-code deals and arrange custom consulting work.

**2000–2002**

**Visual C++ / Windows SDK / Microsoft Foundation Classes**

SENIOR SPEECH RECOGNITION PROGRAMMER — VoiceTech Inc., Augusta, Ontario

- Used C++, MFC, and Windows SDK to build a natural language interface to office productivity tools such as Microsoft Word, WordPerfect, and Lotus 1-2-3.
- Controlled office tools through programmable APIs while processing speech input from programs such as Dragon Dictate and IBM ViaVoice.
- Highlight was VoiceMate for the Internet, which allowed control of Internet browsers, including Netscape, by voice control.

**2000**

SENIOR PROGRAMMER — Rybena Corporation, Pinehurst, Ontario

- Developed photo-realistic desktop communications centre using Visual C++, MFC, and SDK.
- Mentored team members in MFC and debugging skills.
- Interacted with internal QA and usability groups to design and improve components.

continued...

*This resume uses the attractive, clean, highly readable Tahoma font along with a clever design to make it a visual standout.*

JEFFREY J. VANBEEK          (905) 555-6666 • vanbeek@imail.com          Page 2

**1997–1999**    LEAD PROGRAMMER/ANALYST — TaxSystems Canada, Pinehurst, Ontario
- Guided UI subsystem development while building core tax calculation routines.
- Developed shared class libraries in C++ for personal, corporate, and trust tax products.
- Connected TaxSystems' data structures to MFC's document/view architecture using a multiple document/multiple view interface (MDI).

**DOS / C**

**1995–1997**    TAX SOFTWARE PROGRAMMER/ANALYST — TaxSystems Canada, Pinehurst, Ontario
- Conducted full overhaul of TaxSystems' system platform to improve performance and stability.
- Performed troubleshooting, maintenance, optimization, and enhancements.

**1994–1995**    TAX SOFTWARE PROGRAMMER/ANALYST — ABC Systems Corp., Medina, Ontario
- Reimplemented core of existing tax programs to rectify limitations caused by existing segmented architecture design.
- Highlight was design and implementation for "E-Tax," allowing preparation and transmission of electronically filed tax returns with Revenue Canada, Taxation.

## Education

**1992**    **University of Waterloo**
Bachelor of Mathematics – Honours Computer Science / Information Systems option
**Awards:**
Brad J. Sokol Award for Student Leadership
Gates Foundation Scholarship 1991–1992
Réné Descartes Entrance Award

## Training

**2004**    **People Management Course**
- 3-day in-house program conducted by Canadian Management Association
**2003**    **Microsoft Professional Developers Conference**
**2001**    **Project Management Course**
- 2-day in-house program developed for SHL and BC Tel

## References

Personal and professional references available upon request.

# Ryan F. Drury

1984 Maplewood Lane
810-561-9328

Saginaw, Michigan 48630
ryanfdrury@aol.com

## Profile

❏ Experienced IT professional with expertise in programming and systems integration.

❏ Specific areas of interest include software construction and research & development.

❏ Strong communication skills include ability to interpret technical concepts for non-technical users.

❏ Adaptability evidenced by experience in diverse industries: automotive, food service/hospitality, photographic processing equipment, and banking.

❏ Personal strengths include an excellent work ethic, persistence, and strong organizational skills.

## Highlights of Experience

❏ Developed applications for integrating customer systems with control systems and MMI.

❏ Created data-collection applications using MS Access.

❏ Generated user manuals and technical documentation for applications.

❏ Collaborated with customers during project development; trained end users in utilizing systems.

## Technical Inventory

SOFTWARE

*Programming Languages:*
Borland C++ 5.0
MS Visual Basic 3.0/4.0/6.0
VisualAge C++ for OS/2

*Operating Systems:*
Windows 2000 Workstation
Windows 2000 Server
Novell NetWare 4/5.x/6
Red Hat Enterprise Linux 3
UNIX

*DDE Servers:*
Software Wedge/WinWedge 3.0
ModLink
WinLinx

*PLC Programming:*
PLC Workshop for
  Modicon PLCs
RSLogix

*MMI Packages:*
InTouch
Factorylink
PanelBuilder 1400e
PanelBuilder 32
Labview 4.0
RSView32

*Applications:*
MS Access 2.0/97/2000/2003
MS Excel

HARDWARE
PLC-5
SLC500
PLC-2
Reliance A40
Modicon Compact 984

Sun SPARCstation
PanelMate
PanelView

Standard Register
  barcode printers

*(continued)*

*An unusual font, used judiciously, can effectively "spice up" a resume. Note the extensive Technical Inventory that takes up half of the first page, and how details of experience are not mentioned until page 2.*

**Ryan F. Drury**   Page 2        810-561-9328 — ryanfdrury@aol.com

# Relevant Experience

AUTOMATED CONTROLS • Brighton, Michigan                                    2002–Present
**Systems Engineer / Programmer**
- Write PLC programs to control industrial processes.
- Develop operator interfaces for PC and industrial display terminals.
- Develop data collection applications using Microsoft Access.
- Oversee maintenance and back-up of Windows NT 4.0 fileserver.

*Selected Projects:*
- Designed and wrote C programs that were instrumental in the success of two projects.
- Installed and configured Windows-based UUCP mail server.
- Wrote Visual Basic program to record flaws found by engine block test stand.
- Developed Labview application to test fuel pump component.

GENERAL DATA • Detroit, Michigan                                          1999–2002
**Software Engineer**
- Developed C-based Windows programs for food service and hospitality management firm.
- Incorporated point-of-sale software, inventory management, and reservation systems.
- Wrote code for printing reports.
- Implemented module check-out procedure.

J. B. CROSS & ASSOCIATES • Ann Arbor, Michigan                                1999
**Simulation Engineer**
- Developed simulation models for automotive paint and body shops.
- Collaborated with Simulation Group Manager to design and write a chain-pull program using Visual Basic.

QUALITY PHOTO PRODUCTS • Owosso, Michigan                                 1998–1999
**Programmer**
- Designed and maintained programs in C and FoxPro relating to photographic industry.
- Assisted with Novell LAN maintenance and troubleshooting.

NBD BANK • Lansing, Michigan                                              1996–1998
**Computer Technician/Network Administrator**
- Assisted in the installation of a Wide Area Network.
- Troubleshot Novell LAN/WAN.
- Maintained PC/LAN back-up schedule.
- Installed and configured software and workstations.

# Education

SAGINAW VALLEY STATE UNIVERSITY • University Center, Michigan
**Bachelor of Science —— Computer Science**                                     1998

*References available on request*

# CHRISTOPHER WILLIAMS

2075 Exeter Road, #555
Augusta, Ontario A2B 2B2     Email: cwilliams@imail.ca     Home: (905) 555-6666
Mobile: (416) 444-5555

## OBJECTIVE

Programmer / Analyst

## TECHNICAL EXPERTISE

| OPERATING SYSTEMS: | VERSIONS: | YEARS EXPERIENCE: |
|---|---|---|
| Windows 2000 | Server & Client | 5 |
| Windows | 98, 2000, XP | 5 |
| Novell NetWare | 4.1 | 5 |
| OS/2 Warp | 3.0, 4.0 | 2 |
| | | |
| SOFTWARE: | VERSIONS: | YEARS EXPERIENCE: |
| COM & DCOM | - | 2 |
| Visual Basic | 5.0, 6.0 | 4 |
| Crystal Reports | 6.0, 7.0 | 4 |
| Oracle PL/SQL | 7.3 | 1 |
| Oracle Stored Procedures | 7.3 | 1 |
| SQL Server Stored Procedures | 7.0 | 2 |
| OmniBuilder RAD Tools | 2.9 | 2 |
| OmniScript | 2.9 | 2 |
| COBOL | 4.5 | 2 |

## ADDITIONAL QUALIFICATIONS

- Motivated and hardworking with the ability to adapt and work within tight deadlines.
- Highly skilled in troubleshooting, debugging, and problem analysis.
- Proven ability to complete projects according to specifications, on time and within budget.
- Equally comfortable and effective in both team member and team leader situations.
- Excellent verbal and written communication skills, ensuring the highest level of client service and relationship management.
- Effective time management and organizational skills.

## PROFESSIONAL EXPERIENCE

**PROGRAMMER/ANALYST**     2002–2004
LCD Group     Augusta, Ontario
*Technical Skills: Visual Basic, COM & DCOM, PL/SQL 7.0, Oracle 8, C++*

- Led a sub-team of 6 developers in the design and development of a comprehensive operational database for NHLPA.
- Worked closely with program testers to ensure compliance with RFP (Request for Proposal).
- Successfully converted old dBASE programs to Visual Basic and ensured Y2K compliance for Ontario Hydro and CBC—all code tested to specs and user acceptance with no errors.

*(continued)*

*This resume effectively uses a table to display technical expertise. The Additional Qualifications section highlights important but less quantifiable attributes.*

**RESUME 23, CONTINUED**

CHRISTOPHER WILLIAMS                                                  PAGE 2
cwilliams@imail.ca
(905) 555-6666
───────────────────────────────────────────────────────────────

**WEB DEVELOPER**                                                    2001–2002
PLATINUM SYSTRONICS                                         Peterborough, Ontario
*Technical Skills: Oracle Web Server, PL/SQL, HTML, JavaScript, Windows NT 4.0 Platform*
- Integrated a web site with an interactive database (Oracle 7.3) for Human Resources Development Canada (HRDC)—www.ititraining.com

**SYSTEMS ANALYST**                                                  1999–2001
CABLESYSTEM SOFTWARE, INC.                                      Pinehurst, Ontario
*Technical Skills: COBOL*
- Hired to write operating software program for local cable provider, managing all customer tracking, accounting, archiving, billing, etc.—program soon marketed to other small to medium-sized cable providers across Canada.
- Additionally wrote program to track all activities and correspondence between members of Canadian Cable Systems Alliance (CCSA) and cable signal suppliers.

**APPLICATION DEVELOPER** (Co-op)                                    1999
LCD Group                                                     North York, Ontario
*Technical Skills: Lotus Notes 3.0*
- Proposed, designed, and developed internal client tracking system and re-engineered database.

**ASSISTANT LAN ADMINISTRATOR** (Co-op)                              1999
Spotlight, Inc.                                                Pinehurst, Ontario
*Technical Skills: Novell NetWare 4.0*
- Provided primary technical support and troubleshooting for huge corporate network, responding to technical inquiries, resolving problems, and performing daily backups.
- Planned and installed Software Training Centre, including 1 server, 8 workstations, and all cabling.
- Repaired servers, PCs, printers, and cabling as required.

**BUSINESS MANAGER/ CO-OWNER**                                       1978–1996
Dubin Filtration Systems                                        Augusta, Ontario
Manufacturer of custom-made pipes, filters, and equipment for oil and water well-drilling industry. Clients throughout North America with sales of $10 million annually.
- Successfully built company from ground up, including all financing, premises, machinery, sales, production, and operational responsibilities.
- Responsible for managing all day-to-day operations to ensure quick production, product delivery, and client satisfaction.

## PROFESSIONAL / TECHNICAL DEVELOPMENT

| | |
|---|---|
| **Java Development**—Seneca College, Toronto, Ontario | Ongoing |
| **MCSD Certification**—Microsoft | Ongoing |
| **Visual Basic 6.0**—ObjectSystems, Toronto, Ontario | 2003 |
| **Oracle Development Seminar**—Oracle, Mississauga, Ontario | 2000 |
| **Computer Operations**—Seneca College, Toronto, Ontario | 2000 |

References available upon request.

## CHARLES G. SHORT

▶▶▶▶▶▶▶▶▶▶▶▶▶▶▶

11906 Charter Parkway   Ballwin, MO 63011
636.962.8453/mobile   636.965.8299/home
cgshort01@att.net

### SUMMARY ▶▶▶▶▶▶▶▶▶▶▶▶▶▶▶▶▶▶▶▶▶▶▶▶▶▶▶▶▶▶▶▶▶▶▶▶▶

Focused **Senior Programmer/Analyst** with a proven record of contribution in team leadership, system analysis, design, development, and implementation. Particular expertise in client-side and mainframe development. Knowledgeable in supply-chain management, financial accounting, manufacturing, production, asset management, and transportation functions.

- Confident rapport builder; skilled in building positive working relationships based on sincerity, helpfulness, mutual respect, and trust.
- Skilled, versatile communicator and facilitator; effective with business and technical participants at all levels.
- Goal-oriented, systematic planner with a big-picture perspective.
- Relaxed, collegial, and supportive team leader and mentor.
- Adaptable, creative, and tactful problem solver; skilled in identifying the best options and solutions.
- Engaged learner; well-read on current technologies and applications.
- Enthusiastic contributor with a collaborative spirit, a strong work ethic, and a passion for seeing a quality job through to fruition.

| | |
|---|---|
| *Tools* | XMLSpy, IntelliJ Idea, Toad, TSO/ISPF, IMS Expert, Data Expert/FileAid |
| *Databases* | Oracle, IMS, DB2 |
| *Languages* | Java, Java Swing, XML, DOM4J, XSL, XSLT, HTML, DOM, JavaScript, SQL, COBOL, JCL |
| *Software* | Tomcat, Weblogic, MS Office |

### EDUCATION ▶▶▶▶▶▶▶▶▶▶▶▶▶▶▶▶▶▶▶▶▶▶▶▶▶▶▶▶▶▶▶▶▶▶▶▶

M.A., Computer Resources and Information Management
Maryville University, St. Louis, MO

B.S., *with honors,* Information Systems and Data Processing, Minor: Business
Bowling Green University, Bowling Green, OH
  Earned 100% of college expenses.

### EXPERIENCE ▶▶▶▶▶▶▶▶▶▶▶▶▶▶▶▶▶▶▶▶▶▶▶▶▶▶▶▶▶▶▶▶▶▶

1995–present   DYNAQUIP CONTROLS, INC., Washington, MO

*Lead Programmer/Analyst 1/01–present*
Provide team leadership for design/development of supply-chain/inventory-management system incorporating Cayenta Frameworks Java client and Weblogic J2EE EJB server. Participate in task and navigation analysis, paper prototyping, usability testing, and results analysis, providing liaison to human factors/usability project team. Ensure 8–10 developers conform to standards, specifications, and quality expectations.
  Developed graphical user interface (GUI) using Cayenta's Java-based controllers.
  Facilitated user testing and led implementation of user-centered design.
  Mentored several junior developers on standards and principles.
  Maintained server-side EJB (Enterprise Java Beans) components.

*Page 1 of 2*

*This candidate's early work experience, while seemingly unrelated to his new career in technology, provided him with diverse knowledge of business functions—just the kind of practical information a programmer/analyst needs to deliver accurate software solutions.*

**RESUME 24, CONTINUED**

**CHARLES G. SHORT**                                                              *Page 2*
636.962.8453
cgshort01@att.net

*Senior Programmer/Analyst 10/98–1/01*
Participated in a variety of design/development and enhancement projects.

Created GUI for asset-management/tracking system, using Java, Java Swing, and Model-View-Controller framework.

Coded tracking system to accommodate internationalization.

*Programmer/Analyst 5/95–10/98*
Developed and maintained mainframe revenue-accounting systems.

Participated in developing and testing COBOL/IMS/DB2 interface to Revenue Systems Processing (RSP) client/server front-end for existing batch-accounting and waybill-tracking system.

Provided primary support for Accounts Receivable Autocash System accommodating receipt and processing of bank transmissions (Electronic Fund Transfers).

Enhanced and maintained COBOL/IMS/DB2 revenue-accounting, waybill-processing, and collection systems.

1992–1995        PC MALL, Toledo, OH

*Warehouse Support Assistant*
Retrieved, verified, packaged, and shipped computer/electronic equipment to domestic and international locations (part-time during college).

1986–1992        COTTON CLUB, INC., Toledo, OH

*Plant Team Technician*
Learned and performed bottling operations, purchasing, materials management, equipment troubleshooting/maintenance, and distribution functions. Met with vendor sales representatives.

1982–1986        UNITED STATES NAVY

*Sonarman*
Installed and maintained submarine sonar systems. Trained new personnel on procedures, documentation, and equipment-handling for surveillance and precision navigation systems; managed up to five sailors.

**TRAINING** ▸ ▸ ▸ ▸ ▸ ▸ ▸ ▸ ▸ ▸ ▸ ▸ ▸ ▸ ▸ ▸ ▸ ▸ ▸ ▸ ▸ ▸ ▸ ▸ ▸ ▸ ▸ ▸ ▸ ▸ ▸ ▸ ▸ ▸ ▸ ▸ ▸ ▸ ▸ ▸ ▸ ▸ ▸ ▸

*Maryville University, Center for the Application of Information Technology (CAIT):*
Enterprise Java Beans, Graphical User Interface Using Java, Java Servlet Programming, Advanced Java Programming

*Object Computer Incorporated (OCI):*
Extensible Markup Language (XML), Extensible Markup Language Transformation (XSLT)

Dale Carnegie Course

# BRENDAN R. SWENSEN

111 South 222 East
Salt Lake City, Utah 84102
801.555.1212
swensen@email.com

## APPLICATIONS PROGRAMMER

Award-winning programmer with experience in multiple areas of technology and management. Proven track record of providing exceptional customer support across industries. Technically proficient in numerous programming and software applications. Recipient of Cyber Enterprises Employee Excellence Award, 2003.

## TECHNICAL SKILLS

Technologies: PERL programming, shell scripting, VI syntax highlighting, Linux, UNIX, CVS/version control, Ultra-edit, basic networking and troubleshooting.

Software: VI, Microsoft Office Suite: Word, Excel, Outlook.

Operating Systems: Windows 2000, Windows XP, Linux.

## PROFESSIONAL EXPERIENCE

CYBER ENTERPRISES, Salt Lake City, Utah                                    2000–Present
*Multimillion-dollar instant-credit decisioning company*

**Applications Programmer** *(2002–2004)*
Sole criteria programmer for Bank of America instant credit decision-making software applications. Develop programs that parse/read credit bureau information to determine whether credit applicants meet eligibility requirements set forth by client.

- Instrumental in overall design of Bank of America projects including converting from Clipper to SQL and updating systems processes to newer technologies.
- Assist customers outside scope of project; find innovative solutions to meet customer needs.
- Developed bureau error file-parsing script to identify errors in returned files from bureau; validate no errors exist prior to entering production and provide quality control following implementation.
- Run test cases on program according to client specifications; test all aspects of criteria to ensure more accurate representation of demographic is tested.
- Saved hundreds of input hours by developing and implementing Web scripting rules to import customer-specific logic rules from Cyberscript to SQL Server.
- Member of Webrules support team: Address customer issues, answer questions, and resolve problems.

**Technical Support** *(2000–2002)*
Acted as first line of contact for customer support issues and maintained operating systems.

- Answered customer questions, identified proper account if unknown; opened ticket on issue and resolved numerous issues to avoid customer needing to contact project management.
- Acted as first line of defense against system outages: provided system maintenance, created disc space, and rebooted systems when needed.

GOURMET PIES, Salt Lake City, Utah                                         1996–2000
*Specialty pizza restaurant chain*
Oversaw all aspects of restaurant operation.

**Assistant Manager** *(1998–2000)* **Supervisor/Shift Supervisor** *(1996–1998)*
- Managed all aspects of restaurant operation, including scheduling of 40+ employees, customer issues, inventory control and ordering, weekly newsletter; maintained high level of service.
- Worked off profit and loss statements; received numerous bonuses for maintaining cost control.
- Introduced software to simplify daily service reports and increase efficiency; updated Apple to IBM.
- Addressed employee issues including interviewing, hiring, training, and disciplinary action when necessary; created positive working environment to maintain talent.
- Promoted rapidly from supervisor to assistant manager.

## CONTINUING EDUCATION

Online coursework includes XML, Managing Difficult People, Communication, Speech

*Early experience in the restaurant field is included because it highlights management skills that enhance this individual's programming expertise.*

# CHRISTOPHER RYAN

119 Dorothy Place, Lynbrook, New York 11563 • 516-472-8953 • cryan2003@netzero.com

## SOFTWARE ENGINEER / PROGRAMMER

*C++, Perl, and Java / Object-Oriented Design and Development / Windows, UNIX, and GNU/Linux*

## Professional Profile

Software engineering and honors program graduate with 4+ years of hands-on programming and application design experience. Track record reveals exceptional skills in effective and error-free programming, system debugging, and customer-centered service. Demonstrated creativity in utilizing various software tools to develop and perform testing and analysis.

### Core Skills

- Program & Instruction Coding
- User Training
- Web Design & Maintenance
- System Analysis
- Program Logic Development
- Database Design
- High-Level Design
- Program Documentation
- System Administration

### Strengths

- ➤ Software design and development in C++, C, Java, Perl, and PHP in Windows, UNIX, and Linux.
- ➤ Experience working with Microsoft Foundation Classes, OpenGL, and Windows Sockets in C++ and Swing and JDBC in Java.
- ➤ Effective testing of software applications and submission of clear problem reports with solution recommendations.

## Computers

| | |
|---|---|
| **Languages:** | C++, C, HTML, Java, JavaScript, Perl, ASP, PHP, Assembly, UNIX Shell Script, and SQL |
| **O/S:** | Windows 95/98/2000/XP/NT, UNIX, GNU/Linux (Debian), and Macintosh |
| **Applications:** | Microsoft Office 2000 Suite, Visual C++, Visio 2000, Visual SourceSafe, GNU Dia, GIMP, Adobe Photoshop, CVS, GCC, DDD, Nedit, vim, Dreamweaver, FrontPage 2000, and X Windows |

## Experience

KINGSTON REYNOLDS & ASSOCIATES, Far Rockaway, New York                    2003–Present
**Programmer**
- Create and use Perl script to generate XML documentation of SQL stored procedures and ASP pages.
- Develop HTML web pages and modify ASP forms.
- Perform software testing of ASP pages and standalone Visual Basic and FoxPro applications.
- Develop InstallShield script and create StuffIt Installer builds for Macintosh computers.
- Perform research, analysis, and client support.

COLUMBIA UNIVERSITY, New York, New York                    1999–2001
**Web Team / Teaching Assistant / Tutor and Grader**
- Designed Web pages for the university.
- Assisted with software engineering classes and labs.

*(continued)*

*This individual had an outstanding education but had taken a basic job upon graduation. This resume was designed to show off all of his computer skills, briefly mention his work experiences, and list all of his academic achievements because he was practically entry-level.*

**CHRISTOPHER RYAN**                                                  PAGE TWO
119 Dorothy Place, Lynbrook, New York 11563 • 516-472-8953 • cryan2003@netzero.com

LIFE SCIENCE TECHNOLOGY, INC., Valley Stream, New York          Summers 2000–2002
**Administrative Assistant**
- Maintained product database and assembled Drug Master File for submission to the FDA.
- Designed Regulatory Affairs Department brochure.

COLUMBIA UNIVERSITY, New York, New York                          Summer 1999
**Information Technology Intern**
- Developed Web pages for development office.
- Set up networked computer lab.

## Education

Columbia University, New York, New York
**Bachelor of Science—Software Engineering**                     May 2003
➢ Columbia University Honors Program
➢ GPA 3.9—Graduated with Highest Honors
➢ Presidential Scholar for three semesters
➢ Tau Beta Pi Engineering Honors Society
➢ Phi Kappa Phi Honors Society

Career Solutions, Lynbrook, New York
**Computer Support and Maintenance Program**                     1998–1999
➢ CompTIA Certified A+ Service Technician

Hofstra University, Hempstead, New York
**HTML Web Page Design**                                         Summer 1997

# DAVID SUZUKI

Email: davidsuzuki@yahoo.com

145 West Rosecliff Court
Saukville, WI 53080

Office: (414) 629-3676
Res: (262) 344-3449

## TECHNICAL PROFILE

A dedicated and loyal systems professional with 20+ years of hands-on experience as a **database administrator and application developer.** Solid understanding of relational databases. Excellent design, coding, and testing skills. Strong oral and written communication abilities.

| | |
|---|---|
| Databases: | DB2, Oracle, SQL |
| Languages: | COBOL, IBM/AS, Visual Basic |
| Operating Systems: | VM, UNIX, DOS, Windows 98 and XP |
| Third-Party Software: | COGNOS, Impromptu, Informatica, Microsoft Access |

## PROFESSIONAL EXPERIENCE

**Midwest Staffing Inc.,** Milwaukee, WI                                          1984 to Present
  *(A global employment services organization with annual sales in excess of $10 billion.)*

### LEAD DATABASE ADMINISTRATOR AND DEVELOPER
Lead mainframe and Oracle database administrator with 24/7 responsibility for performance, tuning, recovery, and planning. Use various utilities to transfer data to other platforms and build tables/indexes. Respond to end users' requests for information and resolve discrepancies in data reports. Research and interact with vendors in the purchase of third-party software. Train and supervise assistant DBAs. Write user manuals, operating procedures, and internal documentation.

Selected Database Development Projects and Achievements:

- Administer mission-critical payroll and billing database that bills $5+ million per week.
- Designed, developed, and implemented Oracle databank—a duplicate of the mainframe databank. End users now have greater access to data using desktop tools.
- Developed and maintain franchise fee billing application.
- Developed Central Billing consolidation application that bills $5 million per month.
- Researched and recommended purchase of ETL Informatica PowerMart utility. Data movement to the data repository, the Internet, and databases is now accomplished in one step. Previously, data movement involved large amounts of development time.
- Developed mainframe processes using the ESSCON Channel (high-speed data transfer) to move data from the mainframe to the AIX platform. Compared to the old method using Outbound, this has reduced data transfer time by at least 50%.
- Selected by management to train assistant database administrator. Assistant is now a reliable backup on mainframe-related database issues.

## EDUCATION

**Oracle and Oracle Tuning,** Certificate Courses, University of Wisconsin—Milwaukee, 2003

---

*Note how your attention is drawn to the "selected database projects and achievements"—the hands-on experience that will sell this candidate.*

# JONATHAN P. WOODRIDGE

41 Chatham Avenue • Cherry Hill, NJ 08034 • 609-714-8020 • jpw@aol.com

**Programming / Software Training / Technical Support**

## SUMMARY

- High-energy, self-directed professional with a technical / business academic background and 10+ years of successful business experience.
- Frequent recognition for outstanding performance in positions requiring strong planning, analytical, problem-solving, and customer service skills.
- C++ programming experience, using class functions and conversions, inheritance and dynamic memory location, I/O file streams, data files, and data structures: arrays, strings, addresses, and pointers.
- Developer of programs that integrated Visual Basic with Access.
- Extensive background in training and customer service; able to clearly convey information.
- Proven ability to assess and hurdle complex obstacles; viewed as a strong troubleshooter.

**Programming Languages:** C++, Visual Basic
**Software:** MS Excel, Access, PowerPoint, Word, Visio
**Operating Systems:** Windows XP/2000/98
**Hardware:** IBM-compatible PCs

## EDUCATION / PROFESSIONAL DEVELOPMENT

A.S., Computer Science / Business Administration: Dumont County College, Dumont, NJ

Professional Seminars / Training Programs: Customer Service, Training, Interviewing, Employee Relations / Coaching

## SKILLS AND ACCOMPLISHMENTS

### Programming

- Developed an amortization chart in C++ that allowed user to enter input to calculate payments, balances, and interest paid.
- In C++, created a bowling program that recorded score data input by user and stored it in an output data file for later use.
- Developed programs for the real estate and fast food industries that integrated Visual Basic with Access, utilizing the database in the interface and retrieving it using SQL statements.

### Technical Writing

- As project manager, led a team of 6 in the development of a software manual.
- Conducted an analysis of the software program and typical users, assigned responsibilities, completed a task list, developed task completion dates, and performed frequent reviews to assess progress.
- Ensured clarity and integrity of document and use of appropriate terminology.

### Planning / Leadership / Training / Troubleshooting

- Managed the operations of multimillion-dollar retail locations, with responsibility for sales, customer service, cost containment, recruiting, training, scheduling, and inventory.
- Received frequent regional and district recognition for sales volume and expense control.
- Evaluated problems at various sites and devised and implemented solutions.
- Trained managers throughout the region, while maintaining responsibility for store management.
- Conducted group orientation and training sessions for seasonal sales associates.

### Customer Service

- Focused on creating customer-centered environments that inspired repeat business.
- Emphasized quality service with management trainees and staff.

## PROFESSIONAL EXPERIENCE

Store Manager, The Man's Shop, Sea Girt, NJ          1996–2002
Store Manager, Carltons of California, Freehold, NJ          1989–1996

## INTERESTS

Investing and Financial Management

*This is one of the few purely "functional" resumes you'll find in this collection. Notice how the Professional Experience section is bare-bones, whereas the skills and accomplishments are categorized and explained in some detail.*

# Janet Jones

111 Flatlands Avenue
Brooklyn, New York 11111
(718) 394-4444 ▪ jjones@earthlink.net

## Systems Engineer ▪ Project Leader

Thoroughly experienced in the **development and implementation of business systems** within **mainframe** and **micro environments.** Areas of expertise encompass

- ➢ **Data Model / Logical Design**
- ➢ **Coding**
- ➢ **Needs Analysis**
- ➢ **Functional / Design Documentation**

- ➢ **Module / Class Specifications**
- ➢ **Data Security**
- ➢ **Batch / Online Systems**
- ➢ **Test Management**

## Technical Summary

➢ **Mainframes**

| | |
|---|---|
| **Languages:** | COBOL / COBOL II, ISPF Dialog Manager, REXX, SQL (DB2), BMS / SDF / SDF II, Script / GML |
| **Databases:** | DB2, VSAM / IDCAMS / ICCF |
| **O/S:** | MVS / XA, CICS / INTERTEST |
| **Other:** | TSO/ISPF, SPUFI, PRO-EDIT, DATA-XPERT / FILE-AID, LIBRARIAN / PANVALET, ENDEVOR |

➢ **Micros**

| | |
|---|---|
| **Languages:** | Basic (MS and Visual), C/C++ (MS and Visual, Solaris), MS Access, xBASE (dBASE, Clipper), Microfocus COBOL, REXX, SQL (XDB, Sybase, Watcom) |
| **Databases:** | SYBASE, MS Access, Btrieve / Xtrieve, XDB, Watcom, dBASE (III and IV), Clipper |
| **O/S:** | MS-DOS (3.x to 6.x), Windows (98, 2000, and XP), UNIX (Solaris) |
| **Other:** | Galaxy, Rogue Wave Tools.h++, Window Widgets, Crystal Report Writer, PVCS, TLib, Visual SourceSafe |

## Sample of Accomplishments

➢ As a consultant for **Software, Inc.,** participated in a number of major projects within the Financial Services community:

**Columbia Bank / Big Apple Bank** *(post-merger):*

- Enhanced SAS-based Reorg Letter Writing System to accommodate changes in business environment resulting from a prior merger. System subsequently integrated into the Corporate Action Letter Writing System due to further merger activity.

- Added new vendor data feeds to a Corporate Action Reporting facility, which involved changes to both the batch and online processing.

- Member of team that designed, developed, tested, and implemented PC client / server system for the Corporate Action Letter Writing System to replace existing SAS-based system. Developed GUI workstation using Visual Basic 5. Interfaced with the Data Base Administrator (DBA) for the physical design, creation, and maintenance of all Sybase-stored procedures.

- Participated in the design, development, and implementation of an automated input system for the Global Securities Area using COBOL II in a DB2 SQL Batch/CICS environment.

- continued -

*"Ms. Jones is continuing to look for project management positions, capitalizing on her systems engineering experience. Major projects are highlighted, showing her technical skills as well as industry expertise." (Writer's comments.)*

# Janet Jones

111 Flatlands Avenue
Brooklyn, New York 11111
(718) 394-4444  ▪  jjones@earthlink.net
Résumé - Page Two

---

## Sample of Accomplishments

**Big Apple Bank:**

- Involved in the development of a Visual Basic interactive interface of a Securities Lending and Asset Management System. System functions included file maintenance of the underlying MS Access database, daily trade processing, data transmission, and reporting. Reporting functions were created using Crystal Reports for data access and printing.

**Mellon Brothers:**

- Developed audit application written in C++, with Galaxy as the GUI interface and Sybase as the underlying database. The application processes daily delta files downloaded from the mainframe and produces a variety of reports based on user-generated ad hoc report requests.

**Bank of the Americas:**

- Participated in the development of the Global Custody component of a client / server project designed to provide the customers with an integrated Reporting and Inquiry System and an easy-to-use integrated workstation for entering and modifying global instructions. The system was developed under Windows NT using C++, Galaxy, and Sybase on a Sun platform. The Accounting System was a Novell-based system written in Microfocus COBOL using Btrieve.

➢ As technical project leader at **Monolith Insurance Company,** supervised programming staff, streamlined systems, and oversaw enhancements and modifications:

- Within Actuarial / Statistical Reporting Area, streamlined an annual maintenance effort by replacing common hardcoded file and table definitions by COPYLIB members, and utilized PERFORMS to replace hardcoded loops and common field suffixes to identify usage and/or derivation.

- For Schedule F Reinsurance Reporting System, replaced the existing Batch Interrogation System with online IMS System.

- Redesigned and enhanced Automatic Statistical System, which resulted in the merging of the 5 systems into 3 new systems, with an approximate 30% additional savings in operational resource requirements.

---

## Professional Experience

SOFTWARE, INC. (SI), New York, New York                              2000–Present
**Consultant**

MONOLITH INSURANCE COMPANY, New York, New York                      1994–2000
**Technical Project Leader**

MEDICAL INSURANCE CORP., New York, New York                         1989–1994
**Technical Project Leader**

---

## Education

ROCHESTER INSTITUTE OF TECHNOLOGY, Rochester, New York
**B.S., *Cum Laude*, Computer Studies**

## SHAWN GEOFFREYS

**1322 OTTAWA ROAD, APT. #6, TORONTO, ONTARIO, K5M 6L2**

(416) 327-2255 • sgeoffreys@sympatico.ca

### Software Developer • Analyst/Programmer
*Strong acumen for solving coding-level problems of various applications.*

Highly motivated IT professional with proven experience in complex project management capacities. Energized by challenges, steep learning curves, and high-pressure deadlines. Outstanding analysis, development, and installation of high-performance technology solutions. Reliable team player with effective troubleshooting and debugging experience. Strong work ethic coupled with flexibility to adapt to all technical environments.

*Areas of Strength:*

| | | |
|---|---|---|
| ◆ Web Application Engineering | ◆ Online Intranet Applications | ◆ Web Game Creation |
| ◆ Technical Writing | ◆ Technical Support | ◆ Microsoft Products |
| ◆ Military/Aerospace Systems | ◆ Secret Security Classification | ◆ Quality Assurance |

### TECHNICAL SUMMARY

| | | |
|---|---|---|
| ✓ Open GL programming | ✓ HTML/Web page creation | ✓ QNX |
| ✓ Java 2 | ✓ Active Server Pages 2.0, 3.0 | ✓ UNIX/IRIX/LINUX |
| ✓ COBOL | ✓ Macromedia Flash 4.0, 5.0 | ✓ SQL/dBASE 7.0 |
| ✓ Perl | ✓ Kinetix 3D Studio MAXrMX | ✓ Microsoft Internet Explorer |
| ✓ Tcl/Tk | ✓ Cgi/Wincgi scripting | ✓ Microsoft PowerPoint |
| ✓ XML | ✓ Motif/X Windows | ✓ MS-DOS |
| ✓ PHP | ✓ SQL Server 6.5, 7.0, 2000 | ✓ Caligari Truespace 4 |
| ✓ Win Api | ✓ Microsoft Visual Basic 5.0, 6.0, .NET | ✓ Netscape Navigator |
| ✓ Oracle 8i, 9 | ✓ CSS Style Sheets | ✓ Microsoft FrontPage |
| ✓ ASP.NET | ✓ MFC | ✓ Dreamweaver 3.0 |
| ✓ Microsoft Access | ✓ Adobe Photoshop | ✓ Corel WordPerfect Suite |

### KEY PROJECTS AND ACCOMPLISHMENTS

**DATA INTEGRATOR:**
  *Challenge —*  Corporation lacked centralized personnel record, manually tracking information.
   *Action —*  Creatively developed base codes and automated script to act as singular dataflow for company.
   *Result —*  Significantly reduced man-hours needed to sustain crucial personnel information through single data model.

**ROOTS APPLICATION:**
  *Challenge —*  Need to update third-party application within Product & Assembly.
   *Action —*  Spearheaded successful data extraction and development of new application.
   *Result —*  100% customer satisfaction and increased productivity.

**SECURITY APPLICATION:**
  *Challenge —*  Pressing need for internal application in order to terminate usage of Excel.
   *Action —*  Project manager charged with integrating historic data via developed scripts. Exceeded requirements by creating code for inclusion of third-party software "guard card" picture display.
   *Result —*  Project delivered on time, with extra enhancements that ensured increased productivity.

**CONTRACTOR CONTROLLER SOFTWARE:**
  *Challenge —*  Procurement department had no tracking tool to record contactor activity.
   *Action —*  Guided innovation of custom software solution to satisfy business need.
   *Result —*  Increased productivity, efficiency, and interdepartmental relations.

continued…

*Major projects are highlighted on the front page of the resume, utilizing the "CAR" (challenge, action, results) analogy to paint a complete picture of the results achieved.*

# SHAWN GEOFFREYS

| (416) 327-2255 | Page 2 | sgeoffreys@sympatico.ca |

## PROFESSIONAL EXPERIENCE

**GREGORY DEFENSE CANADA,** Toronto, ON                               2002–2004
_(A diversified global enterprise employing a highly trained team of +600.)_
### Software Developer: Information Management Systems

Assigned as lead to assignment involving design of innovative system that managed, supported, monitored, and reported on subcontractors working for Gregory Defense Canada. Required to research current corporate policies and procedures incorporating "best features" from range of systems potentially usable by corporation. Final application integrated data between two data systems and included creation of applicable documentation including Class Diagrams, Relation Database Diagrams, Statement of Work, and Basis of Estimate. Assumed responsibility for total support and installation of new application.

➢ Routinely oversaw application upgrades in .NET using C++ to produce ASP.NET web applications, ensuring up-to-date technology for all departments.
➢ Reduced code-development time 20% by implementing standard custom reusable function libraries.
➢ Achieved $20,000 in adjusted savings by streamlining application development time.
➢ Supervised up to 4 co-op students; responsible for training evaluations, quality control on code revisions, and compliance with corporate standards.

### Programmer/Analyst: System Design and Integration

Participated as integral member of project team developing new system to support and maintain administration of security records for all employee and contractors within Gregory Defense Canada. Examined current policies and procedures in conjunction with previous MS Access application, ensuring data-integration compatibility with third-party software Guardcard systems.

➢ Authored Application Design Analysis for Security Profile and Reception Application System.
➢ Created SQL stored procedures to accommodate technical requirements and migration of old database tables via custom scripts to new SQL server.

**GAMES DEVELOPMENT CORPORATION,** Montreal, PQ                               2001
_(Global leader in software development, employing more than 30,000 IT professionals nationwide.)_
### Beta Tester

Recruited to provide integral support to testing of Internet web-service, troubleshooting various components of highly popular online game. Charged with tracking fault reports and classifying severity of bugs with game software and providing real-time voice communication services.

### EARLY CAREER PROGRESSION

Challenged through a series of technical assignments within government and private companies. Created web games and corporate sites; developed statement of scope and analysis documentation; and assisted in networking of systems. Highlights include

**D.N.D.:** _Contract Web Developer_ (2000) ♦ **GOING GOLD MEDIA:** _Contract Web Developer_ (2000)
**COMPUTING AND DETAILING CORPORATION (CDC):** _College Co-Op_ (1998–1999)

## EDUCATION/PROFESSIONAL DEVELOPMENT

| | |
|---|---|
| **ADO.NET, Intro to ASP.NET, Into to Web Services,** _Canadore College_ | 2002 |
| **Computer Technology—Computing Science Diploma,** _Nipissing College_ | 2000 |
| **Ontario Secondary School Diploma,** _Widdifield Secondary School, Thunder Bay_ | 1996 |

**RESUME 31: BY WANDA MCLAUGHLIN, CPRW, CEIP**

# MARY G. RODRIGUEZ

4411 East Maryland Avenue — Gilbert, AZ 85234
(480) 781-0710 — MRodriguez@aol.com

**FOCUS**  Position as **Software Engineer** where B.S. Degree in Computer Science, experience in Object-Oriented Programming, and knowledge of Internet technology are desirable.

## TECHNICAL EXPERTISE

Program Design / Development / Maintenance

Database & Network Administration

System Upgrades & Enhancements

Hardware & Software Evaluation / Support

**Programming Languages / Platforms:**
Java 1.2, C++, Visual C++, HTML, JCL, CICS, SQL, COBOL, Pascal, BASIC, NATURAL, FORTRAN, MS-DOS, Windows, UNIX

**Software:**
MS Office, CorelDRAW, Harvard Graphics, PageMaker, WordPerfect, Quattro Pro, Novell Network

## RELATED EXPERIENCE

**Programmer / Analyst**                STATE OF ARIZONA, Phoenix, AZ — 2002–2004
Used 4GL programming languages to develop interdepartmental programs. Analyzed data and wrote basic requirements documentation to create databases and programs. Assisted in training end users.
*Achievements:*
— Assisted in upgrading 20-system linked network in Novell.

**Programmer**                ANALYTICAL RESEARCH, INC., Sacramento, CA — 2001–2002
Directly accountable for all facets of programming and system maintenance for market research company providing services for major travel and leisure accounts throughout the world, including America West Airlines, Lufthansa, United Airlines, and Ritz-Carlton Hotels.

Developed and implemented custom marketing research programs; administered 30,000+ database; coordinated user additions, deletions, and system back-up functions for Novell network. Participated in all phases of hardware and software upgrades, enhancements, and maintenance. Occasionally supervised temporary employees.
*Achievements*:
— Developed presentations for visual aids and company books utilizing a variety of graphic packages, including Harvard Graphics, CorelDRAW, ACROSS, and Windows.
— Managed 200+ slide presentations to major clients.
— Member of team that brought existing system, programs, and databases successfully into Y2K compliance.

**Desktop Publisher**                ARTISTRY, INC., Los Angeles, CA — 1997–2000
Assisted customers in the development of visual graphic presentations for custom brochures and marketing materials. Determined client requirements, assisted in selection of special graphic designs and programs, and designed and processed orders.
*Achievements:*
— Developed strong skills in computer operations and creative design.

## EDUCATION / TRAINING

**B.S. in Computer Science,** 2001                CALIFORNIA STATE UNIVERSITY, Northridge, CA
Emphasis: Software Engineering & Computer Mathematics

**Java, Intermediate Java, C++, Visual C++**                SCOTTSDALE COLLEGE, Scottsdale, AZ
— Currently attending
— Developed Mortgage Calculator utilizing Java applets

---

*This efficient, one-page format uses good organization and formatting to clearly communicate the individual's qualifications. The Focus statement at the top is another way of stating an objective.*

# Teresa D. Fisher

8585 Barbara Avenue • Sacramento, CA 95916          (916) 321-5505 • tdfisher@golden.com

## SOFTWARE DEVELOPMENT • PRODUCT MANAGEMENT • TECHNICAL SUPPORT

### PROFESSIONAL EXPERIENCE

GOLDEN COMMERCE, Sacramento, California                                              2002–Present
*A global provider of end-to-end, Internet-based electronic commerce solutions.*

**Product Manager** – Exchange Payment Business Unit (EPBU), Feb. 2003–Present

Promoted to oversee the Cash Management product line—*Exchange: Banker, Exchange: ACH, Exchange: Advice,* and *Exchange Banker for the Internet.* Manage 4 programmers in software development and support activities for these products providing payment systems solutions in and from the client corporation through to the payment network (Federal Reserve Bank, Value-Added Network, or Value-Added Bank).

- Served as effective cross-functional liaison across technical support, sales, development, finance, and management, as well as customer interface for product direction, bug fixes, and enhancements.

- Maximized productivity of high-wage development staff, improved customer satisfaction, and achieved faster project turnaround. Accomplished by working with technical support manager and establishing a process for escalation and tracking of product issues, whereas before support staff routinely escalated problems to Development before validating that the issues were not operator- or environment-generated.

**Client Services Consultant** – Financial Electronic Data Interchange (FEDI), Aug. 2002–Feb. 2003

Conducted onsite installation, training, and support of FEDI software, including EDI mapping and systems integration. Worked with large financial institutions that market and license the software to their own clients.

- Provided valuable, first-hand knowledge of bank operations to help consultants customize installation and implementation of Exchange products for a better fit with the institutions' operational needs.

- Assisted with product testing and guidance of leading-edge *Exchange Banker for the Internet.*

FIRST FEDERAL BANK, Fresno, California                                              1999–2002
*A leading statewide financial services organization offering state-of-the-art electronic technology to process customer and internal transactions.*

**Unit Supervisor** – Technical Support Unit, Electronic Banking (2000–2002)
**Electronic Banking Technician** (1999–2000)

Managed operation, development, and maintenance of sophisticated electronic banking systems that included commercial electronic transactions, telephone transactions, and internal processing. Led the installation of *Exchange: Banker* software and network, customizing the application to interface with existing systems. Supported entire electronic banking department in use of software and hardware, and served as contact with vendors to initiate modifications. Played key role in assessing system upgrades. Directly supervised 3 technicians responsible for hardware and software support functions.

*Selected Achievements:*

- Spearheaded technological upgrade that attracted significant new business to the organization due to convenience, efficiency, and ease of use.

- Integrated commercial financial services software *(Exchange: Banker)* into existing host system using Novell NetWare 5.x. Customized programming with batch files and host link interface, File Express, and script languages to move files to and from host. Examined business workflow to determine how systems would interact for maximum efficiency/reliability.

(continued)

*This is a classic, well-designed resume that includes all pertinent information in an easy-to-skim layout that emphasizes career advancement and accomplishments.*

**RESUME 32, CONTINUED**

# Teresa D. Fisher

(continued)                                          **(916) 321-5505 • tdfisher@golden.com**

**PROFESSIONAL EXPERIENCE (cont.)**

Promoted to unit supervisor to lead implementation of more sophisticated and broad-based technology.

- Supervised expansion of customized *Businesslink* system, increasing total active users fourfold.
- Upgraded hardware and software for *Firstline* telephone banking and information system, and accomplished maintenance using Intervoice programming language. Managed system security and generated utilization reports.
- Conducted development for a PC Banking system, allowing retail customers access via home computer.
- Served (by invitation) on Golden Commerce's User Advisory Committee for *Exchange: Banker* software to provide user feedback, prioritize system modifications, and interact with developer on support and future planning for the product. Identified need for code changes by the Federal Reserve and Golden, as well as a security upgrade and other minor modifications that were implemented by software vendor.

NATIONAL BANK OF NORTHERN CALIFORNIA, Modesto, California               1992–1999

**Programmer / Analyst** (1997–99), **Computer Operator** (1994–96), **Data Control Clerk** (1992–94)

Initiative and rapid assimilation of technical knowledge resulted in fast-track promotion to network administration position providing network and desktop support for 380 internal customers using Microsoft Office and financial services software Maxxus ACH.

- Developed applications using DOS, Visual Basic, and QBasic, and designed a Novell menu system.
- With limited resources, improved availability of support for host applications with a remote access pool.
- Served as primary point of contact on help desk, adjusting communication with users to accommodate their level of technical knowledge.

RETAIL SALES – COMPUTER AND ELECTRONICS EQUIPMENT, Sacramento, California          1986–1992

**EDUCATION & TECHNICAL TRAINING/SKILLS**

| | |
|---|---|
| **Electronics Technology:** | Modesto Community College Coursework (32 credits) |
| **Hardware:** | PC, modems, peripherals, modem pools, host interface cards, voice cards, Token Ring MAUs, routers, bridges, remote access pool, tape backup devices |
| **Operating Systems:** | Novell NetWare 4.x and 5.x, Windows XP Workstation, Windows 9x, DOS, OS/2, Sun/UNIX |
| **Software:** | Word, PowerPoint, Excel, Exchange: Alliance, Electronic Data Interchange (EDI) |
| **Programming:** | DOS QBasic, Visual Basic, ProComm scripting |

# DEBORAH WOOD

4209 Brower Road, P.O. Box 325, Anderson, MA 56209
Phone: (345) 295-7810 ▪ Mobile: (345) 505-5621 ▪ E-mail: dwood@aol.com

## SOFTWARE DEVELOPMENT MANAGER / SENIOR SOFTWARE ENGINEER
### 20+ years of experience in all phases of software development life cycle

Exceptionally well-qualified senior software engineer and manager with sophisticated programming skills and a sincere passion for resolving complex problems and business challenges through technical innovation. Solid portfolio of vertical market software products proving expert hands-on ability in all phases of the software development life cycle—conception to customer delivery and support. Dedicated, results-driven, and energetic leader; extensive experience in small start-up environments. Core strengths in

- Product Conception, Design, & Development
- Project Management
- Product Quality Assurance
- Troubleshooting & Customer Support

- Contract & Licensing Negotiations
- Custom Software Engineering
- Team Building & Leadership
- General Business Management

## TECHNICAL QUALIFICATIONS

**Languages:** Borland Delphi, Borland C++ Builder, MS C/C++, MS Assembler, MS VC++, MS Visual Basic, Mark Williams C, BASIC, Borland C/C++, Turbo Pascal, HP Assembler, Z80 Assembler, Access, dBASE, Clipper

**Libraries & APIs:** Windows 16/32 API, ActiveX, Inso OEM Viewer API, Quick View, Aztec Copy Protection, Cimmetry AutoCAD API, TurboPower Series, Raize, LMD, WPTools, Dream Inspector, Topaz, Rainbow Technologies Hardware Lock, Essentials Series, Genus Series, Greenleaf, and more

**Development Tools & Applications:** Wise InstallMaster, MS Visual SourceSafe, Multi-Edit, EC, DOS Batch files, WinBatch, CodeView Debugger, CodeSmith Debugger, MS Office (Word, Excel, PowerPoint, Outlook, FrontPage, Project) MSIE, Adobe Acrobat, Norton Utilities, PowerDesk, Paint Shop Pro, Photoshop, Netscape, and more

**Operating Systems:** Windows 98, Windows 2000, Windows XP, Windows 2003 Server, Mac OS

## CAREER HIGHLIGHTS

**Alsiksek Software Solutions, Boston, MA**          Nov 2001 – Jun 2004
**New Technologies, Inc., Boston, MA**               Jan 1991 – Oct 2001

### VICE PRESIDENT OF ENGINEERING / DIRECTOR OF PRODUCT ENGINEERING

Cofounded New Technologies, Inc., and directed all software product development, shipping, and customer support efforts. Conceptualized, designed, and managed the development of vertical market software products targeted to the industrial and manufacturing industries. Formulated and implemented quality assurance policies, procedures, and methodologies. Negotiated favorable contracts and licenses for third-party software modules and libraries. Led teams of up to 7 programmers and technicians.

Retained by Alsiksek as Director of Product Engineering following acquisition of New Technologies in 2001. Continued in previous product engineering, project management, and support role; focused on refining and upgrading the cutting-edge document management product developed by New Technologies.

- Conceptualized, designed, developed, and delivered a full line of software products meeting industrial and manufacturing industry needs for computer-based training, file organization and document management, troubleshooting, and shop floor utilities.
    - Products included Trainer Series, Assistant Series, Technical Toolbox, Portable HGR, and the company's most notable product, Virtual Library.
- Earned professional reputation for exceptionally solid, high-quality, and supportable software products through stringent oversight of specifications, code version control, code reuse, documentation, and testing.

*continued…*

*Extremely appropriate for a senior software engineer, this resume includes a detailed profile, lengthy technical skills summary, and experience that highlights accomplishments and contributions.*

**RESUME 33, CONTINUED**

(345) 295-7810         **DEBORAH WOOD** – Page 2         dwood@aol.com

- Invented, designed, and integrated new technologies within software products, utilizing special talent for analyzing customer requirements and creating new, marketable products to meet needs.
- Specified and developed troubleshooting products and played an instrumental development role in custom computer-based training covering a wide range of general and specific industrial topics for Allen-Bradley, GE Fanuc, and Reliance Electric. Assisted in structuring third-party reseller licensing agreements with Rockwell Software and Taylor Software for New Technology's products.
- Productized and delivered fully functional software applications; oversaw licensing enforcement, setup utility development, documentation and packaging creation, and manufacturing/shipping processes.
- Developed a minimally intrusive licensing enforcement/copy protection strategy that enabled the ability to meter software product users in a multiuser environment.
- Redesigned, upgraded, and enhanced Virtual Library for the Windows 32-bit platform, achieving complete backward compatibility and the ability to coexist with earlier versions.
- Created totally innovative feature for Virtual Library that utilizes dynamic pointer technology to provide an advanced, non-database-driven document revision control system with e-mail support for companies seeking to achieve and maintain ISO-9000 status.

**Wood and Associates, Inc., New York, NY**         Jan 1988 – Jun 1991

**PRESIDENT / PRINCIPAL SOFTWARE CONSULTANT**

Built and managed this software consulting company, working under contract with Allen-Bradley to handle CNC custom software engineering engagements as well as support customers through troubleshooting and enhancements for previously developed custom software. Directed a 10-person team of subcontractors. Simultaneously managed other computer consulting projects for a wide range of clients.

- Designed, developed, and tested "Merlin"—Allen-Bradley's first PC-compatible hardware platform for the CNC line; implemented to improve the human interface front end to the 8200AT CNC. Created and integrated new features such as real-time task scheduling and task switching.
- Conceived and developed Desktop PAL, the first and only third-party software product for developing and documenting 8200 and 8200AT CNC PAL on a PC-compatible computer.

**Allen-Bradley Co., Highland Heights, OH / Dusseldorf, West Germany**     Mar 1976 – Dec 1987

**CNC SOFTWARE GROUP SUPERVISOR, MILLS AND ROBOTICS** (1985 – 1987)
**CNC SOFTWARE QUALITY ASSURANCE SUPERVISOR** (1984 – 1985)
**COMPUTER CENTER SUPERVISOR** (1983 – 1984)
**SOFTWARE ENGINEER / TECHNICIAN** (1976 – 1983)

Advanced rapidly through positions of increasing responsibility as a software engineer and supervisor to final management position, leading a team of 5 directly reporting supervisors and approximately 70 indirect reports. Managed all standard and custom software development projects for mill and robotics applications.

- Measurably improved "as shipped" software quality through the implementation of new policies and procedures for testing and shipping. Analyzed and isolated problem areas and developed an innovative preventative method to eliminate problems in new shipments.
- Developed a fully operational and self-sustaining CNC computer department in Dusseldorf, West Germany, achieving corporate goal of establishing a local CNC software development engineering presence in Europe. Completed assignment in just 19 months, 5 months ahead of schedule.
- Designed, developed, tested, and debugged CNC executive software, focusing on operator interfaces, PAL special features, basic control logic, servo control, axis motion, and system configurability.

## EDUCATION

**COMPUTER PROGRAMMING**
Institute of Computer Management, Boston, MA – 1976

Extensive continuing education includes college-accredited courses in software development languages/ techniques, operating systems, and network administration, as well as vendor training with Microsoft, Borland, and IBM/Lotus. Certified as ISO-9000 Facilitator Specialist through Cleveland State University.

# CHAPTER 6

# Resumes for Technology Support Professionals

- Help Desk Administrators and Analysts
- Technical Call Center Representatives
- Technical Support Technicians
- Data Library and Warehousing Specialists
- Technical Training Specialists
- Technical Writers
- Technology Sales and Marketing Professionals
- Technology Business Development Professionals

# JAMES CARRO

408 Springmeadow • Holbrook, NY 11741 • 631-567-9183 • jcarro@aol.com

## PROFILE

**Helpdesk / Desktop Support Specialist** able to provide theoretical and practical customer/user service and support to diagnose, troubleshoot, and repair hardware, software, and peripheral problems. Skilled in applying analytical and technical skills to produce practical solutions. Experienced in the installation of state-of-the-art hardware and software applications. Knowledgeable about equipment bases, digital switches, hubs, patch cables, routers, servers, administrator stations, network closet wiring, and installation procedures.

## TECHNICAL PROFICIENCIES

*Install, Upgrade, Migrate & Configure*

*Hardware:* Pentium 486/586/Pentium IV
*Language:* HTML 4.0
*Operating Systems:* Windows 95/98/2000/XP
*Software:* MS Office 2000 (Word / Outlook / Access) • Lotus Notes • Internet Explorer • Norton Utilities
*Communications:* **Protocol** / SCSI / IDE / MFM / RLL / ESDI • **Interface** / modems / network cards / I/O ports

## EDUCATION

Boston University, Boston, MA
**Windows XP / HTML 4.0**
**Certification (in Progress)**
PC Tech & Support Program, **A+ Certification, 1999**

## EXPERIENCE

MEDICAL GROUP • Oakdale, NY                                                                    **1998 to Present**
**Independent Computer Support Contractor**
Build computers from board level, install operating systems and software, and configure systems. Perform multiple installations of IE 6.0 and Fax Sr. from LAN.
~ *Researched components for value and reliability, resulting in substantial savings to customers.*

CERIDIAN PERFORMANCE PARTNERS • Boston, MA                                            **1995 to 1999**
**Fulfillment Coordinator**
Performed as visibility liaison among company and human resource departments of subscribing Fortune 500 clients. Assured timely and cost-efficient fulfillment of material for affiliate and client events. Worked with UPS Online System and Federal Express Powership, updating and maintaining affiliate and client database. In conjunction with Production Department, defined and maintained online inventory system for offsite service facility.

LAURA ASHLEY GLOBAL DEVELOPMENT • Boston, MA                                         **1992 to 1995**
**Mail Services Supervisor**
Distributed U.S. and interoffice mail, including payroll, to a staff of 300. Operated and upgraded Pitney Bowes mailing systems. Maintained database of 200 North American shops, U.K. headquarters, and European satellite offices.
~ *Contributed creatively to marketing department's nationwide window-display advertising.*
~ *Trained personnel in applications of UPS Online Shipping and Federal Express Powership.*

This resume is easy to skim for essential information—technical qualifications, experience, and achievements.

**RESUME 35:** *BY* **LINDA MATIAS, CEIP, JCTC**

# (Ms.) Furkhunda Rizvi

57 Hofstra Boulevard
Port Jefferson Station, NY 11772
631-555-2425 • frizvi@yahoo.com

## Overview

Skilled **Helpdesk Analyst** with 7 years of experience providing PC and CLIENT/SERVER TECHNICAL SUPPORT. Experience in diagnosing and resolving difficult problems in the area of hardware, applications, and operating systems. Interface with end users handling inquiries regarding system configuration and operating systems. Effectively render technical advice to non-technical personnel. Keen ability to address technical issues and close out customer tickets in a timely manner.

## Technical Capabilities

| **Operating Systems:** | | | |
|---|---|---|---|
| | ▪ Windows NT/XP | ▪ Windows 95/98/2000 | ▪ UNIX |
| | ▪ DOS 5.0/6.0/6.2 | ▪ Novell Client | ▪ AS/400 |

| **Applications:** | | | |
|---|---|---|---|
| | ▪ Windows XP | ▪ Microsoft Office Suite | ▪ PC Anywhere |
| | ▪ WordPerfect | ▪ Lotus 1-2-3 | ▪ Netview |
| | ▪ Lotus Notes | ▪ Arbiter | ▪ Tandem |
| | ▪ Oasis 4.5 | ▪ Deja Win | ▪ Outlook 2000 |

| **Hardware:** | | | |
|---|---|---|---|
| | ▪ HP Brios/Vectras | ▪ Okidata Printers | ▪ Digi Boxes |
| | ▪ HP Printers | ▪ Cisco Routers | ▪ Multiplexors |
| | ▪ Serial Connectors | ▪ CATS Cables | ▪ NIC Cards |

## Professional Experience

**Helpdesk Analyst,** Federal City Bank, Littletown, New York                **1999–Present**
Provide technical support to more than 2,000 branches, back offices, and ATM computer-based systems.

- Provide expedient and appropriate commands to incoming inquiries regarding system malfunctions.
- Dispatch appropriate second-tier support or vendors to solve hardware complications.
- Maintain complete documentation of all daily site outages, LAN outages, and application alerts, allowing corporate headquarters to identify high-error-frequency locations.
- Identified possible technological glitches and offered solutions for a newly installed GUI program.
- Executed, as part of a team, the technical integrity of two computer systems during a merger.

**Helpdesk Representative,** Cable USA, Northport, New York                **1997–1999**

- Resolved daily systematic and operational malfunctions, ensuring minimal loss of work productivity.
- Directed support for complex problems to next-level support, simultaneously keeping users informed as to the status of open calls.
- Assisted end users with connectivity problems, computer lockouts, and printer problems.

## Education

**Associate of Science** – Computer Information Systems, Briarcliffe College, Patchogue, New York, 1999

*The clean, attractive look of this resume is achieved through font selection, horizontal lines at top and bottom, and the three-column format of the Technical Capabilities section.*

# SUSAN SCHAEFFER

3 Vineland Road ✧ Hazlet, New Jersey 07730 ✧ 732-555-4278
SS070313@peoplelink.com

## QUALIFICATIONS PROFILE

**More than 10 years of experience in QA testing, network administration, and customer/technical support.** Adept in computer installation, configuration, maintenance, and administration. Effectively train end users and perform skilled problem resolution. Accurately assess customer needs and specifications by phone and in person. Quickly identify problems and issues and provide fast troubleshooting and problem resolution.

*Highlights include*

- Excellent communication and diagnostic skills.
- Ability to rapidly learn new information regarding technology concepts and tools.
- Solid knowledge of computer-based information technologies and their interrelations with business management processes.
- Proactive self-starter known to initiate process and system improvements to increase stability and staff productivity.

## PROFESSIONAL EXPERIENCE

**ABC Financial ✧ Pennsville, NJ**                                     1997–Present
**SECOND-LEVEL SENIOR HELP DESK TECHNICIAN/QA TESTER**
Troubleshoot approximately 30 second-level calls per day in regards to application support, remote LAN access, Lotus Notes, Internet access, LAN troubleshooting, operating system support, Microsoft Office, mainframe applications, hardware support, and proprietary financial applications for more than 64,000 employees and vendors worldwide. Resolve more than 90% of total call volume. Document and track status of client inquiries, coordinate appropriate responses, and follow up to ensure client satisfaction. Receive excellent customer satisfaction feedback.

*Key achievements:*

➤ Prepared, organized, and conducted Remedy Help Desk Problem Management training enterprise-wide for 1,000+ employees. Created and distributed end-user documentation and training surveys.
➤ Customized, established, and evaluated training criteria for each specific business group.
➤ Wrote biweekly "Remedy Newsletter," ensuring superior support for the application.
➤ Performed QA testing to ensure the product and specifications exceeded standards and were in compliance with business-unit requirements.
➤ Consistently recognized for *superior performance.* Named "Employee of the Month" first quarter 2003.

**HKG Pharmaceuticals ✧ Ortley Beach, NJ**                           1991–1997
**LEAD HELP DESK TECHNICIAN/TESTER/TRAINER/TECHNICAL WRITER**
Involved in successive career progression through the computer and network operations group into a help desk, eventually supporting more than 2,000 sales representatives and internal marketing employees. Supported proprietary software, various operating systems, upload issues via DEC VAX, and software and hardware installations. Tested and error-proofed outgoing software programs in conjunction with designing reference materials for end-user instruction.

*Key achievements:*

➤ Taught home-grown DOS-based application classes to end users for groups of 15–50.
➤ Performed COTS Analysis; studied call logging systems and made final decision to purchase HEAT for the issue tracking tool.

(continued)

*A strong Qualifications Profile sets the tone for this accomplishment-rich resume. Certifications and computer skills are clearly presented in table format on page 2.*

Susan Schaeffer                                                       Page 2

*Professional Experience Continued...*

**Lamar Global Solutions ✧ Allentown, NJ**                              1996–1997
**TECHNICAL RECRUITER**

## CERTIFICATIONS

- Microsoft Word
- Microsoft Excel
- Microsoft PowerPoint
- Microsoft Access

## COMPUTER SKILLS

- Microsoft Word
- Microsoft Excel
- Microsoft PowerPoint
- Microsoft Project
- Microsoft Access
- Visio
- Adobe Acrobat Reader/Writer
- Windows 9x/NT/2000/XP
- Windows NT Server
- Mainframe Applications
- Expert Advisor
- Paint Shop Pro
- Lotus Notes
- Remedy
- Remote LAN Access

## EDUCATION

**University of Phoenix ✧ Online**                                          2004
**MBA**
Technology Management

**Kirk Hall University ✧ Gainsville, NJ**                                     1992
**Bachelor of Science**
Marketing, GPA 3.34

# Bill Rupert

118 Ronan Ct. • Matawan, NJ 07747 • rupert@optonline.net
(Home) 732-739-2480 • (Mobile) 732-750-4687

## INFORMATION TECHNOLOGY LEADER

Talented and accomplished technical leader with five years of success in supervising, problem solving, and training. Experienced leading cross-functional teams with diverse technical backgrounds. Dedicated, hardworking individual with intercommunications skills to work at all levels of an organization. Innovative professional with proven ability to identify, analyze, and solve issues to increase customer satisfaction and raise skills sets of team members through expertise in

- Leading Level-One and -Two technical teams
- Communicating, presenting, and training
- Coaching, mentoring, and managing technical staff
- Developing and implementing projects

## PROFESSIONAL EXPERIENCE

**TEAM LEADER / TECHNICAL SUPPORT SPECIALIST**                    1999–Present
*CBA Financial, Lafayette, NJ*

**Team Leader:** Guide and supervise team of seven members in all aspects of technical and procedural support. Compile daily help-desk statistics; monitor phone calls; address conflicts or performance issues; create agendas for and lead biweekly team meetings. Provide ongoing feedback to team members to help achieve and exceed performance objectives. Dedicate extensive time and energy to improving communications with help-desk analysts, local desktop support, and clientele, while accepting full responsibility for six-month and annual performance reviews, employee motivation, and morale.

**Technical Support Specialist:** Built and currently direct the Lotus Notes Level-Two group, supporting internal help desks to resolve end users' questions and issues. Provide Lotus Notes training at all levels to help-desk analysts via Sametime sessions, conference calls, and classroom programs. Resolve approximately 30 Level-Two Lotus Notes issues per day. Monitor Level-One tickets on a daily basis in search of technical trends to help provide individual or group feedback and update training programs.

**Career Highlights:**
➤ Traveled internationally for two months to train new help-desk analysts on receiving Level-One technical phone calls.
➤ Created, coordinated, and implemented the new-hire training program. Oversee 10 trainers while maintaining and updating all documentation, including midterm and final exams, training outlines, and end-user reference guides.
➤ Developed and currently maintain the department's Lotus Notes troubleshooting guide.
➤ Participated on the "Remedy implementation team," which involved pilot testing, evaluating, and providing feedback to the development team.
➤ Won Help Desk "Employee of the Month" award, first quarter 2002.

**SENIOR HELP DESK ANALYST**                                      1997–1999
*CBA Financial, Lafayette, NJ*
Interpreted, evaluated, and resolved more than 70% of telephone inquiries pertaining to application and network support. Provided technical guidance for domestic, international, and remote end users, along with other systems support units, to identify and resolve complex client problems. Documented and tracked status of client inquiries, coordinated appropriate responses, and followed up to ensure client satisfaction. Participated in the analysis of client-identified issues that required changes to department procedures, standards, or systems.

(CONTINUED)

*The Career Highlights section breaks up the position description and calls attention to notable activities and achievements.*

**Bill Rupert**, Page 2                                                                rupert@optonline.net/732-739-2480
*Professional Experience – continued…*

**RESELLER COMPUTER CONSULTANT / ACCOUNT EXECUTIVE**                                    1995–1997
*Evax Engineering Corporation, Irvine, NJ*
Managed more than 300 accounts nationwide. Negotiated pricing of various computer components
with industry leaders of retail and resell. Assisted upper-level management with marketing ideas in
accordance with current market conditions and trends both domestically and internationally. Authorized
account manager of IBM and Compaq systems and laptops.

## COMPUTER SKILLS

- Microsoft Word
- Microsoft Excel
- Microsoft PowerPoint
- Microsoft Project
- Lotus Notes

- Systems Management Server (SMS)
- Adobe Reader/Writer
- Windows 9x/NT/2000/XP
- Windows 2000 Server
- Mainframe Applications

- Expert Advisor
- Paint Shop Pro
- Visio
- Remedy
- Remote LAN Access

## EDUCATION

**BACHELOR'S DEGREE IN MANAGEMENT SCIENCE**                                             1994
*Kane University, Union, NJ*

**NETWORKING CLASSES**                                                                  1998
*Integrated Computer Management (ICM)*
Administering Microsoft Windows NT 4.0, Supporting Windows NT Core Technologies

# *Jayne Wharburton*

3213 Zenith
Blairsburg, IA 50010

(515) 238-1875
jaynewharb@prairienet.com

## SUMMARY OF QUALIFICATIONS

Solution Center professional with two and a half years of experience interacting face-to-face with students, faculty, and staff. Able to clearly understand problems and find positive solutions through use of problem-solving skills, knowledge, and consultation with other technical support staff. Excellent knowledge of policies and procedures. Willing to learn new skills to continue best serving the needs of the customer and Solution Center.

## TECHNOLOGY SKILLS

Knowledge of Solomon bookkeeping program, FoxPro reference library program, Microsoft Word and Excel, Internet, and e-mail systems.

## WORK EXPERIENCE

### Iowa State University, Ames, IA, 1999–present

**Computation Center,** Clerk III, 2003–present
Interface with walk-in customers (students, faculty, staff) on a daily basis. Explain technical procedures in a clear, precise manner using personal knowledge and expertise, consulting with other support staff, or referring to senior-level technical staff. Distribute handouts on setting up Internet access.

→ Understand and apply the Center's policies and procedures.
→ Explain Internet access registration to students, faculty, and staff.
→ Direct appropriate set-up of Ethernet for dormitories and off-campus modems.
→ Verify Vincent accounts and enter information into database.
→ Develop excellent client relations with internal and external departments.
→ Prepare invoices and process charge orders, sales, and reference materials.
→ Maintain inventory of computer supplies necessary to meet customer needs.

**Extension Distribution Center,** Clerk III, 1999–2003
Balanced cash reports to sales on a daily basis, prepared billing and credits, maintained up-to-date database, and processed orders.
→ Applied problem-solving skills to resolve complicated orders in a timely manner.

## EDUCATION

**Bachelor of Science,** Iowa State University, Ames, IA, 2001
Major: Social Work

*Note how this individual transitioned from a degree in Social Work to a career in technology! The resume does a good job of defining her technical activities along with problem-solving and customer-service skills.*

## RESUME 39: BY ARNOLD G. BOLDT, CPRW, JCTC

### ALEXANDER V. MATTESON

| | |
|---|---|
| 1234 Winterberry Crescent | 407-678-1234 |
| Winter Park, Florida 32793 | AVM123@hotmail.com |

**OBJECTIVE**       Entry-level technical support/programming position utilizing strong computer skills.

**QUALIFICATIONS**

**Programming Experience:**

- Utilized dBASE to create inventory/sales analysis tool for retailer. This program identifies customer buying trends and allows user to project sales of various product lines.
- Designed and implemented Just-In-Time ordering system utilizing dBASE and EDI to directly interface with book publishers' electronic ordering systems. This innovation reduced inventory on hand by 36% for these product lines.
- Familiar with UNIX and dBASE; learning C/C++.

**Software Skills:**

- Implemented and administered UNIX-based integrated inventory, purchasing, and point-of-sale system for local retailer. System handles 100,000 transactions per year and has substantially streamlined inventory/ordering procedures.
- Installed, revised, and administered "One-Write" accounting system.
- Proficient in DOS, Windows 9.x, and Novell NetWare.

**Business Management Experience:**

- Administered payroll, accounts payable/receivable, and all tax filings for retail business.
- Managed $120,000 securities portfolio.
- Restructured organization for retailer, redefining job descriptions and reclassifying job responsibilities.
- Reviewed business insurance policies and instituted changes resulting in 34% savings in annual premiums.
- Reduced costs of direct-mail advertising campaign by 43% through analysis of mailing list and programming designed to minimize postage costs.

**EMPLOYMENT HISTORY**

1995–Present       **Operations Manager/Financial Manager**
                   Enchanted World of Toys, Inc., Orlando, Florida

**EDUCATION**

                   **Graduate School of Business Administration**
                   University of Miami, Coral Gables, Florida
                   *Coursework in Accounting and Economics*

1995               **Bachelor of Science, Aeronautical Studies**
                   Florida Institute of Technology, Melbourne, Florida
                   *Dean's List — 5 Semesters; G.P.A.: 3.4/4.0*

**PERSONAL**       Sergeant-at-Arms, Orlando Rotary Club
                   FAA Certified Commercial Pilot

*References Available Upon Request.*

*The lengthy Qualifications section, subdivided into three distinct areas of expertise, places the focus squarely on these essential qualifications while deemphasizing the candidate's current combined operations/financial management position.*

# KATY F. BERGEN

2564 South 1800 East ▪ Salt Lake City, Utah 84106
(801) 245-9607 ▪ katyfbergen@aol.com

**PROFILE**

## TECHNICAL TRAINING PROFESSIONAL

*Hospital Information Systems / End-User Training & Support*
*Needs Analysis / Systems Installation & Testing / Financial Applications*

*Results-driven professional* with solid experience in the delivery, evaluation, and customization of effective hands-on instructional programs that improve efficiency, increase productivity, enhance quality, and strengthen financial results. Combine strong analysis, planning, and organizational abilities with effective problem resolution and relationship management skills. Proven expertise in hospital information software; accounting/finance applications; and system installation, upgrade, and support.

**VALUE OFFERED**

☑ *In-depth knowledge* of AS400-based SMS financial software for hospital operations. Provide installation, training, and follow-up support for custom systems. Strong background in accounting/bookkeeping. Proficient with Windows 9.x/2000/XP, Word, PowerPoint, and Lotus Notes.

☑ Deliver *intensive hands-on training programs* at client sites using live systems. Ensure that clients understand system functions and can manipulate software to produce desired results.

☑ *Consistently receive highest possible ratings* for training effectiveness. Frequently requested by clients to provide training for add-on products and new employees.

☑ *Analyze business needs,* recommend procedural changes/software customizations, and *adapt training program content* and level for specific end-user training requirements. Provide detailed feedback to software development team.

☑ *Highly articulate and effective communicator.* Excellent team-building and interpersonal skills; work well with individuals on all levels.

☑ Organized, take-charge professional with *exceptional follow-through abilities and detail orientation;* able to oversee projects from concept to successful conclusion.

☑ Effectively prioritize a broad range of responsibilities to *consistently meet tight deadlines.* Demonstrated success in surpassing productivity and performance objectives.

**PROFESSIONAL EXPERIENCE**

### HEALTH SYSTEMS CONSULTANT
**Shared Medical Systems (SMS)** ▪ Salt Lake City, UT          2001 to Present

*$1.1 billion provider of information system solutions for worldwide healthcare industry. Serve 5,000+ customers in 20 countries in North America, Europe, and Asia Pacific, including hospitals, physician offices, clinics, and major health provider networks and organizations.*

Consult on new system implementation for clients in small- to medium-sized hospitals across the U.S. Work with software development team to analyze customer business objectives and develop customized integrated systems to facilitate financial transactions and reporting.

continued

*This attractive format—combining a wide, gray-shaded left column, check-box bullet points, and a clean sans-serif font—creates a very professional resume for an experienced technical trainer. Note the unusual Value Offered section.*

**KATY F. BERGEN,** Page Two    (801) 245-9607 ▪ katyfbergen@aol.com

**PROFESSIONAL EXPERIENCE** (CONTINUED)

HEALTH SYSTEMS CONSULTANT
**Shared Medical Systems (SMS),** *continued*

Travel to customer sites for 4-week installation jobs. Deliver, install, and test systems; interface with hospital administrators and technical staff for troubleshooting and performance assessments. Train end users on live system, providing on-the-job support/Q&A during final week. Compile thorough reports for management and development team on installation events and training outcomes.

*Recent accomplishments:*

- Successfully completed training for 35 users at hospitals in 8 states and the Caribbean during 2004. Provided on-site installation, training, and support for 42 weeks of the year.

- Consistently earned *excellent* and *exceeds requirements* ratings on student and supervisor performance evaluations.

- Selected for SMS Installer's Achievement Club—1 of 20 consultants chosen by management among 150 installer/trainers company-wide.

- Assisted 10-member team in documenting policies and procedures for remote computer operations. Wrote hidden command-line policy for AS400 system, including user profiles and upgrades. Provided feedback to team on hospital environment/situations, staff responsibilities, and trainer interactions.

- Worked with 12-member Process Improvement Team to rewrite extensive SMS system implementation methodology.

- Mentored 3 new SMS trainers. Routinely served as resource person for colleagues, providing materials and advice on training methods.

**PRIOR EXPERIENCE**

BOOKKEEPER
Affordable Fabrics ▪ Omaha, Nebraska

RADIO NEWS & PROMOTIONS DIRECTOR/WRITER/BROADCASTER
KLO-AM, Ogden, UT ▪ KSIT-FM, Rock Springs, WY
KTRS-FM, Casper, WY ▪ KALL-FM, Salt Lake City, UT
AEROTRAFFIC, Salt Lake City, UT ▪ KRVI-FM, Salt Lake City, UT
KYNN-FM, Omaha, NE

OFFICE MANAGER
Spring Air Mountain West, Inc., Salt Lake City, UT
Norm Bishop Volkswagen, Boise, ID

**EDUCATION AND TRAINING**

Boise State University, courses in Business Administration, Boise, Idaho

**Professional Development:**
Completed 100+ hours of SMS training annually. Courses included Consulting Skills, Business Writing, Interviewing Skills, Listening Skills, Communications, Sexual Harassment, and PowerPoint Presentations.

**RESUME 41:** BY MYRIAM-ROSE KOHN, CPRW, CEIP, JCTC, CCM, CCMC

# Bonita Thomas

27851 Altadena Street, Cacillo, CA 91384 • 661-538-9331 • bearsys@aol.com

### Technical Expertise

- Windows 95
- Windows 98
- Windows 2000
- Windows XP
- MS Works
- MS Word
- MS Excel
- MS PowerPoint
- Netscape Navigator
- Internet Explorer
- Freelance Graphics
- Ascend 5.0
- Lotus 1-2-3 5.0
- Lotus Notes
- LAN
- WAN

## Systems Training & Technical Support Professional

Dynamic, passionate, creative, dedicated, and results-driven Training and Support Specialist with proven record of achievement in computer systems training and technical support (groups and individuals). Outstanding project management, networking, presentation, and follow-up skills. Solid abilities in technical training, team building, management development, and customer service. Extensive background in sophisticated networking, client/server, and telecommunications technologies. Excellent troubleshooter; persuasive communicator; superior motivator. Flexible; loyal; strong work ethic; quick learner.

## Professional Experience

CACILLO INSURANCE • Southern Valley, CA • 1990–Present

Senior Fire Claim Automation and Procedures Specialist (3 years)
Senior Auto Claim Automation and Procedures Specialist (2 years)
Auto/Fire Claims Procedure Training Specialist (2 years)
Agency Field Specialist (7 years)

*Consistently promoted based on performance.*

As designated **Instructor,** design instructional system and manage training program. Train claims employees in the use of automated computer system for effective handling of client claims. Conduct group sessions either in office or at central training facility. Perform work flow analysis on clerical support, professional (claims representatives), and management units in each office: Interview and watch them perform, and then review common errors occurring in different situations; lead monthly discussions with superiors and report findings directly to corporate HQ. Keep meticulous records as to who (300+ employees) was trained, when, and in which applications.

In **Technical Support** role, manage, support, troubleshoot, and maintain claims system for five offices. Provide on-site training and telephone support (MIS Help Desk) for multiple offices/departments (clerical, administrative, accounting, claims, agency administration, management). Produce computerized/multimedia presentation materials for employee meetings and other functions. Involved in development, testing, and training of new software programs distributed throughout the region.

- Instrumental in diagnosing major system problem and implementing solution in regional offices affecting 100+ employees. Resolved numerous issues and made recommendations that were adopted office-wide.

- Member of system conversion team when Claim Master Record software superseded Claim Service Record; conversion from mainframe/dumb terminal to distributed client/server PC-based system.

- Lead project team in setup and operation of Disaster Operation Offices for handling of claims. Set up computers (hardware); train and supervise temporary/permanent staff to process claims.

### Community Volunteer

- Big Sisters of Los Angeles
- Santa Clarita Shelter
- United Negro College Fund
- Delhaven Community Center
- Adult Tutor, California Literacy

## Education

**Bachelor of Arts:** University of Redlands, Redlands, CA
- Major: Communications; Minor: Education

**Microsoft Office User Specialist Program**

**IIA** (Insurance Institute of America) Designation

**Department of Insurance,** State of California
- Fire and Casualty Broker/Agent, Life Agent

*This resume packs a lot of information onto one page, yet in a highly readable format thanks to clear, bold headings, brief bullet-point lists, and a readable serif font. The computer graphic adds interest and helps to break up the text-rich sections.*

# LILY P. CHOY

▪ 132-20 82nd St.   ▪ Ozone Park, NY 11417   ▪ 718-275-3232   ▪ 917-848-6627   ▪ lilypchoy@mail.com

### Technical Account Manager/Integration Analyst/Sales and Systems Engineer

▪ **IT Logic**       ▪ **B&D Systems**       ▪ **Data Manager, Inc.**       ▪ **CompAmerica**

- *20+ years of experience as a liaison to corporate clients, marketing teams, and systems engineers; partner with leading Fortune 100 companies in financial services, media, and government sectors.*
- *Success gathering competitive intelligence and incorporating partner products into company solutions to deliver "best in class" infrastructure software applications.*
- *Expertise creating and facilitating demonstrations and prototypes that link product features and benefits to client-specific needs.*
- *Recognized for ability to absorb multiple technologies in short time frames.*

## CAREER HIGHLIGHTS

*Core Competencies*

*Multi-Tier Enterprise Systems*

*Technology Integration*

*Systems Functionality*

*Architecture Solutions*

*Mainframe Applications*

*Systems Implementation*

*Competitive Benchmarking*

*Technical Sales Presentations*

*Solutions Selling*

*Pre/Post Sales Support*

*Proof of Concept*

*Technical Account Maintenance*

*Client Servicing*

### Continuous Process Improvement

- Reengineered IT Logic product demonstration and reduced systems requirements by more than 60%.
- Leveraged industry product knowledge to supply competitive market data for briefing distributed throughout B&D Systems. Recommended procedures for influencing future market share.
- Designed a customer-specific Data Manager product demo that streamlined training capabilities and increased client usability by as much as 98%.

### Customer Focus

- Turned around three at-risk clients at IT Logic by providing "high-touch" service resulting in improved customer service rating and on-time integration testing.
- Spearheaded "tech-day" between customer sales team and IT Logic engineering team; resolved 100% of outstanding systems issues.
- Delivered pre-sales proposal and integration testing on time under extremely tight deadline; applauded by IT Logic and client management for ability to adapt quickly under difficult circumstances.
- Reduced down-time on trading floor by 25% over a two-year period as B&D's on-site support specialist.
- Requested as CompAmerica's point-person for the company's two largest accounts.

### Technology Solutions

- Promoted to integration specialist for IT Logic's financial accounts from pool of more than 65 SEs nationwide based on industry knowledge and solid record of achievement in application and data integration.
- Selected by senior management to be liaison in the B&D Integration and mainframe areas of the company product set. Designated regional mainframe expert.

*(continued)*

*A combined functional/chronological format was used to showcase accomplishments from all phases of this candidate's career. High-profile company names are emphasized in the summary.*

# LILY P. CHOY (page two)

*Business Platforms*

*XYZ Application Server, ABC Integration, XYZ Portal, J2EE, XYZ Enterprise Servers*

*Operating Systems and Database Products*

*Microsoft Windows, Microsoft SQL, Oracle, Linux, AS400*

*Integration Connections*

*Mainframe, Database, HTTP, Peoplesoft, SAP, Siebel*

*Internet Technologies*

*HTML, XML, JSP, JavaScript, Web Services, Web Design*

*Financial Integrations*

*SWIFT, Omgeo, STP, FIX*

*Awards/Recognitions*

*IT Logic Merit Stock Option, 2002*

*IT Logic Knowledge Transfer Award, 2000*

*B&D Merit Award, 1998*

*B&D Innovator Circle Award, 1996*

*Data Manager Field Systems Engineer of the Quarter, 1993*

*CompAmerica Solution Award, 1989, 1990*

*CompAmerica Appreciation Award, 1988*

- Integrated B&D mainframe data into emulation Windows software using Oracle product for NBC coverage of presidential election.
- Pioneered B&D demo center to market services to 300+ local users.
- Piloted initiative at Data Manager to replace expensive leased lines with the Internet for a potential cost savings to the client of $1 million.
- Requested by Morgan Stanley as the CompAmerica representative at the prestigious Las Vegas Comdex industry show on three occasions.

## Business Development

- Delivered 275+ technical sales presentations to 42 Fortune 100 clients on several business platforms over a 20+ year career.
- Presented CompAmerica's new XYZ Personal System and Operating System to 2,300+ customers over a two-week period. Persuaded client to purchase 370 computers on day of announcement, enhancing company revenues by $700,000.

## CHRONOLOGY

**IT Logic, New York, NY**                                  1998 to 2004
*Third-largest applications infrastructure software company providing enterprise software to 1,200+ customers.*
- Integration Specialist (2000 to 2004)
- Senior Systems Engineer (1998 to 2000)

**B&D Systems, New York, NY**                              1993 to 1998
*Provider of innovative integration Web services, and portal and analytic solutions for 1,100 enterprise customers worldwide.*
- Senior Systems Engineer, Eastern Region

**Data Manager, Inc., New York, NY**                        1990 to 1993
*Leading supplier of enterprise information access and management software services to major corporations and government agencies worldwide.*
- Senior Systems Engineer, Northeast Region

**CompAmerica, New York, NY**                              1981 to 1990
*Industry leader in IT business and consultative services.*
- Account Specialist Systems Engineer (1988 to 1990)
- Specialist Systems Engineer (1986 to 1988)
- Customer Service Representative (1984 to 1986)
- Senior Associate Programmer (1981 to 1984)

## EDUCATION

**MBA, Information and Communications Systems**
*Fordham University, New York, NY*                           1987

**BS, Computer Science**
*Cornell University, Ithaca, NY*                             1981

# KYO TANAKA

*75 Hillcrest Drive    East Haven, CT 06512    (203) 469-2320    kyotanaka@netzero.net*

## PROFILE

Experienced technical writer / trainer with demonstrated skill in documenting software used for both non-technical users and technical support staff. Recognized for producing consistently clear, coherent documentation within deadline and with minimal supervision. Accustomed to collaborating closely with programmers during development and testing as an integral part of the software development team.

- ❑ Strengths include communication skills (both oral and written), organization and planning, meticulous proofreading, and project / schedule management.

- ❑ Experienced with computers and, in particular, with word-processing programs and authoring systems (Corel WordPerfect, Microsoft Word, RoboHelp).

## EXPERIENCE

MAAX INDUSTRIAL AUTOMATION AND CONTROLS, New Haven, Connecticut
AUTO-CONTROLS CORPORATION (purchased by Maax IAC, April 2003)
HIGH RIDGE CORPORATION (purchased by Auto-Controls, June 2001)

*Technical Writer / Trainer, 2000–2005*

Wrote detailed online and print instruction manuals for Windows NT–based and OS/2-based industrial gauging equipment.

- ❑ Manuals included a technical reference for setting up and maintaining the hardware, as well as in-depth software documentation for daily use and system setup.

- ❑ Involved in each product during the development cycle and contributed significantly to software testing.

- ❑ Provided software training classes, for both an historical product and newer products, to customers and technical support personnel.

*Technical Writer, 1998–2000*

Researched, wrote, and often illustrated industrial-gauge manuals.

- ❑ Manuals included theory, safety requirements, installation and setup procedures, operator guides, and maintenance requirements.

- ❑ Also wrote detailed instructions for the computerized electronics or personal computers used to operate the gauges.

*(continued)*

*Professional experience as technical trainer and writer is enhanced by freelance writing and editing activities.*

KYO TANAKA                                                      (203) 469-2320

*Page 2*                                                    kyotanaka@netzero.net

FREELANCE

*Writer / Proofreader / Trainer, 1997–Present*

Independently generate diverse professional assignments. Recent sampling includes the following:

- ❑ Teach word processing (Corel WordPerfect and Microsoft Word) classes in the Southern Connecticut Community Education Program.

- ❑ Taught Windows 2000, basic and intermediate, to employees of Kelly Staffing Service, 2003.

- ❑ Revised Policies & Procedures manual for Pratt & Whitney Credit Union, 2 versions, 2001 and 2002.

- ❑ Summarized market research interviews, and edited and consolidated findings into structured reports for Angus Consultants, 1998.

- ❑ Wrote travel article published in *Yankee* magazine, 2003.

- ❑ Feature article writer for local Habitat for Humanity newsletter (volunteer).

YALE–NEW HAVEN LIBRARY, New Haven, Connecticut

*Indexer, January 1996–May 1997*

Assisted with the development of a local history index generated from newspapers dating back to the early 1800s. Focused primarily on individuals and their connections to events.

BUILDERS REVIEW, INC., Derby, Connecticut

*Managing Editor, 1993–1995*

Wrote and assigned feature articles, "spotlights" on local home builder associations, and news items, as well as promotional material for the company. Proofread both the Xerox and blue-line of the 20-plus magazines and all printing assignments. Established the editorial, feature, and production schedules for all the magazines.

## EDUCATION

UNIVERSITY OF CONNECTICUT, Storrs, Connecticut

*Bachelor of Arts, Biology, May 1993*

Minors in both Communications and English. Worked Sophomore, Junior, and Senior years as a Resident Assistant for the University Housing Department. Served one year as a Peer Assistant. Active in intramural sports.

## ACTIVITIES

- ❑ Senior Member of the Society for Technical Communication.

- ❑ Marathoner (qualified for Boston Marathon 2005).

## STEVEN J. THOMAS

**eBusiness Technology Director**

### CAREER PROFILE

**eBusiness/eLearning Management Professional** experienced in the strategic planning, design, execution, and leadership of enterprise-wide technology initiatives that support business systems, strengthen organizational capabilities, and enhance productivity/efficiency. Proven record for delivering cost-effective projects on time and within budget. Expertise in technical training and development combines with equally strong qualifications in project management, operations/department management, and systems integration. Recognized for building, mentoring, and supervising teams responsive to meeting business demands for high-quality training products.

Nominated for the 2004 Excellence Award for creating an electronic knowledge base
for all 300 training personnel across all business lines in company.
Recognized with the prestigious annual eLearning Best Practices Award in 2003.

### PROFESSIONAL EXPERIENCE

**RYAN BECK FINANCIAL SERVICES, INC.**                   SAN DIEGO, CA
**Director, eBusiness Technology Solutions Group**       2002–Present
**Assistant Manager, eBusiness Technology Solutions Group**   2001–2002

Promoted to pioneer and direct Group's development and maintenance of technology-based training initiatives and support functions, including Web-based Training, Online Help, and Electronic Performance Support Systems (EPSS) for 2,000 internal and 20,000 external customers. Provide eLearning expertise/support to technical trainers as well as managers company-wide. Supervised team of 8 and managed vendor relationships and contract negotiations.

**Selected Accomplishments:**

▶ **Chosen to manage a major corporate initiative for development and implementation of training in the release of a new higher-end technical product that prepared new teams to meet aggressive sales goals.**

- Created the Project Management structure and standards for a complex project that included new product, operating model, and technology components.
- Led team of 11 in developing and implementing training materials delivered on time and within budget.
- Forged a collaborative partnership and team environment between 2 separate training departments that had never worked together.

▶ **Championed, persuaded senior management, and introduced innovative eLearning technologies, processes, and trends company-wide.**

- Managed development of and promoted to senior training and business leaders a Process-Based Assessment and Training method from idea generation to successful pilot implementation. Results led to enhanced workflow processes: Improved accuracy by 20% and time to perform tasks by 246%; 96% stated that training would increase their efficiency.
- Led research on new simulation tool products, reducing development costs by an estimated $142K+ per year with a 174% EVA. Presented business case and won approval from senior leadership to implement.
- Spearheaded creation of eLearning standards, processes, and best practices, ensuring application of consistent methodology in program development among new and existing training personnel.

▶ **Led development of and delivered 4 Web-based training programs on time and within budget, effectively overcoming multiple obstacles.**

- Took charge of the design and implementation of 2 concurrent Web-based training projects for 1,600 users that included eLearning, instructor-led training, distance learning, and job aids for Loss Control System. Realized significant savings for the company over prior system rollout strategy.

*continued...*

This resume is peppered with documented business results from e-learning programs this executive has led.

## STEVEN J. THOMAS

**Page 2**

**Director, eBusiness Technology Solutions Group,** *continued...*

- Managed Web-based course design contributing to successful relaunch of Business Objects application for 1,400 users. Led training program development for business insurance analytical platform.
- Provided development direction, mentoring, and consultation on a high-priority project for Web-based and Online Help training initiatives related to a business lines rating tool.

▶ Initiated project, persuaded management, and revamped 1,500-page online product manual providing key data on 48 states for 50,000 users. Streamlined and produced a searchable, more user-friendly Web format that is also easier and faster to maintain than prior version.

**ARRANSON TECHNOLOGY SYSTEMS, INC.**                                   SAN DIEGO, CA
**Training Consultant, Integrated Learning Solutions Group**            **1999–2001**

Collaborated with clients and technical experts to develop Web-based Training (WBT), Computer-based Training, and Instructor-led Training for proprietary ERP systems. Team leader for Web-based Training project, including interaction with internal and external clients, project planning, creation of design structure and standards, and instruction evaluation. Analyzed software design documents to determine system functionality.

**Selected Accomplishments:**

▶ Developed multimedia training for 22,000 users of procurement systems, providing automated, strategic, streamlined contract-management support within a complete workflow-management solution.
▶ Designed multimedia program to train 8,000+ users of a financial system managing $36 billion annually.
▶ Co-designed a central record-keeping database, using Access and Active Server Pages.
▶ Created WBT using Microsoft Visual Interdev and performed HTML/VB Script edits.
▶ Developed user guides, job aids, and train-the-trainer materials for an Ariba 7.0 eProcurement system.

**ELECTRONIC INFORMATION TECHNOLOGIES, INC.**                          NEW YORK, NY
**Technical Trainer**                                                   **1994–1999**
Provided end-user training on a proprietary ERP system to the finance and accounting organization of a government agency with 16,000 employees. Led 12 other training instructors.

**Selected Accomplishments:**

▶ Provided training on accounting systems for paying 5.7+ million people annually; trained personnel on vendor payments (total of $126 billion annually) and computerized accounts payable system.
▶ Contributed to development of instructional design standards for all financial-management courses.
▶ Presented numerous courses on vendor pay; created and instructed a Microsoft Office training course.

### EDUCATION

**M.S., MANAGEMENT INFORMATION SYSTEMS**
University of California, San Diego, CA, 2000

**B.S., WORKFORCE EDUCATION AND DEVELOPMENT**
New York University, New York, NY, 1994

# LOUIS M. DIAMOND

515 Bay Drive                                                                                           Brick, New Jersey 08724
Residence: (732) 295-9803                    email: lmdiamond@home.com                    Mobile: (201) 609-2520

## TECHNOLOGY SALES / MARKETING AND BUSINESS DEVELOPMENT

### Asia, Europe, Middle East, and United States

Solid executive career leading start-up and fast-track growth of high-technology companies. Expert in business development, product positioning, and market expansion with strong operating, financial, and HR skills. Strengths include forging cooperative working relationships; identifying and formulating strategic, revenue-generating partnerships. Proven "intraprenuer" with a track record in championing new organizational initiatives and employing "out-of-the-box" thinking.

## CAREER HISTORY

**XYLINK CORPORATION,** San Diego, CA (2/00–Present)

**Director of Business Development,** 7/03–Present

Full strategic and tactical responsibility for creating and leading a worldwide business development team in the sale of high-technology products, including security software, standalone WAN / LAN appliances, modules, and components. Accountable for planning and orchestrating aggressive market and business development initiatives throughout emerging global markets for this $400 million corporation. Captured vertical industries such as telecommunications (network equipment manufacturers and carriers), health care (payers and providers), and wireless (e-merchants and solution providers). Performed financial evaluation of business development opportunities, including Net Present Value (NPV) and Internal Rate of Return (IRR) calculations. Conceived and developed new product distribution channels that increased market penetration.

   Accomplishments:

- Evaluated competitive activity, competitive products, emerging technologies, and new markets to determine the corporation's global market position. Performed financial evaluation of business-development opportunities, including NPV and IRR calculations.

- Built and led a global business development and sales organization. Spearheaded business development initiatives and marketing strategies that spanned four continents. Trained new sales recruits in international liaison, marketing, and business development skills.

- Negotiated an annual $4 million technology license contract with L3 Communications.

- Performed due diligence and negotiated an Original Equipment Manufacturer (OEM) contract with DICA Technologies for the sale of an ISDN product into the Japanese market; captured $3.5 million in annual sales revenues.

- Negotiated and signed a global purchasing agreement with AT&T Solutions, resulting in $6 million in annual sales revenues.

- Established multichannel distribution networks to expand product reach in health care, wireless, and telecommunications markets.

- Negotiated strategic alliances and signed multiple co-marketing agreements, including the establishment of partnerships with SYMANTEC and IBM / Tivoli.

- Developed Marconi Communications and ADTRAN as a reseller channel for Virtual Private Network (VPN) products; estimated annual revenue of $6.5M.

- Developed business partnership with Nokia and Ericsson to provide wireless security technology.

**Global Account Manager,** 2/00–7/03

- Drove international sales revenues, launched new business development initiatives, and profitably directed account-development programs throughout emerging markets worldwide, including such accounts as Citigroup, AT&T Solutions, MBNA, Chase, Bankers Trust, Credit Suisse / First Boston, and Fidelity Investments.

- Increased sales revenues by 200% over two-year period.

(Continued)

*More than half of the first page of this resume is taken up with sales-related accomplishments. Note that unlike many other computer and Web resumes, technical qualifications are included only within the context of sales achievements.*

**LOUIS M. DIAMOND**, Page Two        (732) 295-9803 • lmdiamond@home.com

## CAREER HISTORY (Continued)

**CINCINNATI ELECTRONICS CORPORATION,** Mason, OH (1/99–2/00)

**Regional Sales Manager,** Eastern United States

Responsible for regional profit and loss, distribution network management, and the coordination of marketing and sales activities within a territory extending from the Caribbean to eastern Canada. Boosted both market penetration and company brand recognition. Increased sales by more than 90 percent. Revamped regional coverage to maximize productivity and enhance efficiency of the distribution network. Tracked sales and analyzed trends and market conditions to develop annual forecasts. Generated market analysis reports. Developed and implemented application-specific seminars and presentations for value-added resellers. Interfaced with advertising and public relations agencies to maximize marketing efforts.

**HUGHES AIRCRAFT CORPORATION (FLIR Systems, Inc.),** Carlsbad, CA (12/93–11/97)

**District Sales Manager,** Northeast Territory

Managed and coordinated infrared imaging system sales to Fortune 500 companies throughout New Jersey and extending to eastern Canada. Cultivated this territory by developing and implementing comprehensive marketing strategies. Increased sales by 74% within a five-year period. Hired and trained independent factory representatives to exceed targeted sales quotas. Tailored an incentive program to optimize productivity.

**AGEMA INFRARED SYSTEMS,** Secaucus, NJ (9/91–12/93)

**Sales / Service Representative**

Introduced thermal imaging systems to the medical marketplace. Performed market research prior to product introduction.

**DATAGRAPHIX,** New York, NY (7/90–9/91)

**Customer Engineer**

Responsible for the installation and maintenance of complex microfiche systems.

## EDUCATION

**RUTGERS, THE STATE UNIVERSITY OF NEW JERSEY,** Newark, NJ
**Executive MBA, Finance Concentration**
**Bachelor of Science Degree, Marketing**

**GAVILAN COLLEGE,** Gilroy, CA
**Associate Degree, Electronic Technology**

## MILITARY HISTORY

**UNITED STATES NAVY** (Honorable Discharge), 9/84–6/90

**Cryptologic Technician Maintenance E-5;** received Top-Secret SBI Clearance

References Furnished upon Request.

# Dwight D. Stephenson

1082 South Street     Natick, Massachusetts 01760
Home: 508-349-9876     Mobile: 508-209-1234     dstephenson@mailcity.com

## IT PROFESSIONAL SERVICES / TECHNOLOGY SALES

- Twenty years of experience in information technology and professional service sales
- Consistently achieve or surpass quota
- Proficient in learning and selling technical products to sophisticated clients
- Exceptional ability to build a region through prospecting and missionary selling
- Strong "closer" with emphasis on strategic selling to major account market
- Leadership qualities and a team player

## PROFESSIONAL EXPERIENCE

**TECHNOLOGY FOR YOU** – Boston, MA                                  2003–Present
**Regional Sales Manager** – *IT professional services to Fortune 500 accounts*

- Place teams of consultants to identify/solve issues of client, e.g., enterprise systems management, Y2K compliance, software distribution, etc.
- Exceeded quota ($3 million) with sales to large corporate and government accounts.

**SOLUTIONS, INC.** – Boston, MA                                  1999–2003
**Account Manager** – *Mainframe and PC development tools and solutions for major accounts in the New England marketplace*

- Closed sales with large corporate accounts, including BankBoston, Fidelity, UNUM, and Allmerica.
- Exceeded quota with 50% of the business coming from new accounts. Developed strong CIO / CTO relationships with client companies to achieve long-term company success.
- Rebuilt Fortune 500 direct end-user account base in New England.
- Established and managed new systems integration partners throughout New England.

**RBN ASSOCIATES, INC.** – Boston, MA, and Providence, RI                                  1997–1999
**Account Manager** – *Routers, bridges, and other internetworking products*

- Built State of Rhode Island territory from $400K ('97) to $2.5 million in sales ('98).
- Top producer of new account business in Eastern Region.
- Successfully maintained key end-user accounts including Fleet Bank, GTECH, Textron, and State of Rhode Island.
- Developed numerous new accounts and reseller channels.

*With a bold, italic description of specific technologies and environments following each job title, it's very clear that Mr. Stephenson's expertise is in technology sales. Note how sales "buzzwords" (quota, prospecting, missionary selling, strategic selling, and so forth) are included in the summary.*

Dwight D. Stephenson, 508-349-9876 — 508-209-1234
Page 2

**DATATEL, INC.** – Boston, MA                                              1994–1997
Senior Account Executive – *Networking management systems, multiplexers*

- Represented company products in the public and private sectors.

- Established strong relationships with new WAN and LAN customers, including State of Massachusetts, BBN, Raytheon, Lotus.

- Rookie of the Year, 1995.

**ENTERPRISE DATA SYSTEMS CORPORATION** – Boston, MA          1991–1994
Account Manager – *IBM plug-compatible CPUs and data storage systems*

- Produced more than $10 million in sales to commercial, education, and public-sector accounts.

- Developed relationships with highest levels of MIS management in Boston.

- Achieved status as highest producing representative in Boston District.

- 1994 Sales Contest Winner (#5 out of 135).

**VITEM CORPORATION** – Albany, NY, and Boston, MA                 1987–1991
Sales Representative – *Plug-compatible storage equipment and 3270 communication products*

- Sold successfully to Albany-area commercial and New York State government accounts.

- Developed significant volume of new accounts; established strong contacts with 50 area data-processing industry executives.

- Managed all sales functions of remote office.

- Achieved Quota Club status: #1 ('88) and #2 ('89). Sold more than $2 million/yr. '88–'91.

**SOFTWARE UNLIMITED** – Boston, MA                                      1983–1986
Account Manager – *IBM 34/38-type minicomputers and software for the manufacturing and distribution industry*
Consistently exceeded quota objectives ('85 through '87). Acquired excellent product and industry training.

### TRAINING, SEMINARS, and WORKSHOPS

| | |
|---|---|
| **Holden Associates** | – Power-Based Selling (1999) |
| **Target Marketing Associates** | – Target Account Selling (1996) |
| **Miller-Heiman** | – Strategic Selling (1992)<br>– Conceptual Sales (1992) |

### EDUCATION

**MBA**, 1989, Bentley College – Waltham, MA
**Bachelor of Arts, Economics,** 1983, Roger Williams College – Bristol, RI

# Michael Roy

5 Fairway Court • Burlington, Ontario, Canada L7M 2S8
(905) 336-5454 • (905) 336-1999 (FAX) • mroy@hotmail.com

## IT BUSINESS DEVELOPMENT PROFESSIONAL

Experienced business development executive with 17 years of success in formulating and implementing high-level strategic business directions within the pharmaceutical, healthcare, and financial industries. Innovative professional with proven ability to successfully analyze client business issues, recommend IT solutions, and convert to sales opportunity utilizing

- Program Development & Management
- Product Development & Marketing
- Client Training & Management
- Team Leadership

Demonstrated skill in assimilating new concepts and technology and capitalizing on the primary competencies of technical and design teams.

## TECHNICAL SKILLS

| **Project Management Tools** | **Special Operating Systems** | **Network/Infrastructure** |
|---|---|---|
| Visio 5.0 | Document Imaging | LAN/WAN |
| Microsoft Project 2000 | Automated Workflow | Wireless Cardiac Telemetry |
| Microsoft Office 98/2000/XP | Electronic Medical Records | Monitoring Systems |

## CAREER HIGHLIGHTS

Compusolutions, Washington, DC                                    2004–Present
**Regional Vice President—Business Development**
Manage a multidisciplinary team of technical professionals in offshore/onshore outsourcing of software development to leading-edge technology firms.

- Increased Software Development outsourcing contracts by $30M in 6 months within the domains of ERP, Customer Relationship Management (CRM), document imaging, workflow, airline reservation systems, and e-learning.
- Collaborated with local and international project leaders to achieve "best practices" in software development life cycle.
- Provided management leadership to multiple teams of professionals such as project managers, business analysts, technical architects, web developers, and quality assurance resources.

ELT, Ottawa, ON                                    2002–2004
**Senior Business Development Executive**
Assumed responsibility for software sales (in excess of $10M) and professional services in an eight-state account base for a Fortune 50 healthcare Information Systems company.

- Collaborated with implementation team to successfully install clinical information, document imaging, and workflow systems in 15 larger hospitals.
- Developed cost benefits and return-on-investment analysis demonstrating the effectiveness of document imaging and workflow on clinical and financial environments.
- Won the approval of key executive stakeholders (CEO, CFO) to convert ROI analysis into sales opportunity.

(continued)

*This resume includes a summary that hits all the right notes to connect with technology companies looking for an experienced business-development professional. The position summaries are brief and results oriented.*

**Michael Roy**, Page 2                    (905) 336-5454 • mroy@hotmail.com

HighNet Systems Inc., Houston, TX                              2000–2002
**Technical Account Executive**
Consulted with key executives in utilization of IT to solve business issues for a developer of
document imaging and workflow systems for the financial and healthcare industries.
- Participated in maintenance of various accounts and projects within the financial and
  healthcare industries.
- Worked effectively as a team member to assemble new technology and information.

SYmPiatic, Ottawa, ON                                        1995–1999
**Director—Information Technology**
Provided technical leadership to a company of 850 employees whose areas of expertise centered
on clinical information systems for the healthcare industry.
- Designed, implemented, and maintained the LAN environment at the corporate level
  and in seven regional offices across Canada.
- Successfully coordinated corporate selection of CRM solutions provider.

Technis Ltd., Toronto, ON                                    1988–1995
**Technical Service Engineer**
Designed and implemented LAN/WAN-based diagnostic and monitoring systems for hospital
critical-care environments.
- Collaborated in the management of multiple complex projects, providing support profit
  growth from $2M to $10M in 1 year.
- Provided project management and technical support, on-site diagnosis, and
  troubleshooting of LAN and wireless cardiac telemetry monitoring systems installations.

J&R Testing, Windsor, ON                                     1987–1988
**Design Engineer**
Worked on all phases of design and development of various industrial and pharmaceutical
testing equipment.
- Consulted with development team on architecture and development tools that enabled
  the on-time, on-budget development of the Hepatitis Testing System.

## EDUCATION & PROFESSIONAL TRAINING

- **Electrical Engineering Technologist:** Algonquin College, Ottawa, ON
- **Electrical Engineering Technician:** Seneca College, Toronto, ON
- **Project Management Skills:** DigitalThink, Inc.
- **Data Communication and Networking:** Learning Tree International, Ottawa, ON
- **Financial and Management Accounting:** Toronto University, Toronto, ON
- **Executive Presentation Skills:** Communispond, Inc., Chicago, IL

### REFERENCES AVAILABLE UPON REQUEST

CHAPTER 7

# Resumes for Network and Systems Technologists

- Network Administrators and Analysts

- Network Engineers

- PC and Computer Specialists

- Systems Administrators

- Systems Engineers and Analysts

- Certified Professional Systems Engineers

# Myra C. Landers

1256 GEYERS LANE, ELLICOTT CITY, MD 21046 — 301.555.5555 — MCL@HOTMAIL.COM

**Network Administrator / Systems Analyst**

## Tech Profile

- ▶ PC Hardware & Software Configurations
- ▶ DOS
- ▶ LAN/WAN
- ▶ Windows 2000 Workstation
- ▶ ADP
- ▶ Microsoft Products

## Awards

- ▶ Received a number of notable awards for excellence in managing computer operations, professionalism, and team leadership. Please inquire as to the nature of the awards.

## Profile

- ▶ Expert knowledge of all Microsoft products.
- ▶ Microsoft Certified Professional, Windows 2000 Workstation, April 2000.
- ▶ Ten years of direct experience supervising critical computer operations.
- ▶ Troubleshoot operations, processes, and networks; determine accurate and timely solutions. Apply quality assurance measures.

## Experience

UNITED STATES ARMY, 1997 to Present                          *Top Secret Clearance*
*Network Administrator/Systems Analyst*, Germany                 **2000 to Present**

- ▶ Supervise two personnel supporting critical computer requirements and ongoing operations. Effectively manage daily operations in a network with 50 computers, two servers (40 offices), and 250 clients.
- ▶ Implement upgrades and policies regarding network security. Excellent ability to research and figure new ways to make applications run smoother. Skilled problem solver. Provide quality service to all customers. React quickly and thoughtfully to ADP problems, applying an experienced knowledge of computer systems to ensure minimal computer problems/downtime. Keep all automation systems free from viruses. Analyze problems/glitches and recommend or implement viable working solutions.
- ▶ Maintain a comprehensive, working knowledge of Windows 2000 Server Workstation and Exchange Server 5.0. Proficient knowledge of PC server hardware and software configurations and LAN/WAN networking.
- ▶ Start new accounts for secure Internet access. Manage and issue PKI email encryption software to best secure military email.
- ▶ Selected by senior management to co-lead a diverse team in providing daily customer service and network administration. Instrumental in getting a new server on-line.

SPECIFIC PROJECT

- ▶ Developed a system policy and implemented network security upgrading software, ensuring compatibility with the fast-paced civilian sector, which was running dual operating systems. Ensured the DOS-based programs operated correctly; then installed more server-based software and services enabling server-based administration of the network, significantly enhancing initial response time to the client.

*Power Generation Section, Team Leader,* **Kentucky**                **1997 to 2000**

- ▶ Supervised a team of six mechanics. Performed direct support, maintenance, repair, overhauling, and rebuilding of power generation equipment.
- ▶ Trained, guided, and offered assistance to a team of mechanics to ensure full mission capability at all times. Reviewed operator's equipment licenses.
- ▶ Conducted troubleshooting of mechanical, electrical, and hydraulic systems and determined faults.
- ▶ Prepared status reports for senior management on equipment and parts tracking. Managed inventory and parts tracking databases. Administered quality control measures.

## Education and Training

- ▶ AA in Computer Science, Central Texas College, 1999
- ▶ Microsoft NT Server 4.0 Core Technologies, New Horizons, 2003 (Certificate of Training)
- ▶ Internetworking Using MS TCP/IP, New Horizons, 2003 (Certificate of Training)
- ▶ Primary Leadership Development Course, U.S. Army, 1999
- ▶ Power Generation Management, U.S. Army, 1997

*This attractive, unusual format does a good job of organizing and presenting the information in this resume so that it remains highly readable. The left column effectively highlights important and distinguishing qualifications.*

# GABE CONNOR

98 Ben Franklin Drive, Cherry Hill, New Jersey 08034
Home: 856-492-0094 • gabec@hotmail.com • Cell: 856-214-3124

## NETWORK ADMINISTRATOR/SENIOR IT SYSTEM COORDINATOR

IT professional with a strong background in the administration and management of computer hardware and software; programming of network systems; and 18 years of experience in the design and repair of electronic devices. Proven record developing solutions that improve efficiency of IT and business operations. Recognized for leadership in planning, project management, scheduling, and definition of scope for information systems projects.

**Fluent in Japanese and Chinese—both verbal and written.**

## TECHNICAL EXPERTISE

**TECHNICAL STRENGTHS:** MS OS ◆ Lotus Domino Administrator ◆ Windows 2000 Server & Windows 2003 Server Base Network ◆ AS/400 Base Network Design ◆ VPN Network Design ◆ Citrix System Deploy ◆ Database Planning ◆ LAN ◆ WAN ◆ Design (DB2) ◆ Thin Client Architecture ◆ Virus Prevention (Worms & Trojan Horses) ◆ Internet & Intranet Security ◆ Disaster Recovery

**PERSONAL STRENGTHS:** IT Support ◆ Systems Administration/Management ◆ Troubleshooting & Problem Solving ◆ Hardware & Software Programming

**OPERATING SYSTEMS:** MS-DOS ◆ Windows XP/NT/2000/98/95 ◆ Windows 2003 Server ◆ AS/400 ◆ Linux

## CERTIFICATION

**AS400 Administrator Control (IBM Certified)**

## PROFESSIONAL EXPERIENCE

YU GUI MOTO, LTD – *Jersey City, NJ*                           Apr 1998 to Present
**Network Administrator/Senior IT System Coordinator**
*Valued team member reporting directly to the Managing Director of Japanese-owned company. Scope of responsibility includes Network Administrator; analysis of, troubleshooting, and programming computer applications and systems for users; evaluation of potential network enhancements; analysis of existing hardware and software; implementation of firewall and anti-virus systems (Netscreen, McAfee, Trendmicro, Etrust); migration and upgrade of AS400; total database planning and design; and deployment of IP phone system between branch offices.*

*Key Contributions:*

➢ **Reduced communication costs by $54,000 annually** by successfully upgrading the Frame Relay Network to an ADSL VPN network, centralizing all applications and reducing client problems.

➢ **Improved productivity** through the deployment of an improved purchase management and sales management system, resulting in a more user-friendly system that became the **benchmark for operational units in New Jersey, Australia, Singapore, and Thailand.**

➢ **Drove continuous process improvements within the company** by successfully designing the Windows 2000 Base Network, Deploy Lotus Domino Server, and Windows 2003 Base Network Deploy (including Active Directory).

*This resume format highlights technical skills at a glance and includes accomplishments that demonstrate value to any organization: reducing costs, improving productivity, and increasing IT efficiency.*

**RESUME 49, CONTINUED**

PROFESSIONAL EXPERIENCE CONTINUED...

➤ **Reduced IT management costs** and **increased company network security** through the implementation of the Windows Terminal Server and Citrix System.

➤ **Extended target market for product offerings** through the introduction of a Web-based stock inquiry menu, **significantly reducing labor costs** and extending product interest to international visitors.

➤ **Worked collaboratively with team members** in developing and submitting an improved plan for the industrial work database (DB2 Database), **significantly improving CRM.** Plan reduced productivity loss to such an extent that corporate headquarters in Japan made it the **company benchmark for operational units both locally and overseas.**

➤ Enlisted as company specialist on database planning (DB2 Database) and design coordinating. **Saved the company more than $50,000** annually through solutions that improved **IT efficiency and business operations.**

SUKI SOKKIA CO. – *Tokyo, Japan*                                          Apr 1987 to Mar 1998
**Electronic Engineer**
*Reported directly to the Division Manager for engineering company developing and making small and medium LCD modules, while supervising a staff of 8. Responsibilities included planning, design, and experimental production of standard and custom LCD modules driver circuit; preparation of manuals for mass production procedures; advice on mass production; internal technical training; and consulting on LCD products.*

*Key Contributions:*

➤ Twice selected as **Company representative** for technology guidance visits to China.

➤ **Trained internal technicians** in the design, testing, evaluation, and troubleshooting of LCD modules.

➤ **Appointed as project leader** for experimental production, evaluation, and mass production preparation of **Toshiba Corporation's LCD module.**

➤ **Selected to consult clients** on designing interface circuits for LCD modules **due to outstanding communication, technical efficiency, and problem-solving skills.** Clients included Sony, Toshiba, Canon, Korg, YOKOGAWA Electric Corp., Sanwa Denshi, and Purdy Electronics.

**Technology Instructor,** CAMDEN EDUCATION INSTITUTE – *Camden, NJ*          Aug 1982 to Mar 1987

────────────── EDUCATION ──────────────

CORNELL UNIVERSITY – *Ithaca, NY*                                          Nov 1986
**BS in Engineering (Electrical & Electronic Engineering)**

────────────── PROFESSIONAL DEVELOPMENT ──────────────

SIP Base VoIP Technologies Seminar                                          Aug 2003
NGN & VoIP Technology Workshop                                          Mar 2003
AS/400 Administrator & Control Course                                          Aug 2002
Compaq IN & SS7 Training Course                                          May 2002
Microsoft COM & DCOM Usage                                          Sept 2000

REFERENCES AVAILABLE UPON REQUEST

GABE CONNOR                          CONFIDENTIAL                          2

# TREVOR COULSON

3113 Tanglewood Lane
Kansas City, MO 64101

tcoul@mo.rr.com

H: (314) 239-1212
C: (314) 876-1313

## INFORMATION TECHNOLOGY PROFESSIONAL
*Network Design, Administration & Analysis ~ Hardware & Software Solutions ~
System Integration / Administration*

Microsoft Certified Systems Engineer (MCSE) • Microsoft Certified System Administrator 2000 (MCSA) •
Cisco Certified Network Associate (CCNA) • Network + Certified • A + Certified • INet + Certified

*Talented professional who is recognized
for consistent ability to:*

- **Transform requirements into solutions.**
- **Ensure continuity of services.**
- **Design and implement efficiency programs.**
- **Employ dynamic resolutions to problems.**

*Core Competencies:*

- Server Security Configuration
- TCP/IP
- ISP & Web Services
- Hardware Configuration
- Router & Server Configuration
- Dedicated Network Servers (DNS)
- Firewall Configuration / Security
- Virtual Private Networks (VPN)

- Network Design & Installation
- MS Exchange 2000
- WANs / LANs
- Software Configuration
- DHCP Configuration
- Group Policy Controls
- IIS 2
- Voice Over Internet Protocol

- Network Resource Mgmt.
- Network Architecture
- User / Technical Support
- Remote Access Equipment
- Terminal Services
- Active Directory
- Domains & Trusts
- Network Printer Setup

**Platforms:** Windows Server 2003, XP, 95/98 and 3.1; Mac OS 8.5 and OS X; Linux 6.0
**Software:** MS Office, MS Project, MS Visio, CorelDRAW, Adobe Illustrator, and Adobe Photoshop.

## PROFESSIONAL EXPERIENCE

**NETWORK ADMINISTRATOR –** *TORRANCE COLLEGE, Kansas City, MO* 1999–2005

Orchestrated the design, maintenance, configuration, installation, and monitoring of eight computer labs with more than 300 units. Adhered to configuration specifications for MCSE, CISCO, and web development courses. Strove to spearhead the streamlining and growth of information technology (IT) operations and capabilities for business offices and student use. *Highlights of contributions:*

▫ **Network Design & Installation:** *Saved organization more than $14,000 in outsourcing costs.*
- Facilitated the design and installation of new network architecture / infrastructure for labs and business offices to include all cabling, routers, switches, and Internet access for more than 300 PCs.
- Installed and configured new CISCO LAB to Networking Academy specifications.
- Set up and configured DNS Services, Domains and Trusts, Group Policies, DHCP Services, Print Services, Active Directory for Domains, MS Exchange 2000, and services for Macintosh.

▫ **ISP & Telephone:** *Saved organization more than $30,000 annually in support and service costs.*
- Upgraded and deployed Internet access T1, negotiating outstanding service savings.
- Introduced Voice Over Internet Protocol (VOIP) services, slashing between-branch communication costs.

▫ **Network Security:**
- Installed Microsoft Internet Security & Acceleration (ISA) Firewall and Network Address Translation (NAT) for security and optimization of Internet access.

▫ **Hardware & Software Management:**
- Serviced, maintained, and upgraded hardware and software of all nodes throughout the network.
- Migrated college to Windows 2000 Server, Professional, and Office 2000. Installed Advanced Server and Windows 95, 98, and 2000 Pro client software.

continued

*The boxed capabilities section toward the top of the resume communicates value that is supported by concise activity/achievement statements in the chronological work history.*

**TREVOR COULSON**     (314) 239-1212     tcoul@mo.rr.com     **Resume Page Two**

## PROFESSIONAL EXPERIENCE continued

**SUPPORT SERVICES MANAGER** – *PASKIL & ROUKE, LLC, Kansas City, MO*     1997–1999

Provided third-tier management with responsibility for directing help-desk personnel and operations in support of 700 users and more than 90 applications in ten offices. Played a key role in identification, roll-out, and deployment of new systems and software to all offices. *Highlights of contributions:*

▫ *Help Desk Operations:* *Streamlined functions through implementation of help-desk software including VPN. Developed escalation processes.*
  - Directed 24/7 team in providing first- and second-tier support for all applications such as Novell, Windows, GroupWise, and ERP systems.

▫ *Software:*
  - Performed extensive research of emerging technology and available resources to upgrade and streamline company.
  - Deployed MS Office upgrades to all offices, providing on-site implementation, conversion, floor support, and training.

## EDUCATION

**Associate of Science (AS), Network Engineering** – Torrance College, Kansas City, MO

**Associate of Science (AS), Computer Information** – Valencia Community College, Orlando, FL

## AFFILIATIONS

Network and Systems Professionals Association, Inc. (NASPA) • Association of Information Technology Professionals (AITP) • Frame Relay Forum

# MATTHEW A. JACKSON

mattjackson@bewellnet.com • (917) 750-5430

### NETWORK ADMINISTRATOR – SYSTEMS & NETWORK ENGINEER – IT SPECIALIST

**KEY VALUE:** Blending technical expertise, business savvy, and relationship-building skills.

**HIGHLIGHT OF QUALIFICATIONS:** Innovative, proactive IT professional with seven years of hands-on experience in Network Administration/Systems Engineering and Network Security. Impressive record of achievement in designing, building, implementing, maintaining, troubleshooting, repairing, and updating state-of-the-art Windows networks. Expertise in legal, financial, accounting, and architectural fields.

### CORE STRENGTHS:

**Selling/Presenting:** Commended by employer for ability to "do things in 1 client visit that others couldn't accomplish in 5 years" related to sales. Effectively present complex concepts to technical and non-technical audiences of up to 15—including executive management—with record of achieving high buy-in ratio.

**Negotiating:** Captured combined savings of $75,000+ in last 20 months through skilled negotiations and by leveraging personal contacts in extensive vendor network, including Dell, Compaq, and HP.

**Client Relationships:** Outstanding history of building and maintaining relationships, earning trust, respect, and business from diverse groups of people through dependability, communication skills, strategic vision, technical excellence, and meticulous follow-through. Reputation for going "above and beyond."

**Problem Solving:** Expert diagnostic and needs assessment skills. Respond to expansive problems by presenting cost-effective, customized solutions appropriate for company's or client's size, scope, and mission. Consistently monitor systems, oftentimes preventing situations from becoming issues.

### TECHNICAL SKILLS

#### Applications/Software

Windows 9x, NT 4.0, 2000 Server and Workstation, XP; Microsoft Exchange 5.5 and 2000; Cisco-based Networking; Novell Network; Office 97, 2000, and XP; iManage DMS; Veritas Backup Software; Disaster Recovery; ArcServe; Citrix Nfuse; DocXchange; Blackberry Enterprise Server and Handhelds; Trend Micro, Symantec, and InnocuLan Enterprise Antivirus Suites; ISDN & TCP/IP Videoconferencing; Voice and Data Communications; Corel Office 6.0, 8.0, and 2000; Peachtree Accounting Software; Lotus Notes Client; MS SQL; Intranet. Exposure to Linux.

#### Hardware

Servers; Workstations; LAN/WAN; Media (CAT 5, MM Fiber); Cisco 2900 and 5000 Series Switches; Hubs; Routers; TCP/IP Printing; NIC; Sonic Wall Firewalls; Entek Firebox Firewall; Mammoth Data Storage.

### PROFESSIONAL EXPERIENCE

**SENIOR SYSTEMS ENGINEER**                                                10/2002 – Present
Allied Technologies, New York, NY

Handle design, construction, implementation, management, maintenance, troubleshooting, and upgrading of internal and external (client) networks for small IT-consulting firm servicing wide variety of clients, ranging from individuals to Fortune 1000 company. Provide IT solutions, encompassing configuration of all network connectivity levels for up to 100-user NT and W2K environments. Handle servers, workstations, backup solutions, mail servers, and connectivity (up to T1). Act as Security Administrator.

- Captured savings of $20,000 within 9 months through vendor negotiations, in addition to 6-month savings of $3,500 by negotiating cost-effective Internet and phone service plans.

*Technical, people, and business strengths are highlighted up front and in some depth, while prior positions are described quite concisely. Notice how education is mentioned in the Prior Experience Includes section to explain employment gaps.*

MATTHEW A. JACKSON Page 2 of 2          mattjackson@bewellnet.com • (917) 750-5430

(continued)

- Selected to lead major internal network upgrade; successfully managed Windows NT & 98 workstation to Windows 2000 rollout, increasing company productivity.
- Delivered 20% productivity increase for financial services company after convincing client in 1 visit to implement Windows 2000 network—predecessor made unsuccessful attempts for years. Designed, purchased, and implemented network with file server, email exchange server, home drives, shared document drives, firewall, terminal services.
- Enhanced employer's reputation by establishing trust and respect based on technical expertise and interpersonal skills, resulting in 30% shift from emergency services to service contracts.

**NETWORK ENGINEER**                                                      1/2002 – 10/2002
Smith & Jones, LLP, New York, NY

Recruited to update 10-year-old network for high-end law firm handling litigation, corporate and tax law, bankruptcy, and trusts and estates. Outdated network caused chaos, lost files, and tardiness. Hired during organizational change—challenged with resistance in senior management. Managed $2.5M project budget and $500K annual IT-budget, 17 servers, and 200+ workstations. Responsible for IT asset management, daily network operations and management, and product research and purchases.

- Key member in network infrastructure rollout: Windows 2000 Server and Workstation, Active Directory, security and policies administration, MS Exchange 2000, Office XP, iManage DMS, ArcServe, Citrix Nfuse, DocXchange, Blackberry Enterprise Server, Trend Micro, InnocuLan Enterprise Anitvirus, and ISDN & TCP/IP videoconferencing.
- Created streamlined, user-friendly network. Commended by senior management for efforts and results in productivity increases.

### Prior Experience Includes:

**FULL-TIME STUDENT MASTER'S DEGREE PROGRAM**                            1/2001 – 1/2002
New York University (NYU), New York, NY

**NETWORK ADMINISTRATOR**                                                5/1998 – 1/2001
Auraria Higher Education Center, Business Services, Denver, CO

**CONSULTANT**                                                           3/1996 – 5/1998
Finmark Consulting, Denver, CO

**FULL-TIME STUDENT BACHELOR DEGREE PROGRAM**                            8/1993 – 3/1996
Metropolitan State College, Denver, CO

**US ARMY HONOR GUARD**, Fort Myer, VA                                   8/1990 – 8/1993
Honorable Discharge; achieved rank E-4

### EDUCATION, AFFILIATION, AND PROFESSIONAL DEVELOPMENT

BACHELOR'S DEGREE—Metropolitan State College, Denver, CO—2000
**Information Systems Management (ISM), Political Science, and English**

**Member (since 1997):** Association of Information Technology Professionals (AITP)

**Professional Development:** MCSE Certification—anticipated November 2005. CCNA Certification—anticipated January 2006. Committed to ongoing training through industry involvement, research, beta tests, and active participation in online IT community.

# Yuval Fischel
■ ■ ■

18 Eloura Lane
Rocklin, CA 95677

Email: yuvalfischel@hotmall.com

Telephone: (916) 624-8735
Mobile: (916) 214-9900

## IT Professional

*MCSE • Technical Support • Networks • Applications • System Security*

**G**eneralist IT professional with multiple strengths in network administration, system security, and advanced desktop and application support. Microsoft Certified Systems Engineer certification combined with 7-plus years in customer-support roles, developing capacity to understand problems intuitively, strategize a course of action, automate daily work tasks, and create robust systems that aid productivity. Acknowledged throughout employment and academic life as an able troubleshooter, a cooperative team player, and an individual willing to share information for improved service delivery. International experience in high-pressure desktop/application support areas; proven skills in dealing with people from a diversity of backgrounds with expediency and courtesy.

**Value Offered:**

- Network Design, Implementation, Security and Administration
- LAN/WAN

- Disaster Recovery, Backups
- System Security
- Application Support
- Process Reengineering

- Hardware Configurations and Troubleshooting
- IT Policy Development
- Customer Service

## Technology Snapshot

*Network:* TCP/IP and Internet networking; Cisco Routers; hubs and wiring

*Server Applications:* Exchange 5.5 /2000/ 2003; Proxy Server Linux Red Hat 6.2; DNS Server, Linux 9; Check Point firewalls; Archserve; Backup; Terminal Server 2003

*Platforms:* Windows 2000/NT/XP/Me/9x; Mac OS X; Linux 9

*Desktop Applications:* Microsoft Office 97/2000/XP/2003, Acrobat, Photoshop

*Hardware:* PC repairs, troubleshooting, peripherals, installations

## Experience Highlights

- Streamlined and automated system tasks that **enabled a 33% reduction in staff with no loss of service levels to end users.**

- **Expedited issue-resolution** by launching remote access software (VNC) that controlled the network across multiple sites in Israel.

- Cut time in restoring faulty hard drives by hours through use of Ghost disk imaging and regular backups.

- **Instigated a series of preventative maintenance** tasks. Composed scripts that automated everyday work routines including the deletion of temporary files, regular disk checks, and defragmentation processes.

- **Managed US$20,000 project,** expanding a local area network for a hi-tech company. Installed personal computers and laid cables for five new stations.

- Influenced clients during on-site visits by displaying professionalism, expediency, and courtesy. **Reputation as a competent technician prompted repeat business** and encouraged word-of-mouth referrals that **increased the client base by 25%.**

Yuval Fischel                                  Page 1                                  Confidential

*A strong and detailed first page "disguises" the fact that this candidate had only two jobs and three years of experience. The idea was to get across his understanding of business benefits from his contributions and to show that he had a multitude of IT skills but was not locked into one particular area.*

---

### Employment Narrative

TEL AVIV TODAY, Israel           1/2003–1/2005
**Network Technician/Administrator**
Confronted upon commencement with a network experiencing substantial problems. Constant crashes and mail congestion from outdated equipment and inadequate security prompted numerous end-user complaints.

In a 24 x 7 production environment with diverse platforms and specialist editorial software, the need to handle complex issues quickly and competently was paramount. Mastered the systems quickly, achieving daily recognition for high levels of service delivery.

**Actions/Contributions:**

- Combated lengthy downtimes following system crashes that severely affected the productivity of end users. Introduced "Ghost" images of central systems that contained critical software—an initiative that allowed rapid restoration. Solution **cut downtime by 35%**, eliminating the need to re-install operating system and applications.

- Initiated transition from existing virus protection to Norton Antivirus. After implementation, **90% of virus issues were eliminated.**

- **Instigated a series of preventative maintenance tasks.** Composed scripts that automated the deletion of temporary files, and routinely launched regular disk checks and defragmentation processes. Deployed PoleEdit policy with administrator rights **preventing the installation of unauthorized software.**

- **Expedited issue resolution** by launching remote access software to control the network across multiple sites in Israel. Created educational tools for end users that provided the step-by-step basics of general problem resolution to employ prior to contacting technical support. **Cut technician time on problem resolution by 33%.**

- Assumed control of back-ups to ensure quick restoration following system crashes.

- Configured Check Point's Firewall-1 to **deflect SPAM.** Expert configuration prevented unnecessary receipt of non-productive mail, prompting **less mail congestion.**

- Streamlined and automated system tasks that enabled a 33% reduction in staff **without loss of service level to end users.** As a team of two remaining technicians, administered the WAN and LAN; oversaw communication lines to 20 branches connected by ATM, ISDN, and Sifranet; provided first-, second-, and third-level technical support on a range of office, specialist, and utility software via telephone from customers locally and internationally; troubleshot hardware issues for 300 personal computers, 50 printers, routers, switches, modems, and 25 laptops.

- Upgraded Windows NT4 environment to 2003 Active Directory **without incident.**

**Summary:**

**Reported to:**
Infrastructure Manager

**Supervised:**
Computer Technician

**Customers:** 500 end-users

**Technologies:**
Windows 2003 Server, Exchange 2000, Linux 9, DNS Server

**Position Tasks:**
- Defining profiles
- Backups
- LAN/WAN connectivity issues
- PC/Peripheral troubleshooting
- Software installations
- 1st, 2nd and 3rd level desktop support
- Subcontractor liaison
- Systems migration / integration

ONLINE LAB
**Senior Network Technician**

- **Managed US$20,000 project,** expanding a LAN for a hi-tech company; installed personal computers and laid cables for five new stations.

- Selected to form two-person team installing 40 personal computers in two days for a banking institution. Completed **project to deadline without incident.**

---

### Education | Training

**Bachelor of Social Science,** *Emphasis: Informatics, Computer Research Tools.* Hebrew University of Jerusalem
**MCSE 2003** (anticipated 2005)

# Irving T. Ventura

48 Valley Field Rd., Manlius, New York 13104
Residence: (315) 245-1290 ▪ Cell: (315) 505-3409 ▪ E-mail: iventura@twcny.rr.com

### IT Professional

**Software Engineering / Systems Administration**

*Professional experience in the following positions:*
Online Content Developer ▪ Systems Administrator ▪ Chief Technology Officer ▪ Research Specialist
Intranet Programming Assistant ▪ Internet Customer Service Agent

### EDUCATION

*Bachelor of Arts Degree in Computer Science,* SUNY at Syracuse, Syracuse, NY
Anticipated Graduation date *12/2005*
Concentration in **Systems Administration** and **Software Engineering.**
*President,* Computer Science Association

### TECHNICAL BACKGROUND

| | |
|---|---|
| **Platforms:** | Sun Solaris 9, Red Hat 9, Fedora Core, Red Hat Enterprise Linux 3, Windows 2000, Windows XP |
| **Tools:** | Macromedia Dreamweaver MX, Adobe Photoshop, WhatsUp Gold, FTP |
| **Web Languages:** | HTML, ASP, VBScript, JSP, PHP |
| **Programming Languages:** | Java 1.5, Java VM, C, Pascal, ML, Fortran |
| **Databases:** | MS Access 2000, SQL, Oracle, QBE |

### CONCURRENT PROFESSIONAL EXPERIENCE DURING EDUCATION

MAHARDY FURNITURE, East Syracuse, NY                 *November 2000 to Present*
**Online Content Developer** (2/04–present)
▪ Maintain the Online Catalog and ensure useful content by contacting more than 50 manufacturers.
▪ Assist in design and implementation of new Online Catalog designs.

**Internet Customer Service Agent** (11/00–present)
▪ Provide instant service to more than 500 customers per week through Web contacts and live chat. Work with upper-level management to devise strategies to improve customer service.

**Intranet Programming Assistant** (12/01–12/02)
▪ Designed and implemented e-commerce shared homepage using ASP and MS Access 2000.
▪ Assisted in developing intranet modules for company associates to share and use.

SUNY at SYRACUSE, Syracuse, NY                 *March 2003 to Present*
**Systems Administrator** (6/03–present)
▪ Administrator assigned to 4 machines; Assistant Systems Administrator for 2 machines. Operating Systems used: Sun Solaris 9, Red Hat 9, Fedora Core, Red Hat Enterprise Linux 3.
▪ Maintain, update, and provide security measures on all machines to ensure optimal performance and security.

**Chief Technology Officer** (5/03–present)
▪ Perform as Webmaster for SUNY Syracuse Student Government. Update, maintain, and provide constant improvement to Web site.
▪ Provide focus groups to gather input from students with different majors to ensure the best site content and features for everyone's use.

**Research Specialist** (3/03–5/04)
▪ Researched and programmed to test real-time Java VM with different criteria. Resulting research to be used by governmental organizations for use in smart weaponry and for space shuttle launch in 2009 to Mars.

### ADDITIONAL ACTIVITIES / AFFILIATIONS

COMPUTER SCIENCE ASSOCIATION, SUNY at Syracuse                 *March 2003 to Present*
**President**—Organize events, fundraisers, and meetings. Provide tutoring and class mentoring to computer science majors/minors. Conduct workshops and teach additional skills. Participate with "Women In Computing At Syracuse" to make CSA approach stronger and more effective. Started Computer Science Library. Organized SUNY Syracuse Computer Science Programming Challenge.

Association for Computing Machinery (ACM), **Member**—Competed in ACM Programming Challenge for 2 years.

Mahardy Furniture, **Personal Internship**—Established network monitored map using WhatsUp Gold.

*Although still a college student, this candidate already had a wealth of experience in the IT field. So his resume positions him as an experienced professional rather than "just" a newly graduating student.*

**Microsoft**
CERTIFIED
*Systems Engineer*

# DAVID PEREZ

601 San Angelo • Ingleside • Texas • 78362 • Phone 361.776.7969 • Cellular 361.550.4561 • dperez@msn.com

**MICROSOFT CERTIFIED • INTERNATIONAL / DOMESTIC IMPLEMENTATIONS**

Twelve years of expertise in troubleshooting, system administration, networking, and programming.

Reliable, Dependable, Committed • Team Player • Tenacious, Ambitious, and Loyal
Driven by Pride, Motivation, and the Achievement of Excellence

### Certifications
Crystal Reports • Microsoft Exchange • Microsoft ISA Server • Microsoft Certified Systems Engineer (MSCE)

### Competent in 100% of IT Languages
C • C++ • Visual C++ • BASIC • Visual Basic • .NET • ASP.NET • ADO.NET • Java • Pascal • C-sharp • COBOL • AS400 • Assembly • SQL • FoxPro • dBASE V • FORTRAN • HTML • DHTML • XML

### Technology
Visual Studio.Net • Modicon Programming • Modsoft Wonderware • MS Back Office • IIS • DNS Server • DCHP • WINS • Web Trends • ASP • ADO • ADSI • SQL 2000 • Clustering SQL Servers • Load Balancing • XML • Active Directory • ISA Server • FoxPro • dBASE V • Microsoft Office Suite 2003 • Access • Excel • HTML • DTML • Java • Visual Basic • J Creator • Net Beans • Network Viewer • Exchange Server • Windows 2000 • Windows 2003 • Datacenter • Adobe Acrobat • Adobe Photoshop • Crystal Reports Report Writer • Ahead Nero • Visual Source Safe • UPS Systems • MGE Management Software • Dameware • Real VNC • FrontPage • Dreamweaver • HomeSite • Visio • Fast Call • Tserver • Witness eQuality • Balance • Witness eQConnect • Data Sac Arena (4 Terabytes) • NICE • Veritas Backup Exec • Cisco routers and switches • Foundry Switch • Fluke Technologies • Multiplexing • DSL • T 1's , T 3's and DS 3's • Egain Mail • Surf Control • Heroix eQ • Connect Direct • Beyond FTP • PC Charge • Reflections • Tiny Term • Avaya G3R Switch • Aspect Switch • Hummingbird • PC Anywhere • Norton Antivirus for Gateways • Norton Antivirus for Exchange • Norton Antivirus Corporate Edition • Remote Desktop

## PROFESSIONAL ACHIEVEMENTS

**Migrated Operation to Panama City, Panama, Call Center Facility**
Key member of Victoria transition team that successfully completed migration of Prepaid Customer Care operation during two roundtrip visits to the Panama facility. Migration tasks included transferring Mail Servers, Egain Servers, Credit Care Protection software, Fraud Protection software, Fast Call, Telephony Server, Hummingbird, Maitland Email, Call Management Systems, and all other applications. Trained IT, HR, and management on the new applications and provided support throughout the year once transitioned. *"David was a major contributor to the success of the Panama project. The staff looked to David and the Victoria IT team for guidance on a daily basis during and after the implementation of the project. David still serves as a mentor to the Panama systems team."* IT Manager

**Migrated from NT Domain to a Windows 2003 Active Directory Domain**
Set up domain controllers, print servers, Software Update Services (SUS) server, DNS, WINS, DHCP, Group Policy Management, Organizational Units, Trees and Forests, Virus Protection Server (Symantec), Ghost Server (images for the workstations); also set up the trust between the existing domains. Designed and planned the implementation and single-handedly completed the project within the deadlines. *"David has done an outstanding job in completing this project."* IT Manager

**Created Storage Area Network for Actions Plus Ingleside (Backup Solution) Expansion**
Created a SCSI array of tape drives, using Veritas Backup Exec, to back up our servers using a separate Storage Area Network that didn't interfere with the existing network to utilize bandwidth. Job definitions and media organization were required. *"This has been a challenge! David has taken take leftover drives and a server and reorganized them to create a reliable backup system."* IT Manager

**Implemented Network Security and Monitoring Systems**
Set up HeroixEQ, HP OpenView, and Big Brother servers to monitor all aspects of our servers and network equipment. Configuration for the new servers was required as well as specifying certain aspects of our network so that these monitoring systems alert the department of any unwanted changes or outages.
*"Heroix has been an asset and an aid in helping monitor the health of our servers and systems. David has taken this system and many others by the hand and has become an expert at them."* IT Manager

**Additional Implementations**
Implemented SQL and Windows Security Patches. Installed 2 Symantec Antivirus Servers (WNort and Snort). Configured data space on the Witness Server (Datasack). Assisted in Foundry implementation.

*INFORMATION TECHNOLOGY PROFESSIONAL*

*Notable elements of this resume are the visual design and the strong Professional Achievements section highlighted by managers' comments. The extensive technology listing is designed more for keyword scanning than for reading by the human eye.*

## DAVID PEREZ

601 San Angelo • Ingleside • Texas • 78362 • Phone 361.776.7969 • Cellular 361.550.4561 • dperez@msn.com

### PROFESSIONAL EXPERIENCE

**ACTIONS PLUS CUSTOMER CONTACT CENTER SOLUTIONS**

Ingleside, Texas—Client: AT&T                                          September 2001–Present

*Forbes magazine recognizes Actions Plus as one of "America's Leading Companies." Call Center magazine has recognized Actions Plus for "Best Call Center" and "Call Center of the Year." Actions Plus is a result of a merger of two major staffing firms—Intellicast and Plus Systems—with headquarters in Ft. Lauderdale and more than 310,000 employees worldwide. The Customer Contact Center Solutions business unit has seven locations throughout the United States and abroad serving major clients such as AT&T, Sprint, and Cisco.*

**SYSTEMS ENGINEER / COMPUTER PROGRAMMER / DATABASE ADMINISTRATOR**
Dual responsibilities for "sister-site" client—The Motor Inn Reservations Center—Berclair, Texas.
Security administration; programming; telecom; Web design; database administration; network administration; supervision of two help-desk employees and virus protection.
- Upgraded NT Domain to Windows 2003 Active Directory.
- Migrated from Proxy Server to ISA Server and from SQL & to SQL 2000.
- Phone line and network additions for training room and call center expansions.
- Key contributor to disaster recovery.
- Set up network security and infrastructure.

**CONTRACT ASSIGNMENTS:**

Ingleside, Texas                                          January 2001–September 2001

Texas Workforce Solutions of the Coastal Bend
Database Administrator / Systems Engineer / Project Manager / Computer Programmer

Web Page Designs, Inc.
Web Page Developer and Designer / Computer Programmer

**INTERNET, INCORPORATED**

Ingleside, Texas                                          February 1997–December 2000
*Awarded Most Valuable Team Player*
**PROJECT MANAGER FOR MULTIMILLION-DOLLAR PROJECTS FOR ALCOA**
**SYSTEMS ENGINEER / COMPUTER PROGRAMMER / WEB PAGE DEVELOPER AND DESIGNER**
- Upgraded from NT to Windows Domain.
- Key contributor to Union Carbide (Dow) EPR project and expansion.
- Built a unit from the ground up—ordered all equipment and parts, hired all project employees.
- Managed multiple projects from start to finish within budgetary constraints and calendar deadlines.
- Documented all documents and manuals and converted to electronic format.
- Implemented virus protection throughout the sites and managed 100% of the computer systems remotely with common operating equipment and locked-down network security.

**ADDITIONAL EMPLOYMENT:**

| | | |
|---|---|---|
| CDP Chemicals—Manpower Assignment | Aransas, Texas | June 1996–February 1997 |
|    Project Manager / Systems Engineer | | |
| Coastal Bend Wireless Cable TV | Ingleside, Texas | August 1995–June 1996 |
|    Regional Sales Manager / Project Manager | | |
| United Cellular | Rockport, Texas | March 1994–July 1995 |
|    Regional Sales Manager | | |
| Texas Eye Center Express | Victoria, Texas | March 1993–February 1994 |
|    Owner/Manager | | |
| Eye Center | Victoria, Texas | January 1992–March 1993 |
|    Sales Manager | | |

INFORMATION TECHNOLOGY PROFESSIONAL

**RESUME 55: BY BEVERLY HARVEY, CPRW, JCTC, CCM, CCMC**

# JUSTIN WILSON

| Phone: 510.524.2557 | | 45 N. Winding River Road |
| Mobile: 510.653.7542 | Email: jwilson@worldnet.att.net | Oakland, California 94605 |

**Microsoft Certified Professional / Certified Internet Architect / A+ Certification**
**3.x, 4.x, 5.x, 6.x, Master CNE / Cisco Certified Network Associate**

## QUALIFICATIONS SUMMARY

➤ Results-oriented technology engineer with more than 18 years of experience in electronics, computer technologies and digital commerce.

➤ Extensive customer service background worldwide.

➤ Expertise in multiple protocols and platforms.

➤ Extensive training and experience using Novell's Directory Services for Directory Tree design and repair (NDS).

➤ Excellent team development, management and leadership skills.

➤ Multicultural and multilingual. Fluent in German, French and Italian.

## PROFESSIONAL EXPERIENCE

TECHNO-SUPPORT USA, La Jolla, California                                    2001 to Present
*The largest independent provider of technology support for the digital world.*

**Senior National Technical Support Engineer**

Oversee the development and execution of customized solutions to help established businesses adapt their IT infrastructures to the changing requirements of the rapidly evolving digital marketplace. Assist major providers of broadband, DSL, cable and wireless technologies meet demands for deployment and support. Manage a team of 92 Technicians in a 24/7 operation.

- Manage Sabre Travel information support for Novell 5.x and 6.x server-based and Win95 peer-to-peer-based networks including modem and frame relay connectivity.
- Provide direct second-level support for Novell, Inc., under contract, including all aspects of client and server, issues dealing with design, and repair of directory services (e.g., 700 servers for the State of California).
- Managed a series of customer service and quality improvement projects to improve customers' experience and create loyalty.
- Conduct monthly classroom instruction in Novell Certification courses.

MEMOREX TELEX, Fresno, California                                          1994 to 2001

**Product Test Supervisor** (1997 to 2001)

Oversaw testing of more than 12 state-of-the-art technology product lines and 30+ technicians.

- Developed and created test plans, organized test resources and schedules, managed execution and oversaw quality control procedures and processes.
- Interfaced with project leads and engineers to define test requirements and develop a database for streamlining processes.
- Interfaced with customers, engineers, technicians and senior executives to resolve and improve productivity, efficiency and quality.

(continued)

*With strong technical credentials leading off this resume, it is sure to catch the attention of employers. It is particularly well written and inviting in appearance.*

**JUSTIN WILSON**     510.524.2557/jwilson@worldnet.att.net     Page 2

MEMOREX TELEX (Continued)

**Electronics Technician** (1994 to 1996)

Instrumental member of an elite electronics team designing and troubleshooting electronic circuits for technologically advanced systems for a series of new product releases.

- Drew schematic circuit diagrams using PC software, designed and built mechanical enclosures, produced drawings for outsourcing and prepared layout of circuits using PCB layout software.
- Oversaw assembly of fine pitch surface mount components and ball grid arrays on printed circuit boards used in oscilloscopes, digital multi-meter, soldering iron, microscope and vacuum-operated de-soldering equipment.

TELETECH/AMERICA ONLINE, Stockton, California                    1990 to 1994

**Technical Lead**

Supervised a group of 32 technicians providing customer service and technical support to incoming callers using America Online, CompuServe, and Internet Mail software.

- Worked with various operating systems and applications including Vantive, Windows 95 and NT, DOS, Lotus AmiPro, Microsoft Office, Microsoft Works and WordPerfect.
- Assisted users worldwide in a diverse range of technical support issues.

BURTEK, INC., Sacramento, California                    1987 to 1990

**Senior Field Service Engineer**

Supervised in-house and on-site assembly, test and customer acceptance of flight simulation training devices to British Air, PSA, TWA and Eastern Airlines.

- Provided close customer contact to resolve product performance issues in a timely fashion.

U.S. NAVY                    1983 to 1986

**Electronics Technician**

Served as communications liaison in NATO fleet exercises. Supervised work of radar and communications technical group, NAS Whiting field. Top Security Clearance. Recipient of numerous awards, medals and commendations.

### EDUCATION

**BBA, Computer and Information Science,** University of California, 1997
**AAS, Industrial Engineering,** TCC Tulsa Community College, Oklahoma, 1987
**AAS, Computer Science,** TCC Tulsa Community College, Oklahoma, 1984
**Graduate,** U.S. Naval Electronics School, Great Lakes, Illinois

Completed 48 technical training, application, systems and technology courses and seminars. Amplified training addendum available upon request.

### PROFESSIONAL AFFILIATIONS

NPA (Network Professionals Association)

NUI (NetWare Users International)

# RICHARD TAYLOR

937 Hillside Avenue, Worcester, NY 12197 • Phone 607-578-5325 • taylor@computerspring.com

### LOTUS NOTES / NETWORK ADMINISTRATOR – COMPUTER CONSULTANT
(Network Installation, Configuration, Computer Installation/Setup, User Training)

**Microsoft Certified Professional (MCP)**
**Certified Novell Administrator (CNA)**
**Certified Lotus Notes System Administrator**
**Certified Lotus Notes Application Developer**

*Innovative and talented computer professional with an impressive record of achievement in data center operations including technical and systems support covering both Microsoft and Novell systems.*

## PROFESSIONAL PROFILE

- Results-driven expert skilled in all phases of computer technologies including **installation, configuration, PC Network backup, virus detection and removal,** and **system upgrades.**
- Accomplished technical professional skilled in building customer rapport, **troubleshooting,** and **problem resolution.**
- **Strong communication skills.** Able to interact with varied personality types from trainees to executives.
- Proven ability to develop procedures to streamline and improve daily operations.
- Extensive experience in a variety of **desktop technology** environments, operating systems, and PC applications including **Lotus Notes** and **Microsoft Exchange.**

## TECHNICAL SKILLS AND QUALIFICATIONS

| | |
|---|---|
| **Hardware:** | Compaq/Dell, Servers and Workstations |
| **Operating Systems:** | MS-DOS, Windows 3.1, Windows for Workgroups, Windows 95/98/2000/XP, Windows NT 3.51/4.0, Novell NetWare, IBM OS/400 |
| **Programming Languages:** | Domino Fax Server, Lotus Pager Gateway, Sametime Server, Rumba, LotusScript, JavaScript |
| **Network Applications:** | Domino Fax Server, Lotus Pager Gateway, Sametime Server |
| **Client/Server Applications:** | Lotus Notes 3.x/4.x/5.x, Microsoft Outlook, Microsoft Exchange Server, Microsoft SMS, Novell Application Launcher |
| **PC Experience:** | Software Installation, Hardware Configuration, PC Repair |
| **NT Experience:** | Enterprise Networking, Domain Model Planning, Workstation Troubleshooting, Server Troubleshooting |
| **Networking Experience:** | TCP/IP Configuration, TCP/IP Troubleshooting, Internet Mail Routing, Web Hosting, Network Configuration, Network Troubleshooting |
| **Software:** | Microsoft & Office Products, Lotus SmartSuite Software |

## PROFESSIONAL EXPERIENCE

**2003–2004**   **American Universal,** Oneonta, NY
**LOTUS NOTES ADMINISTRATOR**

- **Streamlined rollout of Lotus Notes** using Network Application launchers, resulting in reduced manpower of 700 hours per rollout.
- **Pioneered and implemented procedures to establish Help Desk System,** which strengthened end user support.

*(continued)*

*This resume fits the first few lines of important professional experience on page 1, while giving most of the space to technical and professional qualifications.*

**RICHARD TAYLOR**                                                                                           PAGE 2
607-578-5325    taylor@computerspring.com

*(Professional Experience continued)*

- Administered and maintained **Lotus Notes e-mail system** for more than 1,400 system users.
- Developed and **conducted training programs** for daily support of Lotus Notes for up to eight desktop services team members.
- Planned, designed, and **implemented an internal intranet strategy** using Domino Web Servers. Conferred with programming department to develop and maintain website used by more than 7,000 field insurance agents.
- Successfully **implemented Domino Web Mail, SSL, and Java Servlet Manager.**


2000–2003        **Mutual Medical Systems,** Worcester, NY
                 **PRODUCT ANALYST** (2002-2003)
                 **SR. CUSTOMER SERVICE ACCOUNT REPRESENTATIVE** (2000–2001)
- **Coordinated technical pre-sales support** for GroupWare Sales Team, including training and development for new interns.
- **Directed Lotus Notes infrastructure planning** and implementation for clients.
- **Installed NT Servers, Lotus Domino Services, and Lotus Notes and maintained NT Server Administration.**
- Proficient in applications including **Fax Gateways and Pager Gateways** both internally and for hospitals across the country.
- Provided **customer support for more than 40 hospitals** having purchased products from SMS GroupWare Services team.
- Primary Support for **MedSeries 4 Optical Archiving** and **AR/ADT Purging application** running on AS/400.


1997–2000        **Jennings Oil Company,** Middleburgh, NY
                 **MANAGER**
- Managed all phases of store operations for multiple store locations.
- Coordinated processes of accounting, inventory management, training up to seven associates, and customer service.


### EDUCATION

Enrolled in BS Psychology program – **Oneonta Community College**

Completed 2 years in **Computer Information Systems** – SUNY at Cobleskill – 2002–2003

**BA (Business Information Systems)** – SUNY at Cobleskill – 2001

# ANDY DeSALVA

20825 Spinning Circle Drive  ♦  Germantown, MD 20874
E-mail: adesalva@hotmail.com  ♦  (301) 542-3333

## IT PROFESSIONAL

Self-directed technical management professional with more than 10 years of progressive experience in **network administration, UNIX systems administration** and **Windows NT administration**. Combine strong analytical, troubleshooting and technical acumen with solid leadership, project management and team-building skills to consistently deliver productive technological solutions. History of commitment to bottom-line objectives and professional achievement. **MCSE / MCP Certifications.**

## CORE COMPETENCIES

- Network Administration
- Technical Troubleshooting
- Systems Administration
- Customer Technical Support
- Network Installation

- Disaster Recovery
- Quality Assurance
- Y2K Compliance
- Network Troubleshooting
- Staff Technical Training

## PROFESSIONAL HISTORY

**UNIX SYSTEMS ADMINISTRATOR**
Adco Research Laboratories — Adelphi, MD (January 2004 to April 2005)

Maintained UNIX system accounts on Silicon Graphics Onyx and Sun Sparc servers for this government research facility with 250+ employees. Provided UNIX support to division, including maintenance of hardware and software on several Silicon Graphics workstations, Linux workstations and X Window support.

- Guaranteed consistent operations of print queues and print software and ensured daily backups of software and research data.
- Updated operating systems with latest upgrades and patches and created accounts for new users.
- Provided support to research team with installation of software applications and created / maintained NFS file systems on 5 different UNIX systems.
- Credited with replacing backup script and customizing it to work with an automated DLT tape changer.

**IT CONSULTANT II / LEAD CONSULTANT**
Impact Visions Group, Inc. — Columbia, MD (2000 to 2003)

Charged with providing IT support to U.S. Naval Medical Information Management Center projects for this $35M IT consulting firm.

- Configured and deployed client/server system for U.S. Navy hospitals worldwide, known as Ambulatory Data System (ADS), consisting of Information Database, 1–5 application servers and X Window terminals at each clinic. System was designed to retrieve patient appointment data and store information about patient procedures prior to billing insurance provider.
- Led installation and configuration of SCO UNIX on 2–10 servers at 7 Navy sites and performed extensive UNIX troubleshooting at each site.

(continued)

*The highlight of page 1 of this resume is the boldfaced Core Competencies section that includes all relevant keywords.*

# ANDY DeSALVA
Resume, Page 2 of 2

*Continued...*

- Provided on-site technical support to resolve applications software and network projects and assisted personnel in integrating ADS system with existing medical system.
- Performed testing of upgrades to ADS system and also performed the actual upgrades to most sites including Bethesda National Naval Medical Center.
- Saved government thousands of dollars in travel and lodging expenses by developing UNIX shell scripts that were used to perform remote system upgrades.
- Co-led a $1.5M project to research, develop, document and deploy 53 Y2K-compliant UNIX servers in U.S. Navy hospitals and clinics worldwide. Migrated from Interactive (Sun) UNIX operating system to SCO UNIX 5.0.4., exporting data from MUMPS database and importing data into newer version of MUMPS.
- Provided on-site project support to Naval Medical Information Management Center, including serving as Webmaster for 3 Navy projects and UNIX system administrator for 2 Bethesda Naval Hospital Information servers; configured NT servers for shipment to remote sites.

**COMPUTER REPAIR TECHNICIAN**
University Computing Services (Student Intern) — Baltimore, MD (1999 to 2000)

Primarily responsible to diagnose, repair and install workstation platforms of Macintosh, DOS, Windows 95/98 and Silicon Graphics workstations for student labs and faculty. Maintained Novell 5 server, hardware and software of university PC and Macintosh labs and SGI lab hardware.

**QUALITY ASSURANCE TECHNICIAN**
U.S. Army Information Systems Engineering Command — Germany (1994 to 1998)

Responsible for the continued operation of the Wide Area Network for the Army European Command. Accountable to diagnose and repair faulty components of the European Defense Data Network, including Cisco routers, switches, PADs and modems. Provided numerous quick response technical assistance efforts and served as lead tester of Desktop Interface to Autodin Host (DINAH) system, which included workstation, specialized software and digital encryption device.

- Awarded Army Commendation Medal for consistent quality, performance and service.
- Selected as lead technician on technical assistance efforts based on extensive knowledge of systems.
- Coordinated and conducted network performance testing of military communications circuits at communications centers throughout Europe.

## EDUCATION

**BS, Information Systems Management,** 2000
University of Maryland, Baltimore County

Army Communications Computer Systems Repair Course (Computer Technician) — 7 months
Telecom Troubleshooting Seminars

# SARAH LANCER

155 Crystal Road, Hilltop, New York 11787 • (631) 222-0102 • lancer523@earthlink.net

**Manager of LAN Administration** with CNE, MCSE and MCP certifications seeking continuous challenge with a progressive organization. Core strengths encompass:

| | | |
|---|---|---|
| — LAN Administration | — Technical Writing | — Expense Control |
| — Project Management | — Business/Technical Solutions | — Procurement |
| — System Conversions | — Planning & Development | — Inventory Control |
| — Help Desk Support | — Team Leadership | — Vendor Relations |

## PROFESSIONAL EXPERIENCE

MILLER-STENSON FINANCIAL ADVISORS, Miller Place, New York          1/99–present
**Manager, LAN Administration**          1/04–present
**LAN Administrator**          1/99–1/04

### Project Management

- Report directly to the Vice President of Information Services; charged with overseeing the technical support needs of 200 corporate users and 40 users throughout seven remote branch locations.
- Manage the performance of LAN-based hardware and software as it relates to multiple versions of NetWare and Windows NT Servers, to support the management of critical financial data.
- Provide technical expertise and support for multiple Microsoft products encompassing Office Suite 97/2000, Outlook, Exchange, Internet Explorer and various hardware, inclusive of printers, scanners and Palm Pilots.
- Directed the complexities of a Corporate Human Resources system conversion involving the purchase, installation, configuration and migration of confidentially sensitive information to a NetWare 4 Server.
- Guided several mass deployments of corporate-based systems through implementation of Novell's ZENworks, and provided post-installation support with client connectivity issues.
- Collaborate with Sprint concerning service issues, user access privileges and firewall protection for the corporate web site, and monitor the integrity of on-line ethics.
- Remain on call to expeditiously diagnose and troubleshoot a broad scope of technical problems, and serve a key role in the execution of disaster recovery plans 24 hours a day, seven days a week.

### Office Administration

- Requisition the purchase of hardware and software, and monitor data and company-wide user activity reports to track equipment and the use of multiple licensing software.
- Participate in NCUA audits to ensure LAN activities are fully compliant with regulatory procedures.
- Develop technical manuals and documentation for technical teams and company-wide personnel.
- Prepare biweekly status reports for management review.

— continued —

*This resume uses the bulleted style to present diverse experience and accomplishments. It is extremely readable in 12-point Times New Roman font.*

# SARAH LANCER

(631) 222-0102        — Page 2 —        lancer523@earthlink.net

OLYMPIA UNIVERSAL, Lake Calverton, New York        4/98–12/98
**Technical Support Engineer**
- As part of a team of Technical Support Engineers, provided post-installation systems support to 6,000 field service engineers, salespeople and customers for approximately 1,000 networks servicing nationally based medical professionals.
- Diagnosed and supported an extensive product line of Olympia video imaging equipment, printers and voice recognition software utilized during medical procedures.
- Prepared tradeshow exhibit materials, developed technical documentation, and planned LAN designs.
- Compiled field data, maintained activity logs and prepared monthly reports for management review.

GLOBAL AVIATORS, INC., Unionville, New York        5/92–6/97
**Network Administrator**
- Traveled internationally to collaborate with management on the planning of technical breakthroughs.
- Supported diversified network requirements for multiple corporate locations, established data communications capabilities and implemented data backup procedures.
- Guided the analysis, testing, implementation and conversion of multiple entities to an A/P and G/L system to facilitate the preparation of budget forecasts, financial statements and monthly reports.

## COMPUTER / NETWORKING SKILLS

**Operating Systems:** Windows NT 95/98/2000; Novell NetWare 3.x/4.x/5.x
**Hardware:** Extensive hardware and peripheral installation and maintenance
**Software:** Installation and troubleshooting of various Microsoft applications
**Protocols:** TCP/IP, IPX/SPX
**Cabling:** Ethernet 10/100BASE-T

## EDUCATION

COMPUTER TRAINING SOLUTIONS, Miller Place, New York
**Microsoft Certified Systems Engineer (MCSE), 2004**

NAUTICAL HEIGHTS COMMUNITY COLLEGE, Miller Place, New York
**A.A.S., Computer Information Systems, 1997**

## CERTIFICATIONS

Microsoft Certified Systems Engineer, 2004
Microsoft Certified Professional + Internet, 2004
NetWare 5.x Certified Novell Engineer, 1998

# BRIAN JONES

4/23 Smith Street, Rocklin, California 95677     Mobile (407) 784-1265     jonesbrian@bigworld.com

SYSTEMS ANALYST   SYSTEMS DEVELOPER   SYSTEMS SUPPORT MANAGER   TECHNICAL SUPPORT MANAGER

## SUMMARY

Accustomed to supporting large multi-user networks, driving system design and architecture improvements to meet changing business needs, and determining technical, operational, and financial viability of producing client-focused solutions. Specialist knowledge of financial systems, team leadership, and training, providing a balanced mix of business and technical expertise.

## SELECTED ACCOMPLISHMENTS

- Strategically planned, coordinated, and led complete divisional relocation to new site, establishing new structure and developing customer-responsive network; multi-phased relocation process successfully completed over 3 separate stages, on time and on budget.

- Spearheaded and rolled out multi-level training program to raise staff competency levels in using Microsoft Office 2000 integrated product suite; reduced burden on desktop support areas for rudimentary technical information.

- Coordinated major booking system implementation; oversaw diagnostics, testing, rollout, and end user training.

- Designed, planned, and implemented new network hierarchy.

- Instrumental in the career progression of 5 IT trainees.

## TECHNOLOGY SKILL SET

### Key Credentials
- Network Management
- Systems Design & Development
- Accounting Systems
- Formal Documentation for Systems Development
- System Upgrades
- Software & Hardware Support
- Network Security
- Critical Problem Solving
- Staff & End User Training

### Software/Hardware
- Windows 9x, 2000, XP & NT Workstations
- Microsoft Office 2000
- Visio
- Adobe Photoshop
- Visual Basic .NET 2003
- Integrated Accounting Packages
- FileMaker 7
- Novell Networks
- TCP/IP
- UNIX Servers
- NT Server

## CREDENTIALS & TRAINING

CERTIFIED NETWORK ADMINISTRATOR, *ADTD Training*
DIPLOMA IN ACCOUNTING PRACTICES, *University of Rocklin*

- **Visual Basic .NET 2003**
- **MS Access (Advanced)**
- **FileMaker 7**

Brian Jones                                    Page 1                                    Continued Page 2

*Professional experience doesn't appear until page 2, whereas key attributes and accomplishments take center stage on page 1 of this well-organized, attractive resume.*

## CAREER EXPERIENCE

**SYSTEMS COORDINATOR,** *Training & Development Section, Department of Education*          2000–Present
Systems manager leading team of 6 in supporting, creating, developing, and managing systems at the Education Development Center at Rocklin.

Accountable for overall strategy including technology acquisitions and integration, hardware/software support, quality control, vendor selection, scheduling, safety, team training and support, and daily operations.

- Contribute technical expertise in resolving customer hardware/software support issues; provide personal attention to 60+ people across 6 units; troubleshoot and advise customers on technical problems, achieving maximum system utilization.

- Administer Novell and NT servers.

- Established and maintained new computer-training classroom initiative.

**BUSINESS & IT MANAGER,** *Vallejo Community College*, Los Angeles          1994–2000
Challenged to demonstrate fiscally responsible financial decision-making, driving information technology enhancements school-wide. Streamlined financial reporting processes and improved the quality/caliber of financial data.

- Spearheaded the integration of technology advancements; installed and administered Novell network; updated software/hardware; contributed technical support to IBM and Mac end users throughout administration and classroom areas.

- Coordinated and supervised UNIX server installation.

**ASSISTANT ACCOUNTANT/IT MANAGER,** *Mega Manufacturing Works*, Australia          1990–1994
Large manufacturing company. Supervised UNIX server, hardware, and software installations. Provided user support for all mainframe and workstation issues.

Actively participated in planning, implementing, and installing integrated accounting system to streamline tasks, boost productivity, reduce labor costs, and diminish potential for duplications and errors. Dual accounting role. Analyzed and reconciled accounts, prepared journal entries, calculated monthly summaries, led month-end closing and analysis, and prepared financial statements.

**ASSISTANT ACCOUNTANT,** *FTRE Enterprises*, Australia          1988–1990
Financial management accounting. Compiled and produced accounting reports for 2 Victoria-based companies for presentation to Sydney headquarters.

## REFERENCES

Available upon request.

# JACK A. HOLMAN, CNA, CNE

190 East Sidewater Lane ▪ Austin, Texas 77000
(512) 999-7666 ▪ jaholman@spirit.net

## QUALIFICATIONS SUMMARY

- **Efficient CERTIFIED NOVELL ADMINISTRATOR / CERTIFIED NOVELL ENGINEER / MIS SPECIALIST** with **computer operation** expertise using a variety of mainframes and printers and encompassing console operation, tape mounting, and documentation. Experienced in utilizing CA-1 to monitor and control scratch, vault, and disaster tapes; CA-7 to monitor and control batch job processes, schedule run flows, and abend jobs; and CA-11 to restart abended jobs.
- Proficiency in **system troubleshooting**, **malfunction identification**, and **problem-solving**; assist programmers and users in resolving software and hardware problems.
- Excellent **team leadership**, **instructional**, **communication**, and **interpersonal** skills; effectively train, supervise, and motivate operators; interface well with people of diverse levels, backgrounds, and personalities. Work well independently or as productive team member.
- College academic studies with concentration in **Computer Science** and **Computer Networking**.
- High level of accuracy with attention to detail. **Career-** and **goal-oriented**.

## HARDWARE EXPERIENCE

| | | |
|---|---|---|
| IBM 9672 MVS/ESA | 9395 DASD | 4635 Xerox Laser Printer |
| IBM 3090 MVS/ESA | 3390 DASD | 9700 Xerox Laser Printer |
| 3490 Cartridge Tape System | IBM RS6000 | IBM Printers (4224, 4248, |
| 3480 Cartridge Tape System | 1900 Forms Separator | 4234, 6262, 4246) |
| 3420 Reel-to-Reel System | 2000 Forms Counter | 3174 Controllers |

## SOFTWARE EXPERIENCE

| | | | | |
|---|---|---|---|---|
| JCL | CICS | RAPS | Netview | Windows |
| MVS | CA Products (CA-1, | VTAM | Netman | 9x/2000/XP |
| JES2 | CA-7, CA-11) | VPS | Remedy | Windows 2003 Server |
| TSOE | VFTS | VMCF | E-mail | Novell NetWare 6.5 |
| | | | | Microsoft Office XP |

## PROFESSIONAL EXPERIENCE

NATIONAL GROCERY COMPANY, Austin, Texas (1993–Present)

Rapidly advanced from entry-level associate in store setting to I/O Operator to Computer Operator to Senior Computer Operator in MIS-Operations Department of major grocery chain encompassing 140 stores.

**Senior Computer Operator—MIS-Operations Department** (2002–Present)

- Promoted and assumed greater and supervisory responsibility of MIS computer operations.
- Operate console; run production flows and batches of all output generated by 140 stores (tags, payroll, payroll checks, sales and progress reports, end-user reports, price books, bulletins).
- Manage Help Desk operations and offer technical solutions to end-users as needed.

**Computer Operator—MIS-Operations Department** (1999–2002)

**I/O Operator** (1996–1999)

**Produce Associate / Bakery Associate / Checker / Stocker / Sacker** (1993–1996)

▪▪▪

*Key credentials are included as part of the name, in large type. Work experience is listed only minimally, so that more attention can be given to technical experience qualifications.*

# JOHN D. JOSEPH

150 Elm Street
Hartford, CT 06107

john.joseph27@yahoo.com

Residence: 860.249.3409
Mobile: 860.505.2301

## PROFESSIONAL SUMMARY

*Development, standardization, upgrade, & deployment of enterprise-class IT systems & processes*
*– UNIX-based WAN, LAN, and client-server environments –*

**IT project manager, team leader, and individual contributor** with 13+ years of experience supporting a multibillion-dollar company's growth and expansion. Consistently tapped to manage complex, cross-functional technology initiatives and turn around projects. Tenacious problem solver known for "making things happen" at lower costs within strict time constraints. Skilled relationship builder able to achieve project buy-in from stakeholders. **Combine bottom-line business orientation with technical expertise.** Skills:

- IT Operations & Process Management
- eBusiness Content Management
- ERP System Implementation (mySAP ERP)
- Enterprise-Wide IT Desktop Support
- Budget Development

- Architecture-Standards Development
- Data Conversion
- CRM (Customer Relationship Management)
- Systems Integration & Implementation
- Data Warehouse/Reporting Management

## PROFESSIONAL EXPERIENCE

SELECT LIGHTING INC., Hartford, CT      1995–Present
*3rd-largest lighting manufacturer in the world with $3.7 billion in North American annual sales.*

**eBusiness Manager / Data Warehouse Manager** (1997–Present)

Direct corporate-enhancement projects to increase functionality of IT operations for 5 major North American divisions. Manage the Data Warehouse Department and projects in support of Enterprise Business Systems and intranet/extranet initiatives. Oversee application development for R&D. Direct 7 technical staff.

    **CHALLENGE #1:** *SAP Reporting/Data Warehouse Upgrade.* Charged with solving serious reliability, reporting, and cost problems. Assumed management of a 2-terabyte, UNIX-based data warehouse including multiple NT-based datamarts to optimize reporting for North American operations at 19 sales offices, 3 distribution centers, 17 manufacturing plants, and 1 customer service center.

    **Actions:** Enhanced data warehouse architecture. Designed and implemented a data warehouse application-development methodology. Formalized processes, procedures, and standards for establishing and operating reporting subsystems. Automated report delivery.

    **Results:** Delivered a scalable, efficient warehouse reporting system. Decreased emergency-event frequency from daily failures to once in 3 months. Slashed costs, reduced errors, and increased reliability. Reduced report-development cycle time by 50%. Dramatically grew reporting capability while reducing staffing requirements by 66%. Provided cost-efficient capability for adding new reporting modules.

    **CHALLENGE #2:** *Document Management.* Collect and consolidate information stored in various formats in multiple locations. Meet consumer requirements for a single online source for lighting information. Render operable the extranet's online product catalog.

    **Actions:** Implemented a Web-based corporate-document-management system and product catalog in 3 weeks. Collaborated with a business-side colleague to consolidate data and integrate it into Web systems. Provided intensive technical input into software installation, integration, and testing. Identified need for an alternative storage system; purchased and adapted a solution using FileNET. Achieved buy-in from 3 contributing divisions. Coordinated upload to the extranet of thousands of pages in standardized format.

(continued)

*A challenge-action-results format is used to provide significant and relevant detail about major technology projects in a highly readable format.*

## JOHN D. JOSEPH — PAGE 2
JOHN.JOSEPH27@YAHOO.COM — 860.249.3409

**Results:** Automated document management. Played key role in producing a 6-fold increase in Web orders from 5% of North American sales to 30%. Delivered a more efficient approval process for making document changes, thus ensuring conformity to brand identity. Provided e-commerce product-catalog functionality.

### SAP Data Conversion Manager (1997)

Managed the SAP data-conversion effort for a division with $1.4 billion in annual sales. Directed a team of 10 programmers to convert master data from mainframe legacy systems to a SAP client-server environment.

**CHALLENGE:** *Conversion to ERP system.* Restore integrity of a mission-critical project that was in disarray and behind schedule. Solve communication problems between business side and IT.

**Actions:** Closed communication gap, bringing all stakeholders on-board with plans. Worked with programmers to extract data from the mainframe, reformat it, and upload it into SAP. Scheduled and implemented tests to establish benchmarks and correct sequencing in preparation for going live.

**Results:** Successfully converted to a client-server, UNIX-based SAP system within the 3-month deadline. Seamlessly transitioned to SAP over a weekend with full functionality delivered by Monday.

### Technical Services Manager (1995–1997)

Managed IT desktop support and operations at headquarters, customer service center, 19 sales offices, and 3 distribution centers. Managed 10 direct reports. Hardware asset management accountability for 600+ PCs.

**CHALLENGE:** *Hardware asset management.* Correct inefficiencies and inaccuracies.

**Actions:** Established an automated materials-management system to track inventory and purchasing. Converted from a disorganized system with hundreds of personal printers to network printing.

**Results:** Delivered $200,000 in cost savings over a 3-year period. Enabled more accurate planning for hardware obsolescence. Supported improved management decision making and budgeting.

---

## EDUCATION, PROFESSIONAL DEVELOPMENT & SKILLS

UNIVERSITY OF MASSACHUSETTS, Amherst, MA: **Bachelor of Science,** Computer Science

**Recent Technical Training**—Maintain leading-edge skills in **both technology and management:**
*Software/Hardware/Systems:* Linux Systems, Server-Side Web Programming in PHP, JavaScript, Visual Basic, Statistics, Apache Server, MySQL
*SAP Training:* Logistics Information Systems Reporting, Business Information Warehouse Analysis, Business Information Systems
*Architecture:* Data Warehouse Architecture, Client-Server Architecture

**Management Skills Coursework (selected):** Process Management, Team-Oriented Problem Solving, Finance, Time & Priority Management, Supervisory Management, Total Quality Management

**Technology Skills:**
UNIX, Linux, Windows 98/2000/XP, Oracle, MS SQL 2000
SAP R/3, FileNET Document Management
ASP.NET, VB.NET, JavaScript, PHP, MySQL, Visual Basic
Microsoft Project, FrontPage, Office, Access, Visio; Cognos PowerPlay, Impromptu

## PETER BROWN, CCIE

234 Hawking Blvd.
Oakville, Ontario L6L 4T2

Phone: 905.342.2525
Email: pete.brown@luringo.ca

### Lead the Organization into Tomorrow

#### SENIOR DESIGN ENGINEER □ TECHNICAL ARCHITECT

Detail- and task-oriented professional with an exemplary background in conceiving and developing unique initiatives to propel technology to the limit and optimize performance. **Capable of tackling the most challenging networks and delivering results.** Creative and visionary, recognised for keeping on the leading edge of technology and utilizing the latest applications and hardware. Results- and performance-driven; thrive in an environment of constant challenge and diversity. Articulate; break down the technology barrier and act as the conduit between customer and technical experts. Industrious; exude energy and confidence, motivate and mentor team members to succeed and deliver quality work within strict specifications, timelines, and budgets. Core competencies include the following:

| | |
|---|---|
| Project Management | Routers & Switches |
| Routing Protocols | Internetworking, TCP/IP Services |
| Cost-Benefit Analysis | Presales Technical Support |
| Enterprise Architecture Development | Systems Documentation |

### TECHNICAL ENVIRONMENTS

| | |
|---|---|
| Operating Systems: | MS Windows 9x/NT/2000/XP; Novell NetWare 6.5 |
| Cisco Routers & Switches: | 1600, 2500, 2600, 3600, 4000, 7500, 1900, 2900, 3900, 4900, 5000, 6000, 8500, 10000, 12000 Internet Series |
| Routing Protocols: | RIP, IGRP, EIGRP, OSPF, IPX EIGRP, IPX RIP, BGP IS-IS |
| Routed/Bridged Protocols: | IP, IPX, NetBIOS, SNA |
| Telco: | ISDN, Frame Relay, X25, ATM, T1, Dark Fiber, ASDL |
| Other Tools: | Sniffer Pro, Network General Sniffer, Netview (SNMP), DNS, HTTP |

### PROFESSIONAL EXPERIENCE

Roma Tele-Communications, Inc., Toronto, Ontario                    2001–present
Held the following 2 progressively responsible positions:
**SENIOR DESIGN ENGINEERING SPECIALIST, Level II**    2002–present
**SENIOR DESIGN ENGINEERING SPECIALIST, Level I**    2001–2002

- Played key leadership role in conceiving and delivering a national Multi-Protocol Laboratory Switching (MPLS) network for a high-value contract with numerous Government of Ontario ministries secured by Roma despite fierce competition from Bell Canada. Process included
  - Developing the complex system, detailing equipment to be utilized to create the customized and aggregated services, and devising the proof of concept to be accepted by client.
  - Working with the Program Manager to define the business case to capture $9 million in funding to complete the prestigious project, considered one of the top 5 projects in Roma.
  - Placing component orders with Cisco to purchase numerous switches and routers; responsible for monitoring the expenditures.
  - Acting as the team lead, tasked with pre-staging the equipment and configuring prior to shipping to geographically disparate offices for rollout.

(continued)

*Attractive and easy-to-skim tables are used to present keywords, technical skills, and extensive training.*

**PETER BROWN, CCIE**
905.342.2525/pete.brown@luringo.ca

*Roma Tele-Communications, MPLS Project.......continued*

- Working with the space/power/racking group to ensure the power support was adequate.
- Partnering with the transport team to optimize the long-haul connectivity over SONET.
- Scrutinizing documentation with the Last Ride Access Designers to establish the processes for commodity devices.
- Directing the knowledge handoff to local Tier I & II designers, acting as the main troubleshooter and providing support to all Tier III network professionals.
- Interacting with vendor to iron out bugs. Initiative now providing a very high SLA for the Government of Ontario.

- Acted as the lead engineer during the complex process of moving an MPLS project for FTM Bank from pre-sales to post-sales. Involved in the Custom Solution Group to validate the functionality of services delivered to FTM Bank. Designed and delivered final product; dispatched to local design engineers to implement the product on the Roma network, allowing a complete end-to-end solution for FTM Bank. Project recognized as the highest-level initiative undertaken by Roma.
- Provided design engineering and custom solutions for clients, interacting with cross-functional personnel to complete diverse projects according to mandates.
- Reported to Manager, National Service Fulfillment; consistently appraised by manager with the highest ratings and given financial remuneration for work.
- Recipient of the 2002 "President's Award" for being the *Leader of Tomorrow.*

Rienwald Services Incorporated, Mississauga, Ontario                    2000–2001
**SENIOR TECHNICAL ANALYST**
- Played a key technical advisory role during the office and systems move from Montreal, Quebec, to Mississauga, Ontario; designed new systems environment work flow and completed transfer without business interruption.
- Moved the Rienwald Data Centre from a layer II network building to a layer III solution, enabling Rienwald to stabilize network operations and allow for expansion.

SystemsInTel Services, Toronto, Ontario                    1999–2000
**TECHNICAL LEAD**
- Contracted by the Toronto Catholic District School Board to install and roll out the Windows 2000 network across 50 schools. Project recognized by Microsoft Canada as one of the first dozen production networks in Canada.
- Developed and implemented new desktop software system for the TCDSB.

**EDUCATION**

Ryerson Polytechnic University, Toronto, Ontario                    1994
**BACHELOR OF BUSINESS MANAGEMENT—Accounting**

**CISCO CERTIFIED INTERNETWORKING EXPERT (CCIE #21234)**

Strong proponent of continually updating skills and keeping on the leading edge. Attended numerous courses, workshops, and seminars, including

| | |
|---|---|
| Cisco Secure Pix Firewall Advanced (CSPFA) | Cisco Secure Virtual Private Network (CSVPN) |
| Implementing Cisco MPLS (MPLS) | Advanced Cisco Router Configuration |
| NetGun Masters | Expert CCIE Prep |
| Cisco Internetworking Troubleshooting | Designing Cisco Networks |
| Designing Windows 2003 Networking Services | C-Level Systems Integration |
| Configuration Management for Windows 2003 | Windows XP Support |

# CHAPTER 8

# Resumes for Web, Internet, E-Commerce, and Game-Design Professionals

- Video Game Designers
- Web Designers
- Web Graphic Artists
- Web Applications Developers
- Webmasters
- Internet Sales and Marketing Professionals
- E-Business Managers
- E-Commerce/Internet Executives

# Paula Heaton
## VIDEO GAME ARTIST

*"I work to evoke emotion and I strive for perfection, but I also know that it takes more than artistic vision to make a great game. I'm very dedicated and I do whatever it takes to get the job done."*

## professional profile

Creative artist with a recognized talent for conveying personalities, emotions, weight, and motion. Collaborate well with others to generate and execute ideas within tight deadlines. Earned a reputation for dedication, humor, intelligence, and going "above and beyond" to help teammates.

## technical skills

**Software...** 3D Studio Max, Character Studio, Unreal Editor, Illustrator, Photoshop, Dreamweaver, Flash, QuarkXPress, Premier.

**Graphics...** Low- and high-polygon 3D modeling, texture maps, lighting, camera work, character design, modeling, rigging, animation, concept art, and storyboards.

## professional experience

BIG STYLE STUDIOS, Cleveland, OH                                        2001–2004
**ARTIST**

Created concept art, sprite animations, and textures for this newly formed game developer. Reported to the company's founder and developed cityscape concepts, gadgets, weapons, characters, monsters, and objects for a Game Boy Advance role-playing game (RPG).

- Created animation sequences for game's lead character within multi-directional control scheme. Produced sprites, created a running sequence in all eight directions, and converted the art into files for programmers to code.
- Transformed company's website to incorporate Flash animation and a more appealing interface. Designed and programmed a cinematic entrance, created custom soundtrack, and highlighted company's development philosophy through stimulating artwork.
- Volunteered to take on additional texturing work under extremely tight deadlines, helping the team members meet their commitments for work on fantasy RPG.

## education

**Certificate in Multimedia Technology - GPA 4.0** – Ohio Media Institute, Cleveland OH          2003
*Courses: Digital/Audio Video Production, Digital Imagery, Computer Animation, Multimedia Production*

- Created three-minute 3D film within seven weeks. Storyboarded entire film and designed all camera work. Hand-animated biped's actions and applied them using 3DS Max. Independently completed all models, textures, and animation for the four characters. The finished project is now shown to incoming classes to demonstrate what they can accomplish.

Ohio University, Athens, OH
Completed coursework in Studio 2D, Drawing, Art History, and Water Painting

## affiliations

Active Member, International Game Developers Association (IGDA), Cleveland Chapter

45 Mark Lane, Cleveland, OH, 44101 / heaton@net.net / h: (216) 555-5555 / c: (216) 555-5556

*The artist's own work is used to highlight and distinguish this creative resume; the quote beneath her name gives further insight into her unique qualities. Her part-time work for the last three years is the central focus of the resume and helps position her above other recent graduates.*

*Quality Computer Graphics & Web Site Design*

HTML/DHTML

Document Layout/ Construction

Web Design Principles

Page Setup

Scanning/Photo Manipulation

Image Optimization

WYSIWYG Editors

Text & Font Management

Forms/Tables/Frames

Color Theory

Original Sketches

Auto Tracing of Drawings

Client-Server Concepts

Cross-Browser Issues

*Portfolio of samples:*

*http://www.avisto/ rob/portfolio/*

# Robert Berlane

561 Thompson Street ▪ Boston, MA 02116 ▪ (617) 876-3215 ▪ rob@aol.com

## COMPUTER GRAPHICS/WEB DESIGNER

Highly self-motivated and goal-oriented professional committed to pursuing a long-term career in computer graphics and Web design. Offer a 14-year track record demonstrating strong analytical and problem-solving skills, computer proficiency, and ability to follow through with projects from inception to completion.

## Qualifications Summary

- Certified in computer graphics and Web design through an intensive 350-classroom-hour program.

- In-depth experience applying graphic design principles to produce innovative and tasteful print documents and Web sites.

- Intrinsic creative talent and lifelong interest in photography; offer a keen eye for quality design and document/Web site layout.

- Fluent in the MS Windows 95/98/NT operating environments. Proven ability to quickly learn and apply new technologies.

- Completed high-impact graphic and Web design projects including menus, newsletters, logos, postcards, CD covers, stationery, retail packaging, and a 50-page Web site.

- Advanced training and experience in the application and usage of QuarkXPress 6.5, Adobe Photoshop CS, Adobe Illustrator CS, and Microsoft FrontPage 2003.

- Exceptionally well organized; strong work ethic and willingness to work hard to achieve employer objectives.

## Education & Training

**CERTIFICATE IN COMPUTER GRAPHICS/WEB DESIGN**, Jan. 2005
American College of Technology, Boston, MA

**BACHELOR OF SCIENCE, Cum Laude,** Chemistry, May 1990
Dominican University, River Forest, IL

## Employment

Medical Technologist, Boston General Hospital, Boston, MA, 1990–Present

Collect, process, and analyze more than 2,300 patient samples daily in the chemistry laboratory of this large metropolitan hospital. Interface extensively with physicians and other medical professionals. Test, troubleshoot, and perform QA protocols on sophisticated instrumentation.

*This great-looking resume would attract attention even if the individual didn't have strong qualifications! The technical summary in the left column is an effective way to highlight key technical skills. Note the reference to his online portfolio—a wonderful selling strategy for a Web designer.*

# Barry R. Bruce

12321 Peony Circle    Manchester, MO 63021
636.345.9135/h    636.364.0929/c    barryrb63021@aol.com

## Web Graphic Artist

Motivated, productive creative-team member with a comprehensive fine-art education and proven initiative, versatility, and dependability. Committed to delivering assignments on budget and on deadline.

- ▶ Intuitive learner with a quick grasp of software tools and techniques.
- ▶ Applications expert: fluent in Adobe Illustrator, Adobe Photoshop, Adobe InDesign, MS FrontPage, and MS Office applications; familiar with QuarkXPress, Dreamweaver, Flash, Bryce5, Poser, and CorelDRAW.
- ▶ Confident relationship builder; skilled in building productive working relationships based on approachability, coachability, sense of humor, and trust.
- ▶ Systematic and detailed planner.
- ▶ Focused, enthusiastic project manager, effective in managing priorities and multitasking in a dynamic, high-energy working environment to exceed client expectations.
- ▶ Take-charge, creative, and independent problem solver.
- ▶ Accountable team contributor; teachable and easy to work with.

## EDUCATION

B. A., Art, Major: Graphic Design, University of Missouri, Columbia, MO, December 2003
- ▶ Coursework included Drawing, 2-D and 3-D Design, Illustration, Painting, and Photography.
- ▶ Designed and created three CD covers, concert poster, magazine cover, and band logos for Total Chaos (a Columbia band) in fulfillment of Senior Project, demonstrating mastery of design concepts and principles.
- ▶ Awarded First Place Certificate of Merit for Digital Media, 2003 Art Department Spring Student Exhibition; frequently selected to participate in art shows.
- ▶ Pledge Class President, Delta Upsilon social fraternity. Organized major all-Greek fundraising event for house philanthropy.
- ▶ Toured Europe after graduation; visited Santa Guilia City Museum in Brescia, Italy; Galleria dell' Accademia, Pitti Palace, and Uffizi Gallery in Florence, Italy; Musee d'Orsay, Palace of Versailles, and Musee du Louvre in Paris, France; National Gallery in London, England; Musee Picasso in Antibes, France; Museum of Czech Cubist Art and Mucha Museum in Prague, Czech Republic.

## EXPERIENCE

**Intern**
FRUEHOFF PRODUCTS, Columbia, MO                                      June 2003–March 2004

Edited and upgraded company Web site (www.fruehoffproducts.com) for mail-order catalog company marketing woodturning equipment (lathes, tools, and materials) to artist and hobbyists worldwide.
- ▶ Used FrontPage, Illustrator, and Photoshop to develop print, Web, and catalog ads incorporating design, illustration, photography, and typography.
- ▶ Allowed small company to produce professional-quality advertising materials in-house, saving significant dollars in previously outsourced jobs.
- ▶ Worked 20+ hours/week during school; consistently finished projects on time and on budget.

**Intern**
SCHILLING DISTRIBUTING (Miller Brewing Distributor), Columbia, MO                    Fall 2003

Assisted sole Graphic Artist on staff. Conceptualized and executed posters to advertise Miller Brewing beverages for P.O.P. displays. Printed and laminated large-scale, full-color prints.
- ▶ Used Photoshop and Illustrator extensively.
- ▶ Completed assignments with minimal direction and supervision.
- ▶ Worked 10+ hours/week during school; fulfilled all assignments on time and on budget.

*Portfolio available at www.visualparadise.com.*

This resume makes the most of recent education and two relevant internships. Each is explored in some detail to provide a strong qualifications profile for this young Web artist.

# LYDIA MOSBACH

3596 Bogart Avenue
Columbus, Ohio 43240
(614) 766-9844

lydiamosbach@mindspring.com

## ENTRY–LEVEL WEB DESIGNER

Visionary, creative professional qualified by 5 years of academic and professional achievements in Web site production and project management. Combined expertise in graphic design and technical editing with exceptional ability to conceptualize and bring project to full fruition.

### QUALIFICATION HIGHLIGHTS

- Cutting-edge technical knowledge of HTML programming and desktop publishing software.
- Extensive graphic layout, design, production and marketing experience.
- Demonstrated experience in promotion strategies.
- Proven record of effectively managing multiple tasks without compromise to quality.
- Innovative, creative and enthusiastic in approaching projects.
- Recognized for strong work ethic, integrity and commitment to success.

## EDUCATIONAL ACHIEVEMENTS

**Master of Arts,** December 2004
University of Reading – Reading, England

**Visiting Scholar,** 2003
Summer Program in Archaeology, 2002
American Academy in Rome – Rome, Italy

**Internationaler Ferienkurs,** 2002
Universität Heidelberg – Heidelberg, Germany

**Bachelor of Arts,** Art, 2001
Mount Holyoke College, South Hadley, Massachusetts

## SELECTED PROJECT HIGHLIGHTS

**The Parthenet: Internet Resources for Students of Art History** – Conceived in 1999 to assist students in online research. Contains numerous sources of information about art history. Award-winning site highly used and listed in academic Internet guides worldwide. (2002 to Present) www.mtholyoke.edu/parthenet.html

**Digital site emulation at Kenchreai, the Eastern port of Corinth** – Studied the applications of technology in the field and created a multimedia Web site. Manipulated plans into 3D animated sequences of the site's building phases. (2001 to 2003)

**Consultant to the Matrix Project at Yale University and Mount Holyoke College** – Worked with team of medieval scholars to create an online database of medieval women's religious communities in Western Europe. (2000 to 2002)

**The Travels of Mac and Cheese** – Developed as a spoof on the deification of Kraft Macaroni and Cheese. Site involved "reenactment" of box of Mac and Cheese traveling around Europe and photographing journey for the Web site. (2000 to 2001) www.mtholyoke.edu/mandcc/mandc.html

(continued)

*This new graduate has a solid portfolio of interesting projects that are highlighted on the resume. Her strong academic credentials take center stage on page 1.*

# LYDIA MOSBACH

lydiamosbach@mindspring.com

Resume, Page Two of Two
(614) 766-9844

**Matrix: Resources for the Study of Women's Religious Communities** – Developed site's original design, graphics, layout and database format for presentation at national conference. (2000 to 2001) matrix.bc.edu (Can be viewed in present form at Boston University.)

**Hildegard and Clare Resource Center** – Identified need and developed site concerning medieval religious women. Provides resources and links for in-depth study of Hildegard of Bingen (Germany) and Clare of Markyate (England). (2000 to 2001) www.mtholyoke.edu/medieval/resource.html

**Mount Holyoke College History Department** – Commissioned by the History Department to develop their informational Web page, which is now maintained by department secretary. (2000 to 2001) www.mtholyoke.edu/acad/hist

**Birgitta the Wonder Beetle** – Original site narrating the travels and tribulations of Birgitta the Wonder Beetle; provided travelogue, insights and links to new VW Beetle enthusiast sites. (1999 to 2000) lydiamosbach.mindspring.com/Birgitta.html.

## EXPERIENCE

**Online Editor and Member** – *The Journal of the Women's College Art Coalition* (1999 to 2001)
- Published online edition of *The Journal,* an undergraduate scholarly journal concerning women's issues in the fine arts. Designed and maintained Web sites.
- Generated publicity and outreach programs to 83 other women's colleges in the nation.

**Intern – Mount Holyoke College, Development Office** – (1998 to 2001)
- Orchestrated fundraising efforts for the Alumnae Fund of the College. Managed large-scale phone-a-thons; organized callers and donation recordkeeping.
- Developed incentive strategies and events to encourage and maintain caller morale.

**Intern – Columbus Museum of Art, Registrar's Office** – Columbus, Ohio (Summer 1999)
- Catalogued prints and works on paper as part of a full museum inventory and installation of the permanent collection. Researched works to be deaccessioned.

## TECHNICAL KNOWLEDGE

Proficient in many Remote Sensing, GPS, GIS, CAD and GeoPhysics Applications.
Data processing, database development and related archaeological field uses, both Mac and PC.
Networking, hardware/software maintenance, repair and troubleshooting.

**Internet** – Netscape, Explorer, Telenet, FTP

**Graphics/Drafting/Authoring** – Photoshop, QuarkXPress, CorelDRAW, PageMaker, AutoCAD, PageMill

**Basics/Database** – MS Office, FileMaker Pro, $4^{th}$ Dimension, MS Access, ProCite, FileWorks, MS Excel

**Equipment** – Scanners, CD-RW, digitizers, plotters, slide scanners

**Languages** – HTML 4, DHTML, Java, UNIX

# Mark M. Rodriguez

837 Red Fox Road ■ Madison, WI 53703 ■ (608) 555-7826 ■ mark@markrodriguez.net

## Web Applications Development / Graphic Design / General Programming
### Project Management & Teamwork
**Vision ... Leadership ... Collaboration ... Execution ... Results**

➢ Committed professional, qualified by academic and professional successes in Web site production and project management.
➢ Innovative, creative and enthusiastic designer, able to conceptualize and bring projects to full fruition.
➢ Detail-oriented project manager with a proven record of effectively managing multiple tasks without compromise to quality.
➢ Quick learner eager for new professional challenges.

### ■ Technical Summary ■

**Languages:** JavaScript, PHP, HTML, XHTML, XML, SQL, XSLT, Java, C/C++, OpenGL (3D Modeling)
**Software:** MySQL, MS SQL, Oracle, Samba, Apache, CVS, MS Office Suite (Word, Excel, PowerPoint, Outlook), Photoshop, SSH, FTP
**Operating Systems:** Linux administration; proficient using Windows 9x/NT/2000/XP, Linux, UNIX, Mac OS X
**Other:** W3C Standards (CSS, DOM, WAI, etc.), Web for PDAs, Linux Security, Forms and User Interface Design, Cross-Browser Issues/Fixes

## EXPERIENCE

JORELL NETWORK LTD.–Milwaukee, WI — *Integrated data/voice networking products manufacturer.*      2003–present
**Web Applications Developer: Marketing**
■ **Asked by President to come on board full time after initial hire as a six-week contractor.** Develop and manage product for corporate Web site. Maintain corporate Internet, intranet, and extranet sites with key responsibility for creation of product pages.
 ➢ **Enhanced site's overall usability** by redesigning the entire site. Modified sites to adhere to W3C standards, migrated to a CSS-based layout, and enabled support for non-traditional browsers (PDAs, text readers, etc.).
 ➢ **Improved code reliability** by initiating quality assurance programs: Web page, email page, and link validation.
 ➢ **Shortened development time** by establishing a documented code library promoting code reuse.
 ➢ Designed and delivered an interface application **6 months under projected timeframe and $4,500 under budget.**

UNIVERSITY OF WISCONSIN–Madison, WI — *One of the most comprehensive public universities in the U.S.*      1998–2003
**Web Applications Developer: College of Liberal Arts Student Services** (2002–2003)
■ One of 2 students hired to develop Web-based content management system for 43 sites with more than 17,500 users.
 ➢ **Initiated radical security enhancements** to mission-critical servers. **Created user friendly features. Planned and performed all installations, upgrades, and maintenance. Efforts were recognized by Office of Information Technology at its annual banquet.**

**Security Monitor: Security Monitor Program** (1998–2001)
■ Patrolled grounds late evenings/early mornings, investigating abuse, assuring procedural compliance, screening visitors, and performing any other duties to protect the people and property of the U of W community. Trained in First Aid, Body Substance Isolation and CPR.

## EDUCATION

UNIVERSITY OF WISCONSIN–Madison, WI                                                          Degree: 2003
**Bachelor of Science, Computer Science**                                        **Computer Graphics Emphasis**
■ Balanced academic (3.9 GPA), employment (30+ hours a week), and community/campus service (VISTO) commitments.

CONTINUING DEVELOPMENT: Avid print/online reader on technologies. Enjoy Linux-based network administration on my home computers.

*Print Portfolio of Work Samples Furnished upon Request*

*To compete against others with more experience, this candidate included a strong value statement at the top of the resume that communicates what he can offer that others cannot. The Experience section communicates his results and successes.*

## DAMIAN PETERS

3 Blaine Road, Mill Valley, CA 94941
(415) 222-2222 / (415) 555-5555
damianpeters@commnet.net

## Web Production

### Profile

➤ **Award-Winning Content Development:** Transformed under-utilized web site into a vibrant, highly regarded community with more than 270,000 members. Site was selected as a "Webby Awards" finalist for three consecutive years.

➤ **Phenomenal Revenue and Profit Growth:** Grew web site's annual revenues 55% in three years by developing multiple new revenue streams. Delivered 45% increase in profits during the same period.

➤ **On Time, On Budget Project Management:** Consistently applied Six Sigma project management principles to deliver "over and above" expectations, even when working to seemingly impossible deadlines.

### Philosophy

 *I believe in asking the important questions: Is there another way…? What if…? Why can't we…? There is always opportunity for improvement, and creative professionals respond exceptionally well when given the opportunity to challenge the status quo.* 🙶🙷

### Experience

GPA MEDIA LLC, San Francisco, CA                               1999–Present
**EXECUTIVE PRODUCER, MEDIABUZZ.COM**

Promoted to position after former employer acquired GPA. Turned around this unprofitable site by leveraging existing content from the annual Media Conference and *Media Buzz* magazine while also generating marketing leads for both organizations. Built a site that is now recognized as the industry leader.

> *"Damian is single-handedly responsible for the transformation of mediabuzz.com"*
> Jean Raymond, CEO and President, GPA Media

**Value Added: Led fundamental changes that increased revenues by 55% and turned the site from a loss to a 45% profit within 3 years.**

- Added revenue-generating features such as paid job postings, searchable resume database, sponsored links, banner ads, affiliate partnerships, and sponsored seminars.

- Increased site membership by 280%, to 273,000. Created systems to capture key demographic information so that the membership list could be used for targeted cross-promotion to the company's other properties.

- Leveraged existing content to create new revenue streams, such as a set of recorded conference sessions that generated a 50% profit margin in its first year.

- Named one of the "Top Media Influencers of 2002" by *Technology Now* magazine.

- Conceived and planned the implementation of premium membership for the site. For a monthly fee members will be able to access additional multimedia content such as video footage and audio content.

- Built multimillion-dollar partnerships with leading film production companies and TV networks including NBC, ABC, HBO, and Miramax, thereby enhancing content and increasing brand exposure.

(continued)

*A unique feature of this resume is the Philosophy section, which allows the job seeker to speak directly to the hiring authority. Glowing testimonials (taken from his performance evaluations) highlight an Experience section rich with results.*

**DAMIAN PETERS**                                                                 **Page 2**
**Web Production**                          (415) 222-2222 / damianpeters@commnet.net

### Experience (Cont.)

DAVIES SLATER INC., San Francisco, CA                                              1992–1999
**EDITORIAL DIRECTOR, MEDIABUZZ.COM** (1998–1999)

Led editorial direction for the mediabuzz.com family of websites, managing 15 freelance writers and 3 editors and working closely with site designers and programmers.

> *"Damian just doesn't give in … he is relentless when he has a great idea."*
> Peter Shaw, Former Producer – mediabuzz.com

**Value Added: Crafted new editorial strategy that drove 343% increase in web site traffic and 59% revenue growth.**

- Launched annual archive of back issues on CD-ROM, generating incremental revenues of more than $44,000 per year.
- Managed major redesign of mediabuzz.com. The site had previously been managed by external developers which made it expensive and time-consuming to change content. Brought development in-house to allow daily site updates.
- Built affiliate partnerships worth more than $5 million per year in free advertising.
- Implemented a weekly email newsletter that is automatically generated from existing site content and sent to 60,000 subscribers.
- Revamped and communicated style guide to ensure a consistent tone across all sites.

**EDITOR-IN-CHIEF, MEDIA BUZZ MAGAZINE** (1996–1998)

Managed staff of two editors and team of freelancers with responsibility for editorial content and deadlines. Also wrote two monthly columns and created and maintained the magazine's web site.

> *"Your impact on the magazine has been phenomenal – thank you!"*
> Peter Wallis, Editor-in-Chief, Davies Slater

**Value Added: Received 11 awards for editorial excellence from the American Society of Business Press Editors between 1997 and 1998.**

- Key member of the launch team for mediabuzz.com, making editorial and cross-promotion decisions.
- Developed innovative product-launch campaign for mediabuzz.com that generated 50,000 page views on day one.
- Increased magazine ad revenues 30% by designing and executing "advertorial" sections.

**PRODUCT REVIEW EDITOR, MEDIA BUZZ MAGAZINE** (1994–1996)
**PROJECT COORDINATOR, ANNUAL MEDIA CONFERENCE** (1992–1994)

### Education

B.A., Economics. University of California, Berkeley—Berkeley, CA (1991)

### Affiliations/Publications

Advisory Board, Media Buzz Conference, 1997–Present

Board of Directors, International Media Association, 2003–Present

Co-author of the book *Media Marketplace* (Chrysalis Books, 1998)

## LISA M. FITZGERALD
2431 Watt Street, Tucson, AZ 85719 • 520-688-3880 • fitz@msn.com

## WEB DEVELOPER

### PROFESSIONAL PROFILE

**INNOVATIVE WEB DEVELOPER** with hands-on experience combining solid understanding of HTML, VB Scripting and web browser capability across multiple platforms. Excellent knowledge of constraints involved in online media design. Highly creative and equally skilled in back-end complex programming such as Active Server Pages (ASP) as well as graphical design concepts. Able to manage web site development processes from architectural and functional design concept, including page creation authoring, through successful completion. Able to implement site server strategies and multimedia fundamentals. Dynamic dedicated professional with outstanding communication skills, able to focus on customer service and company vision. Core technical skills include:

**Highly proficient writing HTML in Notepad**

**Active Server Pages, VB Scripting, and Java Scripting**

**Web Editors: Home Site, Hot Metal Pro**

**Software: Photoshop, Corel PHOTO-PAINT, Paint Shop Pro, Lview, Access, Visio**

### PROFESSIONAL DEVELOPMENT

| | |
|---|---|
| **Logic and Analysis for Programmers** | **Quantitative Communication** |
| **Programming 1 (in C)** | **Systems Design and Analysis** |
| **Digital Computer Techniques** | **Advanced Systems Management** |

### PROFESSIONAL EXPERIENCE

**Graphic Web Solutions,** Tucson, AZ                                                   2002–present
**WEB SITE DEVELOPER, MANAGER**
- Design, develop and implement new web interfaces, graphics and layouts.
- Create, manage and maintain company web sites.
- Direct all phases of business operation including strategic planning, financial management, client acquisition/retention and marketing.

**Internet Marketing Solutions, Inc.,** Phoenix, AZ                                    1998–2002
**WEB SPECIALIST**
- Developed web sites for company intranet, including Competitive Intelligence Web Site for Marketing and Image Catalog.
- Provided technical support to associations designing sites; created and implemented web forms using ASP.
- Created file structure on company server to assist other departments with web site design and permissions.
- Implemented file structure on production server and uploaded changed files for employees.
- Initiated design and publication of online Café menus resulting in financial savings by eliminating hard copies.

**ADMINISTRATIVE ASSISTANT TO DIRECTOR**                                              1996–1998
- Supported Director of Information Systems; managed schedule and updated calendar.
- Coordinated all phases of company events, including Golf Scramble, Company Picnic, Summer Bowling League.

### PORTFOLIO OF WEB DESIGN
- www.executivefinalcopy.com
- www.kinterlanddogs.com
- www.networksinc.com
- (Full portfolio presented upon request)

### EDUCATION
- **Web Development Certificate,** University of Phoenix — 2003 — Curriculum included 230 hours of study.
- University of Maryland — 30 credits applicable to **AA in Business Administration**

*To support her strong professional qualifications, this designer provides a portfolio of three sites where interested employers can view her work immediately.*

## Kathryn G. Oakes

4862 Greene Lane ▪ Hatfield, PA 19440 ▪ (215) 855-4863 ▪ kathryn.oakes@dotresume.com

**OBJECTIVE**

**Website Coordinator / Project Manager**

**SUMMARY OF QUALIFICATIONS**

- Seven years of web design experience coupled with a degree in management.
- Ability to work well with people at all levels. Experience coordinating with multiple functions and providing training and support.
- Strong organizational skills. Proven ability to manage multiple tasks, develop effective schedules, and deliver work on time.
- Good sense of design. Talent for conceptualizing creative solutions to achieve clients' goals.
- Solid knowledge of industry tools; monitor new trends through research.

**PROFESSIONAL EXPERIENCE**

**BUX-MONT COLLEGE,** Chalfont, PA (1998–present)
SENIOR WEBSITE DESIGNER, 2003–present
WEBSITE DESIGNER, 2000–2003
WEB ASSISTANT, 1998–2000

Design websites and manage day-to-day site maintenance. Determine design goals and specifications based on user requirements, marketing input, and comparative research. Prepare schedules and requirements documents; coordinate with marketing, content administrators, programmers, and others to deliver final product. Create mockups, final designs, templates for content developers, Flash timelines, and other special features. Test content for cross-browser compliance. Provide technical support for content providers and end users.

*"I've just received a wonderful comment re the updated web site from [company] – the president said that we've done more in the past six months to upgrade the site than he has seen any institution in our 'space' so evolve."*

—*College President*

### Accomplishments

- Saved six-figure fee for outside consulting by stepping in to redesign organization's primary website (http://www.buxmontcoll.edu)—well received by customers.
- Served as designer on team that delivered project for remake of organization's main, 4000-page website one month ahead of schedule; met deadlines on all other projects.
- Enhanced quality of sites through improvements in architecture, elimination of redundancy, and incorporation of user-friendly design; maintained quality and consistency by developing and implementing style guidelines.
- Initiated process to streamline content imports with cascading style sheets and templates.
- Improved customer service and saved time for web staff by suggesting that first-level website support be moved to customer service group, and by developing and providing training for the transition.
- Increased productivity of website support services through development of "canned procedures" for frequently asked questions.

(continued)

*This resume highlights management skills as well as design experience to help this Web designer advance to a management position. An impressive quote speaks to her design and project skills.*

## Kathryn G. Oakes

Page 2

**PROFESSIONAL EXPERIENCE (CONTINUED)**

**SIGHT & SOUND,** Philadelphia, PA (1995–1998)
WEBSITE DESIGNER, 1997–1998
ADMINISTRATOR / GRAPHIC ARTIST, 1995–1997
GRAPHIC ARTIST / OFFICE SUPPORT, 1995

Assisted in production of television pilot, stepping in where necessary to ensure desired effect achieved. Redesigned company website; conceptualized logo animation for Tri-State Convention Center; designed signs, fliers, business cards, and other company print materials.

**COMPUTER SKILLS**

Macromedia Dreamweaver MX and Flash MX

Adobe Photoshop CS, ImageReady 7, and Illustrator CS

Swish, Question Mark Perception, Adobe Acrobat Professional 7

Microsoft Office 2000 (Word, Excel, PowerPoint) and Visio 2000

**EDUCATION**

**B.B.A.,** Villanova University, Villanova, PA (1994)
Major: General & Strategic Management   Honors: Dean's List

**PROFESSIONAL DEVELOPMENT**

**PROJECT MANAGEMENT**

Project Initiation and Planning, Penn State Abington (2004)

Franklin Covey Project Management Workshop, Franklin Covey (2001)

What Matters Most Workshop, Franklin Covey (2000)

Communication Skills, Fred Pryor Seminars, Inc. (1999)

**WEBSITE DESIGN**

Editing, Web Publishing, and DVD Authoring on the Avid XpressDV, Future Media Concepts (2002)

Visual Design Fundamentals, Philadelphia University (2001)

Macromedia Flash, Philadelphia University (2001)

JavaScript, Berkeley Computer Training (1999)

Desktop Publishing, Montgomery County Community College (1994)

**RESUME 71: BY SUSAN GUARNERI, NCC, NCCC, CPRW, CCMC, CEIP, MCC**

# John Joseph Derry

176 Woodhaven Drive, Eatontown, NJ 07724    (732) 927-5555    JJDer@bol.com

## Web Applications Management
### E-Commerce    B2B    Project Management

### KEY QUALIFICATIONS

✓ **Technical Strengths**: Up-to-date, diverse training in e-Business Management coupled with years of experience in analytical, technical process engineering profession.

✓ **Project Coordination and Teamwork**: Highly productive in team environments as both member and team leader. Efficient in handling multiple project priorities.

✓ **Communication**: Able to communicate technical information in an easily understandable way. Recognized for relationship-building with team members and clients. An effective listener.

✓ **Personal Attributes**: Innovative problem-solver. Committed to goal achievement. Dependable.

### EDUCATION

☑ Cybersoft Internet Professional — CIP 1, Cybersoft, Inc., Woodbridge, NJ
  August 2004 — **Certified e-Business Architect, e-Business for Managers**
  December 2003 — **Certified Cybersoft Communications 1000** including Fundamentals of Networking, Database, Web Development, Web Design, Multimedia, and Internet Business

☑ Bachelor of Science, Industrial Engineering, Connecticut Institute of Technology

### TECHNICAL SKILLS

**e-Commerce**: e-Business and B2B Infrastructures and Consumer Payment Protocols
**Applications**: ERP, e-Procurement, Selling Chain Management, Customer Relationship Management
**Software Tools**: MS Word, HTML, FrontPage 2000
**Operating Systems**: Windows XP/2000/98/95

### PROFESSIONAL EXPERIENCE

1999-2003 — ENGINEERING SYSTEMS, INC., Astro Space Division, Eatontown, NJ
Manufacturing Engineer, Production Engineering Department

Provided assembly documentation and engineering floor support throughout all phases of production flow, including fabrication, assembly, and test operations, for the manufacture of diverse satellite products contracted by major government clients (USSA and the U.S. Air Force).

### ACCOMPLISHMENTS

- Promoted to Team Leader for the introduction of new equipment and upgrades. Performed research and analysis of new equipment for cost effectiveness and quality. Tested in production mode. Full authority to sign off fully tested equipment to production line engineer.

*Notable on this resume are the checkmark bullets and the strong emphasis on career accomplishments.*

# Jennifer C. Wallach

73 Barbizon Lane • Woodstock, VT 05412
802.885.1111 • jcwallach@hotmail.com

### Qualifications Summary

- Highly motivated and accomplished **Web Page Developer/Technical Communications Professional** with strong project management and implementation abilities; resourceful design and research/documentation specialist.
- Innovative and creative initiative-taker with demonstrated expertise in all facets of web page design, desktop publishing, and computer/Internet technologies; flexible and adaptable in positively responding to changing organizational needs.
- Effective problem-assessment and problem-solving abilities; expert communications and editorial skills.
- Highly proficient with the following web development and graphic tools/skills: HTML, JavaScript, DHTML, and XML; Microsoft FrontPage and Office Suite, Adobe PageMaker and Photoshop, QuarkXPress, and CorelDRAW.

### Professional Experience

2001–Present     ARGON INTELLIGENCE GROUP, INC. (AIG) • Barnard, VT
**Web Page Developer**
- Broad range of creative/technical responsibilities includes development and ongoing product management for corporate web site as well as sites for major clients; maintain corporate intranet and extranet with key responsibility for creation of product pages.
- Corporate/client project scope entails maintaining excellent customer relationships, managing and executing monthly updates, and coordinating/supervising contract designers.
- Successfully initiated, developed, and documented interface designs for company's first completely online HTML help system for retail systems product; implementation yielded substantial cost savings over paper production as well as enabled more timely releases/updates.
- Graphic Designer for corporate marketing materials; design/author user manuals for ancillary retail systems products; provide technical consulting on as-needed basis across all disciplines.

1999–2000     DOBSON COMMUNICATION CORPORATION • South Woodstock, VT
**Marketing/Public Relations Intern**
- Managed production of three monthly newsletters; oversight responsibility included story idea selection (collaborating with market coordinators), story assignments/editing, liaison to ad agency regarding layout requirements and art specifications, and prepress approval of final product.
- Developed and wrote internal as well as external communications including news releases, feature stories, and promotional feature pieces.
- Implemented wide range of creative design assignments, from conducting a web page competitive analysis and implementing a company recycling program to producing a competitive event for employees of eight branch stores and executing a customer essay contest.

### Education

**NEW HAMPSHIRE COLLEGE** • Manchester, NH
**Bachelor of Arts Degree — Journalism/Public Relations** (2000)
- Officer, Public Relations Student Society of America (1998–2000)
- Member, Phi Beta Lambda (Professional Business Leaders)

Continuing development includes attendance at professional seminars/conferences and meetings complemented by subscriptions to professional journals.

### Affiliations

**PUBLIC RELATIONS SOCIETY OF AMERICA**
- Webmaster/Newsletter Editor
**HTML WRITERS GUILD**
**SOCIETY OF TECHNICAL COMMUNICATION**

*This individual transferred her writing, marketing, and PR skills to a career as a Web page developer. Most of her resume focuses on communications strengths and the value she's brought to her employers.*

# Jim Haskins

2300 Main Drive
Apartment B
Miamisburg, OH 45342

Home: 937-555-1234
Office: 937-555-4321
Email: jimh@haskins.com

**Web Site: http://www.jimhaskins.com**

## Senior Web Architect
Programming • Web Development • Graphic Design

### Clients

**The Merry Company**

**County.com**

**Idea Imaging Group, Inc.**

**Marketing-Solutions Group**

**Blue Sky Auction Service**

**Prime Information Source**

**ChiefNet, Inc.**

**Smith Gallery**

**Typographic Services**

**AutoRetailing, Inc.**

**Jazzy Skateboards**

**Tech Industries/
Core Engineering**

**Image Photographic**

**Career Coaching Company**

~

### Representative Work

**www.marketing-solutions.com**

**www.longbow.cc**

**www.jazzyboards.com**

**www.imagephotographic.com**

**www.careerresource.com**

**Additional portfolio samples available**

### Professional Profile

**Creative Web Developer** with 8 years of experience as a programmer and designer • Recognized as an innovative and solution-oriented developer of original program applications

**Experience** managing and collaborating with small or large teams of developers and designers, working in interactive and print media • Project management • System and design integration • Web usability strategizing and testing • Diagramming Information Architecture and interactive design concepts • Database design • Graphic design • Strong client relations and presentation skills • Budget management

### Notable Achievements

**Architect** of Mac OS X Internet Relay Chat (IRC) client noted for its visual design and user-friendliness. More than 3,000 downloads.

**Creator & Developer** of a project management tool that includes real-time feedback on budgets (live tally), project status, distribution of staff effort, deadlines, and remote accessibility.

### Technical Proficiencies

**OPERATING SYSTEMS** Mac OS X • Linux • Solaris • AIX • Windows

**INTERNET** Internet Explorer • Netscape (Mozilla)

**DATABASES** MySQL • MS SQL • Oracle

**LANGUAGES** HTML • XHTML • XML • JavaScript • CSS • Perl • PHP • ANSI C • GNU C • C99 • Objective-C (utilizing Apple's Cocoa framework)

**SOFTWARE APPLICATIONS** QuarkXPress • Apple Motion • Apple DVD Studio Pro Adobe: Acrobat • Photoshop • Illustrator • AfterEffects • InDesign • PageMaker Macromedia: Flash • Dreamweaver • Director • Freehand

(continued)

*The left column provides "live" links to Web sites developed by this individual. The first page of this resume could be used on its own for freelance projects; details of employment are included on page 2.*

**Jim Haskins**—page 2

937-555-1234                                                                                                    jimh@haskins.com

## Professional Experience

MARKETING-SOLUTIONS GROUP, Dayton, OH
**Designer, 2003–present**
Strategize, design, and develop in-house and client visual communication solutions in Web, interactive, and traditional media formats. Project manager and IT system administrator.

**KEY ACCOMPLISHMENTS**

- Conceived and developed a project-management application tool to boost efficiency throughout the company. Application was successfully implemented internally and then presented as a product offering to clients, resulting in a new revenue stream for the company.

- Project manager for a complex multimedia new-product launch for Prime Information Source. Assignment involved concept development, interactive CD design and programming, photo shoot direction, and design of a video wall presentation for trade show. According to Prime Information Source, this was their company's most successful new product campaign.

INCREATION DESIGN STUDIO, Urbana, OH
**Design Lead, 2002–2003**
Led design team in the execution of in-house and client Web-development projects. Planned and managed production processes and workflow. Key member of team that spearheaded the company's re-branding effort.

**KEY ACCOMPLISHMENTS**

- Successfully re-branded the company from ChiefNet to InCreation via the development of its Web site, resulting in establishing the new corporate identity with clients and staff.

CHIEFNET, INC., Urbana, OH
**Web Developer, 1997–2002**
**Customer Service, 1996–1997**
Designed and implemented new Web interfaces, graphics, and layouts.

**KEY ACCOMPLISHMENTS**

- Developed, designed, and managed County.com, a local community portal site that featured local events, weather, and editorial articles. The site became a showcase of ChiefNet's abilities in Web design and development.

## Education

Associate of Applied Business, Clark State Community College, Springfield, OH
**Graphic Art Design**

# Michael R. Jensen

111 East 11<sup>th</sup> Street
New York, New York 11111
(212) 222-2222
mrj@eternalspring.com

## Internet Services ■ Sales ■ Consulting

Service-oriented **Sales professional** offering considerable experience in **Internet consulting** and **broadband data technology.** Consistent producer, at ease dealing with high-level executives and IT professionals. Highly focused individual who enjoys working in a team environment and working toward shared goals and objectives. Areas of expertise and strengths encompass the following:

| | | |
|---|---|---|
| ◆ **Account Development** | ◆ **Presentation Skills** | ◆ **Account Management** |
| ◆ **Relationship Building** | ◆ **Needs Analysis** | ◆ **Problem Resolution** |
| ◆ **Creating Strategic Alliances** | ◆ **Negotiations / Closing** | ◆ **Training & Supervision** |

## Professional Experience

GBX CORPORATION, New York, New York                                    2003–Present
**Internet Consultant**

- Generated $100,000 recurring revenue, year-to-date, in the marketing of data centers, T1 lines, Web hosting services, co-location, and high-speed broadband data technology.
- Targeted, and successfully established relationships with, major firms including Infoseek, Sports Illustrated, The Venator Group, Advanstar Communications, Elite Model Management, Infinity Interactive, 9Net Avenue, E-liance, Big Foot.com, Razor Fish, NetMix, Indignet, Star Diamond Group, Edgar Online, and Screaming Media.
- **Ranked #4 in sales** within the President's Club.
- Successfully created valuable strategic alliances by offering profit-sharing programs and special marketing agreements to various ISPs, Web developers, consultants, and telecom specialists.

MERRILL LYNCH, New York, New York                                    1999–2003
**Senior Sales Representative**

- **Cultivated $50 million in assets** and produced in excess of $400,000 in gross commissions annually.
- Raised capital for two Internet start-up companies that currently trade publicly.
- Consulted extensively with clients, assessing needs and providing investment guidance and recommendations.
- Provided guidance, training, and support to incoming account executives.

AT&T, New York, New York                                    1996–1999
**Senior Sales Representative**

- **Achieved 150% of quota** all eight quarters with company.
- Targeted key accounts in lower Manhattan and provided consultative services on the use of high-end business equipment and telecommunications equipment.

## Education, Training & Skills

SYRACUSE UNIVERSITY, Syracuse, New York
**Bachelor of Arts–Marketing / Economics & Political Science** (double major)                1996

- PSS (Professional Selling Skills) Training
- Achieve Global (sponsored by Time Mirror)
- Well versed in various Internet technologies; knowledge of Word and Excel

*This is a straightforward sales resume for a gentleman who made a career change a few years back, leaning toward Internet and information technology. He wishes to continue within Internet services, and this is emphasized on the resume.*

# RON T. CARTER

Home (905) 286-3380    95 Henry Drive, Toronto, ON M2G 4L9    **Email: getcarter@rogers.com**

## DIRECTOR OF WEB MARKETING
High-Tech Start-Up, High-Growth & Turnaround Organizations
*Specializing in Nontraditional Marketing Strategies*

Award-winning, entrepreneurial, dynamic, and self-directed Web expert with more than 14 years of solid experience in Web-centric design and service. Consistently successful in identifying and capitalizing on market opportunities to drive revenue and profit growth. Deliver key solutions to corporate marketing challenges. Achieve consistently outstanding performances in team building, team leadership, and customer service. Respond to business challenges with confidence, determination, and focus.

- Strategic Planning
- Productivity Enhancement
- Marketing and Contract Negotiations
- Web-Based Solutions
- Market Research & Analysis

- Critical Problem Solving & Analysis
- Mediation & Negotiation
- Customer Relationship Management
- Team Building, Motivation & Leadership
- Corporate Image Campaigns

*Seeking to lead the evolution of Web-centric marketing*

## PROFESSIONAL EXPERIENCE:

**CANADA MAIL**, Toronto, ON *($6 billion company with 300+ product lines)*    2000 to Present
**Senior Manager—Web Team**

*Challenges:*    Plan and orchestrate a complete overhaul of Canada Mail's antiquated Web site, revitalize operations, and lead the corporation's launch into emerging technologies.

*Achievements:*
- Redesigned entire Web site, incorporating emerging technologies designed specifically with technology solutions to meet the needs of complex customer service.
- Achieved/surpassed all turnaround objectives. Increased overall traffic by 40%, attracting more than 4 million visitors, with 400 million hits in just 9 months.
- Solved interdepartmental logistics for implementation of Web site upgrades.
- Left legacy for ASP tools, allowing the building of applications with business units.
- Increased efficiency of server management, including the automation of address changes.
- Interaction with the Privacy Commissioner and barristers, focusing on Web site privacy issues.
- Controlled management and allocation of $2 million in hardware, software, and network technologies.
- Utilized disciplined budget strategies to reduce marketing costs by $400,000.
- Established global systems support to users worldwide.

**SPEED TECHNOLOGIES**, Ottawa, ON *($25 million international company)*    1999 to 2000
**Manager—Web Team**

*Challenges:*    Transition Web site from ineptness to an effective marketing tool. Increase communications of sales teams with both customers and corporate partners.

*Achievements:*
- Pioneered the launch of a new Web site.
- Created, designed, and implemented corporate extranet.
- Delivered 500% traffic increase in 8 months.
- Streamlined operations to reduce costs by $150,000.

**ASK–US–WHY INTERACTIVE**, Ottawa, ON    1997 to 1999
**Project Manager—Web Team**

*Achievements:*
- Architected the creation, implementation, and maintenance of several large Web sites.
- Spearheaded technology pilots and internal training intranets.
- Identified opportunities for client satisfaction that led to renewal of service contracts and awards.
- Integrated nontraditional outsourcing to save an average of $200,000 per project.

(continued)

*Presenting the extensive background of a real "Web guru," this resume emphasizes both deep experience and strong achievements. Note the "Specializing in..." statement at the top that helps to focus the resume.*

**RON T. CARTER**
Page 2

(905) 286-3380
Email: getcarter@rogers.com

**CAROUSEL NETWORKS,** Ottawa, ON
1996 to 1997
**Webmaster**

*Achievements:*
- Realigned the Web site and achieved/surpassed all turnaround objectives. Increased traffic by 100%.
- Engineered traffic growth of 85% in 6 months.
- Optimized budgets resulting in $90,000 savings.

**DOUBLE HELIX, INC.,** Ottawa, ON
1994 to 1996
**Co-Founder/President**

*Achievements:*
- Founded Internet Service Provider, online content provider, and technology consulting firm.
- Instrumental in the formation and launch of 7 subsidiary companies, 1 graphic design firm, and 2 online magazines.
- Designed and built 3 online communities and 2 ISPs.
- Engineered solutions enabling customer communication through online communities.
- Sold 7 companies, one for $230,000 to I-Star in 2001, and others to AvalonWorks.

## EARLY CAREER EXPERIENCE:

**SOLICITOR GENERAL OF CANADA,** Ottawa, ON
1992 to 1993
Graphic Designer/System Administrator

**NATIONAL ENERGY BOARD,** Ottawa, ON
1990 to 1992
Graphic Designer/System Administrator

## TECHNICAL QUALIFICATIONS:

| | |
|---|---|
| **Presentation/Graphics:** | Macromedia Dreamweaver / Macromedia Flash / Adobe Illustrator / Adobe Photoshop / CorelDRAW |
| **Basics/Database:** | Adobe Acrobat / Crystal Reports / Microsoft Office (Word, Excel, PowerPoint, Access) / Microsoft Project / Sawmill / Sonic Foundry Sound Forge / Steinberg Cubase / Web trends / Windows 9x, NT, 2000, XP |
| **Languages:** | HTML / JavaScript / SCO UNIX (UUCP, NNTP, FTP, SMTP) |

## EDUCATION & PROFESSIONAL DESIGNATION:

**Bachelor of Arts in Cognitive Science**—Carleton University, ON
1992

**Registered Graphic Designer (RGD)**

## PUBLICATIONS & AFFILIATIONS:

Creator/Editor of "MacSensible" E-magazine (sold to Ziff-Davis)
Creator/Editor of "PCSensible" E-magazine (sold to Ziff-Davis)

Contributing writer to *Computer Paper* magazine, *Canada Computes* magazine, *Monitor Magazine,* and *Association for Internet Marketing* magazine

Founder: Ottawa Professional Promoters Association

Communications Director/Member: Society of Graphic Designers of Canada

Member: Association for Internet Marketing, Project Management Institute, Association of Registered Graphic Designers of Ontario

Former Board Member: International Webmasters Association
Former Director: Society of Graphic Designers of Canada
Former Member: Human Factors and Ergonomics Society

**RESUME 76: BY DEBBIE ELLIS, MRW, CPRW**

# Bernd Hieber
**c/o Hermann – Koehl – Str. 11**
**89231 NEV - VLM**
**Germany**
Telephone from USA  0113-366-635-5278
Telephone from Europe  +33-666-355-278
**Email career@abc.org**
**Online Résumé Portfolio http://www.abc.org/career/print.html**

## E-Business Specialist / Business Development Strategist / Marketing Executive
*Creating & Driving Winning E-Business Strategies for the New Economy*

Dynamic planning expert offering fresh insight and a passion for innovation; proven record of contribution to high-profile international business. Powerful strategist able to map creative budgeting, resource planning, and business development, empowering organizations with the tools, technologies, and strategies to bridge the digital business gap.

Respected leader, able to build team cohesion and inspire individuals to strive toward ever-higher levels of achievement. Exceptional relationship and management skills; relate and interface easily at the top executive levels. Complete, in-depth understanding of Internet tools, trends, and business models. Solid background and qualifications in all core business functions—finance, marketing, sales, and operations.

## AREAS OF EXPERTISE

- Budget Planning / Management
- Resource Management
- Personnel Training / Supervision
- Team / Group Leadership

- Strategic Planning
- Organizational Planning / Analysis
- Presentations / Public Speaking
- Multilingual; speak 3 languages

## HIGHLIGHTS OF PROFESSIONAL ACHIEVEMENT

Inventoried existing budgetary controls, reinventing goals, strategies, and models to meet the demands of the new digital economy. Achieved increased competitiveness, heightened market valuation, and revenue gains.

Formatted strategies and action plans that have exceeded IPO and shareholder requirements for financial planning and reporting.

Facilitated negotiations and consensus for selection / integration of numerous development plans in company budgets.

Identified opportunities to accelerate monthly financial reporting, resulting in substantial extension of management's response options.

Pioneered and promoted award-winning Total Customer Satisfaction Project, increasing competitiveness through 8% cost reduction in packaging, 17% in storage, and 23% in shipping. Recruited to present model in final round of Motorola's worldwide project presentation competition in Toronto, Canada.

Designed and built creative Internet portal for the high-growth organization abc.org; credited with national awards and recognized by international health-care professionals as an expert in e-business marketing.

Noticed for developing highly complex and effective projecting tools for sales, costs, orders, and manpower planning requirements. Integrated marketing, product, and resource plans in budget models, now being employed as corporate-wide standard.

**Confidential**                                                            **(continued)**

*The resume for this internationally experienced professional is full of achievements, keywords, training, and other professional credentials. It's highly readable due to excellent organization, a clean typeface (Arial), and effective use of horizontal lines and type enhancements. Note the reference to a complete online resume portfolio.*

Confidential Résumé of Bernd Hieber                                                                 Page 2

## PROFESSIONAL EXPERIENCE

### *Arrington Global Travel Distribution—Sophia-Antipolis, France, 2000–Present*

**Senior Officer, E-Commerce Division**

Senior consultant managing all Internet commerce initiatives. Direct long-term planning, budgeting, forecasting, and analysis for online sales and marketing activities in an increasingly competitive global marketplace. Provide reporting support for mergers, joint ventures, and partnership agreements. Coordinate and consolidate all company e-commerce functions including 17 divisions, 62 departments, 158 cost centers, and 185 projects. Lead, motivate, train, and coach team comprising talented cost control officers who produce standard and ad-hoc analysis reporting as input for crucial executive management decisions.

### *Motorola Multiservice Networks—Crawley, United Kingdom, and Darmstadt, Germany, 1988–2000*

**International Financial Assistant**

International financial specialist with collaborative responsibility for the reorganization, centralization, and relocation of administration, manufacturing, and customer support for Europe, Middle East, and Africa Markets (EMEA). Key role in implementation of new tools and management systems in finance and operations. Creative participation in innovation of centralized stock and shipment management.

## EDUCATION AND SPECIAL TRAINING

**M.B.A., Business and Marketing**
University of Tuebingen, Germany
Degree awarded 1999

**Business and Marketing Studies**
St. Olaf College, Minnesota, USA
1994–1995

**Business and Marketing Studies**
University of Tuebingen, Germany
Degree awarded 1995

*Effective Presentation Training*—Motorola University
*Working as a Team / Six Sigma*—Motorola University
*Working Smarter*—Leadership Development Ltd.
*Six Steps to Best Quality*—Motorola University
*Trans-Cultural Competence*—Motorola University

## PROFESSIONAL AFFILIATIONS

Member, International Sales and Marketing Executives
Member, Internet Marketing Association
St. Olaf Career Advising Network

## PUBLICATIONS

*Standards, Certification, and Accreditation in the European Union* 1998, VDE Verlag, Berlin, Germany

Author / Coauthor of 7 scientific and non-scientific articles. Complete list of titles can be found at
www.abc.org/career/publications.html

*Supporting documentation, additional information, and references available on request.*
*View complete online Résumé Portfolio at http://www.abc.org/career/english.html*
*Telephone from USA 0113-366-635-5278 — Email career@abc.org*

**RESUME 77: BY BEVERLY HARVEY, CPRW, JCTC, CCM, CCMC**

# ROBERT ROSSTINE

Home: (407) 987-6543
Mobile: (407) 654-9685

robross@takeout.com

17 Glenn Falls Drive
Orlando, Florida 32700

---

### Electronic Commerce / New Business Development / Sales & Marketing Management Executive

Results-oriented Management Executive with ten years of experience leading successful start-up, turnaround, and high-growth companies. Consistently successful in identifying and capitalizing upon market opportunities to drive revenue and profit growth. Strong Internet, clicks-and-bricks experience. Speak conversational Japanese and Spanish. Areas of expertise include

- Strategic / Tactical Business Planning
- Partnership / Alliance Development
- Capital- / Fund-raising
- Supply Network Development

- P&L Management
- Software Engineering / Development
- Staff Development / Management
- Investment Qualification Requirements

*Recognized for E-commerce Expertise by the* **Orlando Sentinel** *(October 2003),* **INC Magazine** *(September 2002), and* **Small Business Opportunities** *(October 2003).*

---

### PROFESSIONAL EXPERIENCE

FastServe.com, Inc., formerly TakeOut.com, Inc., Dallas, Texas                    May 2003 to Present

*A take-out food delivery operation serving more than 37 major markets in the U.S. and Europe.*

**Director, New Market Development—FastServe.com, Inc.** (May 2004 to Present)

Led the launch of an e-commerce business (TakeOut.com) specializing in a one-hour order delivery operation and grew it to an $800,000 operation within first year. Sold to FastServe.com, assisted in ownership transition, and currently manage new market development.

- Engineered integration of TakeOut.com's software and data into FastServe.com's Delivery Magic within two weeks.
- Assisted in integration of all internal and external operating systems, Internet marketing programs, customer tracking systems, menu guide production, and recruitment strategies.
- Conducted due diligence studies and identified new markets for penetration to meet FastServe.com's business development goals.
- Lead development of restaurant partnerships, order fulfillment/call center operations, menu guide development and production, and staff recruitment.

**President/CEO—TakeOut.com, Inc.,** Orlando, Florida (May 2003 to May 2004)

Built a clicks-and-bricks Internet company based on a newly developed unproven software program and the development of contracts with more than 95 bricks-and-mortar companies.

- Conducted due diligence studies, established company direction, developed strategic business plans, created a marketing program, instituted operating infrastructures, and recruited a management team and staff of 35.
- Raised $250,000 in operating seed capital and pioneered the start-up of an online-based one-hour restaurant takeout and delivery service.
- Engineered solutions and worked closely with software programmers to build the nation's first Web-based restaurant delivery software that was redundant, efficient, effective, and technically sound.
- Overcame customer resistance to Web ordering through development of an online order entry system and averaged 35% of sales via the Internet, slashing labor costs and errors.
- Opened for business on May 2, 2003, and recorded more than $2,300 in sales in first week. Tracking $800,000 sales for 2004 with more than 30,000 unique online customers.

(continued)

*Highlighting accomplishments and starting off with a strong summary and essential keywords, this resume is a powerful introduction for an e-commerce executive.*

# ROBERT ROSSTINE

Page 2

(407) 987-6543 • robross@takeout.com

### PROFESSIONAL EXPERIENCE (Continued)

Delivery By Taxi, Inc., Herndon, Virginia                    February 2002 to May 2003

**Corporate Manager**

Recruited to turn around a failing restaurant delivery business with 128 franchisees that had declined from generating $80 million to less than $50 million annually. Challenged to identify problems and implement solutions within one of three corporate stores, document outcomes, build SOPs, and distribute manuals to corporate offices and franchisees.

- Developed a corporate marketing program and improved the quality of existing business unit marketing materials.
- Implemented new operating management and accounting procedures.
- Instituted database mailing programs used by all corporate stores and spearheaded a series of software improvements.
- Delivered more than 90% revenue increases within six months for two of the corporate stores and a 20% increase for the third store.

Themed Diner, Maitland, Florida                    January 1999 to December 2001

**District Manager**

Hired to manage six privately owned and operated restaurants during a rapid growth period. Developed into a national chain with 26 locations.

- Managed the recruitment, staffing, and training initiatives for a 220-employee operation.
- Built several tracking and food control systems.

Catering & Gourmet Gifts, Inc., Orlando, Florida                    July 1995 to December 1998

**Owner**

Launched catering facility and upscale retail gourmet gift store and marketed a mail-order catalog.

- Achieved profitability after only 10 months.
- Produced $500,000 in sales after only two years; expanded to three locations within three years.
- Managed a catering kitchen, retail store, mail-order warehouse, and 23 employees and drivers.

EARLIER CAREER included General Management positions within the restaurant and retail industries.

### EDUCATION / TECHNICAL TRAINING

Wright State University, Dayton, Ohio—Business Finance Concentration

RETS Technical College, Dayton, Ohio—Hotel and Restaurant Management

### PROFESSIONAL DEVELOPMENT

**Sales and Marketing Technologies Seminar,** S&M Tech, Orlando, Florida, September 2003
(Workshops included Search Engines, Effective Marketing, Redundancy, Advanced Technology)

**Restaurant Delivery Service Association,** Las Vegas, Nevada, May 2002
Marketing, Operational Industry Standards, New Technology Workshops

**Internet Seminar,** Nothing But Net, Orlando, Florida, April 2002
(Workshops included Web Page Sales, Internet Business History, Networking & Partnership Building)

### COMPUTER SKILLS

Operating/Network Systems: MS Windows 3.1/97/98/2000/XP
Software: MS Office XP, Works, PowerPoint, PC Anywhere, QuickBooks, Quicken, Peachtree
Technical Skills: Installation, maintenance, and management of networked systems

**RESUME 78:** BY **LYNN P. ANDENORO, CPRW, JCTC**

# KEITH L. SMITH

keith@estores.com
(510) 542-4567

661 Orchard Road
Berkeley, California 94707

## INTERNET TECHNOLOGIES ENTREPRENEUR
### E-commerce / Software Development / Online Merchandising

Creative, results-driven executive with *proven track record in building profitable start-up ventures,* developing strategic partnerships, and driving revenue/profit growth in electronic commerce and retailing. *Decisive, visionary leader; expert at identifying and capturing Internet market opportunities, creating value and convenience in Internet technologies, and inexpensively acquiring specialty market customers.* Combine expertise in strategic planning, P&L management, marketing, and business development with ingenuity in advanced technology infrastructure and business systems.

*Participative leadership style;* able to build motivation, consensus, and cooperation with cross-functional teams in fast-paced environments. Effectively manage all facets of project life-cycle development, from initial feasibility and market analysis through specification, development, quality review, and implementation.

*Strategic Planning ◆ Marketing Management ◆ Strategic Financial Management
Budget Administration ◆ Risk Analysis ◆ Customer Relationship Management
Service Design / Delivery ◆ Scientific Marketing ◆ Data Mining ◆ Customer Profiling
Internet Media Buying ◆ Advertising ◆ Internet Direct Marketing ◆ Venture Funding
Software Design / Development Management ◆ Business Development*

## PROFESSIONAL EXPERIENCE

**FOUNDER, PRESIDENT, AND CEO**
**I-Commerce,** Provo, UT

2001–2005

*Challenge:*  Lead start-up venture from concept through development and market launch to market leadership. *Capitalize on innovative product and service ideas* to competitively position business, build partnerships, and grow revenues.

Craft marketing strategy, distribution methods, and packaging. Acquire business-to-business and business-to-consumer relationships online.

*Action:*  Founded company to create e-commerce sites for specialty retailers, but quickly *identified opportunity* to build unique software tool allowing merchants to manage site content — ShopSite.

Integrated *viral marketing strategies* to promote ShopSite. *Eliminated product distribution costs* by offering Internet downloads for authorized users. Purchased cooperative advertising to pool online marketing dollars and resources.

Surveyed merchants to assess needs and rate system effectiveness. *Optimized online marketing strategies,* analyzing cost per sale per message per market venue.

(continued on page 2)

*This resume was created as part of a financing package for a start-up e-commerce company seeking venture capital. Note the effective use of the CAR strategy in describing key accomplishments.*

**KEITH L. SMITH**
(510) 542-4567 • keith@estores.com

Page Two

**FOUNDER, PRESIDENT, AND CEO, I-Commerce,** continued

Action:
(continued)

**Recruited talented, high-level managers** from leading technology companies. Instituted disciplined software development practices, including code management, version control, and documentation techniques.

**Forged strategic alliances with key partners,** including Microsoft, Adobe, Verio, and Mindspring.

Results:
- ShopSite user base has grown to more than 35,000, making it the **most widely used small business e-commerce software worldwide.**
- **Pioneered method for protecting software from piracy,** enabling I-Central to attract and forge alliances with hundreds of ISP distribution partners.
- Raised $1 million in venture capital. **Delivered 400% return for investors** in an average of 9 months.
- Utilized **disciplined budget strategies** to stretch resources and grow operations on thin cash. Never missed a payroll. Devised internal accounting system for order management, sales, and billing.
- **Sold company for $11 million in May 1998 to Open Market** (NASDAQ: OMKT).

**GENERAL MANAGER**
**Electronics Education International,** Irvine, CA

1998–2000

Challenge:
Lead aggressive business turnaround for designer, manufacturer, and distributor of educational kits and software for electronics training. Drive revenue and profit improvement for company with slow 10% annual sales growth.

Action:
Streamlined operations and business practices to **achieve profit goals with only half of previous inventory and staffing levels.** Redesigned inventory and accounting processes to optimize inventory levels and reduce costs. Competitively positioned company against larger business ventures.

Results:
- **Doubled revenues in first year.**
- **Increased profits more than 80%** through innovative marketing strategies, internal efficiency planning, and revitalized business processes.

**EDUCATION**

**B.S., Corporate Finance** *(cum laude graduate),* NEW YORK UNIVERSITY, New York, NY, 1995

CHAPTER 9

# Resumes for Project Managers and Technology Consultants

- Technology Project Managers
- IT, IS, and MIS Project Managers
- Telecommunications Technology Managers
- Technology Leaders
- Technology Industry Consultants

**RESUME 79: BY SUSAN GUARNERI, NCC, NCCC, CPRW, CCMC, CEIP, MCC**

## Charles Farrow

27 Central Avenue, Toms River, NJ 08754

(732) 929-5555 Home • (732) 929-8888 Mobile • cfarrow@ole.com

### Project Management
#### *IT Systems Installation and Technology Integration*

Results-driven leader with information systems installation and integration experience. Work closely with end-users during the design, development, and training stages. Expert in full-cycle project planning and implementation. Skilled in applications analysis and back-office operations. Demonstrated business acumen and ability to meet fiscal and deadline commitments. Core competencies include

✓ Strategic Business Planning    ✓ Reengineering    ✓ Project Management

✓ Interdepartmental Coordination    ✓ Change Management    ✓ Resource Management

✓ Management & Administration    ✓ Technology Transfer    ✓ Client Relations

Energetic and decisive business leader able to merge disparate personnel into team-centered project teams. Demonstrated team-building, relationship-building, and communications skills.

### PROFESSIONAL EXPERIENCE

**CCS Systems** (software vendor/ASP to Fortune 500 companies), Toms River, NJ    1994–2005

**Director** (1998–2005), **Training Director** (1994–1998)
Managed multimillion-dollar IT projects for large-scale corporate home office applications. Fully responsible for project P&L. Clients included Westney, Cal-Mart, James, Home Store, Jill Jones, D-Mart, and River Royal. Maintained direct and ongoing client contact to ensure smooth operations.

#### Accomplishments

☑ Achieved productivity gains of up to 50% through the development and implementation of projects on time, on spec, and on budget. Consistently met or exceeded performance criteria.

☑ Vital member of steering committee that identified user needs and developed customized solutions for more than 150 clients. Personable, direct approach contributed to client loyalty.

☑ Led projects through entire project development cycle to develop application-specific systems capable of meeting current and long-range corporate information management requirements. Produced and managed deliverables through formal project plans.

☑ Matrix-managed 20-member cross-functional team (hardware, software, quality control, technical support, and training), assigning team responsibilities and overseeing tasks and timelines. Often called upon to use personal judgment, diplomacy, and analytical sense to troubleshoot problems.

☑ Pioneered innovative team building and cross-functional project management techniques to expedite workflow, simplify processes, and reduce operating costs.

☑ Designed and implemented user setup, end-user training materials, and testing procedures.

**River Royal** (Division of Royal, Inc.), New York, NY    1987–1994
**Divisional Planner** (1991–1994) Promoted from Planner and Senior Planner (1987–1991)

### EDUCATION

B.S., Marketing, 1985: McGill University, Ontario, Canada

### COMPUTER SKILLS

Microsoft Office (Word, Excel, PowerPoint, Access, Outlook); Internet

*With all his professional experience at one company, this individual was able to construct a concise one-page resume that effectively highlights his project accomplishments.*

# PETER S. LANG

4756 Pine Haven Drive
Matthews, North Carolina 28105
**Home:** (704) 847-3524 ▪ **Cell:** (704) 434-2676
plang@peterlang.com

## TECHNICAL PROFILE

A dedicated, customer-focused, and articulate technology professional with four years of hands-on experience in providing IT solutions to small-business customers. Solid understanding of network engineering functions, including systems installation, configuration, programming, testing, and support. Strong background in troubleshooting and repairing hardware and software problems. Technical skills include the following:

| | |
|---|---|
| **Operating Systems:** | Windows 3.1, 95, 98, ME, XP, 2000, and 2003 Enterprise Server |
| **Languages:** | HTML, DHTML, PHP, CSS, JavaScript, VBScript, Flash MX |
| **Hardware:** | VPN (including PPTP and L2TP with IPSec), COMDIAL digital phone systems, 3Com SuperStack manageable switches, WAN/LAN Level III Support, and numerous PC hardware and system components |
| **Software:** | MS Office Suite, Macromedia Dreamweaver, Macromedia Fireworks, Jasc Print Shop Pro, Adobe Photoshop, MS Visio, PowerQuest Deploy Center, Symantec Ghost, Symantec ACT (CRM), Remote Desktop Applications (Dameware, Terminal Server, pcAnywhere), IIS Version 5+ |

## PROFESSIONAL EXPERIENCE

**CASAR Solutions, Inc.**—Charlotte, NC                    2001–2005
(Provider of total computer and telephone network solutions for dental, medical, and small businesses)

**Project Manager** (2/04–3/05)
**Team Leader** (2/03–2/04)
**Field Service Technician** (8/01–2/03)

Advanced rapidly through a series of increasingly responsible positions with this regional telecommunications solutions firm. Initially hired to design, install, repair, and support networks utilizing MS Windows (95, 98, NT, 2000, and XP) operating systems. Performed diagnostics/troubleshooting, setup, and maintenance of networks, servers, workstations, and related peripherals. Performed data conversions and system upgrades. Served as chief network engineer. Provided telephone and on-premise customer support.

As **Project Manager,** coordinated all project phases—from needs assessment, proposal, costing and pricing, establishment of timelines, and daily schedules to checklist and client approval. Created floor plan configurations using Visio. Managed call-center function through logging, documenting, and tracking calls.

As **Team Leader,** supervised installation (3-person team) of voice, data, audio, and video wiring—including oversight of board/rack mount (66 blocks, patch panels, switches, and routers).

As **Field Service Technician,** installed and configured PCs and peripherals, as well as supported hardware for workstations and servers, for clients in North Carolina, South Carolina, and Virginia. Performed various troubleshooting and repair work, including hard-drive replacement, file restoration, and video-card replacement. Provided support for all major practice-management medical software products, including Dentrix, EagleSoft, Softdent, EasyDental, Dexis, PBSEndo, Lytech, SoapWire, PracticeWorks, and Oasys.

(continued)

*This resume makes the most of only four years of professional experience, highlighting leadership and management roles while showing rapid career advancement.*

**Peter S. Lang**                                                 (704) 847-3524 ▪ plang@peterlang.com

*Technical/Leadership Contributions:*

➢ Spearheaded installation of managed switches to facilitate in troubleshooting connectivity and collision issues.

➢ Proposed utilization of Gigabit Ethernet technology, a high-speed data-transfer device for clients requiring faster data movement.

➢ Introduced SATA hard drive, providing faster access times for servers and thereby increasing network performance.

➢ Researched and recommended purchase of new Dell PCs with dual processors using hyperthreading technology.

➢ Designed support documents (how-to scripts) to assist technical support in troubleshooting and repair of common problems.

➢ Developed new disaster-recovery plan using external USB 2.0 hard drives, which provided substantially more storage space, decreased daily backup time, and facilitated diagnostics. Previously, data backup used Travan tape drives.

➢ Led introduction of sophisticated applications to associate dynamic IP addresses with friendly domain names and provide easier, more reliable remote assistance for troubleshooting.

➢ Designed company's first user-friendly Web site for client use.

*Major Projects:*

▪ Managed (as team leader) the installation and setup of a 140-line (data/voice), low-voltage wiring project for Paragon Metals, a metal fabricator. Project included relocation of telephone lines, PCs, and peripherals. Supervised 4-person team in cable termination and connectivity testing, while splitting pairs on standard CAT5 and CAT6 cabling.

▪ Managed installation of network and telecommunications cabling, including telephones, audio, video, and computers (8 PC workstations; 30 voice/data, 10 audio, and 8 video lines) for a state-of-the-art "dental spa." Developed specifications, participated in vendor selection, managed parts inventory, and trained users.

---

**EDUCATION**

**A+ CompTIA Certified Professional,** Tech Train—Charlotte, NC, 2001
**Microsoft Certified Professional,** Tech Train—Charlotte, NC, 2001

# Robert J. Donovan

216 Sierra Drive • East Hampton, CT 06424
860.267.9548 • rjdonovan22@attbi.com

**Senior Systems-development Specialist • IT Consulting • Full-cycle Project Management**
**Applications Analysis • Enterprise / Web-systems Development**
**Object Technologies Experience • Strategic Business Planning and Analysis**

- Accomplished, results-driven **Information-technology Professional** with broad expertise harnessing the power of systems, applications, and client-server technologies to precisely meet client needs. Proven track record of accomplishments on clients' behalf—leveraging technological solutions that consistently exceed client project requirements and expectations.
- Well-developed technical skills and expert project-management abilities complemented by highly effective communication and consensus-building skills.
- Keen strategic business-planning and assessment abilities enhanced by strong leadership skills.
- Talent for creatively applying technology to meet changing business needs and automation requirements.
- Reputation as highly collaborative business partner with ability to understand/interpret client needs.

## Technical Skills Summary

| | |
|---|---|
| **Certifications …** | **Java Programmer Certification** (Learning Tree International) |
| | **Web Development Certification** (Learning Tree International) |
| **Hardware …** | IBM Mainframe and PC Windows Environments |
| **Software …** | WebLogic and MQSeries Servers, IMS DB / DC, DL/1, DB2 / SQL / CICS, Adobe Photoshop, Adobe Illustrator |
| **Languages …** | Java, JavaScript, HTML, JSP, SQL, XML, Smalltalk, ASP, ColdFusion, COBOL |

## Professional Experience

**DONOVAN CONSULTING, INC. • East Hampton, CT**                         **1995–Present**
**Lead Architect / Senior Consultant**

Senior Consultant—advise corporate clients and direct project teams in strategic system enhancements; lead technical consultation, design, and programming. Collaborate with executive-level management in defining project boundaries and providing in-depth analysis from end-user standpoint. Develop project plans and schedules; coordinate programmer/analysts' efforts. From 1995 to present, have consulted on full-time basis under auspices of American Consulting Group to key clients throughout Greater Hartford.

*Key Client Assignments and Project Deliverables*

- **Travelers**—B2B and B2C / XML / Java / WebLogic / MQSeries        8/1999–Present

  As Lead Architect, spearheaded development of mapping framework for Property & Casualty Enterprise Development Department (eService and eSales Group); result: Automobile Quote Processing between Travelers/external partners. Used XML and Java over WebLogic mid-tier server; framework extension facilitated communication with IMS legacy rating transactions through MQSeries by putting object data into mainframe copybook. Currently augmenting framework to support quoting by additional partners and in other states.

(continued)

*For this consultant seeking to transition to a corporate environment, projects are presented in some detail and the names of major corporate clients are boldly identified. A strong summary introduces a broad set of technical and professional skills.*

## Robert J. Donovan
860.267.9548 • rjdonovan22@attbi.com

Page Two

**DONOVAN CONSULTING, INC.** • *Key Client Assignments and Project Deliverables (cont'd.)*

- **Travelers**—IMS DB / DC / DB2 / ORACLE / Smalltalk     1/1997–6/1999

  Pivotal middleware team member supporting Personal Lines Client and Sales Front End/Customer Service; instrumental to successful mapping of relational database (DB2 and ORACLE) and IMS Database logical/physical COBOL copybooks to VisualAge Smalltalk application domain objects; used IBM's Smalltalk Data Gateway (SDG) product. SDG's IMS Adapter managed flow of legacy IMS transactions (client=host). Used IBM's IMS Open Transaction Manager Access (OTMA) as interface between TCP/IP and IMS Control Programs.

- **Verizon Corporate Systems Group**—TOPLink / ORACLE     10/1996–12/1996

  Analyzed, designed, and programmed 6 windows for Strategic Cost Development System; wrote using ParcPlace's VisualWorks; used TheObjectPeople's TOPLink as interface with ORACLE database.

- **The Hartford Benefit Systems Group**—Smalltalk / COBOL / CICS / DB2     2/1996–8/1996

  Maintained Smalltalk and COBOL code for Benefit Information Decision System (BIDS) and Benefit Access applications (BA). BIDS was client-server application that stored local data in Sybase and wrote CICS transaction file (uploaded to mainframe and processed). BA was client-server application that displayed DB2 data (retrieved by CICS program scheduled on mainframe).

- **ITT Hartford**—Smalltalk / Object-Oriented     7/1995–12/1995

  Mentored Object-Oriented (OO) / Smalltalk training program; instructed students in OO Analysis and Design and Smalltalk programming. Coached throughout corporate implementation.

- **Connecticut State Department of Labor**—CICS / DB2     4/1995–7/1995

  Analyzed, designed, and programmed Connecticut Automated Benefits System.

**AMERICAN MANAGEMENT SYSTEMS** • Hartford, CT     **1986–1995**

Lead Consultant from American Management Systems directing software-development projects for strategic client accounts:

- **Telia Mobitel**—Smalltalk Development     5/1994–4/1995
- **Connecticut State Department of Labor**—CICS / DB2 Development     1/1993–5/1994
- **Sikorsky Aircraft**—IMS DB / DC Development     8/1991–1/1993
- **Pratt & Whitney Aircraft**—IMS DB / DC / DB2 Development     7/1986–8/1991

**Earlier Career Background** includes **CICS Development** (Women's Specialty Retailing Group), **IMS DB / DC Development** (Hamilton Standard), and **High School Mathematics Teacher** (Windsor, CT).

### Education and Military Background

RENSSELAER POLYTECHNIC INSTITUTE • Hartford, CT
- **Master of Science Degree, Computer Science** (1983)

EASTERN CONNECTICUT STATE UNIVERSITY • Willimantic, CT
- **Bachelor of Arts Degree, Mathematics**

UNITED STATES ARMY • Fort Hood, TX
- **E-5 Specialist 5th Class**; Honorable Discharge after 2 years of Distinguished Service

# Abby Randolph

5 Timber Lane • Somerset, NJ 08873 • 732-555-1212 • arandolph@yahoo.com

### IT PROFESSIONAL - PROJECT MANAGEMENT AND BUSINESS ANALYSIS
*Consumer marketing, provisioning, customer fulfillment and database marketing*

In-depth expertise in all aspects of business application lifecycles including project management, analysis, design, programming, training and strategic systems planning. Adept in both large and small applications across mainframe and client-server architectures. Highly skilled large-scale project manager able to work with clients to identify their business requirements and translate them to IT.

### KEY ACCOMPLISHMENTS

- Achieved $5M in cost reductions through development and implementation of project plans to continue development of releases and in response to audits in projects of $100K–$1M.
- Provided IT support to ensure accurate processing of 28M orders, 72M fulfillments and 335M promotional responses annually.
- Increased joint fulfillment volumes from 3 to 22 percent, saving $1M per month in fulfillment costs.
- Reduced expense on external vendors by $5M annually.
- Directed system enhancements to support the ordering, enrollment, provisioning and fulfillment of 100+ new marketing offers annually.
- Significantly improved provisioning and fulfillment processes to increase timeliness and reduce costs.
- Produced 27 percent reduction in software defects.
- Significantly reduced run times and costs associated with various applications.
- Developed long-term system plans and championed use of IT for competitive advantage.
- Developed a methodology for converting from a strategic to a tactical plan.

### PROFESSIONAL EXPERIENCE

**Telecommunications Technology, Inc.**                                        1980–2005
*Engaged in key leadership roles that contributed consistent value-added expertise, significant cost reductions and growth with increasing responsibilities and continuous professional development during this period.*

**District Manager, Consumer Communications Services—CIO**                    2002–2005
Led a team of 70+ IT professionals in the development, operation and maintenance of the Residence Market Management System—critical to the company's provisioning of long-distance service. Responsible for order provisioning, marketing program fulfillments and promotional history maintenance for 100M+ customers.
- Supported 100+ marketing offers to strengthen company's position in long distance annually.
- Reduced list generation cycle times by 60 percent.
- Initiated 30+ enhancements to improve provisioning process.
- Implemented significant system enhancements to maintain consumer account information integrity.
- Implemented enhancements that extended the system's joint fulfillment process to other bundled offers.
- Utilized innovative approaches to contain costs of enhancements.
- Significantly improved client satisfaction and employee morale through frequent and open communication, strong teamwork and recognition.

**District Manager**                                                          2000–2002
Managed the relationship between the CIO and the Wireless, Personal Number and Consumer Enterprise organizations to ensure support of client initiatives. Responsible for systems engineering, LAN/Server services, strategic systems planning, financial management and executive support.
- Completed a long-term marketing systems architecture.
- Instrumental in enabling a move of applications from mainframe to client-server platform.                    (continued)

*Note the brief summary underneath the most recent position description. It gives a thumbnail summary of this candidate's activities and accomplishments at the company.*

# Abby Randolph

732-555-1212 • Page Two

**District Manager**      1997–2000

Led the development and operation of various marketing and product management systems. Supported 100+ IT professionals and championed IT support at the executive product round table.

- Led a cross-functional team initiative that resulted in a major redesign of the ability to household 150M consumers 50 percent faster.
- Led a number of data-mining initiatives to acquire and retain customers.

**District Manager**      1994–1997

Spearheaded efforts to form a stronger relationship between consumer marketing executives and IT. Implemented four projects identified by the Consumer Marketing Systems Plan, including early implementation of a client-server application.

- Led a groundbreaking effort to utilize IT for competitive advantage.
- Optimized capability of an advertising system for storage of images and transmittal to agencies.

**Executive Assistant to the VP of Data Processing and Corporate Telecommunications**      1993–1994

Responsible for speech and external customer meeting preparation, conference planning, commitment reviews and employee communication as part of a leadership development assignment.

**Staff Manager**      1990–1993

Responsible for development and marketing of a systems planning process to build enterprise-wide systems plans.

- Managed project to develop a systems tool to support the strategic systems planning process.
- Marketed application of the systems planning process across all organizations.
- Developed tactical planning methods to successfully translate strategic systems plans into projects.

**Manager**      1985–1990

Led various teams of six to eight IT professionals that specialized in systems analysis, design services and methods.

- Established and managed a team that spearheaded prototyping and Joint Application Design (JAD) services to engage users in the developing requirements.
- Marketed services interdepartmentally, successfully completing 15–20 prototypes and JAD workshops annually.

**Manager**      1983–1985

Managed a team of 10–12 IT professionals responsible for payroll system development. Managed a team responsible for database design consultation, training material development and manual publication.

**Member of Programming Staff**      1980–1983

Responsible for various programming positions in system development, technical support and training. Project leader for inventory management and general decision support systems. Developed and delivered three courses.

---

### EDUCATION
BA—Mathematics—Douglass College—1980

### EXECUTIVE EDUCATION
Advanced Management Program for Telecommunications—University of Southern California
Leadership Development Program—University of Maryland

### CERTIFICATIONS
Joint Application Design (JAD)
Project Management (In Progress)—Stevens Institute of Technology

### PUBLICATIONS
"How to Solicit User Requirements"—*Communications Monthly*—June 1995

# ADAM SANDS

1111 South Court ✧ Los Angeles, CA 90001 ✧ (213) 211-4444 ✧ adam@aol.com

## SENIOR BUSINESS ANALYST / PROJECT MANAGER

### ~ BUSINESS PROCESS IMPROVEMENT ~ APPLICATION ARCHITECTURE DESIGN ~ PROJECT LEADERSHIP ~

Highly accomplished Senior Business Analyst/Project Manager with a verifiable track record of managing complex IT projects and exceeding expectations. Practiced in clarifying business requirements, performing gap analysis between goals and existing procedures/skill sets, and designing process and system improvements to increase productivity and reduce costs. Extensive experience in the implementation of Financial Accounting, CRM, Employee Relationship Management, and Partner Management systems for financial services firms. Strong interpersonal skills and ability to diplomatically facilitate discussions and negotiations with stakeholders. Recognized project management skills, consistently delivering complex, large-scale projects on time and within budget. Additional areas of expertise:

- Process Analysis & Redesign
- Management of Cross-Functional Teams
- Project & Delivery Methodologies
- Project Management & Tracking
- System Solution Architectures
- Change Control Management
- Budgeting & Planning
- Cost & Resource Estimates
- Project Risk & Scope

## PROFESSIONAL EXPERIENCE

SOLUTIONS ARCHITECT                                                        JUL 2000–FEB 2005
SIEBEL SYSTEMS ✧ LOS ANGELES, CA

One of a select group of individuals assigned to large complex engagements designing application architectures and improving business processes for integration of Siebel systems with existing client systems. Specialized in financial services clients, leveraging extensive experience in banking industry. Assigned to special "Red" accounts indicating troubled or highly sensitive projects.

Demonstrated skills in interviewing business and technical leaders to gather and clarify business requirements. Developed CRM strategy and roadmap vision, and oversaw business process and technical mapping. Authored detailed project/deployment plans and schedules. Took lead role in numerous projects and consistently exceeded customer expectations. From senior management of major client, Banker's Trust, earned Siebel Customer Certification—an independent validation from a client that a Siebel employee was critical to their success. Gained Certification in Siebel 2000, Siebel 7 Applications suite, and Siebel 7 Analytics.

*Notable Projects:*

- **CRM Strategy Project Manager**—*Siebel eInsurance strategy development for Prudential.* Delivered a CRM strategy and roadmap to Prudential's senior management, under a Tom Siebel–led initiative to assist MetLife in transforming the company's sales and service operations. Managed cross-functional team of sales, services, and product marketing personnel to evaluate existing technologies and business processes. Final presentation highlighted areas in Prudential's business where Siebel best practices could transform operations.
- **CRM Strategy Analyst**—*Siebel eHealthcare strategy development for Blue Cross/Blue Shield.* Developed the application architectural vision for marketing, enrollment, maintenance, and renewal operations. Analyzed and documented system and business workflows, designed improvements based on industry best practices, and authored CRM strategy document presenting ROI of new process flows and integrated Siebel solutions.
- **CRM Strategy Project Manager**—*Siebel Financial Services roadmap for The New York Stock Exchange.* Oversaw development of new CRM strategy. Directly engaged with NYSE sales force to assist in improving sales process. Presented findings to C-level executives and helped close sale.
- **Engagement Manager**—*Siebel Financial Services deployment, Credit Suisse First Boston.* Oversaw deployments across several lines of business for Siebel Financial Services, Employee Relationship Management, and Call Center applications. Managed multiple projects valued at $3.5M across numerous locations. Launched and managed Center of Excellence to ensure a sound architecture, track progress, and stay true to CIO's long-term goals.
- **Project Manager**—*Siebel Financial Services implementation, Banker's Trust.* Managed critical $11M project directing a 20-member team including resources from Siebel, several subcontractors, and assigned client resources for a 4,000-seat implementation of Siebel Financial Services suite. Highly visible project as this was Siebel's first implementation on an IBM mainframe. Challenged by tight deadlines, stepped into several roles, such as quality assurance liaison, during peaks in product development lifecycle. Achieved high level of customer satisfaction resulting in client volunteering to be a reference for product and professional services.

(continued)

*Specific cases (projects) are used to illustrate this person's skills not only in managing projects, but also in developing strategic solutions and presenting them at the boardroom level.*

**ADAM SANDS** (213) 211-4444 ✧ adam@aol.com                    **Page 2 of 2**

**SENIOR CONSULTANT**                                            **OCT 1998–JUL 2000**
**ORACLE CORPORATION** ✧ **LOS ANGELES, CA**

Senior consultant specializing in Oracle's financial accounting applications for financial services firms in banking, investment banking, and insurance sectors. Assigned to engagements based on demonstrated skills in business analysis, project management, and customer relationship management. Additionally chosen to lead educational seminars for clients.

*Notable Projects:*
- **Project Manager**—*ERP implementation for Canadian Subsidiary of Merrill Lynch.* Assisted in global unification effort for Merrill's General Ledger system. Assumed project responsibility for full financial suite (GL, AP, AR, and Fixed Assets) rollout in Canada. Managed $6M budget and coordinated migration/integration of Canadian accounting procedures consistent with global reporting standards. Delivered project on time and under budget.
- **Project Manager**—*ERP Y2K testing at Merrill Lynch.* Managed Y2K testing on heavily customized ERP application. Project responsibility included 30 cycles of testing with interfaces feeding data from legacy systems and other third-party software.
- **Team Lead**—*ERP rollout, ING Barings.* Led financial application module rollout for enterprise-wide project. Managed all phases of project from requirements gathering through user acceptance testing and documentation development. Presented project status in daily briefings to client CIO.
- **Business Analysis Lead**—*Pre-sales opportunities at insurance companies and banks.* Worked on several rapid Proof-of-Concept projects in pre-sales engagements including a B2B procurement application. Collaborated closely with sales force and prospective clients to assess needs, acquire data, and configure products to prospects' needs.

**COUNTRY RISK ANALYST**                                         **AUG 1995–OCT 1998**
**MELLON BANK** ✧ **PITTSBURGH, PA**

Researched and prepared macroeconomic analysis of Asian and Middle Eastern economies. Accountable for underwriting foreign institutional-risk and trade-finance analysis. Managed commercial-bank risk portfolio in excess of $18 billion.
- Established internal risk ratings for Sovereign and Institutional risk for bank. Coordinated product rollout effort in Southern Asia for Trust and Commercial Banking divisions.
- Led effort to keep Mellon out of the Asian bank crisis of the mid '90s. Where other banks were pumping more money into Southeast Asia, provided detailed analysis supporting withdrawal position.
- Helped reestablish Mellon as a name in Asia, resulting in development of very close ties with Japanese, Korean, and Australian banks for co-branding/marketing of products overseas.

**CONTROLLER/CFO**                                               **JUN 1991–AUG 1995**
**THE ABC CONCERN (USA)** ✧ **NEW YORK, NY**

Managed the North American office for an Asia-based garment and textile manufacturing company. Oversaw $7M operation and provided strong fiscal leadership in managing cash, costs, and risk.
- Led management negotiations with asset-based lenders including major factoring institutions.
- Established financial management standards and implemented a computer-based inventory and accounts receivable tracking system.

## EDUCATION & CREDENTIALS

Master of Public and International Affairs ✧ International Finance & Economics, University of Pittsburgh

Advanced Certificate in Asian Studies ✧ University of Pittsburgh

Bachelor of Business Administration, Management ✧ Kent State University

**Additional Coursework:**

Information Systems Management, CASE Tool Management ✧ Columbia University

Certificate in Managing Information Technology Projects ✧ The George Washington University

Chairman, Technology Committee ✧ The Frick Museum, New York, NY

Board Member ✧ Carnegie Mellon University Center for Strategy Simulations

# CRAIG LAND

699 River Drive
Narberth, PA 19072

craigland@dotresume.com

Home: (610) 677-5733
Cell: (484) 626-1005

## Executive Summary

**Senior-Level IT Project Manager/Business Analyst** with history of achieving cost savings and enhancing system functionality. Track record of tackling—and solving—tough business and technical problems for companies in transition. Strong leader; demonstrated ability to work effectively with people at all levels and in all functional areas. Experience managing full system development life cycle (phase methodology), from requirements gathering to final implementation and customer training. Integration specialist with mainframe, client-server, and Internet experience. Solid knowledge of IT tools, methods, and standards, as well as financial, sales, and manufacturing systems.

## Professional Experience

**Project Manager,** 2004–present
TANDY BAKERY, Wayne, PA; Computer Consultants, Inc. (agency), Philadelphia, PA
*The number-one dessert bakery in the Northeast, with 24-hour data processing at 15 locations.*

Tasked with integrating accounts receivable and production applications on OS/390 system into Internet-based/client-server AS/400 system following company acquisition. Served as liaison between business and technology groups at different locations, gathering requirements, overseeing definition of specifications, coordinating implementation, and verifying integration test results against requirements. Currently managing final report-building phase and training legacy users on new system.

*Accomplishments*

- Achieved on-schedule integration into one Oracle data warehouse and one application with customized reports for 15 locations.
- Delivered substantial cost savings with integrated system: IT workforce reduced by 80%; accounting and production staff reductions estimated at 50% on project completion.
- Retained all required business functionality for mainframe users on new system.
- Received good reviews on training and accompanying documentation.

**Project Manager,** 2002–2004
NETLEARN CORPORATION, King of Prussia, PA
*A Web-based provider of digital learning resources for the K–12 market.*

Oversaw integration of sales and accounting applications with Oracle database for one-year-old company in data warehouse environment. Met with department managers to determine business needs, developed high-level design requirements and specifications, and created project plan. Directed third-party company in rebuilding database to support requirements. Managed in-house implementation, working with executive management; IT specialists; and data warehouse, operations, sales, and accounting staff.

*Accomplishments*

- Successfully completed project on schedule and in accordance with requirements.
- Automated numerous sales and accounting functions with XML procedure that merged APPLIX sales application, Great Plains accounting software, and Oracle database.
- Empowered sales and marketing staff with system that generated 20 critical reports required for tracking state of business and increasing sales. (continued)

*This resume emphasizes business skills and accomplishments to give this individual a competitive edge over other candidates with equally strong technical capabilities.*

# CRAIG LAND

(610) 677-5733       Page 2       craigland@dotresume.com

**Information System Integrator/Business Analyst,** 2000–2001
CAR-TOUCH ENTERPRISES, Horsham, PA
*An auto-detailing franchise with 300 locations throughout the United States and Canada.*

Led team in migrating AS/400 legacy systems to client-server environment. Gathered requirements, investigated existing hardware and software, and researched third-party solutions. Designed and developed Visual Basic GUI application with Oracle back-end, which performed inventory control, purchasing, sales and marketing, vendor development, and R&D financial management. Implemented remote service enabling franchises to access central database, as well as a telephone system enabling customers to reach any franchise via a single number.

*Accomplishments*

- Saved $50,000 annually and improved quality of reports with updates to telephone application.
- Proposed system conversions and application updates potentially yielding savings of up to $1 million and improving operations with automated, on-demand, up-to-date reports.

**Project Manager,** 1999–2000
FORD CONSULTANTS, Princeton, NJ
*An IT consulting firm providing solutions for Global 1000 corporations.*

Managed development of client-server applications in three areas: construction, project evaluation and facilitation, and employee/financial/purchasing reports.

**Project Manager/Programming Manager,** 1991–1998
GRANGE MARKETING, Philadelphia, PA
*One of the largest direct-marketing companies in the metropolitan Philadelphia area.*

Led multiple, short-term direct-marketing projects from beginning to end in fast-paced environment: developed project proposals, obtained customer approval, and oversaw development and support. Simultaneously managed long-term accounts with insurance companies and federal agencies, supplying payroll and other data services. Supervised staff of 15 in IT, operations, customer service, and marketing.

*Accomplishments*

- Consistently increased sales and achieved profits in line with objectives—15%–20% per project.
- Successfully managed government accounts with strict time frames and security requirements.

## Education, Certification

**B.S., Accounting,** Temple University, Philadelphia, PA

**Project Management Certificate,** Penn State Great Valley, Malvern, PA

**Computer Programming Certificate,** Philadelphia Training, Philadelphia, PA
COBOL II, RPG, Assembly, BASIC, FORTRAN

**Additional IT Courses,** Drexel University, Philadelphia, PA
Basic Windows NT, PL/SQL, PRO*C, Oracle 10g, C++, PowerBuilder, Visual Basic

# Jackie Cardiff

10007 Shoreline Avenue NW ▪ Seattle, WA 98000
(206) 523-1090 ▪ businesssystems@yahoo.com

## Objective: Senior Business Systems Analyst / Documentation Lead

*Experienced IT solutions analyst and matrix-team tech leader with strong IT / analysis / tech writing / documentation / user training skills and 10+-year success record on private & public sector COTS projects.*

| | |
|---|---|
| **QUALIFICATIONS** | Two+ years of experience in technical writing with more than 10 years of experience in information technology consulting in public and private sector environments. Eight years of experience in systems analysis of complex business systems, including documenting business and system process flows, creating logical data models, and writing user and functional requirements. |
| *Experience* | |
| *Business & Systems Analysis* | Currently work with business users at IKON to create business and system requirements for Molsen. Worked with 47 business experts representing 18 businesses in 5 divisions to establish business and system requirements for purchase of FDM software by Puget Fire Department. |
| *User Training* | Created training plan and curriculum materials including system user guides, job aids, seminar outlines, and oral presentations to accommodate diverse audiences at McCaw Wireless. |
| *COTS Implementation* | Worked with Puget Fire Department to plan integration of commercial off-the-shelf (COTS) FDM software enterprise-wide. |
| *Vendor Evaluation* | Evaluated FDM software for Puget Fire Department for their 8 lines of business. |
| *Software Testing* | Managed test teams that performed systems and user acceptance testing. |
| *Documentation* | Excel at synthesizing complex information into high-quality, highly usable documents that fit the needs of the target audience, utilizing proven writing, editing, layout, and organizational skills. |
| *Vertical and Horizontal Communication* | Ten-year success record working at all levels, internally and with multiple vendors/agencies to drive positive change, gain acceptance, meet deadlines, and resolve problems in a timely manner. Excel at motivating matrixed teams to embrace value of business process improvement. |

| | |
|---|---|
| **EXPERIENCE** | **SENIOR BUSINESS ANALYST / CORPORATE TRAINER** |
| **VULCAN TECHNOLOGY PARTNERS,** 1997 to Present | Manage multiple concurrent assignments on-site for technology consulting firm's clients. Create change-management plans, executive summaries, and training curricula. Train staff in change-management methodologies through group and individual training, job aids, and quick user guides. Develop corporate standards and reengineer systems to comply with industry standards. |
| *Areas of Achievement:* | *Select Business & Systems Analysis Projects:* |
| Business Requirements | • **Puget Department of Transportation (IKON):** Current project—Working to collect business requirements for permits and inspections for use of right of way (ROW). |
| Business Process Redesign | |
| System Automation | Previous Project (October 2004–February 2005)—Team member of successful business process redesign and system automation that improved availability of street design information from 8 months to 10 days. Developed and delivered end-user guide and training materials for city's street network database and GIS. |
| End-user Guide Development | |
| Application Integration | |
| Enterprise-wide Business Analysis | • **Puget Fire Department:** Established strategic threshold for application integration and laid foundation for future integrated IT development. Planned and conducted enterprise-wide business analysis across 8 lines of business for potential integration of more than 78 stand-alone applications into central repository. Facilitated joint requirements planning sessions with 47 business experts representing 18 units across 5 divisions. Created business process models integrating 8 lines of business. Identified information exchanges defining content/business rules. |
| Creation of Business Process Models | |
| Content & Bus. Rules | |
| COTS Implementation | |
| Bus./Fee Requirements | • **Puget County Department of Development and Environmental Services:** Implemented COTS (Permits Plus), a specialized client-server construction and land-use permit-management system for PC networks. Defined business and fee requirements to track billing. Designed screen layouts/fee computations. Built application logic. Fulfilled critical deadlines and delivered Y2K-compliant system. |
| Screen Layouts | |
| Application Logic | |

*This hybrid format emphasizes both functional skills areas (in the left column) and business performance and results. It helped this candidate secure an interview from among 350 applicants for a job with the City of Seattle.*

**Systems Analyst**                                                     **Jackie Cardiff** • Page 2
(206) 523-1090 • businesssystems@yahoo.com

Bus./System Process
Documentation

Change Control Processes

Service Quality Improvements

Market Analysis

High-level Presentations

IT & Bus. Solutions

Change Management Plans

Fit & Gap Analysis

Interviewing

Facilitating Multi-level
Meetings

**OTHER
EXPERIENCE**

Technical/Procedural
Documentation

End-user Documentation
Online Help Systems

Procedure Manuals

Organizational and Personnel
Management

Leadership, Mentoring &
Supervision

Budgets & Financial
Administration

Matrixed Team Leadership

- **McCaw Wireless:** Analyzed and synthesized business and system process documentation for customer-care database to increase development productivity by 80%. Developed and implemented change-control processes, and facilitated cross-functional change control boards.

- **Vulcan Technology Partners:** Led strategic marketing initiative to improve quality of product delivery and reduce time to market from 3 months to 6 weeks. Enhanced attractiveness of consulting team in highly competitive market. Performed market research and analysis, interviewed 34 business experts, developed business strategy, prepared and delivered presentations supporting business case, wrote executive summary, and conceived software solution.

- **Puget County Superior Court:** Avoided $3 million in system development costs by writing change-management plan based on operational, technical, and economic feasibility. Conducted fit and gap analysis comparing juvenile-justice information-management system to proposed state system. Interviewed individual business experts and facilitated cross-functional meetings to identify critical business process in 6 juvenile-justice practice areas.

- **The Snohomish Ledger:** Planned, defined, and tracked all tasks and milestones. Estimated time and completion costs for converting from evening to morning distribution. Met all critical deadlines and delivered enhanced system to support product for home delivery.

**Business Systems Analyst—King City Light, Seattle** (1988–1993)
**Program Coordinator—Puget County Department of Public Health, Seattle** (1984–1988)

Held increasingly responsible management positions with an emphasis on organizational development, business analysis, customer service, and program management. *Highlights:*

- Developed end-user documentation and online help systems for new software. Analyzed customer service and wrote new customer-service procedure manuals.

- Developed end-user documentation and online help systems for customer information system. Analyzed customer-service procedures. Led one-year project, writing first-time customer-service procedure manuals and providing written basis for all operations.

- Evaluated and defined processes, tools, methods, and critical success factors impacting processes. Calculated ROIs. Hired, trained, and supervised 16 union-represented employees. Analyzed, developed, and standardized job procedures. Liaison with high-level executives in other agencies.

- Recommended and prepared justifications for $2.2 million budget. Reconciled annual $6 million cash intake by branch office. Supervised financial reports for city treasurer's office. Managed $500,000 annual cash flow for commercial real estate firm.

- Pioneering leader on team of 5 multi-county administrators credited with planning and building business foundation that became nationally recognized program for public education and service to the AIDS population.

**EDUCATION &
CREDENTIALS**

**B.S., summa cum laude, Stanford University**
Certificate in Dependable Strengths Articulation

# BRIAN D. DE BOER

123 Pheasant Court
Liberty, Missouri 64068
816-555-5555 • bdeboer@aol.com

## CAREER PROFILE

**Telecommunications professional** with 20+ years of experience in Project Management/Design, Sales/Service and Purchasing/Billing. Indispensable in financial turnaround of major telecommunications company's cabling business from negative revenues to **million-dollar-per-year profits.** Concurrent responsibilities in sales force instruction and collaboration with track record of motivating others to act upon technical and customer-related initiatives. History of strategic technology deployment to streamline processes, slash expenses and drive profits. Highly communicative in relating and monitoring expectations.

Computer skills: MS Word, Excel, Exchange and Explorer; ABC Technologies DOSS 5, WACSA, FSAC-SS, WirePro, HTML; familiar with SAP. Honest, with a high level of integrity and proven work ethic.

- ➤ Project Management
- ➤ Purchasing / Inventory Management
- ➤ Contractor Management
- ➤ Sales and Marketing / Presentations
- ➤ Custom Wiring / Cable Contracting
- ➤ Customer Relationship Management

## CAREER ACHIEVEMENTS

### Project Management
- Spearheaded ground-up construction of a large contractor database (40+ contractors) over four states. **Results:**
  - ➤ **95% contractor-membership** in the ABC Technologies authorized service program.
  - ➤ **35% climb** in company's **cabling margin**, primarily through analysis/reduction of expenditures.
- Boosted sales force productivity by training team on key customer questions and methods to identify sales opportunities. **Result:** 50% increase in new business lead generation.
- Streamlined job bid turnaround time from one week to 2–3 days by maximizing technology utilization.
- **Slashed** accounts receivable **paperwork** approximately eight hours weekly by successfully implementing direct billing method.
- Successfully **engineered a contract** with a major **17-location account,** culminating in accountability as national account contact for all Systimax cabling. **Results:**
  - ➤ Upgraded all production/box plants nationwide.
  - ➤ Project-managed all locations and sourced nationwide to attain a single point of contact.
  - ➤ Delivered finished product that exceeded client expectations and increased future business.
- Nominated by account executives (based on outstanding accomplishments) to attend first XYZ Communications Elite meeting.
- **Increased profit** margin 25+%; tagged by ABC Technologies to present success strategies (on generating a profitable cabling business) at wiring conference.

### Sales
- **Exceeded sales quota 175%,** two years (Millionaires Club).
- **Achieved 150% of sales** quota, two years (Superachievers Club).
- Recruited to ABC Technologies Network Systems National Task Force that originated a pricing structure for Global Emerging Market organization.

*Continued...*

*Here is a primarily functional format, showcasing achievements under key subheadings and placing details of work experience on page 2.*

# BRIAN D. DE BOER

816-555-5555 • bdeboer@aol.com
Page Two

## CAREER PROGRESSION

*Steady telecommunications career progression (each change a desk-to-desk business transfer). Initiated career with National Communications and presently perform project management at XYZ Communications—each transition generated from company / divisional "spin-offs" (mergers, acquisitions, purchases, etc.).*

**XYZ COMMUNICATIONS** (ACQUIRED A DIVISION OF ABC TECHNOLOGIES), Olathe, Kansas, 2004–Present
**Regional Wiring Coordinator • Contractor Manager • Provisioning Coordinator**
*Charged with supervising 40 contractors in four states. Project-plan and execute custom cabling jobs from order to installation to billing to customer satisfaction. Participate in design meetings at customer sites. Negotiate with suppliers for optimum material prices and continually streamline processes/procedures resulting in declining expenses and climbing profits. Accountable for purchasing and inventory management.*

**ABC TECHNOLOGIES** (ACQUIRED A DIVISION OF MIDWEST TELEPHONE), Olathe, Kansas, 2000–2004
**Provisioning Coordinator • Contract Manager • Wire Design Specialist / Account Executive**
*Similar to prior Account Executive position at Midwest Telephone.*

**MIDWEST TELEPHONE** (A SPIN-OFF FROM NATIONAL COMMUNICATIONS), Lenexa, Kansas, 1988–2000
**Account Executive • Systems Technician**
*Consistently exceeded sales quotas, earning placement in Millionaires and Superachievers clubs. Originated a profitable cabling business from ground up to 40 contractors in four states by effectively networking, accruing leads, generating proposals and closing sales.*

**NATIONAL COMMUNICATIONS,** Lenexa, Kansas, 1980–1988
**System Technician • Repair Technician • Installer**

## COMMUNICATIONS EDUCATION / KNOWLEDGE

**Bachelor of Science in** Telecommunications, University of Missouri, Columbia, Missouri

➤ Graduate, **ABC Technologies Career Path program,** 2003
➤ **Certifications:** Panduit, Mohawk, Bertek, Belden and ABC Technologies fiber optics, ABC Technologies Systimax Certification in Installation, Sales and Design/Engineering
➤ **Training:** New Bridge on basic LAN environments, Bay Networks and AT&T Pardyne DSU/CSU
➤ **Installation/Repair:** System 75/G3, Merlin and Partner; Dimension PBX 100, 400 & 600 installation and repair of Tier 1/Tier 2 levels
➤ **Call Center Applications:** UCD & DGC groups
➤ **Other:** All Comkey products; all other AT&T vintage PBX switches; UNIX language; basic/advanced electronics

## PROFESSIONAL AFFILIATION

➤ **Member,** BICSI, 1999–Present

**RESUME 87: BY HELEN OLIFF, CPRW, FRWCC, CGECI**

# SAM RAWWA

5657 Glade Drive, Reston, VA 20191 • Phone: (703) 264-5657 • E-mail: srawwa@yahoo.com

## IT PROJECT MANAGER / WIRELESS NETWORK ENGINEER
Telecom • Research / Problem Solving / Data Analysis • International Markets

*Objective: Project Manager or Analyst for a growing telecom organization with international reach.*

**TECH MANAGEMENT PROFILE:**

Organized team leader with 10 years of experience in telecom, engineering, R&D, and project management. Wireless-network consultant and project manager for major manufacturers (e.g., Communications Next, New Wave Telecom, and Telecom Network). Experienced with Nextel, Ericsson, and Motorola equipment/vendors. Exceptional skills in research, analysis, data analysis, problem solving, and decision making. Strong interest in leadership, organizational development, and business requirements. Proficient with UNIX, Windows 2003 Server, databases, and geo tools.

- **Network Specialties**—GSM/GPRS, iDEN, IS-136, and CDMA wireless standards and networks (Global System for Mobile Communication/General Packet Radio Service, Integrated Digital Enhanced Network, Integrated Services-136, and Code Division Multiplexed Access), wireless antennas, SS7 signaling, switch translations, call routing, RF (radio frequency) hardware, CellCAD propagation modeling, and ODBC (Open Database Connectivity).

- **Project Management**—Complete project management and evaluation for wireless networks, from team lead, coordination, and budgeting to engineering design, technical review, and oversight. Meet design and business requirements for public, private, national, and international customers in the wireless networks, telecom, and manufacturing industries.

- **Research/Analysis**—Data analysis, trend monitoring, and information sharing. Quality assurance for database reporting, information sharing, engineering R&D, cost reduction, and office functions. Team-based problem solving to meet business requirements.

**AREAS OF EXPERTISE:**

- Project Management/Team Leadership
- Collaborative Decision Making
- Quality Assurance & Improvements
- Budgeting & Cost Reduction
- Metrics, Monitoring & Solutions
- Shared Information Mapping

- Wireless-Network Design & Deployment
- Mobile & Digital Network Integration
- Spectrum Feasibility & Optimization
- Cell-Site Propagation Modeling
- Frequency & Network Capacity Planning
- FCC Regulatory Requirements & Licensing

**PROJECT MANAGEMENT & ORGANIZATIONAL RESULTS:**

- **Directed the entire drive test for an iDEN network** in Florida. (Communications Next)
  - Planned, tracked, and managed project to integrate cell sites into an existing subscriber network over a 6-month period.
  - Cost-justified a network expansion; enabled an increase in network traffic.
  - Analyzed engine data to support acquisition for an ongoing diagnostic system.

- **Managed project to design a GSM wireless network for subscribers** in the Northern Region of Netherlands. (Telecom Network)
  - Team lead for GSM, telecom, and mobile network designers/programmers.
  - Coordinated cell-site deployment with 3 separate departments at Telfort (e.g., construction, transmission, and site acquisitions).
  - Migrated the cell-site tracking database from MS Access to Oracle CellTracker, and trained the radio planning engineers on the new interface and functionality.
  - Designed/produced project tracking reports on the status of cell sites; used MS Access, MapInfo geographical mapping, and an ODBC link to the database.

- **Led teams/projects to increase plant capacity and engineering quality.** (Toledo Motors)
  - Led the effort to expand the dynamometer test labs in Toledo's Engine Plant. Wrote the specs, selection criteria, and evaluation requirements. Increased the total number of labs.
  - Led collaborative problem resolution, as a Quality Liaison for manufacturing groups.
  - Led a quality-improvement effort to improve manufacturing, after researching and analyzing several persistent engine problems and solutions. Reduced warranty cost and achieved quality improvement by coordinating an engine exchange program.

(CONTINUED)

*To help this individual shift from network design to network project management, his resume emphasizes project-management and analytical skills linked to his technical experience.*

# SAM RAWWA
Résumé—Page Two

**TECHNICAL RESULTS:**

- **Optimized a 900-MHz iDEN network** using Motorola equipment. (Communications Next)
  - Analyzed test data and reset system settings to optimize performance. Researched and analyzed trending data to determine cell sites that needed more capacity.
  - Assessed and tuned the level of indoor RF coverage at major shopping malls, airports, and convention centers in Boston.

- **Designed an 1800-MHz GSM mobile network** using Ericsson CME 20 equipment. (Telecom Network)
  - Analyzed and selected the cell site; researched and selected the antenna and base-station equipment, tested the radio frequency tuning, and performed cluster and data analyses to problem-solve RF coverage and quality issues.
  - Provided project support and technical guidance for the engineering team.

- **Designed a 1900-MHz CDMA network** for the City of Kettering. (New Wave Telecom)
  - Reviewed/approved A&E drawings and obtained municipal approval for site placement.
  - Identified, evaluated, and selected cell-site candidates; conducted isolation/obstruction studies to test signal interference for provider-shared sites

**WORK HISTORY:**

WIRELESS INTERNATIONAL, INC.—East Coast Region (www.wirelessint.com)
*One of the world's leading wireless telecommunications, service provider, and consulting companies.*

**IT Project Manager/Network Consultant, Telecom Network,** 2002–Present
**IT Project Manager/Network Engineer, Communications Next,** 1999–2002
**Design Engineer, New Wave Telecom,** 1997–1998
Currently plan, lead, develop, and manage telecom network design and connectivity; cell-site deployment, integration, and testing; and data analysis for executive and technical reporting.

TOLEDO MOTOR COMPANY, INC.—Toledo, OH (www.tmc.com)
*One of the world's leading consumer companies for automotive products and services.*

**Quality Assurance Liaison/Engineer, Essex Engine Plant,** 1994–1997
Led quality-assurance projects, engineering-problem resolutions, and diagnostic-data analyses.

**EDUCATION & TRAINING:**

THE OHIO STATE UNIVERSITY—Columbus, OH
**B.S., Electrical Engineering,** 1994

**Training & Proficiencies:**

- **Management**—Collaborative Decision Making, Assertive Communications, Time Management, Writing on Target, Project Management, Team Leadership.

- **Networking**—Wireless Engineering; Qualcomm CDMA; Direct Sequence Spread Spectrum; CellCAD; ANET and Design; GSM Protocol & Operation; AMPS, IS-54, and IS-136; Antennas and Link Budget Analysis; and UMTS Terrestrial Radio Access (UTRA).

- **Engineering**—dB Planner and MapInfo for geographical information sharing, Vbscan virus checker, CAMAZE, TEMS Drive Tester GSM, and GIMS (Geochemical Information Management System) RF intercept and propagation tools. Also UNIX, PLC5 (programmable logic control) design/programming, EEC V (electronic engine control), and assembly design.

**PROFESSIONAL AFFILIATIONS:**

**IEEE (Institute of Electrical & Electronics Engineers),** 1997–Present
**SPMN (Software Program Managers Network),** 1996
**PMI (Project Management Institute),** 1995–Present

Contact Data—E-mail: srawwa@yahoo.com • Phone: (703) 264-5657

**RESUME 88: BY JACQUI BARRETT, MRW, CPRW, CEIP**

| | | |
|---|---|---|
| 19522 Antioch Road | **KATE C. BALDWIN** | H: 913.555.3467 |
| Overland Park, Kansas 66211 | kcb@everestkc.net | C: 913.555.2925 |

### UTILITIES / PUBLIC WORKS / TELECOMMUNICATIONS INDUSTRIES
#### Engineer ■ Project / Program Manager ■ Contract Negotiator

DETAIL-ORIENTED AND QUALITY-FOCUSED PROFESSIONAL with 15+ solid years in the utility industry. **Instrumental leader in Secure Communication Services' 17-year success history** of project management, maintaining a stellar track record of client satisfaction, follow up on work sold, and assignment completion on time and **under budget as much as 25%.** Focus is improving service for residential and commercial customers in diverse carrier service areas. Exceptional critical-thinking abilities positively impact technically complex projects. Willingness to listen and compromise has contributed to results in logical decision-making and conflict resolution.

#### —Areas of Knowledge and Experience—

| | | |
|---|---|---|
| ■ Engineering Design | ■ Easement Research/Procurement | ■ Requests for Proposal/Quotation |
| ■ Quality Assurance | ■ Written/Oral Communication Skills | ■ Complex Project Management |
| ■ Marketing Programs | ■ Interpretation of Building Plans/Specs | ■ Resource Management/Utilization |
| ■ Contractor/Supplier Negotiation | ■ Construction Cost Estimates | ■ Field Notes/Measurements |
| ■ Contract Preparation/Execution | ■ Profile Drawings on Wiring/Riser Diagrams | ■ Cross-Functional Team Management |

### PROFESSIONAL EXPERIENCE

**SECURE COMMUNICATION SERVICES, INC.,** Leawood, Kansas       1994 to 2004
DESIGN ENGINEER / PROJECT MANAGER

**Performed hands-on management** of this **design engineering, construction estimating, and project management** enterprise serving the telecommunications industry. Areas of focus include Provisioning Contracts; Marketing; Personnel Recruitment/Supervision; Quality Monitoring; Material Prepare Drawings; Installation Notes; Cost Estimates; and Budget Management. Key clients: Sprint, Everest Communications, and local school districts.

**Marketed contract service to local providers,** secured provisioning contracts, and managed the ensuing projects, ranging from nine months to one year per project. Recruited and managed public/independent contractors on clients' diverse job sites. Detailed engineering specifications and ordered material prepare drawings, installation notes, and cost estimates for a multiplicity of projects. Negotiated permanent easements with property owners for equipment sites, buried cable, and blanket and strip easements in new or existing subdivisions or in rural environments. Collaborated weekly with customers to maintain project integrity.

#### —Achievements in Negotiation—
- **Negotiated *all* project contracts** with Sprint, Everest Communications, Kansas University, local school districts, and other clients.
- **Achieved 100% success in negotiating** hundreds of permanent utility easements with property owners.
  - Applied knowledge of procurement practices, including legal aspects: researched ownership, accessed current warranty deed, performed chain-of-title search, and located existing easements.
  - Negotiated a diversity of easements, including cell sites that sometimes involved enlarging existing sites to accommodate the (larger) cell sites.

#### —Achievements in Budget Management—
- **Continually ran 98% of budget** on Sprint jobs, exceeding contract expectations.
  - **Led major, $125M project** that involved linking seven central office locations via fiber-optic cable.
  - Managed complicated project from initial engineering specifications to final construction inspection.
  - Faced with and successfully overcame numerous challenges, including identifying appropriate location in bedrock to place cable, crossing rivers, and working around oil company pipelines.
  - Collaborated with inspector, city, and highway department to ensure cable was placed at proper depth; met with Corps of Engineers; interfaced with companies such as Panhandle Eastern, Texaco, and Enron for proper specifications for crossing their easements; and orchestrated a number of other details to ensure project was built on time and as designed.
  - Achieved project outcome **within 2% of forecasted budget.**
- **Consistently remained 18% to 25% under project budget** on all other projects.
- **Developed quality checklist,** and then achieved buy-in, improving efficiency of engineering projects that eventually led to **35% reduction in bid prices.**       *(continued)*

*Subheadings are used to call out achievements in specific areas that will be of interest to hiring authorities. The format makes it easy to quickly skim the resume for key information.*

Kate C. Baldwin, Page Two                                    H: 913.555.3467 ▪ C: 913.555.2925

—Achievements in Personnel / Project Planning and Management—

- **Successfully recruited/directed project managers, engineers,** transmission engineers, construction inspectors, and CAD drafters for varied assignments across four states, cultivating a solid network of contractors and referrals.
  - Managed human resources details for up to 20 employees, including health care and regulatory requirements and performance evaluations.
- **Saved 100% on future relocation costs** by identifying clearance problems and then planning reroute of entire communications, initially adding to project cost, but dramatically curbing long-term spending.

—Other Achievements: Service Delivery, Presentations, Awards—

- **Optimized service delivery and specifications** by contributing to new engineering, estimating, and construction procedures for long-distance fiber routes.
- **Delivered presentations to local service providers/employees** on Long Range Outside Plant Planning (LROPP), easement procurement, and fiber routes from Central Office to Central Office.
- Awards: **Young Engineer of the Year** Award, Midwestern Society of Telephone Engineers; **Small Business of the Year,** Leawood Chamber of Commerce.

**BLUE DESIGNS,** Lenexa, Kansas                                              1985 to 1993
TELECOM ENGINEERING SUPERVISOR

- **Created and implemented internal staffing processes** for Long Range Outside Plant Planning for Southwestern Bell projects.
- **Managed Outside Plant Engineering projects** from routine work orders to customized estimates.
- **Applied engineering concepts** such as resistance design, loading, pressurization, dedicated plant, underground cable, buried cable, aerial cable, pair gain, pole lines, fiber cable, and outside plant mechanized computer programs.

**U.S. Electric,** Topeka, Kansas                                              1982 to 1985
TECHNICAL WRITER ASSOCIATE

- **Challenged with concept-to-completion** engineering projects: captured all field notes, secured right-of-way easements, and monitored the proper specification of drafts.
- **Promoted to satellite office manager** at remote location.

## PROFESSIONAL DEVELOPMENT

**Bachelor of Science in Telecommunications**
DeVry University, Kansas City, Missouri

- Outside Plant Engineering Course, Western Electric
  - Multiple Right-of-Way Courses

**Affiliation:** Past Treasurer, Antioch Avenue Betterment Association

**Selected Technical Knowledge:** Microsoft Word, Excel, PowerPoint, and Outlook Express; T1 Integrator; T1 Complete; T1 Mighty Mouth; SDSL Endeavor; Birchlink T & D; PRI/PBX Connect; Alcatel; Wavesmith; DACS.

## Juan Dominguez
3 Rose Lane, Utica, New York 14617
315-767-9089 (Home) / 315-456-0989 (Office)
E-mail: jdomingu@yahoo.com

### SUMMARY

*IT Professional with demonstrated project management and systems implementation capabilities. Excellent ability to assess user needs, establish project specifications, evaluate hardware/software solutions, and supervise installations. Strong hands-on experience with a variety of hardware platforms and software applications, including networking, peripherals, and database management. Experience troubleshooting system problems, providing user training and help desk support, and serving as Systems Administrator for network and database applications.*

### TECHNICAL PROFICIENCIES

| | | |
|---|---|---|
| PC Workstations | UNIX System Administration | Windows 98 / 95 / NT / XP |
| AS/400 Systems | Oracle System Administration | Office Suites (MS / Corel) |
| Peripherals | Novell NetWare 5/6 | Access databases |
| Networks / Telecommunications | Lotus Notes | Project 2000 |
| | HTML | |

### PROFESSIONAL EXPERIENCE

NORTHSIDE CORRECTIONAL FACILITY; Rome, New York (1996–Present)
**Information Services Business Analyst**                                          **2002–Present**
- Direct IT implementation projects related to new facilities, relocation of offices, and upgrade of information systems for department with more than 1,100 employees.
- Manage projects from concept through launch, including developing systems specifications, overseeing vendor and contractor activities, and validating system prior to handover to end-users.
- Confer with management team to assess needs and establish scope of projects.
- Coordinate activities with Tri-County Information Systems (TCIS) to review competitive bidding process and provide bidders with project walk-throughs.
- Function as System Administrator of Sun Solaris UNIX and Oracle Database in support of Jail Management System (JMS). Administer MoRIS system for Sheriff Police Bureau.

**Major Projects:**

*Spearheading project to automate various departmental forms in an effort to reduce large volumes of paperwork. Evaluate potential hardware and software solutions for compatibility with existing platforms and for desired functionality.*

*Defined user and department needs and recommended software solution to provide Sheriff's Quartermaster with improved operating efficiency and enhanced customer satisfaction.*

*Managed the installation and setup of 200+ user data network for the Tri-County Jail and Northside Correctional Facility. Developed specifications, participated in vendor selection, and monitored vendor compliance with contractual commitments.*

*Coordinated the installation, training of personnel, and "go-live" launch of MoRIS system for Sheriff's Zone Offices throughout the county.*

*Established interfaces between MoRIS / JMS and outside agencies, including DCJS, NYSPIN, and Rome Police Department, to facilitate sharing of information among agencies.*

*Managed the relocation of offices for 80 people, including general layout, network and tele-communications cabling, and installation of PC workstations. Supervised contractor activities.*

*(Continued on Page Two)*

*Note how "major projects" are highlighted for this IT project-management professional; the format clearly distinguishes achievements from job duties.*

**Juan Dominguez**                                                                      Résumé–Page Two
315-767-9089  ·  jdomingu@yahoo.com

**PROFESSIONAL EXPERIENCE (continued)**

NORTHSIDE CORRECTIONAL FACILITY (continued)
**Systems Support Technician**                                                          2000–2002
- Coordinated equipment acquisition and installation for AS/400 terminals and IBM Token Ring workstations.
- Scheduled installation, relocation, and repair of computer equipment.
- Managed inventory of departmental hardware and software.
- Installed, configured, and troubleshot LAN hardware and software.
- Assisted with installation and management of a Novell 4.1 LAN serving department's A-Zone facility.
- Supported data communications for Sheriff's Department.

UTICA DEPARTMENT OF TRANSPORTATION; Utica, New York (1993–1996)
**Assistant Project Manager**                                                           1999–2000
- Served on Project Team that designed, installed, and supported automated system for gathering data from road sensors throughout a seven-county region.
- Defined departmental needs for the region and recommended appropriate technology solutions.

**Network Administrator**                                                               1997–1999
- Installed and configured LAN hardware and software supporting 25 locations in seven counties.
- Served on statewide Regional Automation Technical Support Committee.

PORTICO LABORATORIES; Baton Rouge, Louisiana
**Technical Support Manager & Communications Specialist**                               1987–1997
- CNA Certified (1989); WangNet Certified (1985).
- Defined user needs and recommended solutions.
- Planned and managed implementation of integrated manufacturing shop floor management application.
- Supervised and scheduled more than 20 system consultants.
- Supported sales activities through technical support.
- Managed Help Desk activities.

**EDUCATION**

ST. BONAVENTURE UNIVERSITY; St. Bonaventure, New York
**Certificate in Project Management**

ST. BONAVENTURE UNIVERSITY; St. Bonaventure, New York
**Bachelor of Science, Computer Science** *(In Process)*

*References Available Upon Request*

# LEE CARRION

58172 Georgia Hwy. 736 ◆ Townsend, Georgia 31714

Home: 816-937-7270
E-mail: lcarrion@stechu.tec.ga.us

Cell: 816-937-1141
Pager: 1-800-591-7371, PIN# 691 5379

## VISIONARY TECHNOLOGY LEADER

*Project Management* ◆ *Research & Development* ◆ *Strategic Planning & Analysis* ◆ *IT Consulting*
*Team Leadership* ◆ *Product Development* ◆ *Staff Training*

Focused, dedicated and highly motivated professional offering 10 years of solid contributions and blended background in technology management and accounting. Exceptional dedication to growing with cutting-edge technologies and seeking to achieve beyond expectations in every endeavor. Motivational leader and communicator, capable of building cohesion and project engagement across all levels of staff, management, vendors and customers.

Proven expertise in lifecycle project management from conception to completion, driving process improvements at all levels with forward-thinking, strategic-planning attitude to surpass expectations and goals. Accomplished trainer, developing online classes and delivering diversified training to more than 600 professionals. Strong belief in training and education as path to success and positive change.

**Areas of Strength & Expertise:**

- Technology Management
- Networking & Infrastructures
- Change Management
- Virtual Team Leadership
- Customer Service

- Strategic Planning
- Technology Training
- Security Policies
- Regulatory Issues
- Evaluation & Testing

- New Product Development
- Budgeting
- Team Building
- Media, Firewalls & Servers
- Hardware & Software

## TECHNICAL SKILLS

Highly skilled in troubleshooting, resource capitalization, documentation, policies and procedures and new technology launch. Fully fluent in

**Software:** Windows NT 4.0 & Windows 2003 Advance Server, Exchange 5.5, MS Office 2000, Macromedia, Peachtree, Checkpoint Firewall-1, Cisco Basic Routing, Virus Application

**Hardware:** Routers, servers, PCs, media

## PROFESSIONAL EXPERIENCE

**Southeast Technical Institute**                                                    2002–Present

### TECHNOLOGY SPECIALIST

Drive new technologies, coordinating networks in multiple locations. Manage media, firewall, servers and computer labs. Direct projects through virtual teams; supervise and train Information Technology staff. Provide internal customer service, computer troubleshooting for instructors and executive personnel, and external customer service, supporting and training local business community on software and hardware. Collaborate with campus executives and staff to track project progress and ensure fulfillment of IT goals. Develop budgets.

*Achievement Highlights:*

- ◆ Cultivated campus network to support 400–500 students, setting up labs, servers, firewall, routers and Internet access. Designed media labeling for patch panels, implemented policies and procedures, instituted test centers, ordered all technical supplies and trained IT staff.

*(continued on Page 2)*

*The headline and subheading that lead off the resume demonstrate an effective placement of key-words, further supplemented by the "areas of strength" at the end of the profile.*

816-937-7270      LEE CARRION - Page 2      lcarrion@stechu.tec.ga.us

**PROFESSIONAL EXPERIENCE continued (Southeast Technical Institute)**

- ◆ Initiated numerous technology and process improvement measures including scanning forms for campus-wide accessibility, implementing fax online, designing online short-cut learning, planning for phone locations and number schemes and preparing for pending installation of Exchange 5.5.
- ◆ Achieved savings of more than $100,000 through effectively managing extensive Y2K project, devising plan to integrate 1,000 new PCs, operating systems, software upgrades and drivers.
- ◆ Consolidated numerous operating systems to single Windows 2003 Advance Server/Professional 2003, facilitating tech support efforts.
- ◆ Converted main campus from Token Ring to Ethernet, networking labs to accommodate 600 PCs and peripherals.
- ◆ Selected PCs for fullest utilization of computerized lab resources; feature removable drives enabling instructors to have drive information related only to class being taught.

**Atlanta Sports Therapies**      1998–2002

ACCOUNTANT

Trained and supported companies on planning and setting up accounting software, maintained spreadsheets, performed audits on equipment, and set goals to decrease debt ratios, constantly updating on accounting regulations and technology improvements. Managed purchases, sales and rental of property and coordination of international trips. Created 3D images for presentations and maintained digital camera images and scanned images on PC.

**Charlois, Shepard, Pruyn & Black, CPA Firm**      1994–1998

JUNIOR ACCOUNTANT

Supported clients in accounting, training clients and staff on accounting software, ensuring proper use of software, planning budgets and managing accounting books for several companies. Maintained complex spreadsheets, coordinated loan application forecasts and projections, completed tax returns, performed audit procedures on non-profit organizations and supervised bookkeepers.

## EDUCATION & TRAINING

**Bachelor's in Accounting**—Valdosta State University
**Associate's in Business Administration**—Abraham Baldwin College

**Professional Development:**
Extensive **Technical Training** including NetWorld Interop Conference, Windows NT 4.0, Windows Advance Server 2000, TCP/IP, Exchange 5.5, Cisco Basic Routing, Checkpoint Firewall-1, MS Office 2000, NetMeeting, DOS 6.2, Basic Oracle—Introduction Class, Basic Linux—Introduction Class, Mastering the Secrets of VPNs, Voice over IP, Accounting Creative Solutions, Peachtree, QuickBooks Pro.

**Management Training** including Over the Top Zig Ziglar, Becoming a Team Leader, Business & Personnel Management, Dale Carnegie How to Handle Difficult People, How to Be a Supervisor in a Competitive World.

**Pending Certifications & Training in MCSE 2000 & CCNA.**

## PROFESSIONAL AFFILIATIONS / PRESENTATIONS

**Member:** CPA Association, Chamber of Commerce, Toastmasters, Kiwanis

**Presentations:** Technology Mission—2001, Becoming a Leader—2000, Telephone Techniques—1999

## KAULANI MAKINO

507 Bedford Drive, Camarillo, California 93010
Home: (805) 555-1212 | makinopc@hotmail.com

**Systems Engineer / Network Administrator/Analyst with more than 10 years of experience in Secure Wired/Wireless Secure Networks. Computer degree and multiple certifications.**

### PROFESSIONAL EXPERIENCE

**SYSTEMS ENGINEER / NETWORK SECURITY CONSULTANT**      1999–2005
COMPUTER SCIENCES CORPORATION, INDUSTRY SERVICES GROUP, El Segundo, CA

Key technology advisor to health-industry clients during their wireless LAN migrations. Produced life-cycle cost and security analyses involving system requirements determination, modeling, and trade-off studies; baseline configuration; and test plan, criteria, and procedures development.

➤ Collaboratively designed and set up a secure IP broadband-based satellite system that delivered global communications and positioning (GPS) to more than 50 corporate enterprise partners and 10,000 employees.

**NETWORK ADMINISTRATOR/ANALYST**      1995–1998
CONCURRENT COMPUTER CORPORATION, Laguna Hills, CA

Charged with providing secure networking solutions and technical support to industries including academic, aerospace, and scientific. Performed advanced analysis and optimization of network, server, and workstation performance.

➤ Reengineered the company's archaic backup system, replacing it with super-sized shared-disk arrays and pooled devices connected within a secure storage-area network (SAN). The results were reduced backup costs, zero data loss, and a 30% cut in overtime labor.

**SYSTEMS ENGINEER I**      1993–1994
ELECTRONIC DATA SYSTEMS CORPORATION (EDS), Folsom, CA

Performed wireless network feasibility studies for government-specific applications.

➤ Baselined a local prison's wired/wireless network infrastructure. This baseline became the backbone of a bid for a multi-year, multimillion-dollar state prison communications network.

### TECHNICAL SKILLS SUMMARY

**CORE STRENGTHS:** Project planning and management for wired/wireless connectivity (e-mail/groupware/Internet/intranet); hardware/software configuration; RSA-compliant security/firewalls

**PLATFORMS:** Windows NT/2K/XP, Exchange, Active Directory, Linux, UNIX (Solaris, HP-UX, IRIX), Banyan VINES, Macintosh, OS/2/WARP, Cisco, Novel NetWare

**SECURITY SOLUTIONS:** Norton Internet Security Corporate, McAfee Enterprise, Sun Identity Server, Oracle Application Server, Citrix Metaframe Password Manager, Datakey CIP, IBM Client Security, Cisco Secure Access Control

### EDUCATION and CERTIFICATIONS

| | |
|---|---|
| **University of California at Los Angeles CA** | 1992 |
|    *Bachelor of Science in Computer Science (BSCS)* | |
| **Microsoft Certified Systems Engineer (MCSE)** | 1999 |
| **Cisco Certified Internetwork Engineer (CCIE), Security+** | 2002 |
| **Certified Information Systems Security Professional (CISSP)** | 2003 |

*A brief headline-style introduction immediately communicates focus and key qualifications. One key project or achievement is called out for each position.*

# STEVEN I. SACHS

2110 Valley Lane ~ Newton, TX 77479 ~ (281) 855-4252 ~ stevsachs@techtrak.com

*Career Goal:*
## LEAD DEVELOPER / TECHNICAL ANALYST / SENIOR CONSULTANT

## SUMMARY

A dedicated **Information Technology Professional** with experience as an IT consultant, website developer, programmer analyst, and test analyst working with clients in a variety of industries. Effective leadership and client relations skills combined with extensive technical expertise (especially Internet-related). Proven ability to quickly learn and apply new technologies and translate client requirements into valid technical solutions. An effective communicator with clients and team members, easily interfacing between the technical and non-technical. Willing to take on any task and well-respected by peers, clients, and management.

## TECHNICAL SKILLS

*Operating Systems:* **Windows 95/98/NT/XP, UNIX (HP-UX)**

*Languages:* **C++, Visual Basic .NET, COBOL, HTML, JavaScript, Perl, Assembler, UNIX ksh, PowerScript**

*Development Tools:* **Borland C++, Visual C++, MicroFocus COBOL Workbench, ColdFusion Studio, Spectra WebTop and COAPI, PowerBuilder 6.5, S-Designer, SPIM Assembler Simulator**

*Special Technologies:* **SQL, Oracle, Microsoft SQL Server, Allaire ColdFusion 4.5, Allaire Spectra, Rational RequisitePro, Visual SourceSafe Administration, Arena Simulation Modeling**

*Special expertise in Internet technologies*

## PROFESSIONAL EXPERIENCE

WOW CONSULTING—Newton, TX                                                                 2003 to Present
*(A $7 billion global information technology consulting firm)*

### Consultant

Work with cross-functional project teams consulting on technology projects for client companies in a variety of industries. Meet with client representatives and research existing IT strategies to determine requirements and identify opportunities for improvement. Create logical database design, write programs, create test plans, and execute test scripts. Conduct code reviews of junior developers and administer source code control for development teams. Serve as technical resource for Internet-related technologies. Organize documentation for client review and obtain client sign-off on deliverables. Train end users on new applications. Manage junior developers and subcontractors and train junior developers in programming, ColdFusion, and Spectra, as well as in client relations techniques.

*Worked on 5 projects and project phases to date, delivering excellent results to each client company and maintaining a track record of client satisfaction, follow-on work sold, and assignment completion on time and under budget.*

*Selected Accomplishments:*
- Instrumental in securing one of company's first multimillion-dollar custom development Internet projects.
- Received unsolicited *Team Delivery* award from a satisfied client for a project completed under extreme deadline pressures.
- Received several company awards, including *Peer Respect Award, Unsung Hero Award,* and *WOW Values Award.*

*This resume leads off with a Career Goal (or objective) to clearly identify the candidate's goals at this point in his career.*

**Steven I. Sachs** ~ Page 2
(281) 855-4252 ~ stevsachs@techtrak.com

<u>WOW CONSULTING</u> *(continued)*

*Project Highlights:*
- Developed a Knowledge Management prototype of a web-based knowledge management system for an oilfield services firm. Presentation of the prototype won a $5 million contract. First release of the software will allow more than 200 engineers to interact with one another through a Request Tracking system. Final release will have an audience of more than 12,000 and will include content managers.
- Ensured Year 2000 compliance of 5 systems for a financial services firm as Test Analyst. Project phase came in $20,000 under budget, and follow-on work was sold to client.
- For a surgical instrument manufacturer, created 2 PowerBuilder applications that increased productivity of the human resources and engineering departments. Converted 3 DCL scripts to UNIX korn shell scripts. Project phase was completed under budget and accounted for approximately $40,000 of the project baseline. Follow-on work was sold to client.
- Implemented an upgrade of a benefits and payroll package that affected the payroll and benefits delivery for 13,000 employees of a business forms manufacturer. Analyzed 1300 custom-built components and made modifications where necessary.
- Wrote Perl scripts with multipart error-checking routines, allowing more than 500,000 users of an online brokerage firm to perform complex stock option ordering strategies.

<u>TEAM ALPHA CONSULTING GROUP</u>—Oxford, TX                    1999 to 2003
*(Independent contracting group providing website development services for businesses)*

**Lead Internet Developer**

Directed up to 3 developers creating dynamically generated Internet websites for businesses. Served as point of contact for clients to determine requirements and resolve problems. Designed and coded HTML and ColdFusion, wrote Perl scripts, established standards and graphically manipulated images.

*Projects:*
- Created prototype for an Internet-based hotel room reservation system for a conference center. Determined and converted detailed requirements into a logical database and application design. Wrote all scripts in the reservations module. The prototype allowed for increased flexibility of room assignments and checkout, as well as a Year 2000 solution.
- Developed a website for a data warehousing consulting firm. Wrote all HTML, created graphics, and set scope.

<u>NATIONAL INSURANCE COMPANY</u>—Colbo, TX                    1998 to 1999

**Programmer / Analyst** (Internship)

Member of data conversion team that wrote data cleansing and validation programs for a new system that affected 3 million policyholders upon implementation. Accessed validation/data-cleansing software to validate customer addresses and standardize name format.

*Project:*
- Wrote 7 COBOL programs to perform data cleansing and conversion. Programs were written to allow concurrent use in order to improve performance.

## EDUCATION & TRAINING

UNIVERSITY OF HOUSTON—Houston, TX
**Bachelor of Science, Applied Science** ~ Major: Systems Analysis (1999)

*Specialized training:* Advanced ColdFusion Development

# CHAPTER 10

# Resumes for Technology Managers and Executives

- IT, IS, and MIS Managers
- Technology Operations Managers and Executives
- CIOs, Vice Presidents, and Directors of Technology
- Telecommunications Industry Executives
- Technology Industry Management Executives

# MICHAEL JAMES

1845 P Street, NW, #310-C, Washington, DC 20036
Home: (202) 638-1920, Cell: (202) 243-1001, E-mail: mj1207@isp.com

## QUALIFICATIONS SUMMARY

Customer-centric manager with nine years of experience progressing from front-line **software-development positions** to **strategic business unit (SBU)-management positions**. Demonstrated history of success in positioning SBUs for optimal profitability and performance through process maturity using leading-edge concepts such as **Six Sigma** and **Software- and People-Capability Maturity Models (S/P-CMMs)**. Adept at leveraging human capital by identifying organizational and customer needs and developing staff to achieve the optimal skills mix.

| Technical Expertise: | |
|---|---|
| | • Principal Certified Lotus Professional (CLP) Application Developer |
| | • Principal Certified Lotus Professional (CLP) System Administrator |
| | • Certified IBM Government Business Partner |
| | • Certified Microsoft Government Business Partner |
| | • Notes/Domino Development |
| | • Rational Software (Requisite Pro, ClearQuest, ClearCase, SoDA, Robot, Rose) |
| | • LotusScript and Domino Architecture Design and Deployment |
| | • cc:Mail and cc:Mail to Notes Messaging Co-existence and Migration |
| | • Domino.Doc |
| | • SameTime |

| Areas of Strength: | | |
|---|---|---|
| | • Consultative Selling | • Technical Writing |
| | • Requirements Gathering | • Project Scoping |
| | • Project Management | • Liaison Roles |

## PROFESSIONAL EXPERIENCE

**TECHNO SOLUTIONS WORLDWIDE,** Washington, DC                                        1995–Present

Promoted rapidly through increasingly responsible positions during a nine-year career with this global, best-in-class company with a broad portfolio of technology, outsourcing, and equipment lease products and services.

**Senior Manager, Business Applications** (2000–Present)

Administer all aspects of daily operations of this SBU including sales administration and personnel management activities such as staffing, training, performance management, and compensation.

<u>Key Achievements</u>:

Trained in **Carnegie Mellon's Software Engineering Institute's (SEI's) Software and People-Capability Maturity Model (P-CMM),** subsequently implementing key P-CMM practices.

- Defined and integrated more effective and mature processes for work activities, increasing our group's expertise and further differentiating ourselves within the industry.
- Implemented key practices from the Software-CMM focused on the process areas of project planning, requirements management, configuration management, and project tracking and oversight.
- Achieved standardization of software project-lifecycle tools by implementing Rational Software tools.
- Achieved no turnover during a 30-month period, as compared to double-digit averages company-wide.
- Trained corporate software-development teams on maturing their developmental practices.
- Selected by the Divisional General Manager to lead a Divisional process improvement effort.

*Continued*

*Process improvements and process maturity were the areas of deepest interest for this technology manager, so the keywords and achievements that illustrate this expertise are emphasized in his resume.*

**Michael James**                                                   Cell: (202) 243-1001

**Managing Consultant, Business Applications** (1999–2000)

Supervised all projects with full responsibility for the projects' lifecycle—scoping, estimating, closing, risk identification and mitigation, and fulfillment.

Key Achievements:

Refocused the Group to narrow its overly broad product/service offerings to perform only project-based work using web-based technologies and Internet standards and protocols.

- Created new project manager and business analyst positions, transitioning from horizontal markets to vertical markets.
- Identified two optimal platforms/specifications (J2EE and Microsoft .NET framework) and developed staff's technical expertise in these areas.
- Established a highly lucrative market niche as industry experts in our areas of specialization.
- Fostered pipeline growth from $1 million to $8 million and increased the average project size from $70,000 to $325,000 within four years.

Secured and managed the first IBM Websphere J2EE project, with a first major release value of $455,000+.

- Created a viable platform for the company at a time when J2EE web-application servers represented previously unexplored technology for the company.
- Participated in deploying an entire Notes/Domino environment consisting of 700 users and 12 Domino servers to generate substantial savings of time and money for the client.

**Engineering Consultant, Business Applications** (1998–1999)

Served as a technical advisor in support of the selling process, conducting inception and discovery phases to thoroughly evaluate customers' business processes.

- Consulted on technology direction, trends, and solutions for 25+ diverse clients.
- Developed proposals, performed project scoping, created statements of work (SOW), and collaborated with clients on discovery, design, development, testing, implementation, and project management.
- Served as the Practice Area Leader for Operational Improvement with efforts based on P-CMM.
- Served as one of seven members on the business-strategy team, which played an integral role in competitively positioning the company during the Internet revolution.

Previous Positions: **Senior Engineer** (1997–1998); **Engineer** (1996–1997); **Associate Engineer** (1995–1996)

**EDUCATION & DEVELOPMENT**

**BS, Mechanical Engineering,** University of Virginia (UVA), Charlottesville, VA          1995

Introduction to the **People-Capability Maturity Model (P-CMM)** (Three-day course)          2001

Extensive **independent study** on topics including **Six Sigma** and its application to **software development; management; use cases; UML explained/distilled; programming; Rational Unified Process; Peopleware.**

**AWARDS**

- Recognized with a **Horizon Award** for work in developing a new system to distribute system releases and fixes to 15 company locations.
- Nominated twice for the **Technology Excellence Award** for exceptional revenue production.
- Awarded a finalist **Stratosphere Award for "Best eBusiness Solution."**

# MARILYN KOCINSKI

606 Limetree Drive, Morrisonville, NY 12962 ~ (518) 643-3782 ~ E-mail: mk321@gateway.net

## INFORMATION TECHNOLOGIES MANAGEMENT

### QUICK PROFILE:

Creative and results-driven expert in the design, development, and delivery of cost-effective, high-performance technology solutions. Client oriented; an accomplished leader and entrepreneur capable of building motivated and productive teams. Extensive qualifications in all facets of project life-cycle development, from initial feasibility analysis and conceptual design through documentation, implementation, user training, quality review, and enhancement. Experience is balanced and spans a wide spectrum of industries, e.g. electronics, telecommunications, manufacturing, health care, insurance, law enforcement, transportation, and distribution. Excellent verbal and written communications skills.

- **LANGUAGES:** COBOL, Algol, Pascal, Simula, RPG, FORTRAN II, FORTRAN IV, 370 Assembler, PDP-11 assembler, VAX assembler, 8086 assembler, C, C++, BASIC, Visual Basic .NET, Progress, Informix, Dibol, DBL synergy, PowerBuilder, Web Speed

- **DATABASES:** Progress, Oracle, Informix, Ingress, DB2, SQL Server

- **OPERATING SYSTEMS:** EXEC 8, OS/MVS, RSTS, VMS, AIX, UNIX, HP UX, SCO UNIX, CTIX, Windows XP/NT, Windows 95/98/2000, OS/400

- **MISCELLANEOUS:** Visual Basic for Applications, Outlook, Word, Power Builder Data Architect, YACC, LEX, MTS, MQ

### BUSINESS BACKGROUND:

1985–Present    Adams & Cross, Inc., Schenectady, NY
**Technical Director—Information Technology**

Led this organization (a systems solution provider) through a series of upgrades to capitalize on emerging technologies and application enhancements. Concurrently serve as CEO. Established key business relationships with various upper-level managers and technical and financial officers and, on their behalf, have conceived and implemented numerous mission-critical systems and services, examples of which are cited below:

- ➤ 2003–2005: Built version 8.2 of MGA Master installed at Ameraset Assurance Co., Urban Underwriters (Robert Plan), and Material Damage Corp.

- ➤ Directed the re-engineering of a ticketing system for scalability and performance for Lasergate Systems. Installed at American Skiing Corp., Biltmore Estate, and Regal Cinemas game facilities.

**Design allowed Lasergate to take small peer-to-peer network-based application and re-engineer to a high-transaction-volume system that allows American Skiing to function effectively. ($1.5 million project).**

*(continued on Page 2)*

*Note how something as simple as a distinctive font used for the name, combined with a wide horizontal rule, makes this resume stand out. Results of each project and position are highlighted in bold, underlined text.*

continued     Adams & Cross, Inc.
**Technical Director—Information Technology**

➢ 2001–2003: Progressive Insurance—Using Automation Resources MGA Master, built a usage-based auto insurance policy-writing and accounting system. System uses GPS and cellular technology to rate based on time and position risk. Information is then gathered from the insured vehicle and compiled into a bill. System also provides statistical reporting based on a mixture of traditional property insurance and usage-based insurance.

**Significantly, Internal I/S quoted $10 million and 5-year project duration. We did it in 1½ years and for just under $1 million.**

➢ 1994–2000: Brooke Corporation—Using Automation Resources Agency Master, constructed large WAN-based agency cluster resulting in a client/server system with UNIX-based databases and NT-based databases to handle insurance agency policy management, accounting, and imaging.

**The benefit gained by Brooke was a system allowing them to readily acquire 60 agencies throughout Kansas, Colorado, and Nebraska, thus building one of the first agency clusters.**

➢ 1997: MGA Master—Instrumental in the design and construction of a complete policy-writing system with integrated imaging and workflow management for a paperless office. System also had integrated MVR and CLUE lookup. Installed at Connecticut Specialty.

**System allowed MGA to sell and service more than $20 million in premiums (PIP and PD) with fewer than 20 people.**

➢ 1996–1998: Nokia—Designed, built, and delivered a quality control tracking system for Nokia's Telecommunications Division.

➢ Installed an accounting system for the company's U.S. operations.

➢ Designed and built a customs export control system to track purchase of electronic components.

**The benefit to this client was that it allowed them to more effectively manage and control all parts installed in their computer and telecommunications equipment.**

➢ 1987–1992: Shands Hospital (University of Florida), University of North Carolina, Atomic Energy of Canada—Designed, built, and delivered a computer-controlled imaging system to assist physicians in locating tumors. Designed and built a system to control radiation therapy machines used to treat tumors.

**This was significant, as it allowed users to design new therapies for patients with cancers in the head and neck areas. With the new system, patients could be treated with greater dignity, not having to be marked with a grid in ink.**

1980–1985     Wingate & Associates (a Digital OEM retailer)
**Vice President**

**EDUCATION:**

■ Case Institute of Technology, Cleveland, OH: BS in Physics, 1983
*Honors:*
■ Awarded Dayton C. Miller Prize for thesis.
■ State of Ohio Awards: 1st Place, Earth Science; Honorable Mention, Chemistry
■ Recipient of the National Science Foundation Scholarship to Georgia Tech

**MARILYN KOCINSKI ~ Page 2**
**(518) 643-3782 ~ E-mail: mk321@gateway.net**

## RICHARD C. TOBER

147 Windsor Drive, Rossford, Ohio 43460
419-666-6224    rctmismaster@aol.com

### Information Systems Management

Results-driven **MIS DIRECTOR** with project management expertise overseeing information system functions, computer operations, and systems programming. Maintain excellent rapport with senior management team to analyze computer system and plant needs, submit recommendations and proposals, and develop plans for systems development, operations, installation and implementation while maintaining system integrity. Skilled at empowering end-users and translating technical information in non-technical terms to achieve quality and maintain efficiency. Excellent project / process leadership skills and proven ability to lead organizational change.

Project Management ~ Systems Integration ~ Process Improvement ~ Quality Assurance
Strategic Planning ~ End-User Training ~ Procedures Development ~ Troubleshooting
Relationship Management ~ Facilitation / Presentation ~ Budget Management / Analysis

| | | |
|---|---|---|
| **TECHNICAL OVERVIEW:** | IBM AS/400 Model 500 RISC | Printer Languages: QMS, RJS, ZPLII |
| | Languages: RPG400, CL, AS/400 Query, VB | Barcode Languages: Intermec IRL, EZ Builder |

### CAREER HISTORY

| | | |
|---|---|---|
| **DIRECTOR OF MIS** | **CSX PRODUCTS – Walbridge, OH** | **1983–Present** |

*Recruited to CSX Products in 1983 as Manager of Data Processing and promoted to Director of MIS in 1994. CSX Products is a multifaceted company that produces wrap products used in the construction, automotive and packaging industries. Randall Corporation in Monroe, Louisiana, recently purchased CSX.*

High-profile position reporting directly to Vice President of Finance. Accountable for development and maintenance of operations and procedures for information processing at all CSX facilities. Assess needs to develop new information processing systems and improve existing program designs. Successfully interfaced corporate offices and off-site locations to align strategies and achieve goals. Provide training and assistance to end-users to ensure peak levels of performance. Lead Process Improvement Teams to improve accounting and cost accounting systems. Facilitator for plant-wide process improvement programs. Responsible for 2 direct reports and 80 end-users at 4 remote sites.

Took over IS department in 1983 with existing IBM System 3 that ran all applications in batch environment. In 1986 converted to IBM System 38, enabling CSX to shift all applications online, giving users control and eliminating data entry. Converted to AS/400 Model B30 in 1994; currently using Model 500 RISC. Major applications include order entry, shipment posting, bill of lading, invoicing, A/R, A/P, G/L, hourly payroll, production / inventory, print plate tracking system, and bar-coded product identification tags.

SELECTED HIGHLIGHTS AND ACCOMPLISHMENTS:
- Played leadership role in driving information systems through acquisition process.
- Spearheaded conversion from IBM System 3 to IBM System 38 in 6 weeks, achieving reduction in annual hardware lease cost of $60K and leading to $40K reduction in personnel costs.
- Relocated CSX AS/400 data center and had remote sites operational in two hours. Entire process, including local users, completed over weekend for business operation on Monday.
- Guided conversion from batch to online processing, transforming most applications. Reduced order entry time from 3- to 4-day cycle to *immediate* and invoicing from 3–4 days to day of shipment, saving substantial time and significantly decreasing chance of error.
- Developed and implemented physical inventory system that reduced inventory process from 3-day, handwritten, manual input procedure with plant downtime of 2 days to 1-day process utilizing Intermec Trakker 2420 ANTARES portable scanners and uploading data to AS/400.

### EDUCATION

B.S., INFORMATION SYSTEMS: University of Toledo, Toledo, Ohio

| | | |
|---|---|---|
| ADDITIONAL TRAINING: | Situational Leadership | Qual Pro Coursework: Process Improvement, Design of Experiment |
| | Visual RPG Seminar | DMC Coursework: RPG 400, Database Design, Control Language |

*This is a concise presentation of an accomplished career. It's easy to pick out the keywords and significant accomplishments.*

# VALERIE VAN GOGH

11710 Old Georgetown Road, Apt. 7C, Rockville, MD 20852
Home: (301) 770-3232, Work: (703) 729-6066, E-mail: vvangogh@isp.net

## INFORMATION TECHNOLOGY (IT) SERVICES MANAGER

**IT professional** with a demonstrated ability to lead cross-functional technical and non-technical groups in developing and implementing cost-effective and efficient applications. **Specialized experience in developing, administering, and supporting global human resources information systems (HRIS).** Skilled at establishing, deploying, and supervising helpdesk operations, onsite and remotely. Experienced in formulating and executing technology budgets and in implementing key initiatives under budget and within deadlines.

### Areas of Strength:

- Analytic Problem Solving
- Collaborative Teams
- Leadership/Training

- Troubleshooting
- Helpdesk Administration
- Technology Solutions

- Systems Design/Development
- HRIS and Management IS (MIS)
- Policy/Procedures Development

### Technical Skills Summary:

**HRM Software/Databases:**

Personnel Quality System (PQS), ExecuTrack (E/Track) Database, PeopleSoft 8.0, HRM Software Package, E-Performance Appraisal Database, Cyborg 3.2/4.5/5.0, Authoria Web Authoring Software, HR Web Charter

**Software:**

MS Office XP/00/97, Adobe Photoshop CS, Netscape, Mac Draw, Lotus Notes R4/R5, Adobe Acrobat 6, Hot-Sync, Macromedia Dreamweaver MX, MS Photo Editor, Lotus Smart Suite Millennium, Visio 2002, Lotus Easy-Sync, HTML, Adobe Illustrator CS, Exchange 5.5, MS Project 02/00/98, Adobe PageMaker 7 for Windows, ColdFusion, MS Outlook, MS Explorer, McAfee, NetObjects Team Fusion 4.0, Java, WinZip, Easy CD Creator 4/5, NetObjects Team Fusion Client 2000, Adobe PageMaker 6.5 & 7.0 for Mac, Adobe Acrobat Distiller 5.0, Remedy, Internet Explorer, MS FrontPage, Mac Typestyler, Citrix ICA Client

**Network:**

Local Area Network/Wide Area Network (LAN/WAN), Internet, Intranet

**Client Operating Systems (O/S):**

Windows XP, 2000, Professional, NT, 98, 95; Mac OS X

## EDUCATION

Candidate, **MBA (Technology Management),** Strayer University, Sterling, VA, May 2005

**BA, Computer Science,** University of Maryland, College Park, MD, 1996

Academic Honors:

Graduate Fellowship, 1996–1998

Member, Academic Honor Society

Dean's List

Continued

*A broad technical and professional overview is presented on page 1, followed by position details and relevant achievements on page 2. Good design makes it easy to absorb key information in a quick read.*

**Valerie Van Gogh**                    **Home: (301) 770-3232**

## PROFESSIONAL EXPERIENCE

**ARIEL ENTERPRISES, LLC,** Ashburn, VA                              2000–Present
**HR Services / HR Information Systems (HRIS) Project Manager** (2002–Present)

Administer lead responsibility for all helpdesk procedures, policies, and operations for human resources information systems (HRIS) among six Northeast Region locations in four states.

- Supervise onsite and remote helpdesk operations, working with the global HRIS group.
- Develop, track, and monitor helpdesk budgets for use by top managers, including the Executive Vice President (EVP) of HR, the Vice President (VP), and the Chief Financial Officer (CFO).
- Collaborate with supervisor to formulate the annual budget of approximately $1.8 million, incorporating cost-center funding allocations delineated by top-level management.
- Serve as the webmaster and project lead for the corporate Internet Vendor Diversity Initiative (VDI) website with responsibility for creating the site's infrastructure, layout/architecture, and graphics.
- Provide global technical-administration support for two key databases.

Key Achievements:

- Improved efficiency and eliminated operational obstacles by establishing helpdesk policies/procedures.
- Trained staff among operational companies on resolving minor in-house issues to prevent escalation.
- Participated on the User Acceptance Testing (UAT) Team to test the helpdesk system before going live.
- Participated in the design of a website on the corporate intranet to enable applicant recruiting, screening, and selection.
- Implemented web-based online-assistance center for questions regarding benefits and HR policies and procedures.
- Implemented a web-based tool for processing travel requests, replacing a labor-intensive system.

**Management Development Specialist** (2000–2002)

Managed a national, 15-person staff in maintaining/securing/administering the two mission-critical databases. Served as the U.S. Regional Manager providing daily coordination of scheduling, planning, and troubleshooting of end users' functional and technical problems.

- Supported 50 end users, nationwide; assessed staff training needs and evaluated performance.
- Oversaw development and implementation of all technical standards and policies/procedures.
- Served as the U.S. Regional Lead for the Management Development & Training Group.

Key Achievements:

- Led an eight-member cross-organizational integration team for two applications.
- Served as the co-leader for quarterly and yearly management development reviews organization-wide.
- Managed an eight-person team to implement an extensive training initiative.

**GRADUATE SCHOOL FOR CONTINUING EDUCATION,** Washington, DC                  1997–2000
**Program Training Specialist,** HR Resource Management Team

Managed the Equal Employment Opportunity (EEO) and classification curricula, which consisted of 30 courses.

- Oversaw training delivery to federal employees, military personnel, and private-sector participants.
- Served as Project Manager for a contract with the military to train 5,000+ personnel nationwide.
- Planned curricula, scheduled instructors, established guidelines, and developed training materials.

Key Achievements:

- Served as co-designer/administrator of the school's website, establishing its web presence.
- Directed multiple project phases in implementing a web-based course-registration process.

**Page 2**

# FRANK P. MEYERS

414 Lincoln Avenue • Bay Shore, NY 11706 • (631) 949-2722 • dataman@sys.net

## *Senior Manager* — Data Center Operations

Information Technology professional with a steadfast career ensuring the integrity of IBM mainframe operations within a Dual Site Data Center environment supporting the global travel industry. Select qualifications include

| | | |
|---|---|---|
| – Data Center Management | – Production Control | – Data Migration |
| – Crisis Management | – Project Management | – Systems Conversions |
| – Mainframe Operations | – Change Process Management | – Technical Documentation |
| – Disaster Recovery Procedures | – Upgrades / Installations | – Vendor / Client Relations |
| – Automated Operations | – Data Safety / Climate Control | – Quality Control |

## PROFESSIONAL EXPERIENCE

Global Mainframe, Rego Park, NY                                                      1985–2005
*— subsidiary of New York and American Stock Exchanges*
**Senior Manager of the Shared Data Center**

### DATA CENTER MANAGEMENT
*— Batch Operations, GSCC Operations, Network Support, and Middleware Operations*
- Managed Shared Data Center operations with full accountability for the cost-effective, on-time management of mainframe functions with a focus on input/output trade data supporting the travel industry.
- Served as primary point of contact on a 24-hour, 7-day-a-week basis, in charge of coordinating critical disaster-recovery procedures directly impacting the stability of data-center operations.
- Developed and revised departmental procedure manuals to assist staff in all aspects of mainframe operations.
- Implemented Quality Control methods to ensure full compliance with company policies and procedures.
- Interfaced extensively with Help Desk teams to provide immediate support on pressing technical issues.
- Generated weekly statistical and department performance reports for senior management review.
- Delivered excellent customer service through situation analysis and timely resolution of escalating problems.

### STAFF MANAGEMENT & TRAINING
- Guided all aspects of personnel management and leadership of shift operators in areas of interviewing, hiring, training, supervision, delegation, evaluation, and promotion recommendation.
- Provided continuous hands-on training of operators to promote the development of skills in anticipating, identifying, and troubleshooting technical problems.
- Ensured a committed support team through cross-training of Computer Operations and Production Control staffs on system upgrades, disaster-recovery tests, and data-migration projects.
- Coordinated weekly staff meetings to discuss departmental issues, project initiatives, and action plans.

### PROJECT HIGHLIGHTS
- Directed crisis-management efforts in response to 9/11, serving as point of contact for the major clients.
- Worked diligently to generate and upload (emailed as an auxiliary method) several weeks of Listed, Over-the-Counter, Surveillance, Netting, and Night of Comparisons trade data to the global travel community.
- Utilized Autoroute (output) to provide Internet services (Artmail) to more than 100 firms.
- Provided in-service training in areas of Datatrak (input) operations with an emphasis on downloading data to mainframes utilizing TCP/IP, data re-blocking (ISPF/PDF), JCL creation, and data verification procedures.

— continued —

*The chronological experience section of this resume is broken down into functional areas to show this candidate's broad technical and managerial expertise.*

# FRANK P. MEYERS

(631) 949-2722 • dataman@sys.net
Page 2

**PROJECT HIGHLIGHTS, continued**

- Delegated instructions to Tech Support, Network, Batch Operations, and Middleware Operations (9/11).
- Led mission-critical software implementation initiatives, overseeing all phases of beta testing cycles and revision of operational procedures in accordance with new system functions and requirements, as follows: ***RTTM GSCC** (2000–2001)*; ***Y2K** (1997–1999)*; ***Beta T+3 Settlement** (1993–1995)*
- Played a vital role in the parallel testing and implementation of outsourcing acquisitions.

**Computer Operator,** Swiss Watches, New York, NY                                        1980–1985

- Joined this watchmaker as a Distribution Clerk working in the I/O Control Area and Micrographic Department overseeing a broad scope of reports processing and distribution services.
- Recognized for ability to master DataGraphix, Allen, and Bruning equipment and IBM systems, receiving an accelerated promotion to Computer Operator assisting with diverse mainframe operations.

# TECHNICAL EXPERTISE

### *Mainframe Hardware*

| | |
|---|---|
| ***Processors:*** | 3090-200, 400, 600, 3084-Q96, 4381-P12, 3038-J24, 3033 AP, 3033 UP, 158-3, IBM 9672 (dual sites), Stratus, DEC (Compact) |
| ***DASD:*** | 3380 (including D & E models), 3350, 3330-11, 3330-1, STC 4305, EMC, Shark |
| ***Tapes:*** | 3480, 3420 |
| ***Printers:*** | 3800-3, 3800-1, 4348, 3211, 3211, 1403, 3900 |
| ***Communications:*** | 3725, 3705, 3174, 3274, 3745, 3172, Cisco, BCN |
| ***Other:*** | 8100, 3890, 3044, IBM 2914 and various T-Bar switching units, DataGraphix Computer Output Microform (COM), Network Systems Corp. Hyper Channel equipment, controllers, redundant coupling facilities |

### *Mainframe Software*

MVS, ESA, OS/390, VM, VTAM, JES2, TSO, CA-1 (Tape Management), CA-7 (Job Scheduling), CA-11 (Re-run, Re-start), TCP/IP, MVS/SP2 (XA) MVS/SP1, JES2 MAS, JES2 RJE, JES2 NJE, ACF/VTAM, BTAM/SP, CICS/VS, IDMS, NCCF, NPDA, JES328X, 8100 HCF, Hyper Channel (HO15, NETEX, BFX), BDT, FTP, NDM, JCL, UCC 7, UCC 11, TLMS II, Super Console, STAM, SAR, SYSPLEX, ACF2, Omegamon/MVS, Information Management, TSO, ISPF/PDF, SDSF, AF/Operator, Tivoli Netview, SOLVE, CA-7, CA-11, FDR/ABR, RACF, z/OS 1.2 with JES2, CICS/TS version 2.2, DB2 version 7, MQSeries version 5.2, Boole/Babbage, IMS, RACF, DCL, DVP, RTTM

### *Data Storage / Tape Management*

Storage Tek Tape Silo Systems: Timberline 9490, 488, 4410

### *Networking / Desktop*

Windows 9x, 2000, NT, XP; LAN/WAN; UNIX; TCP/IP; Microsoft Office Professional; Remedy

# PROFESSIONAL DEVELOPMENT

15+ years of company-led training in broad areas of mainframe operations and general management

# NORMAN STEVENS
6701 Murietta Ave. ◆ Valley Glen, CA 91405
(818) 994-6655 ◆ Fax (818) 994-6620 ◆ NS5555@aol.com

### IS / MIS MANAGEMENT ◆ TECHNOLOGY DEVELOPMENT
*Voice & Data Communications / Integration ◆ Information Technology*
*Project / Budget Management ◆ Strategic Planning*

Expert in the design, development and delivery of technology and communication solutions to meet challenging business demands. Extensive qualifications in all facets of projects from initial feasibility analysis and conceptual design through implementation, training and enhancement. Excellent organizational, budget management, leadership, team building, negotiation and project management qualifications.

*Certified in Lucent, Octel, NEC & Northern Products*

## PROFESSIONAL EXPERIENCE

FOODCORP INTERNATIONAL, Valley Glen, CA ◆ 1996 to Present
*Achieved fast-track promotion through positions of increasing responsibility for multi-billion-dollar international company with 30,000 employees worldwide.*

**Manager of Telecommunications** — 2002 to Present

Technology Executive responsible for management of $15 million department budget. Fully accountable for overall strategy for telecommunications technology acquisition and integration, vendor selection and negotiation, usage forecasting, workload planning, project budgeting and administration. Plan and direct implementation of emerging telecommunications solutions at all FoodCorp domestic locations consisting of 125 facilities. Provide direction regarding telecommunications technology to FoodCorp affiliates throughout U.S. Lead cross-functional project teams; supervise technical and administrative staff with 20 direct reports. Fully accountable for department's strategic vision and leadership.

Representative achievements include the following:
◆ Directed $40 million annual MCI Network conversion at 200 locations within six months, saving company $15 million over a three-year period.
◆ Designed and managed implementation of network utilizing Lucent and Octel at more than 100 locations in 12 months, realizing annual cost savings of $1 million.
◆ Served as Technical Project Director for $12 million consolidation of East Coast Headquarters with West Coast location.
◆ Facilitated move of corporate headquarters, involving 3,000 employees, over a 4-day weekend.
◆ Implemented videoconferencing technology at more than 60 sites.
◆ Built a 4-digit dialing network for FoodCorp locations within a four-month period.

**Assistant Manager of Telecommunications** — 1997 to 2002
**Management Trainee / Intern** — 1996 to 1997

## EDUCATION

**B.S. in Political Science** ◆ UNIVERSITY OF CALIFORNIA, Berkeley, CA

**Professional Development / Continuing Education:** Various American Management Association Workshops and Courses; BCR Technical / Technical Management Courses

*Detailing only one professional position in his resume, this individual includes "representative achievements" that imply he could certainly add to this list. His one-page resume makes a strong statement.*

# Robert Sandoval

5555 East 55th Street
Brooklyn, New York 11213
(718) 657-9871

## Management ▪ Technical Architecture ▪ Global

Collaborative manager with more than 13 years of experience in the development and implementation of mainframe and distributed applications. Recognized for skill at evaluating, recommending and selecting information technology. Areas of expertise and accomplishment encompass

- ❏ **Start-up Operations**
- ❏ **Project Management**
- ❏ **Critical Production Support**
- ❏ **Strategic Planning**
- ❏ **Needs Assessment**
- ❏ **Design Validation**
- ❏ **Database Administration**
- ❏ **E-Commerce Solutions**
- ❏ **Vendor Relations**

## Professional Experience

Argabrite Financial Brokerage, New York, New York                 1994–Present
**Vice President / Manager—Corporate Systems Technology Services** (2003–Present)

Selected to oversee the start-up of the Corporate Systems Technical Architecture Group and develop a three-year Technology Plan. Collaborate with partners to understand business requirements and identify technological solutions to business problems. Provide technology vision and direction, evaluate and research emerging technology and validate technical architecture alternatives. Furnish high level of service to clients in the delivery of technical architecture services. Build key vendor relationships to enhance support, influence product direction and exploit functionality.

Serve as a member of the Enterprise Applications Technology Governance Committee that evaluates and selects standard software products for application development. Manage **strategic initiatives** in three key areas of the organization: Financial Systems, Global Human Resources and Office of the General Counsel.

**Financial Systems:**
- ❏ Develop and maintain plans, formulate strategy, coordinate project activities and review status of critical deliverables.
- ❏ Oversee the evaluation, planning and selection of the hardware to support the Oracle Financials 11.0 release upgrade. Identify hardware and network requirements for infrastructure testing. Schedule vendor evaluations and research Oracle's Network Computing Architecture.
- ❏ Direct performance stress test, evaluating network and hardware resource utilization from strategic locations, network predictive modeling and hardware capacity planning. Evaluate intelligent storage devices for scalable, cross-platform data sharing.
- ❏ Participate on the Books and Records technical evaluation team to review FTI application architecture and recommend technical architecture, as well as on the E-Commerce team to evaluate and implement the Ariba/E-Commerce solution with Oracle Financials applications.

**Global Human Resources:**
- ❏ Evaluate global technical architecture and recommend deployment strategy. Perform design validation and determine requirements for network performance test to evaluate the global architecture for scalability, availability and performance.
- ❏ Coordinate network upgrades, outstanding requests and related network issues. Evaluate ETL and OLAP tools for data mart implementation and define the global architecture.
- ❏ Formulated data strategy with project team and collaborated with project planning team. Direct global network redundancy and business resumption testing.

**Office of General Counsel:**
- ❏ Assist the project team with Web architecture alternatives, content management and text search tools, and document management software evaluation.

**Vice President / Manager—Private Client Information Management** (1999–2003)

Directed distributed and mainframe database administrators (DBAs) providing database support services to facilitate database development and implementation. Oversaw data integration, high-priority issue resolution, business and technical planning, allocation and management of resources and status reporting. Created and managed work plans, technical solutions and documentation and developed database management services. Managed critical production support for more than 80 distributed and 15 mainframe databases.

*(continued)*

*"Mr. Sandoval was looking for a senior technology position within a global environment. His resume is designed to highlight his leadership and start-up skills, along with his technical competencies."*
*(Writer's comments.)*

# Robert Sandoval

5555 East 55th Street
Brooklyn, New York 11213
(718) 657-9871
Résumé—Page Two

---

### **Professional Experience** (continued...)

**Financial Systems Strategy:**
- Standardized and consolidated the firm's General Ledger and SubLedger applications using Oracle Financials ERP applications.
- Directed team of DBAs to manage all database changes; establish, configure and maintain the application and database environments; define and implement database and application migration procedures; and formulate the change management process and procedures.
- Established off-site standby database disaster environment; implemented Neonet messaging software to synchronize data across platforms; and completed benchmark testing of Web reporting application.

**Corporate Library Electronic Archiving & Retrieval:**
- Coordinated selection and design of database to store historic statements on optical disk storage. Oversaw database design, tuning and implementation.

Additional projects included database evaluation, selection and production database implementation for the Human Resource Data Mart, and database support of the PeopleSoft database implementation for Global Human Resource Information Processing.

**Vice President / Manager—Enterprise Information Management & Technology** (1994–1999)

Managed group of DBAs providing database support to Global Systems & Technology. Provided all aspects of database management services. Implemented mainframe database disaster recovery process for business resumption, Distributed Relational Database Architecture (DRDA) data sharing, and database system software installations and upgrades. Initiated distributed database support and negotiated distributed database support services with clients.

---

## Technical Skills

| | |
|---|---|
| **Hardware:** | Sun, Sequent, IBM, Amdahl, Hitachi, DEC, Compaq |
| **Software:** | DBMS: Oracle, Oracle Express, DB2, IDMS, ADABAS, SQL/DS |
| **Operating Systems:** | Solaris, SunOS, MVS, Windows NT, Windows 98, Windows 2000/XP |
| **Front Ends:** | PowerBuilder, Developer/2000, Visual Basic .NET |
| **Web:** | Oracle WebServer, Netscape, IIS |
| **Languages:** | Java, C, C++, PL/SQL, Pro*C, COBOL, CICS |
| **Network:** | SQL*NET, Net8 |
| **Protocols:** | TCP/IP, SPX/IPX, ODBC, DRDA |
| **Middleware:** | Neonet, Shadow Direct, MDI Gateway |
| **Case Tools:** | IEW, ADW, PowerDesigner |
| **ERP:** | Oracle Financials General Ledger, Accounts Payables, Purchase Orders, Fixed Assets, Project Accounting, PeopleSoft Human Resources |
| **System Management:** | Enterprise Manager, Patrol, Autosys, PVCS, NetDeploy |
| **Data Warehouse / ETL:** | Informatica |
| **OLAP:** | Impromptu, Powerplay |

---

## Education

Pace University, New York, New York
*Currently pursuing* **M.B.A.** in **Strategic Management**

Baruch College, New York, New York
**B.A.** in **Finance**, June 1992

# MICHAEL HEWITT

215 Broadway, Apt. 2G • New York, NY 10005
212.398.2349 Res • 212.654.1325 Cell • mhewitt@hotmail.com

## IT DIRECTOR / CHIEF TECHNOLOGY OFFICER

10+ years of IT experience including 8+ years of broad-based management in Systems Design and Development, Implementation, and Support. Strategically and cost-effectively utilize technology in alignment with corporate goals. Consistently improve delivery times and service levels while reducing costs. Excel at strategic planning, high-performance team-building, project management, and implementation of best practice methodologies and continuous improvement programs. Certified Six Sigma Black Belt. Proven areas of expertise include

- Strategic and Business Planning
- Vendor Negotiations & Management
- Best Practices/Continuous Improvement
- Budget Development & Management

- Infrastructure Architecture & Support
- Organizational Development
- Project Management
- Data-Center Management

- Applications Development
- Rapid Deployments
- Structured Methodologies
- Large-Scale Deployments

## PROFESSIONAL EXPERIENCE

**VP INFORMATION TECHNOLOGY**                                       2001–PRESENT
**AMERICAN TELEPHONE ✧ NEW YORK, NY**
*Provider of residential and commercial telecommunications services.*
**SERVICE DIRECT ✧ NEW YORK, NY**
*Provider of telemarketing services to such customers as AT&T, MCI, Direct TV, and Harris Publishing.*

Reporting to the President/CEO, recruited to manage IT and telephony operations for American Telephone and quickly awarded added responsibilities for sister company, Service Direct. Oversee all IT functions including data-center management, vendor relationships, technical support, application development, financial monitoring, and disaster-recovery planning. Manage $10 million operating budget and direct activities of 20+ staff.

Challenged to improve productivity and reduce costs through improved uses of technology. Utilized Six Sigma methodologies and collaborated with department managers to analyze and document process and system workflows. Authored plan to improve software development process, consolidate/upgrade servers, and establish consistent hardware/software standards to eliminate unstable, highly mixed operating environment.

Installed redundant servers and increased line capacity. Launched massive effort overseeing teams of programmers (using C and 4GL in UNIX environment) to review and rewrite more than 75 key software applications. Implemented change control and process documentation for all aspects of the business including new software and telephony upgrades. Deployed hardware monitoring system including multi-tier paging alerts for system issues. Initiated Knowledge Repository and Project Management Office to share best practices.

*Notable Accomplishments:*
- Consolidated and stabilized servers, improving hardware uptime from 70% to 99%.
- Reduced software downtime from 50% to <2%.
- Transitioned firm to employ reusable object-oriented programming modules for applications development, slashing time-to-deliver by 50%.
- Implemented rigorous development and testing processes and decreased software defects by 60%.
- Slashed manual processes by 50% with resultant reductions in overhead costs.
- Altered staffing model to include third-shift operations; improved on-time delivery of data to clients by 50%.
- Reanalyzed network traffic, eliminated unnecessary routing and equipment, and reduced costs by 33%.
- Completed migration of all servers from SCO UNIX to RedHat Linux, reducing UNIX-based application development time 25% by standardizing on single operating system.
- Implemented centralized system for corporate Quality Assurance group to monitor call-center activity; decreased call-rejection rate by 5%.

**Page 1 of 2**

*Changing the resume focus from telecom-specific to cross-industry expertise enabled this individual to appeal to hiring authorities from different industries. Accomplishment statements are loaded with numbers.*

**MICHAEL HEWITT**
212.398.2349 • mhewitt@hotmail.com                                                    **Page 2 of 2**

**APEX SERVICES ✧ CEDAR RAPIDS, IA**                                                  **1992–2001**
*$650M telemarketing firm with 90 call centers and approximately 14,000 employees.*

Earned successive promotions to positions of greater responsibility based on consistently exceeding targets and goals.

### DIRECTOR OF APPLICATION DEVELOPMENT ✧ 1998–2001

Managed, directly and indirectly, 60 personnel (Managers, Programmers, Programmer Analysts, System Analysts, Team Leads, EIS Support Specialist, and Project Managers) accountable for the ongoing maintenance, development, and implementation of projects for 90 outbound Call Centers supporting $650 million in revenues. Challenged to improve responsiveness and ROI of efforts, increase quality of work as defined by quicker development times and fewer software defects, and integrate disparate technologies arising from recent company acquisition.

Developed and managed $6 million budget. Aligned IT team with business units to develop business expertise and improve quality and responsiveness in support of 400+ new monthly work orders. Qualified new business opportunities, drafted responses to RFPs, and oversaw the design and implementation of software for new clients to send/receive data. Led architecture direction strategies and promoted Visual Basic, Java, C, and HTML development in an UNIX/Oracle DBMS environment. Established data warehouse providing customer access through secure Internet site.

*Notable Accomplishments:*
- Increased efficiency of development group by 25% through matrix organizational structure that allowed for responsive shift of experts to meet user needs.
- Reduced software defects from 450/month to 35 by assigning developer accountability, establishing firm rules for object-oriented module reuse, and introducing advanced code-generation tools.
- Reduced staffing by more than 25% within first 6 months while supporting increased business requirements.
- Managed core team of 18 for successful Y2K program converting 90 client applications in less than 6 months.
- Decreased the amount of trouble tickets by 90% using new quality and development procedures.

### INTERNAL BUSINESS MANAGER ✧ 1996–1998

Managed staff of 12 responsible for all internal business-systems development including payroll, timekeeping, data modeling, and request-processing software. Represented the company throughout the entire sales process to ensure that internal IT capabilities were communicated effectively and implemented according to company standards. Evaluated profitability and viability of new business opportunities presented by independent business units.
- Managed selection and implementation of Lawson Financial Package to on-time delivery.
- Implemented TCS timekeeping system used by 90 call centers in support of 14,000 employees; eliminated payroll errors, improved labor tracking, and aided decision-making.
- Developed automated interview system, reducing HR interviews by 70%.

### AT&T SYSTEM MANAGER ✧ 1994–1996

Led staff of programmers developing customized outbound telemarketing applications in support of AT&T client producing $60 million in revenue. Served as company liaison on IT matters. Managed 100+ new project requests monthly.
- Developed plans for 500-seat AT&T center and implemented auto-load system allowing 10 simultaneous data feeds, reducing process time from 8 hours to 1.
- Set up redundant 3780 communication servers, increasing uptime with third-party verifies by 25%.

---

### EDUCATION

University of Pennsylvania ✧ BA, Management Information Systems
Six Sigma Certification ✧ Black Belt ✧ 2000
Oracle Designer 2000 Certification ✧ 1997

# THOMAS C. BURRELL, MCSE, CNE, CCNA

5687 Brookstone Drive
Chicago, IL 60601
Phone: (213) 786-8083 ▪ Email: tom@burrellhome.com

---

### INFORMATION SYSTEMS DIRECTOR / NETWORK SERVICES MANAGER
#### Proven Technical & Management Expertise in a Career Spanning 15+ Years

Technically sophisticated and business-savvy management professional with a pioneering career reflecting strong leadership qualifications coupled with "hands-on" IS and networking expertise. Maintain focus on achieving bottom-line results while formulating and implementing advanced technology and business solutions to meet a diversity of needs. Superior record of delivering simultaneous large-scale, mission-critical projects on time and under budget. Team-based management style and excellent interpersonal/communication skills.

*IT Strategic Planning / Business Solutions / Team Leadership / Budgeting / Project Management*
*Capital Expenditure Planning / Contract Negotiations / Vendor Relations*

---

## Professional Experience

**INFORMATION SYSTEMS MANAGER**, Avery Clinic Health System, Chicago, IL                    **1997–Present**

Recruited to upgrade and replace obsolete technologies at this world-class health care organization with more than 2000 users in 15 remote locations. Hire, train, develop, and lead a 20-person technical team. Manage a $2 million capital budget and $1.2 million operating budget. Scope of position is expansive and includes departmental direction and full design, installation, engineering, implementation, support, training, administration, and management authority for:

- LAN/WAN Network Services
- 24x7 Data Center Computer Operations
- Applications Systems
- Web/Internet Design & Operations

- PC Desktop Systems
- UNIX Systems Administration
- Database Administration
- Help Desk Operations

Spearheaded transition from outdated organization-wide and departmental technologies to highly functional, streamlined, and cost-effective client-server technologies and business solutions that have dramatically improved efficiency, decreased expenses, and optimized data integrity and safety.

### Key Projects & Achievements:

- Directed design and installation of the complete $8 million LAN/WAN infrastructure. Utilized state-of-the-art technologies to provide network connectivity of disparate mainframe, AS/400, UNIX, Windows NT, Novell, and PC systems.

- Completed, in just 8 months—22 months ahead of schedule—a complex $15 million project forecasted to take 2.5 years and involving replacement of more than 30 systems.

- Delivered $2 million in cost savings through aggressive negotiation of contracts and pricing on a budgeted $10 million for hardware/software purchases and consulting services.

- Saved more than $1.2 million in technical consulting fees by negotiating complimentary network design services from vendors.

- Performed the work of 3 full-time equivalents, slashing labor expenses substantially by expanding personal responsibility to include UNIX, network, and database administration.

- Decreased inventory, application pricing, and licensing expenses $750K by establishing standardization for applications, PC desktops, and networking systems.

- Defused and resolved long-standing conflicts and department problems; elevated morale and decreased high employee turnover rates, achieving the best retention rate in the company.

(continued)

---

*The subheading "Key Projects & Achievements" helps to break up what could be an overly dense Professional Experience section. Important technical certifications are noted at the very beginning and detailed at the end of the resume.*

**THOMAS C. BURRELL** ▪ Page 2
(213) 786-8083 ▪ tom@burrellhome.com

**INFORMATION SYSTEMS MANAGER**, 1997–Present, continued

- Managed from planning through completion a $2.4 million Windows NT workstation and network printer implementation project. Delivered on time and $600K under budget.
- Attained consistent 99% up time by implementing disaster recovery and fault tolerance plans. Instituted the first highly reliable corporate-wide, centralized backup system.
- Championed introduction of Internet/intranet/Web technology, corporate-wide email, shared calendaring, and online meetings. Set up and managed a TCP/IP environment, installed a Novell network, and implemented a data warehouse database.
- Collaborated on numerous management committees including the Systems Application Selection Team; Chair of the Network, Operations, and Security Team; and the Y2K Implementation Team.

**NETWORK MANAGER**, Stillings, Inc., Akron, OH                                         1997

Managed and delivered, ahead of schedule, a nationwide, $10 million+ network project involving development of a fully redundant credit verification system. Administered a multi-server LAN supporting Novell, UNIX, and Unisys systems, and supported 2000 users in 850 remote sites.

**DIRECTOR OF TECHNICAL SERVICES**, ProComp U.S.A., Inc., Cleveland, OH                1994–1996

Built and managed Information Systems, Technical Support, Production, and Repair Departments for this start-up Novell Reseller and PC manufacturing firm. Supervised staff, oversaw computer operations, and managed budgets. Saved $2 million the first year by renegotiating manufacturing contracts and relocating production to reduce costs and improve shipping schedules. Developed and trained a team to provide support to a culturally diverse international customer base.

**COMPUTER TECHNICIAN**, MTI Systems, Beachwood, OH                                    1993–1994
**SENIOR SYSTEMS SUPPORT SPECIALIST**, A.B. Dick Company, Brecksville, OH             1989–1993

## Education & Credentials

**AMERICAN INSTITUTE OF COMPUTER SCIENCE**—Chicago, IL
**B.S. candidate in Computer Science**, completed 3 years of study

**TOTAL TECHNICAL INSTITUTE**—Chicago, IL
**Computer Systems Support Certification**—Intensive 2-year program

**Technical Certifications:**

- **MCSE**—Microsoft Certified Systems Engineer
- **CNE**—Novell Certifed NetWare Engineer
- **CCNA**—Cisco Certified Networking Associate
- **CNA**—Novell Certified NetWare Administrator

**Recent Technical Training:**

- Cisco Router Programming & Internetworking
- Network Administration for UNIX Systems
- ATM—Asynchronous Transfer Mode
- Windows NT 4.0 Network Administration
- AIX UNIX Advanced System Administration
- Cisco Enterprise Management Solutions

- Bay Networks—TCP/IP, SNMP, FDDI
- EDI—Electronic Data Interchange
- Windows 95 Support
- Windows NT 4.0 Technical Support
- Internet Information Server
- SQL Server 6.5 Database Administration

## MICHAEL BEATON

133 Fuchsia Way, Toronto, Ontario M4R 5T6
Phone: 416.567.4081   Cell: 416.436.0333   E-mail: mike.beaton@triptik.ca

### CHIEF INFORMATION OFFICER

**The conduit between IT and Business Operations**

Highly successful, industrious, hands-on senior IT executive with an exemplary record of realigning underperforming IT departments. Conceive and implement unique strategies to optimize business operations, elevate productivity, and boost revenue. Deliver solutions as a change agent, visionary, and forward thinker, capable of critically evaluating and responding to diverse information technology issues. Thrive in a fast-paced environment of continuous challenges. Proactive leader, coach, and mentor; gain employee confidence and utilize their talent and knowledge. Shrewd and tenacious business strategist who exudes energy and confidence to excel and deliver. Core business competencies include:

| | | |
|---|---|---|
| • Executive Leadership | • Change Management | • Solutions Delivery |
| • Matrix Management | • Business Continuity | • Yield Management |
| • Web-Based Technology | • Project Management | • Sarbanes-Oxley |
| • Mergers & Acquisitions | • Strategic Direction | • Business Transformation |

### PROFESSIONAL EXPERIENCE

M.B. I.T. Consulting, Toronto, Ontario                                   2003–present
**MANAGING DIRECTOR**

Provide IT leadership, direction, and support in the following core business areas: outsourcing, IT and business infrastructure, realignment, strategic delivery, and Sarbanes-Oxley Act. *Key contracts have included the following:*

***Reed Bailey & Associates***
- Researched and compiled the Project Charter relating to the Sarbanes-Oxley Act for a Fortune 500 company.

Avalon Media, Toronto, Ontario                                            2002–2003
**GROUP VICE PRESIDENT—Information Technology (CIO)**

*Recruited to implement a corporate Information Technology Strategic Plan for the broadcast (ATV), print (the* Toronto Tribune*) and Internet (TTI) divisions and to boost financial performance.*

- Secured approval for an $11 million automated newsroom system to replace obsolete technology for the *Toronto Tribune,* maintaining their advantage in a competitive environment.
- Conceived and executed a capital-requirement cost-reduction strategy, reducing expenditures by 50%. Prioritized capital projects based on benefits, cost, flexibility/investment, and risk.
- Reduced project costs by 100%; achieved by eliminating projects, establishing standards, promoting reuse, and streamlining common services.
- Played the lead role in renegotiating supplier contracts across all areas: telecommunications, software, hardware, and consulting, leveraging the company's purchasing power.
- Co-represented Avalon Media in consultations with PriceWaterhouseCoopers to establish process controls for the implementation of Sarbanes-Oxley, ensuring risks were mitigated and full compliance achieved.
- Instrumental in reintegrating two primary business units during a massive restructuring plan to improve financial performance.
- Accountable for devising and monitoring a $30+ million operating budget, managing $15+ million base capital budget, and leading 180 employees, tasked with supporting 4,400 customers in Canada and abroad.

**Page One of Two**

*A clear focus and unique "branding statement" lead off this resume. Positions are highlighted by strong, specific achievements.*

MICHAEL BEATON Page Two

ATV Television Network (ATV), Division of Avalon Media, Toronto, Ontario 2001–2002
**VICE PRESIDENT—Information Technology**

- Directed a complex integration of Dragon Communications and ATV IT departments after a recent acquisition, using best practices of modern organizational design. Refocused the new unit to function as an external professional service, reversing a negative perception of the IT department.
- Designed, developed, and implemented the technology relocation for 650 Dragon employees into the ATV facilities without business interruption.
- Reduced a spiralling IT operating budget by 10% each year during the integration of CKCC, CKCY, and BORTv.
- Partnered with the V.P. Sales Operations to consolidate 3 advertising-support revenue systems, saving $4.5 million and enhancing productivity and customer service.
- Charged with selecting 70 employees and sourcing external consultants tasked with building a $44 million, 15-year business case. Secured approval from senior management team; selected and negotiated agreement with international vendor. Established a unique joint venture with BlockStar, ATV's largest competitor, during the final stages of the business-case project.

Dragon Communications, Toronto, Ontario 1997–2001
**CHIEF INFORMATION OFFICER & VICE PRESIDENT**

- Recruited to realign an underperforming and disjointed business unit after significant senior-level terminations. Hired skilled replacements, refocused IT to prioritize projects, and acquired additional funding to sustain positive business contributions.
- Appointed as Dragon key representative to the ATV Integration Team with representation from external consultants. Ensured Dragon's technology, process, and human resource requirements were addressed.

British Broadcasting Corporation (BBC), London, U.K. 1980–1997
*Held the following progressively responsible Directorships:*

| DIRECTOR—Corporate IT Planning | DIRECTOR—Regional IT Support, Overseas Dept. |
|---|---|
| DIRECTOR—Corporate Telecommunications | DIRECTOR—National Data Centre |
| DIRECTOR—Applications Development & Support | |

*Selected accomplishments include:*
- Played the pivotal IT leadership role during a complex 3-year corporate rightsizing, meeting the mandated 30% target.
- Reduced the 1994 IT operating budget by 37%, while increasing values to core business units.
- Worked with Deloitte Consulting to plan, acquire, and implement a new SAP corporate finance system to meet cost-reduction initiatives and Year 2000 compliance.
- Consistently acknowledged for the ability to break down the communication and technology barrier, enhance the perception of IT, and work with all stakeholders to optimize technology, boost productivity, and reduce costs.
- Contracted and oversaw numerous external suppliers to assist with IT operations and keep pace with the corporation's need for cost constraints. Drove the importance of IT as an integral and valuable entity across the corporation.
- Managed teams appointed to design and implement multimillion-dollar IT projects to gain competitive advantage.

## EDUCATION

University of Waterloo, Waterloo, Ontario 1979
**BACHELOR OF COMPUTER SCIENCE**

Strong proponent of continuing education. Completed numerous technical and leadership programs.

# PETRA BRANDT

183 VALLEYVIEW DRIVE, BELLE VERNON, PA 15012 ~ 724.872.9030 ~ petra@home.com

## Senior Director, Information Technology

Set Standards in Information Services and End User / Supervisor Training… Improved Customer Satisfaction…
Planned, Managed and Rolled Out High-Profile Projects—All On Time, On Budget

~ Cost Control ~ Budgetary ~ Productivity Enhancement ~ Custom Applications Programming ~
Process Automation ~ Program Planning / Evaluation ~ Resource Planning ~ Quality Assurance /
Quality Control (QA / QC) ~ ISO 9001 Certification ~ Marketing Program Development ~ Sales /
Marketing Training ~ User Training ~ Client Connectivity ~ Internal / External Clients ~ Vendor
Selection and Negotiation ~ Multidisciplined Team Leadership ~ Clinical Research ~ Clinical Testing
~ Clinical Trials ~ Health Care, Oil Industry Experience ~

## Quality Improvements, Process Automation, Project Management Success

STEWART COMPANY, BELLE VERNON, PA                                              2000 to Present
Leading U.S. Provider ~ Esoteric and Routine Clinical Testing, Clinical Trials ~ $200M Division

**Senior Director, Information Technology**                                    2002 to Present
$200M Division ~ 7 Direct Reports, 65 Indirect ~ First Site Y2K-Compliant ~ $13M Annual Budget Always Met
~ Boosted Morale ~ Direct Report, Regional Information Technology Director

— **RETAINED STAFF:** Reduced IT employee turnover from 36% to less than 7% in first year…

— **INITIATED LONG-TERM STRATEGY:** Selected a vendor who authored short-term and long-term LAN
improvement / expansion strategies—nonexistent prior to my involvement…

— **STANDARDS IN PLACE:** Led 10-person team defining software life cycle development SOPs, secured
ISO 9001 certification for laboratory with no carry-overs—involved lab staff in design reviews, defined
time lines and software requirements up-front, and standardized documentation / validation…

— **EXPANDED TRAINING:** First person in IT to conduct team-building workshops—with minimal budget,
launched a team agreement incorporated as a model for IT that improved customer and staff
satisfaction… developed sales training in 1 month that streamlined technology and got 500+ IT,
sales / marketing and business administration decision-makers up to speed seamlessly…

— **IMPROVED QUALITY:** 1 of 8 senior leaders on Quality Management System Steering Committee—
results improved customer satisfaction and quality…

— **CUT THE EXCESS:** Shaved $60K while negotiating telecommunications, PC support, customer and
laboratory systems support contracts…

— **OVER / ABOVE:** Adept at translating technical aspects of connectivity options, regularly requested by
sales / marketing team to detail client non-technical staffs in features…

**Director, Customer Systems**                                                2000 to 2002
Staff of 22, 4 Managers ~ $4M Budget ~ Improved Customer Assistance ~ Reported to Senior IT Director

— **SET COMPANY STANDARD:** Rolled out Web-based system generating 90% ROI in first year—saved
$200K+ annually… directed 7-person team who replaced DOS-based systems and created mechanism
guaranteeing 3-month upgrade at customer site… negotiated $45K savings on original bid… product
adopted as corporate standard for hospital customer systems… 400+ systems in use today…

— **EXTERNAL CUSTOMER HELPDESK 24 X 7:** Created single point of contact for customer connectivity
issues, led implementation for round-the-clock technical support…

(continued)

*Highly relevant results are highlighted at the beginning of each accomplishment statement, making this
a hard-hitting, easily skimmed resume. Note the original heading that replaces the traditional
"Professional Experience" wording.*

| 724.872.9030 | **PETRA BRANDT – 2 of 2** | petra@home.com |
| --- | --- | --- |

**Director, Information Systems** ... STEIN LABS, PITTSBURGH, PA — 1995 to 2000

Esoteric Testing Laboratory and Diagnostics Manufacturing Company ~ Staff of 5 ~ Direct Report to CEO ~ Implemented First CPU Interfaces and Customer Connectivity ~ Highly Visible Role with Clients

- **RESUSCITATED CONVERSION:** Because a consultant fell short of expectations, took over project and had it in place in 4 months—managed 2 programmer analysts who converted 2 CPT/UNIX systems into a MUMPS-based system expediting customer processing...

- **COMPETITIVE EDGE:** Brought in customer inquiry / reporting system on time, on budget—created first online access to test criteria and automated patient report printing, keeping Stein "cutting edge"...

- **UNIQUE OFFERINGS:** Led implementation of first bidirectional customer interface (HL-7 and ASTM) and rolled it out with a targeted marketing program... successfully introduced Internet-based database of antibiotic-resistant organisms, enabling end users to upload, track and trend data against entire U.S....

**Project Manager** ... HILL ARCHITECTS, PITTSBURGH, PA — 1993 to 1995

Software Vendor, Turnkey Distribution Systems ~ Successfully Facilitated DEC System Conversions for Multi-Billion-Dollar, Fortune 500 Clientele ~ All Projects On Time ~ Domestic Locations ~ IS Project Teams, Up to 16 Members

**Programmer / Analyst** ... THE CANCER CENTER, BELLE VERNON, PA — 1991 to 1992

World-Renowned Cancer Research Center ~ Section for Infectious Disease ~ Designed First MUMPS Medical Research Database for Clinical Trials Replacing "3 x 5 Card" Cataloging ~ Wrote Laboratory Tracking System Maximizing Storage while Better Tracking Specimens / Cultures ~ Trained Technicians through Pharmacist, Secretarial and Physician End Users

**Programmer** ... SIGMA OIL COMPANY, DHAHRAN, SAUDI ARABIA, and EL PASO, TX — 5 Years

#1 Oil Producer Worldwide ~ Improved Real-Time Electrical Power System Control Efficiency ~ Instrumental in Developing a Purchasing / Traffic System Expediting Shipments to Saudi Arabia

### Education

UNIVERSITY OF PITTSBURGH, PITTSBURGH, PA
Bachelor of Science in Business Computer Information Systems

CONTINUING EDUCATION—STEWART COMPANY: Project Management, 2003... Supervisory Skills Certificate Process, 2001... Leading Your Team, 2000... Innovation Process, 2000

### Publications

Brandt, Petra. "Human/Computer Interfaces: A Randomized Trial of Data Entry and Editing Formats," SCAMC Proceedings, The Computer Society of the IEEE, Washington, DC, August 2004.

Brandt, Petra. "A Database for Clinical Research in Infectious Diseases," Proceedings Quarterly of the MUMPS Users Group, New Orleans, LA, June 2003.

Brandt, Petra. "User-Interface Design: A Study in Data Entry Methods," AAMSI Congress Proceedings, San Francisco, CA, May 2002.

## JOSEPH C. CARTER

7713 Hilltop Terrace
Kansas City, Missouri 64113

jcarter@alpha.com

Home: 816-444-5551
Cell: 816-367-2290

### Senior Management Executive — Technology
### MBA — Marketing & Finance / MSEE — Telecommunications

**Contributed to the Growth & Strategic Direction of Highteck for the Past 20 Years**

### Qualifications, Profile & Career Highlights

Vision, Strategy, Execution & Leadership
Profit & Loss Management
Operations & General Management
Start-up & Turnaround Leadership
Global Sales & Marketing Management
International Business Development

Strategic Alliances & Partnerships
New Business Development
Contract Negotiations
Team Recruiting & Training
Consensus Building & Team Motivation
Sales Force Management

Executive with a career highlighted by consistent achievements in driving revenues, competitive advantage, and profitability. Recognized for drive, determination, and willingness to challenge the status quo, and for outstanding leadership talents — create proactive business environments where others can be successful, and where synergy can be achieved in support of business objectives. Dedicated to goal attainment and to giving unselfishly to others.

**Developed a start-up business within Highteck with $2 million in seed money that grew to $17 million in revenues within six months — continued to build the business to $200 million in sales, a net profit of 17%, and 400 employees over a four-year period.**

**Took over a failing business with a growth rate of 5% CAGR and a profit rate of -11% — turned it around into a business that grew 10-fold in three years and continuously maintained an 11% profitability.**

**Overcame market downtrends and continued to maintain a $750 million business while competitors have experienced a 75% decline — added services that grew to 41% of total revenue in four years.**

**Outstanding personal sales record — honored with the *Foundation Club Award*, Highteck's most prestigious award given to only 24 individuals in the history of the company.**

### Professional Experience

HIGHTECK TECHNOLOGIES — Palo Alto, CA                                    1984 to Present
*Advanced through sales, marketing, and general management positions as this leading technology company grew from $1 billion to $50 billion.*

**Vice President / General Manager — Telecommunication Sales** (1999 to Present)

Manage a sales force (600 sales and support professionals; 24 representative organizations) responsible for $750 million in sales to telecommunication companies in 29 countries in Europe, Asia, and Australia/New Zealand. Hold P&L responsibility; manage a $130 million budget.

Transitioned primary focus from product to service sales to overcome market downturns — **added services to the product mix that in four years grew from 6% to 41% of total revenue — continued to maintain sales at $750 million while competitors experienced a 75% or greater market decline.**

**Reduced cost of sales from 17 to 11 cents per order dollar (35% reduction from historic norms)** by instituting more efficient sales models and updating sales-force automation. Led team implementing the field portion of an Oracle system for order placement, quotations, billing, and order tracking.

Initiated the utilization of third-party representative organizations that generated an additional $50 million in sales and are continuing to yield results.

Cultivated strategic partnerships for joint ventures and technology sharing and negotiated contracts as large as $100 million for products, systems, professional services, and support.

(continued)

*Skills, qualifications, strengths, and examples of specific accomplishments are highlighted up front in the summary, while quantifiable achievements are printed in bold further down in the document.*

**JOSEPH C. CARTER**
816-444-5551 • jcarter@alpha.com                                                                  **Page Two**

*Highteck – Continued:*

**Division General Manager – Communications Test Division** (1996 to 1999)

Selected to turn around a failing business selling $25 million in test equipment while achieving a growth rate of only 5% CAGR and a profit rate of -11%. Refocused the business on products targeting high-growth markets; held responsibility for P&L management, R&D, finance, marketing, product support, manufacturing, and HR.

> **Grew the business 10-fold to $250 million and outsourced $74 million in manufacturing to third parties. Maintained an 11% net profit** during a three-year period.
> Leveraged technologies that reduced product design cycles from two years to nine months and eventually outsourced non-critical product manufacturing to third-party overseas manufacturers.

**Division General Manager – Technology Management Services** (1992 to 1996)

Envisioned, started, developed, and built a new service business for a product-oriented company – the position was responsible for managing all core business functions including P&L, R&D, manufacturing, sales support, marketing, finance, and HR. Managed a $14 million R&D budget and a $56 million operating budget.

> Sold the concept of Highteck's capability of delivering a service-based business that delighted customers while achieving the highest level of sustained profitability of any good/service ever provided by the company.
> Provided an outsourcing model that was both profitable for the company and cost effective for customers, with services resulting in a **30% to 50% reduction in customers' expenses.**
> **Grew the service-based business from start-up and $2 million seed money/zero revenues to $17 million in revenues with a net profit of 17% in just six months, progressing to 400 employees worldwide and to $200 million revenues** over a four-year period. **Continued to maintain a 17% profit margin** for all four years.
> Managed $3 billion in other companies' test-equipment assets.

**Group Marketing Manager** (1988 to 1992)

Managed worldwide marketing initiatives for the RF/microwave products portion comprising several divisions representing $500 million. Responsibilities included market analysis, product definition, marketing materials, sales procures, sales force training, and technical support to the sales organization. Reported in to four Division Managers, with 75 staff members worldwide.

> **Achieved a CAGR of 13% per year and a 10% net profit.** Led the introduction of 50 new RF and microwave test products (with a $50,000 average cost per product) over a four-year period.
> Established a common format for marketing materials and reduced time to competency for the field sales team by developing improvements in sales-force training and new-product introductions.

**Previous Experience** (1984 to 1987): Sales Engineer/District Manager/Area Sales Manager ending with a reporting structure of 5 District Managers and 60 Sales Engineers and responsibility for a $150 million total sales volume.

> **Recognized as a top sales producer** and for never failing to achieve a sales quota. Qualified for *President's Club* for sustained performance and for setting examples for others to follow.
> Received numerous other awards including Highteck's *Foundation Club* (Highteck's most prestigious sales award that has been given to only 24 people in the company's history) and *Top Sales Engineer, Top District Sales Manager*, and *Area Sales Manager*.

## Education

MBA, Marketing & Finance – Northeastern University (1984)
MSEE, Telecommunications – Massachusetts Institute of Technology (1982)
BSEE, Telecommunications – Boise State University (1980)

# ALEX C. SESMYO

4431 McBride Grove
Houston, Texas 77008                     acsesmyo@txl.net                     713.595.5291 Residence
                                                                             713.309.5293 Cellular

## PROFESSIONAL FOCUS

Managerial / leadership role where broad-based experience in business and technology
will produce positive, profitable results in a constantly changing, challenging work environment.

## PROFESSIONAL PROFILE

- Highly effective business executive, manager, and leader with an entrepreneurial edge for success.
- Passion for technology to create improved operating efficiencies and a competitive market position.
- Diverse and successful sales and marketing background in both goods and services—solid grasp of accounting, finance, business operations, and team leadership.
- Personally bootstrapped, built, and recently sold a vastly profitable small business that achieved recognition in *INC Magazine*'s 500 Fastest Growing Private Companies.
- Broad knowledge of both hardware manufacturing and software development utilized to reduce risks in implementing information management systems throughout an organization.
- Willingness to accept challenges and identify cost-effective, functional business solutions.
- Unquestioned commitment to business integrity, regulatory compliance, and customer-service excellence; penchant for details with drive, motivation, and initiative in any endeavor undertaken.

## KEY AREAS OF CIO & BUSINESS EXPERTISE

### MANAGEMENT FOR A BALANCED OPERATION

- Pattern of continuous improvements in systems, policies, practices, and procedures to enhance organizational efficiency with success in gaining team-member support to make needed changes.
- Solid understanding of cost and pricing relationship and its impact on sales growth and profitability.
- Maintained accounting systems and practices to ensure sound financial management company-wide.

### COST-EFFICIENT UTILIZATION OF TECHNOLOGY

- In-depth understanding of applying technology to maximize operational success and profitability.
- Highly skilled in selection and implementation of cost-effective computer software/hardware.
- Directed development and documentation of proprietary software projects in diverse environments.
- Preferred environments: Visual Basic .NET, SQL Server, Microsoft BizTalk Server, XML, AS400, and UNIX.

### TEAM-BUILDING FOR ORGANIZATIONAL STABILITY

- Extensive team-leadership experience in building and/or supporting organizational stability.
- Skilled in recognizing teams' competencies and leading members to attain realistic goals.
- Communicate organizational goals with clarity, vision, confidence, and a roadmap for success.
- Keep team members focused by apprising of progress toward both short- and long-term goals.
- Readily identify and resolve challenges inherent with goal achievement.
- Consistently earned trust / respect of team members by recognizing / rewarding their contributions.

### STRATEGIC PLANNING FOR LONG-TERM SUCCESS

- Maintain a "big picture" view of an organization's operations.
- Ability to develop and support a vision of where an organization can best operate to serve the interests of the group.
- Experienced in formulating and sustaining an effective, ongoing strategic plan.

*Core competencies are highlighted in box format and are followed by specific business results. Career history appears on page 2.*

# ALEX C. SESMYO
### Page Two

acsesmyo@txl.net                                          713.595.5291

## MARKETING AND SALES FOR GROWTH AND EXPANSION

- Long-term successful track record in sales and sales management—have consistently taken goals seriously and exhibited relentless commitment to reaching / exceeding desired results.
- Led new start-up venture to *INC. 500* status by developing and directing a successful marketing effort, identifying prospective customers, and developing the means to sell both *to* and *through* them—a cornerstone of my marketing philosophy.
- Directed numerous individual marketing campaigns to competitively position products and elevate perceived value.

## PRODUCT DEVELOPMENT / MANAGEMENT FOR COMPETITIVE ADVANTAGE

- Skilled at assessing market potential for a proposed product by performing market analysis and evaluating potential success at a price necessary to be profitable.
- Experienced in all facets of product development from inception through market introduction, including coordination of product development, packaging, support, and marketing materials to deliver a complete product in a timely manner.

## LEADERSHIP / MANAGERIAL EXPERIENCE

**PRESIDENT / CIO / PARTNER—IGLIO TECHNOLOGY SYSTEMS, INC.**
**The Woodlands, Texas, 1990–Present**
- Founded and managed company throughout its 15-year business cycle; specialized in providing servers, software, complex hardware integration, and logistical support to software developers.
- Developed / promoted client / server package marketed through more than 200 independent dealers.
- Achieved recognition in *INC Magazine*'s 500 Fastest Growing Private Companies list.
- Led company through a successful acquisition by XLNC, a Phoenix-based software developer.
- Transitioned into role of External Executive Consultant—increased sales by 48% during integration phase, increased gross profit margins by 33%, and reduced product warranty claims by more than 93%.

## RELEVANT EXPERIENCE

- Prior to starting a business in 1990, employed in Sales / Developer positions with two start-up computer service companies in the Dallas–Fort Worth area, 1985–1990.

## EDUCATION / MILITARY

- The University of Iowa, Iowa City, Iowa—MBA, 1985; BBA, Finance, 1982
- United States Army Special Forces—Green Beret; Honorable Discharge
- Military service as an Intelligence Analyst

## COMMUNITY INVOLVEMENT / INTERESTS

- The Woodlands Council—Four Years. Involved in a major reorganization that resulted in significantly improved customer service, stringent financial discipline, and the completion of a new City Hall, Art Center, Aquatic Center, and youth athletic complex—all completed without a property tax increase.
- Member—The Woodlands Technology Commission—Four Years.
- Interests: Family, technology, golf, and professional baseball.

# Allison Brown

2345 Marcus Avenue, Apt 611

| Phone: 305-123-1234 | Miami Beach, FL 33140 | abrown@aol.com |

## INFORMATION TECHNOLOGY / BUSINESS SYSTEMS EXECUTIVE
*Aligning Information Technology with business to create solutions and opportunities that drive change*

Dynamic, innovative professional with proven track record designing, developing, and delivering successful **cost-effective, high-performance technology and information systems solutions.** Results-driven, analytical problem-solver with extensive experience in identifying opportunities and developing new business strategies and implementation framework to meet challenging multinational business demands. **MBA, fluent in Spanish,** conversant in French. **Particular areas of expertise** include **strategic planning, staff motivation,** and

| | | | |
|---|---|---|---|
| • Financial Services | • Project Management | • Internet / Website | • Auditing |
| • Leadership | • Customer Service | • Securities Issuance | • Cash Management |
| • Risk Management | • Systems Administration | • Crisis Management | • Change Management |
| • Presentation | • Negotiation | • Budget / P&L | • Latin America |

**Keyword summary:** Internet Security, LAN/WAN, Fast Ethernet, contingency/disaster recovery, CRM, RAS, SAS, RDBMS, Sun platform, troubleshoot, UNIX, client/server, data warehouse, OLAP, Oracle, internal technical operations, desktop support, global integrated financial system, asset management, website development and marketing

---

## PROFESSIONAL EXPERIENCE & SELECTED ACCOMPLISHMENTS

**VISA INTERNATIONAL,** Miami, FL                                                        2002–Present
*Vice President, Information Systems,* **Latin America & Caribbean Region**
Provide day-to-day leadership and direction in all aspects of technology for a region of VISA known for its innovation and change management. Technology unit supports more than 450 users including 5 remote sites in Latin America, and includes project management, consulting, programming and development, infrastructure (LAN/servers), and desktop and help desk support. Manage 20 employees and 5–10 consultants.
- Redirected, restructured, and turned around under-performing internal technology division into strong, successful, customer-focused, results-oriented strategic unit.
- Identified problems, provided viable solutions, persuaded senior management to accept proposals, and improved employee morale and involvement, which increased internal customer satisfaction by 55%.
- Initiated, created, and spearheaded several large-scale, high-profile enterprise projects:
  - Data Warehousing: accessing regional transaction-level data from multiple mainframes.
  - Paperless Office: strategized, planned, and implemented pilot to reduce paper flow and storage.
  - Customer Resource Management: evaluated and piloted tools; selected instrument and implemented.
  - Migration from Token Ring LAN to Ethernet: became model for other regions to follow.
- Developed processes, procedures, and guidelines for project documentation, process flows, RFPs, pilot programs, hardware and software licenses, and purchases; reduced costs by $500,000.
- Member of several high-profile technical and change management teams working to improve global systems.

**FEDERAL FARM CREDIT BANKS FUNDING CORPORATION,** Jersey City, NJ                    1991–2002
Financing and Securities Issuer Division of Farm Credit System, $75 billion nationwide network of banks/associations
*Director and Vice President,* **Information Systems & Securities Operations** (1994–2002)
Managed 12 professionals: securities processing analysts, programmer/systems analysts, systems administrators. Recruited to turn around troubled Securities Processing Unit and create a Technology Department.
- Founded and developed high-performing technology group that identified business problems, recommended technical solutions, assessed business/technical risks, worked with users to instill ownership, and delivered projects on schedule and at budget.
- Planned and implemented corporation's access to Internet: developed Internet plan, security policy, and firewall product; provided Internet training; implemented and maintained Internet connection.

*(continued)*

*The slogan beneath the headline is an eye-catching, concise, effective summary of this individual's executive philosophy.*

**ALLISON BROWN**
abrown@aol.com

## PROFESSIONAL EXPERIENCE & SELECTED ACCOMPLISHMENTS

**FEDERAL FARM CREDIT BANKS FUNDING CORPORATION,** Jersey City, NJ
*Director and Vice President* (1994–2002) (Continued)
- Special Assignment: Built and launched Corporate Website (January–September 2001)
  - Identified and formulated site content and marketing of website; interviewed business units and translated business needs into creative web content; created website layout; established technical parameters and programming standards; worked closely with web programmers, graphic artist, and Internet lawyers.
  - Saved company more than $110,000 in project costs.
  - Consulted/advised other FFC banks and outside Board Member corporation on website development.
- Developed interactive financial application which increased productivity by 30%.
- Planned and established corporate disaster "hot" site providing immediate recovery of all critical systems.

*Assistant Vice President* (1992–1994)
- Formulated and directed long-range plan to change corporate architecture from proprietary minicomputer environment to company-wide client/server model, which reduced support costs by 50%, improved service quality by 75%, increased access to critical information by 100%, and ensured future adaptability.
- Created training program for technical staff to develop account management and consulting skills; reduced project delays by 30% and increased cross-functional awareness.
- Managed major systems projects through entire life cycle, including
  - Implementation of online allocation database handling monthly bond auctions.
  - Origination and design of debt-tracking and payment system that provided online historical information on all outstanding fixed-income securities totaling more than $63 billion.

*Manager* (1991–1992)
- Reorganized and redirected problem-ridden operations unit, saving more than $200,000.

**CITICORP, N.A., Domestic Funding Services (DFS),** New York, NY                    **1984–1988**
*Manager,* 1988—*Assistant Manager,* 1986–1988—*Management Associate,* 1984–1986
- Managed daily operations for Citicorp and three subsidiaries, serving as liaison between Citicorp traders/Citibank operations and Chief Financial Officer/investors. Managed and trained 10 employees.
- Played a key role in development of new DFS Self-Audit Business Unit, which identified and solved broad range of financial/accounting problems, increasing departmental efficiencies between 50% and 70%.
- Turned around problem-ridden subsidiary, resulting in first acceptable audit in three years.
- Sent to Aruba to start up foreign exchange and cash management unit for overseas subsidiary.
- Managed Citicorp cash management function totaling $2 billion daily.

## PROFESSIONAL AFFILIATIONS

Association for Women in Computing (AWC)
National Association for Female Executives (NAFE)
Kellogg Alumni Association

## EDUCATION

**MBA,** Finance & International Economics, **J.L. Kellogg Graduate School of Management,** Northwestern University, 1990
**BA,** Economics and French, **Fordham University,** 1984

# ANTHONY HIGGINS

1345 Lois Lane
Stockton, California 95206

(209) 688-4384
anthony@gotnet.com

## CHIEF INFORMATION OFFICER / INFORMATION SERVICES MANAGEMENT

Senior manager with 20+ years of experience in Information Services (IS) Management. Proven track record of increasing operational efficiencies, improving customer service levels, and implementing and maintaining IT initiatives to support successful business processes. Provide vision and dedicated leadership for key technologies, including enterprise systems architecture, networking, desktop, and database management systems. Possess strong functional and systems knowledge of banking systems and software, financial accounting, budgeting, contracts management, human resources, and legal and related government regulatory compliance.

**Key areas of strength include**

FINANCIAL SERVICES INFORMATION MANAGEMENT

IT OPERATIONS MANAGEMENT • VENDOR RELATIONSHIP MANAGEMENT

MERGERS AND ACQUISITIONS • PROCESS ENGINEERING

## CAREER HIGHLIGHTS

BANK OF STOCKTON, Stockton, California

1996-Present

### *CHIEF INFORMATION OFFICER*

Direct the development and implementation of strategic planning to modernize information systems and infrastructure at the corporate office and 18 branches in central California for this $850 million bank operation. Provide leadership and framework to actively identify IT needs of all corporate departments and each branch and respond to critical issues. Supervise and direct a 12-member technical staff and 16 other employees. Oversee the management of data processing services, proof and item processing, records research, telecommunications, personal computers, and local area networks. Direct major reengineering projects and develop new processes to position institution for advanced growth. Establish support operations for all areas; create Desktop and Telecommunications Technical Support functions. Administer annual budget of more than $4 million.

*Selected Accomplishments*

- Implemented new account-processing software and problem resolution of on-line/batch processing resulting in improved IS Departments.
- Introduced new technologies such as ATM terminals, driving and switching software on the existing legacy mainframe to favorably enhance customers' ability to use the bank's ATMs and other ATMs.
- Directed the conversion and implementation of UNIX-based banking core account processing, ATM switch processing, general ledger software, and other related software.
- Saved 30% annually in maintenance expenses through effective budget analysis, purchasing, and IS problem resolution.
- Led upgrade of AT&T System 75 switch to Lucent Definity G3 and directed installation of Intuity Audix PBX system.
- Structured and negotiated vendor partnerships to facilitate joint systems development projects.
- Implemented LAN/WAN infrastructure improvements and led conversion from Novell to Windows NT environment.

(continued)

*An attractive typestyle and good organization make this an inviting resume. Job titles stand out quite prominently, showing strong career progression.*

**ANTHONY HIGGINS**
(209) 688-4384

**Page two**
anthony@gotnet.com

**CAREER HIGHLIGHTS** (continued)

PRIME CONSULTING SERVICES, Austin, Texas                1993-1996

### *SENIOR CONSULTANT*

Consulted with officers and management of commercial banks, savings and loans, and other financial institutions on strategic management of Information Systems actions and integrations. Directed successful conversions and installations of NCR's Universal Financial System (UFS), including interfaces to other customer platforms. Streamlined use of diverse standardized software applications resulting in consistency of banking systems processing. Trained internal departments in services for UFS to include MIS, tellers, and administrative terminal training with the preparation of appropriate manuals.

AUSTIN SAVINGS AND LOAN, Austin, Texas                1989-1993

### *VICE PRESIDENT/MANAGER*

Managed a team of 9 analysts and programmer/analysts and a documentation librarian in the development, enhancements, maintenance, and user support actions for all systems supporting the Deposits and Operations divisions.

- Administered support and modifications for all deposit systems, including check and item processing, ATM systems and software, telephone voice response, ACH and EFT software, and interfaces to the General Ledger, mortgage/consumer loan system, and software.
- Directed and managed the project planning, budget management, and administration for all projects within this development and support group.
- Led IT in the development of Systems Development Life Cycle plan and assisted in the development of the Disaster Recovery plan.

BRIEF HISTORY OF EMPLOYMENT PRIOR TO 1989:

### *CHIEF INFORMATION OFFICER/VICE PRESIDENT*
*The First National Association • Miami, Florida*

Reported to President and Chief Executive Officer. Coordinated and directed the design, development, selection, and implementation of company-wide information systems. Partnered with Operations department to recruit and hire professional systems staff. Devised user training and support programs.

### *PROJECT LEADER/SENIOR ANALYST/PROGRAMMER*
*Ohio Savings & Loan • Cincinnati, Ohio*

Designed, coded, and implemented NCR mainframe software systems marketed to the mainframe market. Two of many systems developed were On-line Integrated Deposits and Loans System (Savings and Loan Account Processing Software). Over 400 S&Ls and Service Bureau installations, and Integrated Banking Central Information File System (CIF). Spearheaded 600+ Commercial Banking installations.

### TECHNICAL EXPERTISE

| | | | |
|---|---|---|---|
| Windows NT | IBM Systems | Unisys Mainframe | Windows 9x |
| LAN/WAN | TCP/IP | Novell NetWare | COBOL |
| SQL Server | UNIX | NCR NEAT/3 | NEATVS |

### EDUCATION

**Bachelor of Science,** University of Cincinnati, Cincinnati, Ohio

Major: Industrial Management—Minor: Accounting

# Denny G. Wong

11650 W. Shepherd ▪ Houston, Texas 77088 ▪ (281) 966-7276
email: denny@flex.net

### INTERNATIONAL TELECOMMUNICATIONS & INFORMATION TECHNOLOGY

*New Business Development & Advanced Technology Networks / General Management*
*Voiceover IP / System Design & Integration / E-commerce Solutions*
*Start-up, Turnaround & High-Growth Operations*

Trilingual (Vietnamese/Chinese/English) IT Management Professional with extensive experience building and leading domestic and international business development initiatives within the telecommunications industry. Consistently successful in identifying and capturing market opportunities to accelerate expansion, increase revenues and improve profit contributions. Extensive experience developing partnering alliances throughout Asia and the Pacific Rim. Conversational in Spanish and Thai. Core management qualifications include the following:

- ➢ Strategic Sales & Market Planning
- ➢ Staff Training & Development
- ➢ Key Account Relationship Management
- ➢ International Market Development
- ➢ New Product & Service Launch

- ➢ Market Research & Analysis
- ➢ Product & Market Positioning
- ➢ Sales Forecasting & Reporting
- ➢ Budget Development & Control
- ➢ Global Commercialization

*Led the start-up and development of two international telecommunications companies, and spearheaded their launch in the United States, Thailand, the Philippines and Mexico.*

Equally strong technical expertise in the design, development and delivery of cost-effective, high-performance technology solutions to meet challenging business demands. Heavy design and programming experience with Windows, UNIX, Linux, HTML, ASP, Java, FTP, SAS, Turbo Pascal, FORTRAN and Visual Basic. Software and database proficiency in MS Office and Access, Lotus SmartSuite, Lotus Notes, SQL and Oracle. Voiceover IP Telephony includes gateways, gatekeepers, billing solutions and unified messaging. Protocols include PSTN networks, ISDN, BRI/PRI, T1/T3, E1/R2, SS7, TCP/IP, H323, SIP, HTTP, MGCP and RTP.

### PROFESSIONAL EXPERIENCE

**WONG.COM, INC.,** Houston, Texas                                                2004–Present
**Cofounder / Vice President of New Business Development / Chief Technology Officer**
Partnered with two other entrepreneurs in the development of a telecommunications company designing Web-based technologies to support global communication networks. Assumed leadership role in international business development, marketing, sales, systems engineering and operations. Identified and secured seed funding through venture capital and private investor groups. Designed internal and external technology infrastructures to ensure affordability, reliability and durability. **Developed and built strategic partnering alliances with Cisco Systems, Vocaltec, AT&T, UUNet international telco companies, broadband providers, ITSPs and ISPs.**

*(continued)*

*For a multilingual executive with extensive global experience, the resume leads off with a lengthy summary encompassing both executive and technical skills. Then it highlights the key accomplishments of each position in bold type at the end.*

| | |
|---|---|
| **Denny G. Wong** | **Page Two** |
| (281) 966-7276 | denny@flex.net |

### PROFESSIONAL EXPERIENCE
*(continued)*

**QUESTEL COMMUNICATIONS, INC.,** Houston, Texas  2003–2004
**Cofounder / Vice President of Network Engineering**
Established and built a global voiceover IP network services company from inception. Full responsibility for strategic business planning, engineering, network architecture, risk management and capacity planning. **Spearheaded voiceover IP expansion and deployment throughout Asia Pacific. Opened and managed operations in the United States, Thailand, Philippines and Mexico.** Designed and implemented Cisco-powered voiceover IP global communication networks.

**INFORMATION SCIENCE CORPORATION,** Houston, Texas  2002–2003
**IT Consultant**
Assigned exclusively to Dupont/Conoco to expand their global business operations. Created extensive WAN network using T1 and Frame Relay technology to connect all company locations, and developed their Internet e-mail systems.

**H.T.I.S. TELECOMMUNICATIONS, INC.,** Houston, Texas  2000–2002
**Manager of Systems Engineering**
Assumed full responsibility for the design and installation of LAN/WAN technologies, client/server architecture, Windows NT and Novell Networks operating systems and applications software. Proposed integrating voice processing servers and telephony gateway equipment to customer specifications.

**RELIANT ENERGY,** Houston, Texas  1998–2000
**Corporate Information Network Specialist**
Recruited to assist IT Director in upgrading and enhancing LAN/WAN technologies. Prepared budgets and made appropriate recommendations on hardware and software equipment. Configured Cisco, 3Com, Asanta, WellFleet and SynOptics networking systems.

**WILLIAMS COMMUNICATIONS,** The Woodlands, Texas  1997–1998
**Corporate Operations Analyst**
Established workstations and file and print servers and installed Windows applications. Configured Northern Telecom (PBX) and Octel telephone systems. **Recipient of Williams Communications Systems Team Service Award.**

### EDUCATION

Sam Houston State University, Huntsville, Texas: **BS, Engineering,** 1996
*Specialization in Computer Science*

### CONTINUING PROFESSIONAL DEVELOPMENT

Extensive technical training on Cisco and Lucent Voiceover Internet Protocol and other technologies

### PROFESSIONAL AFFILIATIONS

Association of Communications Enterprises
International Engineering Consortium / Cisco Houston User Group

# HAROLD WAINWRIGHT

400 Filbert Road
Saratoga, CA 95070

408-555-5555
hwain@yahoo.com

## EXECUTIVE MANAGEMENT PROFILE

**Strategic & Tactical Planning / Project Management / P&L Responsibility
Customer Relationship Management / Team Building & Leadership / Staff Development
IT System Controls & Processes / Applications Development / Database Administration**

Results-driven senior executive with proven ability to gain cooperation and build consensus among diverse groups with conflicting business objectives. Nationally recognized as an IT expert within the healthcare industry.

## ACCOMPLISHMENT HIGHLIGHTS

- Negotiated a 10-year contract expansion and extension worth $80 million, including desktop support, business recovery, voice and data network, application development, and system operations.

- Secured $4 million project at Premier Health Systems by establishing and maintaining a strong relationship with the head of their executive team during projects at other locations.

- Met or exceeded all revenue and profitability targets set by Top Tier by controlling costs and expanding the scope of project contracts.

- Turned around poor customer satisfaction at two locations, raising the ratings from 4 of 10 to 10 of 10. Established an industry-leading position for that aspect of business operations by resolving technical problems and developing a positive relationship with the executive team.

- Maintain high employee morale and retention in a tight labor market by setting clear standards and providing assistance and encouragement to employees in meeting those standards.

## PROFESSIONAL EXPERIENCE

### Top Tier Global Services:

*Project Executive / Chief Information Officer, Bridgewater Hospital*, San Jose, CA, 2001–Present

- Manage a full outsource contract for application development / maintenance, systems integration, and database administration, which includes voice and data network support, telephony, desktop and help desk management, and strategic planning.

- Provide executive leadership to many areas at the hospital, including the committee that prepares for JCAHO audits and the medical information systems committee. Viewed as an extension of the management team and consulted regarding requirements that may impact data flow in the hospital.

- Maintain P&L responsibility, budgeting, forecasting, monitoring, and reporting of finances for the $80 million El Camino project and the new Premier project.

- Address critical strategic and tactical planning issues, interacting with the information management committee and hospital administration to develop effective plans.

- Direct a staff of 40 Top Tier employees and contractors at the hospital. Hired Bridgewater employees and transitioned them to Top Tier by investing in significant retraining and skills upgrading.

- Oversee approximately 12 employees at the service delivery center in Arizona and 6 employees working on the Premier project in Colorado.

- Assist Marketing teams with accounts to be used for corporate references by advising them regarding critical content and structure of proposals.

- Prepare and submit operating reports periodically to senior Top Tier management.

PAGE 1 of 2

*The Accomplishment Highlights technique allows this candidate to present his success stories at the very beginning of his resume; the Professional Experience section that follows gives more details and additional achievements.*

HAROLD WAINWRIGHT                                          PAGE 2

*Project Executive, Premier Health Systems*, Denver, CO, 2004–Present

- Oversee on-site project manager and assist the organization in developing a strategic plan and building a data center.
- Provide expertise on computer operations, which includes developing processes and procedures.

*Project Executive, Health Care Ventures*, Santa Clara, CA, 1996–2001

- Managed daily operations for a joint venture between two major healthcare organizations, including finance / budgets, contract expansion, customer satisfaction, and strategy compatibility.
- Directed Top Tier–supplied services that included business applications, network, telephones, help desk, and strategic planning assistance.

*Manager, Application Development and Support*, Houston, TX, 1993–1996

- Managed the Production Services department, which involved installation, scheduling, and monitoring of all batch production programs to meet service level agreements.
- Led delivery of service to internal Top Tier groups as well as Central Mobile Communications and the World Access airline reservation system.

*Advisory Programmer / Project Leader*, Houston, TX, 1990–1993

- Led and performed systems analysis for all project phases, including audit readiness, business justification, design, tracking, project controls, and customer satisfaction.

**Previously held various technical positions within Top Tier, including application and systems programming**, 1977-1990.

## AFFILIATIONS, CERTIFICATIONS, & AWARDS

- Information Management Systems Society (20,000 members): Annual Conference Committee, 2002–2005; Annual Conference Committee Chair for Information Systems, 2003–2004; Information Systems Advisory Committee Chair, 2003–2004; frequent presenter at conferences
- Board of Directors, Bridgewater Hospital Foundation: Fundraising Committee Chair—raised approximately $500,000 through charity events over a five-year period
- Information Management Committee Chair, 2002–2005
- College of Healthcare Information Management Executives
- American Medical Informatics Association
- Project Management Institute
- ISSC Leadership Conference, 1998–2000
- Top Tier Project Management Certification, 1997; recertified 2000
- Top Tier Departmental Center of Excellence Award: resulted in assignment to lead a project that rolled out batch processes to five major computer centers throughout the United States

*Professional References Available upon Request.*

## BRIAN T. DANTON

89776 Ellington Drive
San Diego, CA 92127

858.487.6561

E-mail: briand@mpr.net

### INFORMATION TECHNOLOGY EXECUTIVE

*10+ years of consistent achievements in providing vision, innovation, strategic planning, and execution to IT organizations in high-growth global companies.*

### CORE COMPETENCIES AND STRENGTHS

✓ Business-oriented IT professional with hands-on experience who champions business process improvements/cost reductions and identifies the most cost-effective, value-added IT solutions.

✓ Full project life cycle experience as a developer, consultant, and manager of large-scale IT projects, consistently producing quality deliverables on schedule and well under budget.

✓ History of excelling in introducing organizational change and leveraging existing technology and knowledge base with internal resources to facilitate business excellence and competitive advantage.

✓ Supervisory and budget experience, combined with excellent communication skills, enable building and continually driving focused IT/cross-functional teams involving different cultures to accomplish results.

✓ Proven effectiveness in consensus building, partnering with senior business leaders and working collaboratively at all levels to assess, plan, and implement IT solutions.

### PROFESSIONAL EXPERIENCE

**ELMAK MANUFACTURING**, San Diego, CA                              1999 to Present
**Director of Applications**

Direct the development, maintenance, and support of all standardized business applications at 14 plants worldwide in a rapid-growth environment (60% growth rate during 1999–2000). Diverse responsibilities encompass development of applications and e-commerce strategies, IT policies/procedures, and partnering with senior executives company-wide.

Supervise 7-member team in 3 application groups: E-commerce, ERP Systems, and Supply Chain. Collaborate with site resources in the delivery of IT solutions. Develop and manage relationships with enterprise software vendors, including Baan, i2, Agile, Oracle, Hyperion, GE, and Valor. Manage $1.7 million budget. Perform applications due diligence and lead system installation teams for new acquisitions.

#### Key Projects & Results:

- **Baan ERP Implementation:** Envisioned, pioneered the design, and leveraged existing internal technology and resources to implement Baan ERP system at company's German plant in record time (5 weeks) at a fraction of the cost ($100,000) of prior implementations. **Results:** Enabled company to retain $40 million account and provided foundation for rapid Baan implementation methodology.

- **Customer Portal Implementation:** Salvaged a failed e-commerce project and delivered results that restored confidence while retaining largest, $350 million–a-year account. Currently utilizing the solution as an enterprise standard to provide cost-effective Web access for all customers.

- **MES Strategy/Solution:** Established consistent strategy throughout company for Manufacturing Execution System (MES) from requirements definition through vendor selection and successful implementation. Instrumental in capturing $100 million–a-year account by architecting a solution to service avionic, medical, and industrial customers that required advanced product-tracking capabilities.

- **Development Cost Reduction:** Reduced Baan development costs $200,000 a year by replacing outside consultants with internal developer.

*Key projects are called out to provide depth and detail to this resume. A headline and two-line achievement statement establish focus and create impact.*

## BRIAN T. DANTON – Page 2
858.487.6561 ▪ briand@mpr.net

**DELMAR SOLUTIONS, Dallas, TX**  1996 to 1999
**Manager of Information Systems**

Recruited to realign IT organization with company's accelerated growth from $36 million to $60 million (33% annual growth rate) in just 3 years. Modernized division's IT infrastructure, standardizing on SAP, Microsoft, Oracle, Compaq and Cisco—all accomplished with a staff of 2. Initiated and managed partnerships with key application and infrastructure vendors. Maintained IT costs under 2% of sales throughout tenure (well under parent company's 7% of sales average).

### Key Projects & Results:

- **SAP/R3 Implementation:** Spearheaded the Accelerated SAP/R3 implementation project at 2 sites, including leadership of cross-functional management and technical teams. **Results:** Awarded for delivering project in just 5 months—on schedule and under budget—at a total cost of only $900,000.
- **Infrastructure Improvements:** Replaced Novell NetWare with Microsoft Windows 2003 Server and cc:Mail with MS Exchange, as well as all switches and routers with new Cisco equipment. Planned and implemented IT infrastructure at new headquarters. **Results:** Complied with mandate without any adverse impact to the business.
- **E-commerce:** Initiated and launched delmar.com, product micro-sites, and surgeons' forum (online discussion group focused on use of company products).
- **Sales Force Automation:** Deployed laptops, provided training and Web-based CRM solution to more than 100 remote sales reps. Created automated Sales Force Tool Kit, providing sales force with same-day research and delivery of technical articles to customers, quote development, and other tools.

**HANOVER CORPORATION, Dallas, TX**  1991 to 1996
**Assistant Manager—Information Management**  1992 to 1996

Promoted to provide divisional IT strategy and leadership in support of Corporate Procurement and Accounts Payable departments' systems, users, and re-engineering initiatives. Developed and managed annual $1.3 million budget. Directed a team of 9 in a mixed technical environment, including MVS, VM, VMS, and client server. **Key Projects & Results:**

- Re-engineered interface between central procurement system and ERP systems at the plants. **Results:** Streamlined manufacturing purchasing and receiving processes while averting production downtime.
- Implemented several integrated self-service requisition applications for MRO.
- Earned Total Quality Ownership Award for duty drawback audit that saved company $200,000.
- Promoted from **Senior Systems Analyst** (1991 to 1992).

## EDUCATION

B.A. (Computer Systems), University of Texas, Dallas, TX, 1991

## TECHNICAL SKILLS

**Applications:** BaaN IV ERP, SAP/R3 (SD, MM, PP, FI, CO), ASK MANMAN, Made2Manage ERP, BaaN E-Collaboration, BaaN E-Sales, Hyperion Enterprise, Valor Trilogy, GXS EDI/XML, Agile Sourcing, i2/ Aspect Development CSM/SSM, Kewill Clippership, Nextlinx TradeCollaborator, MS Exchange, MS IIS, Access Fundraising, Access Financial Management & Control. **Databases:** Oracle, DBMS32, IMS, DB2, SQL Server.

**Languages/Development Tools:** Oracle 9i Application Server, Java, HTML, XML, FrontPage, Crystal Reports, Oracle Discoverer, System Architect, ABAP/Query, ABAP/4, Visual Basic .NET, Access, DCL, UDMS, C, PowerBuilder, Lotus Notes, Borland ObjectVision, Focus, ADMINS/V32, Pascal.

**Server Operating Systems & Hardware:** HP-UX, NT4, WIN2K, Novell NetWare, MVS, VM, VMS, HP PA-RISC, HP Intel servers, Compaq Proliant, IBM Mainframe, DEC VAX.

# PART III

# Cover Letters for Computer and Web Jobs

CHAPTER 11

# Writing a Winning Cover Letter

Now that your resume is written, you may think that you're all set to launch your job search. If it were only that easy! Just as critical to the effectiveness and success of your job search campaign is your cover letter. To begin our discussion of this vital element in your search, let's start with a concise definition:

> **Cover Letter:** A document that accompanies your resume and is used to highlight your specific skills, qualifications, competencies, achievements, and more that *relate directly to the position for which you are applying.*

That's right—the best cover letters are letters that are targeted to specific positions (for example, network administration position with a large university, programming and systems design position with an emerging Internet venture, technology training position with an international company). Targeted letters allow you to selectively include information about your past work experience, technical qualifications, training and education, affiliations, professional activities, and more that directly support your candidacy for a particular position. In essence, you're taking everything about your career, laying it out on the table (so to speak), and then selecting only that information which is most important to your current job objective.

Here's an example of a wonderfully written cover letter that is targeted to this candidate's specific objective—a position as an Applications Support Specialist.

**George Murray**
48 Mountain View Road
Providence, RI 68995
(404) 858-9980
georgem490@home.com

February 4, 2005

P.O. Box 677
Detroit, MI 56788

Re: Applications Support Specialist

As a proficient computer professional with four years of experience in software applications design, development, testing, and maintenance for clients, I am particularly qualified for the Applications Support Specialist position at your company.

Currently an Applications Consultant with a company specializing in health-care software applications, I offer a solid background in system applications, development, customer support, and project management.

In my present role, I manage the implementation of our clients' nursing applications for client/server and other platforms. Client evaluation, product demonstrations, design/development of application solutions, support throughout the implementation cycle, and on-site client training in system customization and use, as well as system audits, are among my primary responsibilities. With solid project planning, coordinating, and management skills, I have a successful track record in delivering results within deadlines.

In addition, my position involves strong analytical and research skills and writing/updating technical documentation for applications. I test, troubleshoot, and maintain software applications on a daily basis, working closely with our QA group. An excellent problem solver, I am able to quickly get to the root of an issue and design a solution. In providing technical support, one of my strengths is to treat each customer as a key account that deserves outstanding service and response.

As part of a team-oriented environment, I also mentor new employees, providing ongoing coaching and training to assist them in professional development. I plan to relocate back to the Detroit area and would welcome the opportunity to join your team. I am confident that I possess the necessary technical knowledge and skills to add value to your company. May we meet to discuss your needs further?

Sincerely,

George Murray

*A targeted cover letter (submitted by Louise Garver, CPRW, CEIP, MCDP, CMP, JCTC).*

All too often, job search candidates write what we refer to as general cover letters—letters that can be used to apply for any position with any type of organization. In essence, these letters simply summarize information that is already included on your resume and tend to be not nearly as effective as targeted cover letters that are customized to each position to which you apply. Because you do not have a specific position in mind when you write a general letter, you are not able to highlight information that would be most essential in a particular situation. As such, we strongly urge that you stay away from general letters and devote the time that is necessary to develop targeted cover letters that will sell you into your next position.

Another a real advantage to targeted cover letters is that the recipient will notice that you have taken the time to write an individual letter to him or her; and, of course, that leaves a great impression. When you are able to integrate specific information into your letter about the company to which you are applying, it clearly demonstrates your interest in the position and the organization, before you've ever had the opportunity to speak with anyone there. Just think how impressed a prospective employer will be when he or she realizes that you've spent the time and energy necessary to research and "get to know" their organization. This, in and of itself, will give you a distinct advantage over the competition.

## Six Steps to Writing Better Cover Letters

To help guide you in writing and designing your own winning cover letters, we've created a step-by-step process and structure that will allow you to quickly and easily write letters that will get you and your resume noticed, not passed over:

1. Identify Your Key Selling Points
2. Pre-Plan
3. Write the Opening Paragraph
4. Write the Body
5. Write the Closing
6. Polish, Proofread, and Finalize

Now, we're going to explore each of these steps in detail to provide you with an action plan to write your letters with ease and confidence. Our most detailed discussion will be of Step 1: Identify Your Key Selling Points, which is the entire foundation for your cover letter.

### STEP 1: IDENTIFY YOUR KEY SELLING POINTS

What qualifications, experiences, achievements, and skills do you bring to a school or company? It's time to evaluate and quantify what it is that makes you unique, valuable, and interesting to potential employers.

#### *Know Your Objective*

The best place to start is by clearly identifying *who* you are and what your job objective is. Are you a C++ programmer, a database administrator, a Web designer, a CIO, a project manager, or a corporate training and development professional? It is critical that you be able to clearly and accurately define who you are in an instant. Remember, an instant is all that you have to capture your reader's attention, encouraging him not only to read your cover letter in full, but to read your resume and contact you for a personal interview.

### Summarize Your Experience

Just as important, you must be able to clearly identify why an organization would be interested in interviewing and possibly hiring you. Is it because of the schools or universities you've attended? The industries in which you've been employed? The positions you held? The promotions you earned? Your accomplishments? Your technical expertise? Your specific skills and qualifications? Your licenses and educational credentials? Your leadership skills? Your foreign-language skills and international experience? Why would someone be interested in you?

### Sell Your Achievements

Your achievements are what set you apart from others with a similar background. They answer the reader's all-important question, "What can you do for me?" because they tell precisely what you have done for someone else. Cover letters and resumes without achievements are simply dry compilations of position titles and responsibilities. They don't sell your unique attributes, and they don't compel readers to pick up the phone and invite you in for an interview.

In thinking about your achievements, ask yourself how you've benefited the organizations where you've worked. In general terms, you can help an organization by

- **Making money** (revenues, profits, earnings, ROI/ROA/ROE increases, new customers)

- **Saving money** (cost reductions, streamlining, automating)

- **Creating new things** (courses, programs, techniques, methodologies, systems, processes, and more)

- **Improving existing things** (reengineering, redesigning, developing new processes, consolidating)

- **Improving staff, departmental, and/or organizational performance** (productivity, efficiency, quality, delivery, and customer service)

- **Winning honors, awards, and commendations**

In writing your achievements, think about the two key pieces of information you want to convey about each of your successes: what you did and how it benefited the organization. It is the combination of both of these components that will make your achievements—and, in turn, you—shine.

Who you are, what you have achieved, and why an organization would want to hire you are critical questions you must ask yourself before you ever begin to write a cover letter. The answers to those questions will directly impact what you write in your cover letter and how you present that information. You must determine what you have to offer that relates to that organization's specific needs, what will be of interest to them, and what will entice them to read your resume and offer you the opportunity for an interview. That information then becomes the foundation for every cover letter that you write.

## STEP 2: PRE-PLAN

Before you begin writing a single word of your cover letter, you must determine the appropriate strategy for that particular letter. You're not ready to write until you can clearly answer the following questions:

- **Why am I writing this letter?** Am I writing in response to a print or online advertisement, sending a cold-call letter to companies, contacting someone in my network, writing to an organization at the recommendation of someone else, or writing a follow-up letter to a company to which I already sent a resume? The answer to this question will significantly impact the content of your cover letter—the introduction in particular.

- **Have I researched the organization and/or the position?** There will be instances where you know, or can find, information about an organization you are writing to, the services and products it offers, the positions that are open, the types of candidates it hires, the hiring requirements, and so much more. Do your research! The more you know about a company and the position, the more on-target you can write your letters, relating your experience to their identified needs. If you know the company has critical hardware issues, be sure to stress your success in resolving those same types of problems and restoring systems integrity. If you know that the company is struggling with its technical support organization, focus on your success in building strong customer-service centers. Your goal is to find common ground between you and the company and then leverage that to your advantage.

- **Do I have a contact name?** Have I double-checked the correct spelling of the name and the person's job title? Do I have the full mailing address or e-mail address? The fact is that if you write to the Human Resources department of a company, you'll never quite know where your letter and resume have landed. However, if you write to a particular individual in a particular department with particular contact information, you not only know who has your resume and cover letter, you also know who to follow up with. This is critical for job search success in today's competitive market!

## STEP 3: WRITE THE OPENING PARAGRAPH

The opening paragraph of your cover letter is your hook—your "sales pitch"—that tells your reader who you are and why you are of value to that specific organization. It should be written to entice the recipient to read your letter in its entirety and then take the time to closely review your resume. And, because it is so critical, the opening paragraph is often the section that will take you the longest to write.

**TIP:** If you're having trouble writing the opening paragraph of your cover letter, leave it for the time being and move on to the body of the letter. Once you've written the rest, the opening paragraph will usually flow much more smoothly and quickly.

There are three specific questions you must address in the opening paragraph of your cover letter:

1. Who are you?

2. Why are you writing?

3. What message are you communicating?

Your answers to these questions, combined with the specific reason you are writing (for example, in response to an advertisement, on recommendation from a network contact, or because of an Internet job lead), will almost always dictate the type of opening you select. Review the introductory paragraphs for the sample cover letters in chapter 14 to help you get started developing your own introduction.

## STEP 4: WRITE THE BODY

Now you're ready to tackle the real task at hand: writing the body of your cover letter—the substance, key qualifications, technical expertise, accomplishments, successes, and whatever other information you choose to highlight that will entice the reader to closely review your resume and offer you the opportunity for a personal interview.

In order to sell yourself (or any product) as "the answer," you must highlight the attractive *features* and *benefits* of that product. Put yourself in the shoes of the buyer and ask yourself

• What will catch my attention?

• What's interesting about this candidate?

• What's innovative or unique about this candidate?

• Why is this candidate different from (or better than) other competitive candidates?

• Do I understand the value I'll get from this candidate?

• Do I need this candidate?

• Do I want this candidate?

Whether or not you're conscious of it, every time you buy something, you ask yourself these questions and others. It's the typical process that everyone proceeds through when they're deciding whether to make a purchase. It is imperative that you remember this as you begin to write your cover letters. Understand that you must clearly communicate the answers to these questions in order to get people to want to "buy" *you.*

**TIP:** Your cover letter *should not* be written as "Here I am, give me a job," but *should be* written as, "Here I am; this is why I am so valuable; give me a chance to solve your problems." Focusing on the value and benefits you have to offer is a good way to capture the reader's attention. Remember, the employer's most compelling question is "What can you do for me?" not "What do you want?"

Your challenge, then, is to convey your value in a short and concise document—your cover letter. Unfortunately, there are no rules to guide you in determining what to include in each specific cover letter that you write. It is entirely a judgment call based on the specific situation at hand—the position, the organization, and the required qualifications and experience. What you include in your letter is not necessarily based on what you consider to be your most significant responsibilities and achievements from throughout your career, but rather what is *most relevant to the hiring company and its needs.*

Achievements, accomplishments, contributions, and successes are the cornerstone of any effective cover letter. It goes without saying that you want to demonstrate that you have the right skills, qualifications, and experience for a particular job. However, you do not want your letter to be a "job description"—a mere listing of job responsibilities. First of all, you've addressed a great deal of that information in the resume that you'll be sending along with your cover letter. You do *not* want your letter to simply reiterate what's in your resume. The challenge is to write a cover letter that complements the resume and brings the most notable information to the forefront.

Depending on the format of your letter, you can convey this information in a paragraph format, a bullet-point format, or a combination of both. Use whichever you feel is most appropriate to convey the particular information. If you decide to use full paragraphs, make sure that they are fairly short to promote readability. Edit and tighten your copy so that every word and phrase conveys information that relates to the employer's needs and your most relevant qualifications.

## STEP 5: WRITE THE CLOSING

Now that you've written your introductory paragraph and the body of your cover letter, all you have left to do is the closing paragraph. Simple enough; in fact, this is generally the easiest section of your letter to write. To get started, ask yourself these two simple questions:

- What style of closing paragraph do I want to use?

- Is there any specific personal or salary information I want to include that was requested in the advertisement to which I am responding?

When it comes to choosing style, closing paragraphs are easy. There are basically only two styles—Passive and Assertive—and the distinction between the two styles is evident:

- **Passive:** A passive letter ends with a statement such as "*I look forward to hearing from you.*" With this sentence, you are taking a passive approach, waiting for the hiring company or recruiter to contact you. This is *not* our recommended strategy.

- **Assertive:** An assertive letter ends with a statement such as "*I look forward to interviewing with you and will follow up next week to schedule a convenient appointment.*" In this sentence, you are asserting yourself, telling the recipient that you will follow up and asking for the interview!

We strongly recommend that you end your cover letters with an assertive closing paragraph. Remember, the only real objective of your cover letter is to get an interview, so *ask for it!* Furthermore, we also advise that you outline an agenda that communicates you will be expecting their call and, if you don't hear from them, you will follow up. This puts you in the driver's seat and in control of your job search. It also demonstrates to a prospective employer that once you've initiated something, you follow it through to completion. This is a valuable trait for any professional.

Inevitably, there will be instances in your job search when you will not be able to follow up:

- If you are responding to a blind advertisement with a P.O. box, you won't know who to call.

- If you are responding to an advertisement that states "No Phone Calls," don't call.

- If you are sending out 1,000 letters to recruiters across the nation, don't waste your time calling them. If they're interested or have an opportunity for which you are suited, they'll call you.

- If you know that you'll never get the individual you want to speak with on the phone, don't waste your time or money.

The closing paragraph of your cover letter is also the preferred placement for any personal or salary information you will include. There are generally only two times you will want to include this type of information:

- **When it has been asked for in an advertisement.** Common requests include such things as salary history (what you have made in the past and are currently earning if you are employed), salary requirements (what your current salary objectives are), citizenship status, or geographic preference.

- **When you are writing "cold-call" letters to recruiters.** When contacting recruiters, we recommend that you at least minimally address your salary requirements (a range is fine) and any geographic preferences in the closing paragraph of your cover letter.

## STEP 6: POLISH, PROOFREAD, AND FINALIZE

The process we recommend for writing your cover letters suggests that you first craft the opening, then the middle, and then the closing of each letter. Although the step-by-step process makes the task fairly quick and easy, you will probably find that your letters need final polishing, wordsmithing, and tweaking to ensure that each section "flows" into the next and that you have a cohesive-sounding whole.

Take the time to proofread your letter thoroughly and carefully. Read it for sense and flow; then read it again to check for spelling errors, punctuation mistakes, and grammatical inconsistencies. We cannot emphasize this point enough. The people who receive your cover letter and resume *do* judge your professionalism based on the quality and accuracy of these documents. In fact, in a survey of hiring authorities we conducted for a prior book, *90 percent of respondents* mentioned quality and appearance factors (such as typos, misspellings, smudged print, and low-quality paper) as reasons for *immediately discarding a resume*. Don't take a chance that your carefully written letter and resume will end up in the circular file before your qualifications are even considered.

Here are a few things to look out for during the polishing phase:

- **Spelling:** Use your computer's spell-checker, but don't rely on it totally. The spell-checker won't flag an "it's" that should be "its" or a "there" that should be "their." Make triple-certain you've correctly spelled all names: people, organizations, software programs, and so on.

- **Grammar and punctuation:** If you're not confident about your grammar and punctuation skills, purchase an all-purpose reference guide and use it as often as you need to. Don't let your cover letter be discarded because of basic grammar and punctuation errors.

- **Interesting language:** As much as possible, avoid cliches and outdated language (such as "Enclosed please find my resume"). It's difficult to find new ways to express familiar sentiments (such as "I would appreciate the opportunity for an interview"), and it's certainly not necessary to come up with unique language for every phrase. But make sure that your cover letter doesn't sound like a cookie-cutter, one-size-fits-all letter that could have been written by any job seeker.

## Authors' Best Tips for Writing Winning Cover Letters

Here's our most important cover-letter advice, gleaned from our experience writing thousands of cover letters over the years.

### DON'T REINVENT THE WHEEL

A great amount of our discussion has focused on the fact that your cover letters should be written individually based on the specific situation. And that is quite true. The more focused your letters, the greater the impact and the more likely you are to get a response and opportunity to interview. However, you *do not* have to reinvent the wheel with each and every cover letter you write. If you're a help-desk administrator writing in response to advertisements for other help-desk positions, you can very often use the same letter with just a few minor editorial changes to match each opportunity. Remember to use your word-processing program's "copy and paste" function. It's a great, labor-saving tool!

## SELL IT TO ME; DON'T TELL IT TO ME

Just like resume writing, cover letter writing is sales—pure and simple. You have a commodity to sell—yourself—and your challenge is to write a marketing communication that is powerful and pushes the reader to action. (You want him to call you for an interview!) Therefore, it is essential that when writing your letters you "sell" your achievements and don't just "tell" your responsibilities.

Here's a quick example. If you are a JAVA programmer, you could "tell" your reader that you've developed more than 10 new JAVA scripts. Great! Or, you could "sell" the fact that you've led project teams that developed and delivered new JAVA scripts that have supported a 200 percent increase in shopping-cart purchases within just two months. Which letter would capture your interest?

## GET OVER WRITER'S BLOCK

Very often, the most difficult part of writing a cover letter is getting started. You can sit and look at that blank piece of paper or computer screen for hours, frustrated and wondering whether the whole world has such a hard time writing cover letters. If writing is part of your daily work responsibilities, the process might not be too arduous. However, if you do not have to write on a regular basis, cover letters can be an especially formidable task. That's why it is so important to follow the step-by-step process we have created. It is guaranteed to make cover letter writing faster, easier, and much less painful!

If you're still having trouble, consider this simple thought: **You do not have to start at the beginning.** Even after writing thousands and thousands of cover letters, we'll sit stumped, unable to come up with just the "right" opening paragraph. Instead of wasting time and brain power, and getting frustrated, we'll just leave it alone and move on to another section in the letter that we feel more confident writing. You'll find that once you get going, new ideas will pop into your head and the more difficult sections will come much more easily and confidently.

## ANSWER THE EMPLOYER'S MOST IMPORTANT QUESTION: "WHAT CAN YOU DO FOR ME?"

A powerful cover letter can help you get what you want: a new, perhaps more advanced, and more satisfying position. It is certainly important that you understand what you want to do, the kind of organization you'd like to work for, and the environment in which you'll be most productive. Yet you must remember that employers aren't really interested in you. They're interested in *what you can do for them*. If you do not keep this thought in the forefront of your mind when writing your cover letters, you're likely to produce a self-centered-sounding "here I am" letter that probably won't do much to advance your job search.

When writing your cover letters, consider the employer's needs and make sure that you communicate that you can add value, solve problems, and deliver benefits for that employer. You can do this through a strong focus on accomplishments ("Ah, she did that for Acme Technology; she can do the same for me.") and through careful attention to the wording and tone of your letter so that you appear to be more interested in contributing to the organization than satisfying your own personal needs.

Then, be sure to review the Cover Letter Checklist on the next page to be sure that your letters meet all of our requirements for style, appropriateness, quality of text, quality of presentation, and effectiveness. Follow our rules and we guarantee that your letters will open doors, generate interviews, and help you land your next great professional opportunity.

# Cover Letter Checklist

Before mailing, faxing, or e-mailing each cover letter you prepare, complete the following checklist to be sure that you have met all the rules for cover letter writing. If you cannot answer "yes" to *all* of the questions, go back and edit your letter as necessary before mailing it. The only questions for which a "no" answer is acceptable are questions #5 and #6, which relate specifically to the organization to which you are writing. As we have stated previously, there will be instances when you can find this information, but there will also be instances (for example, when writing to a P.O. box) when you cannot.

|  |  | YES | NO |
|---|---|:---:|:---:|
| 1. | Do I convey an immediate understanding of who I am in the first two sentences of my cover letter? | ❏ | ❏ |
| 2. | Is my cover letter format unique, and does my letter stand out? | ❏ | ❏ |
| 3. | Have I highlighted my most relevant qualifications? | ❏ | ❏ |
| 4. | Have I highlighted my most relevant achievements? | ❏ | ❏ |
| 5. | Have I included information I know about the company or the specific position for which I am applying? | ❏ | ❏ |
| 6. | Have I highlighted why I want to work for this company or school? | ❏ | ❏ |
| 7. | Is my letter neat, clean, and well-presented without being over-designed? | ❏ | ❏ |
| 8. | Is my letter error-free? | ❏ | ❏ |
| 9. | Is my cover letter short and succinct, preferably no longer than one page? | ❏ | ❏ |
| 10. | Do I ask for an interview in the letter? | ❏ | ❏ |

# CHAPTER 12

## Sample Cover Letters

What follows are six more sample cover letters for your review. Look at them closely. Select opening paragraphs, closing paragraphs, formats, and styles that you like, and then model your own cover letters accordingly. You'll find that by using these sample letters for hints, your letter-writing process will be much easier and faster. To see even more samples and get more help with writing your cover letters, see our book *Cover Letter Magic* (JIST Publishing).

## JOHN D. JOSEPH

150 Elm Street
Hartford, CT 06107

john.joseph27@yahoo.com

Residence: 860.249.3409
Mobile: 860.505.2301

September 30, 2005

Dr. Saul Holden, Vice Chairman and CEO
TRTL Bank Limited
Business Park
Cross Road
Bristol
England BR4 9FB

Dear Dr. Holden:

Expanding and enhancing a world-class company's IT infrastructure, systems, and processes are my areas of strength. As an IT professional with Select Lighting for more than 13 years, I have contributed to major technology initiatives that have been critical to supporting the company's growth to $4 billion in North American sales. I understand from my research that TRTL is poised for explosive growth and is developing IT expansion plans in Bristol to support that growth. My extensive experience would translate into significant benefits for your organization.

TRTL's multi-system IT environment will require the technical skills of highly qualified individual contributors, team leaders, and project managers as the company moves forward with expansion plans. I am experienced in all three roles. I have supported implementation of a major ERP system and integrated a variety of software and hardware solutions to facilitate a range of operations (including CRM, finance and accounting, document management, and data-warehouse reporting). My IT skill set is both broad and deep and includes systems architecture, IT operations, infrastructure development, applications development, IT budgeting, and hands-on technical tasks. My colleagues, managers, and reports know me as a strong team leader, motivator, and player who can work cross-functionally to push projects forward.

If I had to isolate the core reason for my success at Select Lighting, I would say that it is my ability to deliver on time, and with full functionality, the most challenging IT projects. During my career to date, I have been repeatedly called in to solve critical technical problems in both large- and small-scale projects. Some examples include the following:

- I was assigned full management responsibilities for turning around a 2-terabyte, UNIX-based data warehouse that was failing to meet the extensive and sophisticated reporting needs of all North American operations. By reengineering systems architecture, fully automating functions, and establishing standardized processes and procedures, I provided a system that exceeded functional requirements, operated almost error-free, slashed operating costs by two-thirds, and cut reporting time in half.
- As an individual contributor, I designed and implemented a document-management system that enhanced knowledge sharing, reinforced brand identity, and enabled the company to grow its online sales by 600%.
- As Technical Services Manager, I led a team that standardized hardware management in a 600-desktop, client-server environment and delivered $200,000 in cost savings in three years.

I will be in Bristol between 25 October and 14 November to organize my family's relocation to the area. My wife is an English citizen, qualifying me for employment in the U.K. I would like to talk with you in person during that week to discuss possible roles I could play in your IT expansion plans. I can be reached at either phone number or by e-mail prior to my visit to England, but only by mobile phone during the time I am in your area. Thank you for your time and consideration. I look forward to meeting you.

Sincerely,

John D. Joseph

Enclosure

*While emphasizing accomplishments and other value to the employer, this letter also includes relevant information about personal attributes and reason for making a job change (by Jean Cummings, MAT, CPRW, CEIP, CPBS).*

# MATTHEW A. JACKSON

mattjackson@bewellnet.com • (917) 750-5430

September 9, 2005

Michael Portman
Founder/Vice President
Data101, Inc.
1919 Colfax Avenue
Denver, CO 80112

Dear Mr. Portman:

Alvin Jacobson, one of your clients who is very familiar with my background and expertise, alerted me to your job openings since he felt that I would be a great match with your needs.

With seven years of experience in systems and network engineering and a unique combination of technical, interpersonal, and business skills, I have consistently delivered cost-effective, leading-edge IT solutions to a wide variety of clients in both small- and large-scale environments.

Here is how I can contribute to Data101:

- **Problem Solving:** Expertise in diagnostic and needs analysis as well as project planning and management.
  **Results:** I frequently thwart potential problems and consistently deliver customized client solutions. Recently, I helped increase productivity for a financial firm by 20%.
- **Bottom-line Improvements:** Using my big-picture vision and business savvy in decision making.
  **Results:** I negotiated combined savings of $75K+ in the last 20 months by leveraging my vendor network.

I have enclosed my resume for specific technical qualifications and additional achievements.

Having spent the last few years in New York City, I am eager to return home to the Denver area and am excited about potentially becoming part of your team. I am able to make myself available for employment, once hired, after giving suitable notice to my current employer and taking a reasonable amount of time to move from New York City to Denver. My salary expectations are competitive, and I would be happy to discuss them with you in a personal meeting.

A good next step might be to discuss in further detail Data101's specific needs and how I can meet—or exceed—them. I would like to suggest a teleconference, and will follow up with you within a week of your receipt of this letter to schedule a mutually convenient day and time.

Sincerely,

Matthew A. Jackson

Enclosure

*Notice the personal referral that opens this letter; this is a sure attention-getter. Later, this writer uses bold type to emphasize specific examples of how he can contribute to the company. Companion resume: #51, Chapter 7 (by Ilona Vanderwoude, CPRW, CEIP, CCMC, CJST).*

## Yuval Fischel
■ ■ ■

18 Eloura Lane
Rocklin, CA 95677

Email: yuvalfischel@hotmall.com

Telephone: (916) 624-8735
Mobile: (916) 214-9900

November 4, 2005

Mr. B. Smith
Human Resources Manager
APO, Inc.
Canterbury Road
Rocklin, CA 95677

**Re: Network Support Professional**

Dear Mr. Smith:

As an IT professional with more than seven years of experience working in high-pressure environments, I am confident I have the skills, background, and experience it takes to make a positive contribution to your team.

Far from a narrow field of specialization, I have in-depth knowledge of multiple areas—such was the requirement of my background in Israel where I worked for one of the largest newspaper publications in the country.

In a 24x7-production environment, it was critical to get the publication out on time—without fail. Anything that had the potential to impact those deadlines was not an option; consequently, the IT team had to be a "jack-of-all-trades"—from providing first-, second-, and third-level desktop support to rebuilding operating systems after system crashes, eliminating security issues, educating end users, upgrading the network, and managing any and all points in between.

This experience, although demanding, provided the true foundation for my growth as an IT professional, and it is the sum of those strengths that I offer APO today.

Please take a moment to review my resume. As you will see, when first employed by Israel's top-selling newspaper, *Tel Aviv Today,* I was confronted with a network that was plagued with security problems. System crashes were a regular event severely impacting the productivity of staff, and other office locations suffered service delays, often waiting hours for on-site support to fix the most basic of issues. Three years later, most of my recommendations have been successfully deployed. The system deflects spam through a carefully configured firewall; incidences of viruses have been cut by 90%; and delays for on-site technical support have been eliminated through the installation of remote access where IT staff can resolve issues without leaving their desks. Staff are fully educated in the basics of troubleshooting before calling for support, and end-user complaints have dropped dramatically.

Whether you need my advanced experience in troubleshooting applications to respond to desktop support calls from people of all levels of computer literacy, my ability to set up and administer a local- or wide-area network, or my success in establishing system maintenance that ensures optimum uptime, I believe I can make a positive and enduring contribution.

I will follow up with you early next week to see whether we can establish a mutually convenient time to meet. Thank you.

Sincerely,

Yuval Fischel

resume enclosed

*This letter writer talks about his performance in demanding environments in his last several jobs, using a storytelling technique that keeps the reader interested from start to finish. Companion resume: #52, Chapter 7 (by Gayle Howard, CERW, CCM, CPRW, CRW).*

## ALEX C. SESMYO

4431 McBride Grove
Houston, Texas 77008

acsesmyo@txl.net

713.595.5291 Residence
713.309.5293 Mobile

January 28, 2006

Mr. John Linton
Executive Vice President, Human Resources
Courtier Business Campus
23 River Oaks Drive
Houston, Texas 77056

Dear Mr. Linton:

In response to your recent advertisement in the *Houston Post* for a Chief Information Officer (CIO), I believe you will find my credentials a good match with your requirements.

Given that you seek an experienced CIO to lead your Management Information Systems group, I am eager to share my background with you, as follows:

- 20+ years of experience in MIS with a major focus on business systems
- Proven track record of documented accomplishments and contributions in diverse environments
- Outstanding track record in team leadership, strategic planning, departmental direction, and goal achievement
- Vast expertise in computer operations, systems and programming, technical support, and Internet services
- Experience in distributed processing with large numbers of attached devices, utilizing industry-standard protocols

In all aspects of business operations, I am deeply committed to continuous improvement and enhanced operating efficiencies. I am experienced in reporting to boards, senior management, and regulatory agencies. My management style is one of leadership by example with a commitment to high standards, quality, and responsiveness. Regarding salary, my requirements are in the range of $150,000 to $175,000.

My resume is enclosed for your review. I will call on Friday to answer any questions you might have and, if you agree my skills are a good fit, to schedule an in-person meeting.

Sincerely yours,


Alex C. Sesmyo

Enc.

*The bullet points briefly but powerfully call out qualifications that are an exact fit for the position requirements. Notice how salary requirements are stated as a range rather than a specific figure. Companion resume: #105, Chapter 10 (by Billie Sucher, MS, CTMS, CTSB).*

## Joan E. Rickman

348 James Avenue SE
Grand Rapids, MI 49503

616-555-8740
joanier@isp.net

February 20, 2005

Mr. Robert Kramer
Citizens Insurance
645 West Grand River
Howell, MI 48843

Dear Mr. Kramer:

In the five years I have been a Systems Analyst with Metropolitan Insurance Company, I have received three Special Effort Awards and have been promoted twice. A year ago management granted my request to transition from an on-site employee to a remote employee two states away. These accomplishments are an indication, I believe, of my performance and work ethic. Steven Kleinsmith (a former coworker) suggested I contact you about an appropriate position at Citizens Insurance.

When you take a look at the enclosed resume, you will notice I have a broad-based foundation in MIS. My capacity to learn what I don't know is demonstrated by the list of technologies and applications I have taken upon myself to study. Hopefully it goes without saying that I am technically savvy and analytical, but I also have the skills to communicate with colleagues and users at their diverse levels of understanding. My track record indicates a committed, methodical approach to projects (of which I manage several simultaneously) and problem resolution (for which I have been recognized).

Although I have enjoyed my employment with Metropolitan, I am eager to meet new challenges in a smaller organization, and therefore would appreciate an opportunity to speak with you directly, to elaborate on my qualifications and how they might match your current needs. I will give you a call in hopes of arranging a convenient time. I appreciate your consideration and look forward to speaking with you soon.

Sincerely,

Joan E. Rickman

Enclosure

*This letter starts off with some powerful achievements, and then goes on to reference a mutual acquaintance. The second paragraph describes soft skills that offer added value beyond the core job requirements (by Janet Beckstrom, CPRW).*

# DAVID KENT

1623 St. Louis Way     Honolulu, Hawaii 96813
808-555-6255     dkent@alohanet.com

March 14, 2005

John Jones, M.D.
Dean, School of Medicine
University of Honolulu
1234 College Circle
Honolulu, Hawaii 96822

Dear Dr. Jones:

Perhaps you remember our chance meeting at the Bio Asia-Pacific Conference at the Sheraton Waikiki earlier this month. In our brief conversation, I shared with you the idea of utilizing Web development as an administrative tool. You expressed interest in the possibility of implementing such a system within the School of Medicine.

May I suggest a formal meeting to explore the idea?

I have some exciting and creative ideas that may encourage you to take the next step toward realizing the positive impact a content-management system would have in the School of Medicine. This would also be a great opportunity for us to discuss your goals and how an administrative intranet would help you reach them in a more timely and cost-effective manner.

In addition, there has recently been spirited discussion within the IT community on the topic of organizational continuity and its potential vulnerability due to advances in technology. I think you'll find the specific strategies I have to share with you worthy of consideration.

If you recall, my background is in Web planning and development, with specific skills in developing administrative intranets, creating public Web sites, and designing Web-based software to address the internal and external reporting needs of organizations.

Enclosed is my resume attesting to my experience and specialties. I will contact you within the next few days to discuss the possibility of meeting with you.

Respectfully,


David Kent
Computer and Information Systems Manager

Enclosure: Resume

*Notice how this letter opens by making a connection from a brief personal meeting at a professional conference. Because no specific job is being discussed, the letter provides a broad overview of skills and possibilities rather than a point-by-point qualification match (by Peter Hill, CPRW).*

# APPENDIX

# Internet Career Resources

With the emergence of the Internet has come a huge collection of job search resources for technology professionals. Here are some of our favorites.

## Dictionaries and Glossaries

Outstanding information on keywords and acronyms.

| | |
|---|---|
| Acronym Finder | www.acronymfinder.com |
| Babelfish Foreign-Language Translation | http://babelfish.altavista.com |
| ComputerUser High-Tech Dictionary | www.computeruser.com/ resources/dictionary/ dictionary.html |
| Dave's Truly Canadian Dictionary of Canadian Spelling | www.luther.ca/~dave7cnv/ cdnspelling/cdnspelling.html |
| Dictionary of Investment Terms (Australia) | www.county.com.au/web/ webdict.nsf/pages/index?open |
| Duhaime's Legal Dictionary | www.duhaime.org |
| InvestorWords.com | www.investorwords.com |
| Law.com Legal Industry Glossary | www.law.com |
| Merriam-Webster Collegiate Dictionary & Thesaurus | www.m-w.com/home.htm |
| Refdesk | www.refdesk.com |
| TechWeb TechEncyclopedia | www.techweb.com/ encyclopedia/ |

| | |
|---|---|
| Verizon Glossary of Telecom Terms | http://www22.verizon.com/ wholesale/glossary/ 0,2624,P_Q,00.html |
| *Washington Post* Business Glossary | www.washingtonpost.com/ wp-srv/business/longterm/ glossary/index.htm |
| Webopedia: Online Dictionary for Computer and Internet Terms | www.webopedia.com |
| Whatis?com Technology Terms | http://whatis.techtarget.com |
| Wordsmyth: The Educational Dictionary/Thesaurus | www.wordsmyth.net |

# Job Search Sites

You'll find thousands and thousands of current professional employment opportunities on these sites.

### TECHNOLOGY/ENGINEERING CAREERS

| | |
|---|---|
| American Institute of Architects | www.aia.org |
| American Society for Quality | www.asq.org |
| Center for Women and Information Technology | www.umbc.edu/cwit/ |
| Chancellor & Chancellor Resources for Careers | www.chancellor.com/fr_careers.html |
| CIO Jobs | http://jobs.cio.com |
| ComputerJobs.com | www.computerjobs.com |
| ComputerWork.com | www.computerwork.com |
| Computerworld Careers Knowledge Center | www.computerworld.com/ careertopics/careers |
| Dice | www.dice.com |
| Harry's Job Search Internet Hot List | http://jobinfo.freeyellow.com/ index.html |
| IDEAS Job Network | www.ideasjn.com |
| IT Jobs | www.itjobs.com |
| Job-Hunt.org | www.job-hunt.org/computers |
| Jobserve | www.jobserve.com |
| Monster Technology Jobs | http://technology.monster.com |

| National Society of Professional Engineers | www.nspe.org |
| National Technical Employment Services | www.ntes.com |
| Nationjob | www.nationjob.com/computers |
| Quality Resources Online | www.quality.org |
| Resulte Universal | www.psisearch.com |
| Tech-Centric.net | www.tech-centric.net |
| Tech-Engine.com | www.tech-engine.com |
| Techies.com | www.techies.com |
| Ten Links | www.tenlinks.com |

## GENERAL SITES

| 6FigureJobs | www.6figurejobs.com |
| AllStar Jobs | www.allstarjobs.com |
| America's CareerInfoNet | www.acinet.org/acinet |
| America's Job Bank | www.ajb.dni.us |
| BestJobsUSA | www.bestjobsusa.com/ |
| BlackWorld Careers | www.blackworld.com |
| CareerBuilder | www.careerbuilder.com |
| Career.com | www.career.com |
| CareerExchange.com | www.careerexchange.com |
| Career Exposure | www.careerexposure.com |
| The Career Key | www.careerkey.org/english |
| Careermag.com | www.careermag.com |
| CareerShop | www.careershop.com |
| CareerSite.com | www.careersite.com |
| ChiefMonster.com | www.chiefmonster.com |
| *Contract Employment Weekly* | www.ceweekly.com |
| EmploymentGuide.com | www.employmentguide.com |
| Excite | http://careers.excite.com |
| FlipDog | http://flipdog.monster.com/ |
| Futurestep | www.futurestep.com |
| GETAJOB! | www.getajob.com |
| Help Wanted | www.helpwanted.com |

| | |
|---|---|
| HotJobs.com | http://hotjobs.yahoo.com |
| JobBankUSA | www.jobbankusa.com |
| Job Circle | www.jobcircle.com |
| Job-Hunt.org | www.job-hunt.org |
| JobHuntersBible.com | www.jobhuntersbible.com |
| JobOptions | www.joboptions.com |
| KiwiCareers (New Zealand) | www.careers.co.nz |
| Monster.com | www.monster.com |
| MonsterTRAK | www.monstertrak.monster.com/ |
| NationJob Network | www.nationjob.com |
| NCOA MaturityWorks | www.maturityworks.org |
| Net Temps | www.net-temps.com |
| The Riley Guide | www.rileyguide.com |
| Saludos Hispanos | www.saludos.com |
| TrueCareers | www.careercity.com |
| Wages.com | www.wages.com.au |
| WorkTree | www.worktree.com |

## ENTRY-LEVEL CAREERS

| | |
|---|---|
| CampusCareerCenter.com | www.campuscareercenter.com |
| College Grad Job Hunter | www.collegegrad.com |
| College Job Board | www.collegejobboard.com/?1100 |
| MonsterTRAK | www.monstertrak.monster.com/ |

## GOVERNMENT AND MILITARY CAREERS

| | |
|---|---|
| Federal Jobs Net | www.federaljobs.net |
| FedWorld | www.fedworld.gov |
| FRS Federal Jobs Central | www.fedjobs.com |
| GetaGovJob.com | www.getagovjob.com |
| GovExec.com | www.govexec.com |
| USAJOBS (United States Office of Personnel Management) | www.usajobs.opm.gov |

## INTERNATIONAL CAREERS

| | |
|---|---|
| EscapeArtist.com | www.escapeartist.com |
| International Career Employment Center | www.internationaljobs.org |

| | |
|---|---|
| LatPro | www.latpro.com |
| OverseasJobs.com | www.overseasjobs.com |

## Company Information

Outstanding resources for researching specific companies.

| | |
|---|---|
| 555-1212.com | www.555-1212.com |
| Brint.com | www.brint.com |
| EDGAR Online | www.edgar-online.com |
| Experience | www.experiencenetwork.com |
| *Fortune* Magazine | www.fortune.com |
| Hoover's Business Profiles | www.hoovers.com |
| infoUSA (small business information) | www.infousa.com |
| Intellifact.com | www.igiweb.com/intellifact/ |
| OneSource CorpTech | www.corptech.com |
| SuperPages.com | www.bigbook.com |
| U.S. Chamber of Commerce | www.uschamber.com/ |
| Vault Company Research | www.vault.com/companies/ searchcompanies.jsp |
| Wetfeet.com Company Research | www.wetfeet.com/asp/company resource_home.asp |

## Interviewing Tips and Techniques

Expert guidance to sharpen and strengthen your interviewing skills.

| | |
|---|---|
| About.com Interviewing | http://jobsearch.about.com/od/ interviewsnetworking/ |
| Bradley CVs Introduction to Job Interviews | www.bradleycvs.demon.co.uk/ interview/index.htm |
| Dress for Success | www.appearance.com |
| Job-Interview.net | www.job-interview.net |
| Northeastern University Career Services | www.dac.neu.edu/coop. careerservices/interview.html |

# Salary and Compensation Information

Learn from the experts to strengthen your negotiating skills and increase your salary.

| | |
|---|---|
| Abbott, Langer & Associates | www.abbott-langer.com |
| America's Career InfoNet | www.acinet.org/acinet/select_occupation.asp?stfips=&next=occ_rep |
| Bureau of Labor Statistics | www.bls.gov/bls/wages.htm |
| Clayton Wallis Co. | www.claytonwallis.com |
| Economic Research Institute | www.erieri.com |
| Janco Associates MIS Salary Survey | www.psrinc.com/salary.htm |
| JobStar | www.jobstar.org/tools/salary/index.htm |
| Salary and Crime Calculator | www.homefair.com/homefair/cmr/salcalc.html |
| Salary Expert | www.salaryexpert.com |
| Wageweb | www.wageweb.com |
| WorldatWork: The Professional Association for Compensation, Benefits and Total Rewards | www.worldatwork.org |

# INDEX OF CONTRIBUTORS

The sample resumes and cover letters in chapters 4 through 12 were written by professional resume and cover letter writers. If you need help with your resume and job search correspondence, you can use the following list to locate a career professional who can help.

You will notice that most of the writers have one or more credentials listed after their names. In fact, some have half a dozen or more! The careers industry offers extensive opportunities for ongoing training, and most career professionals take advantage of these opportunities to build their skills and keep their knowledge current. If you are curious about what any one of these credentials means, we suggest that you contact the resume writer directly. He or she will be glad to discuss certifications and other qualifications as well as information about services that can help you in your career transition.

**Georgia Adamson, CPRW, CCM, CCMC, CEIP, JCTC**
A Successful Career, a div. of Adept Business Services
Campbell, CA
(408) 866-6859
E-mail:
success@ablueribbonresume.com
www.ABlueRibbonResume.com

**Lynn P. Andenoro, CPRW, JCTC**
President, My Career Resource
1214 Fenway
Salt Lake City, UT 84102
Phone: (801) 883-2011
Fax: (801) 582-8862
E-mail: Lynn@MyCareerResource.com
www.MyCareerResource.com

**Ann Baehr, CPRW**
Best Resumes of New York, Long Island, NY
(631) 435-1879
E-mail: resumesbest@earthlink.net

**Jacqui Barrett, MRW, CPRW, CEIP**
Career Trend, Overland Park, KS
(913) 451-1313
E-mail: jacqui@careertrend.net
www.careertrend.net

**Bruce Baxter, CPRW, MS**
Baxter Communications
4186 Gemini Path
Liverpool, NY 13090
Phone: (315) 652-7703
Fax: (315) 652-7758
baxtercom@juno.com

**Janet L. Beckstrom, CPRW**
President, Word Crafter
1717 Montclair Ave.
Flint, MI 48503
Phone: (800) 351-9818
Fax: (810) 232-9257
E-mail: wordcrafter@voyager.net

**Arnold G. Boldt, CPRW, JCTC**
Arnold-Smith Associates
625 Panorama Trail, Building One, Ste. 120
Rochester, NY 14625
Phone: (585) 383-0350
Fax: (585) 387-0516
E-mail: Arnie@ResumeSOS.com
www.ResumeSOS.com

**Carolyn Braden, CPRW**
Braden Resume Solutions
108 La Plaza Dr.
Hendersonville, TN 37075
Phone: (615) 822-3317
Fax: (615) 826-9611
E-mail: bradenresume@comcast.net

**Paula Brandt**
The Resume Lady, Belle Vernon, PA

**Alice Braxton, CPRW, CEIP**
Accutype Resume & Secretarial Services,
Burlington, NC
(336) 227-9091
E-mail: accutype@triad.rr.com

**Jacqueline Brett, CPC, JCTC**
WorkLife Design
4320 Dutch Garden Ct.
Raleigh, NC 27613
Phone: (919) 510-5950
Fax: (919) 510-5951
E-mail: jbrett@workliferesource.com
www.workliferesource.com

**Martin Buckland, MRW, CPRW, CPBS,
JCTC, CJST, CEIP**
Elite Resumes
1428 Stationmaster Ln.
Oakville, ON L6M 3A7, Canada
Phone: (905) 825-0490
Fax: (905) 825-2966
E-mail: martin@aneliteresume.com
www.aneliteresume.com

**Diane Burns, CPRW, CCMC, CCM, CEIP,
JCTC**
Career Marketing Techniques
Phone: 011-49 (0) 9335-997647
E-mail: diane@polishedresumes.com
www.polishedresumes.com

**Freddie Cheek, M.S.Ed., CCM, CPRW,
CRW, CWDP**
Cheek & Cristantello Career Connections
4511 Harlem Rd., Ste. 3
Amherst, NY 14226
Phone: (716) 839-3635
Fax: (716) 831-9320
E-mail: fscheek@adelphia.net
www.cheekandcristantello.com

**Kristie Cook**
Absolutely Write, Olathe, KS

**Jean Cummings, MAT, CPRW, CEIP, CPBS**
A Resume for Today
Damonmill Square
Concord, MA 01742
Phone: (978) 371-9266

Toll-free: (800) 324-1699
Fax: (978) 964-0527
E-mail: jc@aresumefortoday.com
www.aresumefortoday.com

**Laura A. DeCarlo, CERW, CECC, CCMC,
CCRP, CWPP, JCTC, CCM**
A Competitive Edge Career Service, LLC
1665 Clover Circle
Melbourne, FL 32935
Phone: (800) 715-3442
Fax: (321) 752-7513
E-mail: success@acompetitiveedge.com
www.acompetitiveedge.com

**Michelle Dumas, NCRW, CPRW, CCM**
Executive Director, Distinctive Documents
Somersworth, NH 03878
Phone: (800) 644-9694
Fax: (603) 947-2954
E-mail: resumes@distinctiveweb.com
www.distinctiveweb.com

**George Dutch, CFP, CCM, JCTC**
JobJoy
750-130 Slater St.
Ottawa, ON Canada K1P 6E2
Phone: (800) 798-2696 or (613) 563-0584
Fax: (613) 594-8705
E-mail: jobjoy@sympatico.ca
www.jobjoy.net

**Nina K. Ebert, CPRW/CC**
A Word's Worth, New Egypt/Jackson, NJ
Phone: (609) 758-7799 and (732) 349-2225
Phone and Fax: (609) 758-7799
E-mail: keytosuccessresumes@comcast.net
www.keytosuccessresumes

**Debbie Ellis, MRW, CPRW**
Phoenix Career Group
Phone: (800) 876-5506
Fax: (859) 236-3900
E-mail: debbie@phoenixcareergroup.com
www.phoenixcareergroup.com

**Donna Farrise, JCTC**
Dynamic Resumes of Long Island, Inc.
300 Motor Pkwy., Ste. 200
Hauppauge, NY 11788
Phone: (631) 951-4120
Fax: (631) 952-1817
E-mail: donna@dynamicresumes.com
www.dynamicresumes.com

**Louise Fletcher, CPRW**
Blue Sky Resumes
Bronxville, NY 10708
Phone: (914) 337-5742
E-mail: info@blueskyresumes.com
www.blueskyresumes.com

**Ann Flister, CPRW**
Alaska Career Center
Phone: (907) 561-9311
E-mail: success@alaskacareercenter.com
www.alaskacareercenter.com

**Art Frank, MBA**
Resumes "R" Us, Palm Harbor, FL
(727) 787-6885
E-mail: AIF@tampabay.rr.com
www.powerresumesandcoaching.com

**Judy Friedler, NCRW, JCTC, CCM**
CareerPro International
Toronto, ON and Amherst, NY
(905) 828-0599
www.rezcoach.com
Judy@rezcoach.com

**Louise Garver, CPRW, CEIP, MCDP, CMP, JCTC**
Career Directions, LLC
115 Elm St., Ste. 203
Enfield, CT 06082
Phone: (860) 623-9473
Toll-free: (888) 222-3731
Fax: (860) 623-9473
E-mail: CareerPro@cox.net
www.resumeimpact.com

**Don Goodman, CPRW**
About Jobs
21 Duncan Rd.
Ho-Ho-Kus, NJ 07423
Toll-free: (800) 909-0109
Toll-free fax: (800) 877-3627
E-mail: dgoodman@gotthejob.com
www.gotthejob.com

**Susan Guarneri, NCC, NCCC, CPRW, CCMC, CEIP, MCC**
President, Guarneri Associates
1905 Fern Ln.
Wausau, WI 54401
Phone: (866) 881-4055
Fax: (715) 355-1936
E-mail: Resumagic@aol.com
www.resume-magic.com

**Michele Haffner, CPRW, JCTC**
Advanced Resume Services
1314 W. Paradise Ct.
Glendale, WI 53209
Phone: (414) 247-1677
Fax: (414) 247-1808
E-mail: michele@resumeservices.com
URL: www.resumeservices.com

**Beate Hait, CPRW, NCRW**
President, Resumes Plus
80 Wingate Rd.

Holliston, MA 01746
Phone: (508) 429-1813
Fax: (508) 429-4299
E-mail: bea@resumesplus.net
www.resumesplus.net

**Alice Hanson, CPRW**
Aim Resumes
P.O. Box 75054
Seattle, WA 98175
Phone: (206) 527-3100
Fax: (206) 527-3101
E-mail: success@aimresumes.com

**Cheryl Ann Harland, CPRW**
Resumes By Design, The Woodlands, TX
(888) 213-1650
E-mail: CAH@resumesbydesign.com

**Beverly Harvey, CPRW, JCTC, CCM, CCMC**
Beverly Harvey Resume and Career Services
P.O. Box 750
Pierson, FL 32180
Phone: (386) 749-3111
Toll-free: (888) 775-0916
Fax: (386) 749-4881
E-mail: beverly@harveycareers.com
www.harveycareers.com

**Loretta Heck**
All Word Services
924 E. Old Willow Rd. #102
Prospect Heights, IL 60070
Phone: (847) 215-7517
Fax: (847) 215-7520
Siegfried@ameritech.net

**Peter Hill, CPRW**
Distinctive Resumes
Honolulu, HI
Phone: (808) 384-9461
E-mail: distinctiveresumes@yahoo.com
www.peterhill.biz

**Maurene J. Hinds, MFA, CPRW**
Right-On Resumes
Bozeman, MT
Phone and fax: (406) 586-1416
E-mail: rightonresumes@msn.com
www.rightonresumes.com

**Jan Holliday, MA, NCRW, JCTC**
Arbridge Communications
Harleysville, PA
Phone: (215) 513-7420
E-mail: jan@arbridge.com
www.arbridge.com

**Gayle Howard, CERW, CCM, CPRW, CRW**
Top Margin Resumes Online
P.O. Box 74
Chirnside Park 3116
Melbourne, Australia
Phone: 613 9726 6694
Fax: 613 9726 5316
E-mail: getinterviews@topmargin.com
www.topmargin.com

**Deborah S. James, CPRW, CCMC**
President, Leading Edge Resume & Career
Services
1010 Schreier Rd.
Toledo, OH 43460
Phone: (419) 666-4518
Toll-free: (800) 815-8780
Fax: (419) 791-3567
E-mail: djames@leadingedgeresumes.com
www.leadingedgeresumes.com

**Marcy Johnson, NCRW, CPRW, CEIP**
President, First Impression Resume & Job
Readiness
11805 U.S. Hwy. 69
Story City, IA 50248
Phone: (877) 215-6009
Fax: (515) 733-9296
E-mail: firstimpression@iowatelecom.net
www.resume-job-readiness.com

**Fran Kelley**
President, The Resume Works
71 Highwood Ave.
Waldwick, NJ 07463
Phone: (201) 670-9643
E-mail: TwoFreeSpirits@worldnet.att.net
www.careermuse.com

**Bill Kinser, MRW, CCM, CPRW, CEIP,
JCTC**
To The Point Resumes
P.O. Box 135
Fairfax, VA 22038
Phone: (703) 352-8969
Fax: (703) 991-2372
E-mail: bkinser@tothepointresumes.com
www.tothepointresumes.com

**Ann Klint**
Ann's Professional Résumé Service
2130 Kennebunk Ln.
Tyler, TX 75703
Phone/Fax: (903) 509-8333
E-mail: resumes-annk@cox.net

**Myriam-Rose Kohn, CPRW, CEIP, JCTC,
CCM, CCMC**
JEDA Enterprises
27201 Tourney Rd., Ste. 201
Valencia, CA 91355
Phone: (661) 253-0801
Fax: (661) 253-0744
E-mail: myriam-rose@jedaenterprises.com
www.jedaenterprises.com

**Rhoda Kopy, BS, CPRW, JCTC, CEIP**
President, A HIRE IMAGE®
26 Main St., Ste. E
Toms River, NJ 08753
Phone: (732) 505-9515
Fax: (732) 505-3125
E-mail: rkopy@earthlink.net
www.jobwinningresumes.com

**Louise Kursmark, MRW, CPRW, JCTC,
CEIP, CCM**
Executive Master Team—Career Masters
Institute
President, Best Impression Career Services, Inc.
9847 Catalpa Woods Ct.
Cincinnati, OH 45242
Phone: (513) 792-0030
Fax: (877) 791-7127
E-mail: LK@yourbestimpression.com
www.yourbestimpression.com

**Diana C. LeGere**
Executive Director, Writing Flair
P.O. Box 634
Colonial Heights, VA 23834
Phone: (804) 720-7236
E-mail: DianaLeGere@aol.com
www.dianalegere.com

**Linsey Levine, MS**
CareerCounsel, Ossining and White Plains, NY
Phone: (914) 923-9233 or 914-948-9286
E-mail: LinZlev@aol.com
www.4careercounsel.com

**Kim Little**
Fast Track Resumes, Victor, NY
(716) 742-2467
E-mail: kimresume@earthlink.net
www.fast-trackresumes.com

**Ross Macpherson, MA, CPRW, JCTC, CEIP**
President, Career Quest
131 Kirby Crescent
Whitby, Ontario
L1N 7C7 Canada
Phone: (905) 438-8548
Toll Free: (877) 426-8548
Fax: (905) 438-4096
E-mail: ross@yourcareerquest.com
www.yourcareerquest.com

**Linda Matias, CEIP, JCTC**
Executive Director, CareerStrides
37 E. Hill Dr.
Smithtown, NY 11787
Phone: (631) 382-2425
Fax: (631) 382-2425
E-mail: linda@careerstrides.com
www.careerstrides.com

**Wanda McLaughlin, CPRW, CEIP**
Execuwrite, Chandler, AZ
(480) 732-7966
E-mail: wandaj@cox.net
www.execuwrite.com

**Jan Melnik, MRW, CCM, CPRW**
Absolute Advantage
P.O. Box 718
Durham, CT 06422
Phone: (860) 349-0256
Fax: (860) 349-1343
E-mail: CompSPJan@aol.com
www.janmelnik.com

**Nicole Miller, CCM, CRW, CECC, IJCTC**
Mil-Roy Consultants
Petawawa, Ontario, Canada
Phone: (613) 687-2708
E-mail: resumes@milroyconsultants.com
www.milroyconsultants.com

**Doug Morrison, MRW, CPRW**
Career Power
2915 Providence Rd., Ste. 300
Charlotte, NC 28211
Phone: (704) 365-0773
Fax: (704) 365-3411
E-mail: dmpwresume@aol.com
www.careerpowerresume.com

**Helen Oliff, CPRW, CFRWC, Certified Executive Coach**
Turning Point
2307 Freetown Court #12C
Reston, VA 20191
Phone: (703) 716-0077
E-mail: helen@turningpointnow.com
www.turningpointnow.com

**Jean Oscarson, M.Ed.**
Career Resumes
P.O. Box 509
Goldens Bridge, NY 10526
Toll-free: (888) 808-6949
Fax: (413) 294-7508
E-mail: jeanoscarson@aol.com
www.career-resumes.com

**Barbara Poole, CPRW, CRW, CCMC**
Hire Imaging
1812 Red Fox Rd.
St. Cloud, MN 56301
Phone: (320) 253-0975
Fax: (320) 253-1790
E-mail: barb@hireimaging.com
www.hireimaging.com

**Anita Radosevich, CPRW, JCTC, CFRW, CEIP**
President, Career Ladders
9401 E. Stockton Blvd., Ste. 100B
Elk Grove, CA 95624
E-mail: anita@abcresumes.com
www.federalresumewriter.com

**MeLisa Rogers, MS, CPRW, CPBA, CVLSDT**
Ultimate Career
16 Linda Ct.
Scroggins, TX 75480
Phone: (903) 860-3963
Toll-free: (800) 573-7863
E-mail: mrogers@tisd.net
www.ultimatecareer.biz

**Jennifer Rushton, CRW**
Keraijen—Certified Resume Writer
Level 14, 309 Kent St.
Sydney NSW 2000, Australia
Phone: 61 2 9994 8050
E-mail: info@keraijen.com.au
www.keraijen.com.au

**Barbara Safani, MA, CPRW**
Career Solvers
980 Madison Ave.
New York, NY 10021
Phone: (212) 579-7230
Toll-free: (866) 333-1800
Fax: (212) 580-2388
E-mail: info@careersolvers.com
www.careersolvers.com

**Laura Scheible, CCMC, CJST, JCTC**
Job Search Academy, Clinton, MT
(888) 685-3507
E-mail: laurascheible@earthlink.net
www.JobSearchAcademy.com

**Kelley Smith, CPRW**
President, Advantage Resume Services
P.O. Box 391
Sugar Land, TX 77487
Phone: (281) 494-3330
Fax: (281) 494-0173
E-mail: info@100kresumes.com
www.100kresumes.com

**Ann Stewart, CPRW**
Advantage Services, Roanoke, TX
(817) 424-1448
E-mail: ASresume@charter.net

**Billie Ruth Sucher, MS, CTMS, CTSB**
Billie Sucher and Associates
7177 Hickman Rd., Ste. 10
Urbandale, IA 50322
Phone: (515) 276-0061
Fax: (515) 334-8076
E-mail: betwnjobs@aol.com

**Lonnie Swanson, CDF, CPRW, IJCTC**
A Career Advantage, Poulsbo, WA
(360) 779-2877
E-mail: resumes@nwinet.com

**Sheryl Teitelbaum**
Write Way Resume
450 Shewsbury Plaza #377
Shrewsbury, NJ 07702
Phone: (732) 542-1119
Fax: (732) 264-6467
E-mail: contactus@writewayresume.com
www.writewayresume.com

**Vivian Van Lier, CPRW, JCTC, CEIP, CM, CPRC**
Advantage Resume & Career Services
Valley Glen (Los Angeles), CA
(818) 994-6655
E-mail: vvanlier@aol.com
www.cuttingedgeresumes.com

**Ilona Vanderwoude, CPRW, CEIP, CCMC, CJST**
Career Branches
P.O. Box 330
Riverdale, NY 10471
Phone: (718) 884-2213
Fax: (646) 349-2218
E-mail: ilona@careerbranches.com
www.careerbranches.com

**Ellie Vargo, CPRW, CFRWC**
Noteworthy Resume Services
11906 Manchester Rd., Ste. 112
St. Louise, MO 63131
Phone: (314) 965-9362
Toll-free: (866) 965-9362
E-mail: ev@noteworthyresume.com
www.noteworthyresume.com

**Roleta Fowler Vasquez, CPRW, CEIP**
Wordbusters Resume and Writing Services
433 Quail Ct.
Fillmore, CA 93015
Phone: (805) 524-3493
E-mail: resumes@wbresumes.com
www.wbresumes.com

**Janice Worthington, MA, CPRW, JCTC, CEIP**
Worthington Career Services, Columbus, OH
Phone: (614) 890-1645
Toll-free: (877) 973-7863 (877-9RESUME)
www.worthingtonresumes.com

# INDEX

# The Very Quick Job Search,
### Third Edition
*Michael Farr*

**The best and most thorough career planning and job search book ever written!** Excellent for job seekers, students, and the professionals who work with them. Job seekers who need immediate advice on one or more essential job search topics can concentrate just on the topics that are most relevant to their needs.

ISBN 1-59357-007-4 / Order Code LP-J0074 / **$17.95**

# Job Search Magic

*Susan Britton Whitcomb*

**Available December 2005!** Condenses all of the groundbreaking job search guidance from JIST best-sellers *Résumé Magic, Interview Magic,* and *Cover Letter Magic* into one all-inclusive volume—plus a no-fail system for finding and landing the perfect job for you. Includes sample resumes and cover letters, before-and-after interview responses, career-choice guidance, helpful job search Web sites, salary negotiation tips, job success tips, and much, much more!

ISBN 1-59357-150-X / Order Code LP-J150X / **$18.95**

# Seven-Step Job Search, Second Edition

*Michael Farr*

**Available December 2005!** The latest addition to the *Help in a Hurry* series presents Mike Farr's most essential job search advice—condensed into a concise and handy format! In seven easy steps, readers learn what it takes to land the right job fast. Quick worksheets help readers identify their skills, define their ideal job, use the most effective job search methods, write a superior resume, organize their time to get two interviews a day, dramatically improve their interviewing skills, and follow up on all job leads effectively. Includes sample resumes and an *OOH* tutorial.

ISBN 1-59357-239-5 / Order Code LP-J2395 / **$8.95**

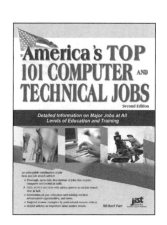

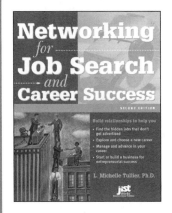
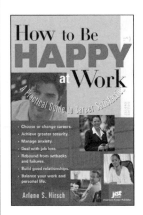